CRIMINAL LAW AND COLONIAL SUBJECT
NEW SOUTH WALES, 1810–1830

Studies in Australian History

Series editors:
Alan Gilbert, Patricia Grimshaw and Peter Spearritt

Convict Workers   Steven Nicholas (ed.)
Origins of Australia's Capital Cities   Pamela Statham (ed.)
A Military History of Australia   Jeffrey Grey
The Invisible State   Alastair Davidson
The Price of Health   James A. Gillespie
The Rule of Law in a Penal Colony   David Neal
Woman Suffrage in Australia: A Gift or a Struggle   Audrey Oldfield
Land Settlement in Early Tasmania   Sharon Morgan

CRIMINAL LAW AND COLONIAL SUBJECT

NEW SOUTH WALES, 1810–1830

Paula J. Byrne

CAMBRIDGE
UNIVERSITY PRESS

Published by the Press Syndicate of the University of Cambridge
The Pitt Building, Trumpington Street, Cambridge CB2 1RP, UK
40 West 20th Street, New York, NY 10011-4211, USA
10 Stamford Road, Oakleigh, Melbourne, Victoria 3166, Australia

Printed in Hong Kong by Colorcraft

National Library of Australia cataloguing in publication data
Byrne, Paula-Jane, 1959–
Criminal law and colonial subject: New South Wales 1810–1830.
Bibliography.
Includes index.
ISBN 0 521 40379 0.
1. Criminal law – New South Wales – History – 19th century. 2.
Criminal justice, Administration of – New South Wales – History –
19th century. 3. New South Wales – Social conditions – 1788–1851.
4. New South Wales – History – 1788–1851. I. Title. (Series:
Studies in Australian history (Cambridge, England)).
345.944

Library of Congress cataloguing in publication data
Byrne, Paula-Jane, 1959–
Criminal law and colonial subject: New South Wales, 1810–1830
Paula-Jane Byrne.
(Studies in Australian history)
Includes bibliographial references
ISBN 0-521-40379-0
1. Criminal law – Australia – New South Wales – History –
19th century. I. Title. II Series.
KUC379.5.B97 1992
345.944–dc20   92-11457
[349.4405]   CIP

A catalogue record for this book is available from the British Library.

ISBN 0 521 40379 0 hardback

CONTENTS

Part 4: The Courtroom

FIGURES

TABLES

AUTHOR'S NOTE

Sources

All of the surviving records of the activities of complainants, constables, magistrates and defendants from the period 1810 to 1830 have provided the basis of this book.

Overall, 5910 cases have been closely examined. I have also examined the records of benches where cases are listed but no depositions remain, particularly records of the Sydney benches and the Parramatta bench for the 1820s.

The records which remain are as follows. For full details, see Appendix.

Minutes

Judge Advocate's Bench, 1810–20.
Police Magistrates' Bench, Sydney, 1812, 1815–16, 1820–21.
Liverpool Bench of Magistrates, 1824, 1826.
Goulburn Bench of Magistrates, 1828–29.
Argyle Bench of Magistrates, 1826–27.
Newcastle Bench of Magistrates, 1823–27.
Bathurst Bench of Magistrates, 1825–26.
Court of Criminal Jurisdiction, 1810–15.

Depositions

Quarter Sessions, Sydney, 1824–30.
Quarter Sessions, Parramatta, 1825–30.
Quarter Sessions, Windsor, 1824–30.
Quarter Sessions, Campbelltown, 1828–30.
Quarter Sessions, Liverpool, 1824–28.

Quarter Sessions, Newcastle, 1826–29.
Court of Criminal Jurisdiction, 1816–24.
Supreme Court of Criminal Jurisdiction, 1824–31.

Returns

Petty Sessions, Sydney, 1824, 1828 (3 months).
Parramatta Bench of Magistrates, 1815–16, 1822, 1824, 1826.

Language

Depositions include words and phrases common to early nineteenth-century New South Wales, e.g. to 'dress' meaning to cook, to 'plant' meaning to hide. I have footnoted these and explained their meaning where necessary.

Depositions were taken by the clerk of the court. They are, then, a transcript of speech. The early nineteenth-century clerk did not play the role of the modern police in deliberating on evidence given, and asking further questions. He simply transcribed the proceedings of the magistrates' bench. If spoken evidence in a later court appearance differed from the initial deposition, the trial was stopped and the speaker was in danger of being tried for perjury. Thus there is close alignment between spoken and written word in these court papers.

I have left the language and spelling of letters and depositions verbatim. In some, it is possible to see accent, hesitation and drunkenness.

The term 'deponent' means 'the person speaking'; 'the prisoner' means 'the person against whom the case is brought'.

Currency

Although many forms of currency circulated in the colony of New South Wales, monetary values were generally expressed in terms of pounds sterling. There were 12 pennies (d.) in one shilling (s.) and 20 shillings in one pound (£). The sum of £1 10s. was also written as 30/-. A half-crown was equal to 2s 6d.

Measurement

Metric equivalents for imperial measures used in the text are as follows.

Length
1 yard = 0.914 m
1 mile = 1.61 km

Volume
1 gallon = 4.55 L
1 bushel = 35.2 L

Mass
1 pound (lb) = 454 g

Area
1 acre = 0.405 ha

ACKNOWLEDGEMENTS

The Clerk for Public Prosecutions allowed me access to the criminal records which provide the basis for this book. Dawn Troy of the New South Wales Archives Office made records awaiting restoration available for my research; she also provided me with lists of cases. Di Rhodes of the Dixson Library assisted me in locating police bench records for Sydney. The staff of the New South Wales Archives Office were also most helpful in locating records, advising copying procedures and tolerating my requests. Though I spent less time in the Mitchell Library, staff there were similarly helpful.

Beverly Kingston supervised this work as a thesis and I am most grateful for her assistance and criticism. This book has also been assisted by Marion Aveling's advice. Alan Atkinson suggested the order of chapters. These historians were involved in assessing the thesis. Over the years there have been numerous people who encouraged me to persist. Many useful discussions were had with Australian and English legal historians, particularly Alex Castles and David Neal. Though this is not a work of legal history, it is they who were most familiar with the territory of this research. I have also received valuable feedback from my colleagues at the Australian universities where I worked.

I also thank Phillipa McGuinness and Robin Derricourt of Cambridge University Press. This book was carefully typed by Linda Maynard and she was most helpful in design of tables and diagrams. Linda has worked patiently for many years on this project and I am most grateful. Janet Mackenzie, a freelance editor for Cambridge University Press, edited this book; I wish to thank her for the extensive work she put in.

This book is dedicated to Jimmy Byrne.

ABBREVIATIONS

A.B.M.   Argyle Bench of Magistrates
C.C.J.   Court of Criminal Jurisdiction
G.B.M.   Goulburn Bench of Magistrates
H.R.A.   *Historical Records of Australia*
J.A.B.   Judge Advocate's Bench
P.M.B.   Sydney Police Magistrates' Benches
Q.S.   Quarter Sessions
S.C.C.J. Supreme Court of Criminal Jurisdiction
S.P.S.   Sydney Petty Sessions

1

INTRODUCTION

In 1822 Eleanor Walsh gave evidence to the magistrate at Bringelly of how she and her husband discovered that Henry Crane, servant to Oxley, had killed their heifer and taken the meat: 'I went with my husband to the spot and told him to track the shoemarks on the ground. There were three men, one with very long nails on the side of each shoe, another barefoot, we tracked them to Mr. Hooks.' Her husband could find no evidence of the heifer and so went further, with a constable, to Hassall's farm and then to Oxley's. At Oxley's they went to the carpenter's shop and observed Henry Crane. They saw he had a shoe with three long nails on the side. He tried to swap his shoes with another man in the carpenter's shop but he was arrested and brought before the Bringelly bench with his shoe; the case was sent to the Court of Criminal Jurisdiction. Crane pleaded not guilty, was tried and acquitted.[1]

These events leading to the arrest of Crane were recounted at Birling, the farm of Robert Lowe, magistrate. Eleanor Walsh and her husband stood before Lowe and gave their version of suspicion, evidence and guilt. Her use of tracking, her husband's suspicions of convicts on neighbouring farms and their perceptions of what constituted evidence of Henry Crane's involvement all produced the case. The magistrate Lowe passed the case to the Judge Advocate. Three months later Henry Crane appeared before the Court of Criminal Jurisdiction. To recount tracking and produce a shoe was not sufficient evidence and Crane was acquitted.

In going to court to give evidence, Eleanor Walsh invoked her own understandings of law. The shoemarks and her husband's tracking were enough indication of guilt for her. In studies of early colonial New South Wales historians such as Alan Atkinson, Marion Aveling, Michael Sturma and Portia Robinson have recognised that convict and free had their own notions of morality, marriage and the workings of the convict system.[2] Such an approach may be extended to a study of criminal law in the early colony. Ordinary people, convict and free, made their own law; they mapped their own boundaries of legality and illegality. They both clashed with and supported the magistrates, judges and juries who interpreted statute law.

The convict system meant that criminal law had greater access to personal life than in England. It also meant that vagrancy law was easily accepted. But freed and free persons also stressed their freedom and argued that they should not be subjected to law. Also, among both administrators and the ordinary population there was different valuing of what it meant to be 'male' and 'female'. This meant that women were more likely to appear before the courts as vagrants than men; they were subject to far more suspicion than men; and they used the courts more for personal disputes than men.

J. B. Hirst in his book *Convict Society and Its Enemies* initially intended to study the free population; but he discovered that the informal workings of the convict system meant 'this was not a society which had to become free: its freedoms were well established from the earliest times'.[3] This study does not reject Hirst's findings. According to legal records; male convicts were able to have their work valued and sell it themselves. Moreover, I argue, the convict system and its informal workings contributed considerably to the modernising of the meaning of 'work' and the criminal law assisted this process as well as, in the countryside; validating a paternalism reminiscent of the colonial plantation. Administrators struggled with measuring and weighing convict labour; 'value' was fraught with difficulty for them, even if we find it an easy term in the twentieth century.

David Neal, a legal historian, has criticised the inadequacy of Hirst's use of the term 'free'; he wants a more solid definition and argues that institutional restrictions on convicts and the lack of legal protection and representation meant that the colony could not be considered free but was a penal colony.[4] While Neal and Hirst work from different paradigms, it may be said that it is true that people in early colonial New South Wales lacked freedom as Neal defines it. However, as we shall see, 'free' and 'freed' were difficult terms also for magistrates and administrators. And, like convicts, the free and freed population made their own definitions of the meaning of freedom. They created their own 'free' world and were prepared to use the law in such a making.

When we consider how 'free' people used the courts, it may be suggested that it was far easier to be convict in early colonial New South Wales than it was to be free. This is because of precisely those difficulties revealed in etymology: the meaning of labour was unclear; the separation of commerce from personal life was far from complete; as in any colonial port the struggle to survive was enormously competitive, and use of criminal law could be incorporated into commerce. The concept of commerce does not have the narrow modern meaning of trade, but was linked to emotion, love, friendship and deceit.

The difficulties of studying the meaning of 'work' also relate to the history of early colonial women.[5] It has been well recognised that the administration held different expectations for the women of early colonial New South Wales. Sexuality was considered far more important than work value. In feminist historiography there has been emphasis on revaluing domestic labour and prostitution: women's work contributed to the economy but was not recognised. It is difficult to separate 'work' in its historical sense from other aspects of life: the meaning of 'work' for women might cross several spheres of behaviour and emotion. In relating prostitution to a cash nexus, we may neglect its meaning for those who practised it. When we analyse the appearances of domestic servants before the courts in the colony, it is clear that the perspective of employers was not necessarily shared by servants. While their work resembled the cash nexus emerging in domestic service in the late nineteenth century in England, convict women wished to get out of service and 'be on their own hands'. To describe domestic servants as good skilled workers is perhaps to blur several meanings of work in one phrase. Work value and sexuality obsessed colonial adminis-trators; these issues were at the forefront of new fashionable meanings which were being considered in English parliamentary debate. We need not react to them and implicitly follow their definitions in rejecting them. What emerges in a study of the courts and women is not their lack of involvement in commercial dealings—the wide scope of these, including barter and exchange, certainly allowed space for women to be involved—but the harsh realm of suspicion and accusation related to their sexuality. This is the realm in which men and women isolate other women. While legal or common law marriage was valued, as Portia Robinson has recognised,[6] the male's place in that marriage lent him more protection against such accusation.

The interest in etymology is relatively recent in social history in England and Europe.[7] It is history which challenges accepted meanings and assumptions concerning the emergence of the modern state. This has not yet been reflected in Australian historio-graphy for this period. Ethnography has been influential in the detailed study, *Australians 1838* edited by Marion Aveling and the related journal *Push from the Bush*.[8] These approaches to the writing of history have also influenced this author.

This work also emerges from dissatisfactions with Marxist terminology which are evident in Marxist anthropology and history. 'Structure' and 'agency' have been seen as inadequate if not outworn tools to work with.[9] A more subtle approach to analysis of change is required. People do influence the everyday workings of institutions: there is a 'battleground', as Ignatieff suggests, between institutions and those subject to them. If one adopts this perspective one is liable to accusations of emphasising popular agree-ment with the institutions of an impartial criminal law—as the legal historian Langbein has done.[10] This book rejects the notion of law as impartial or as capable of being impar-tial: it is bound up with property relations and interest groups. Legal historians have been dogged by the assumption of impartiality and also by the notion of 'crime', both of which are obstacles to analysis.

Historians of law have used court records in several ways. One way is to 'look through' the courts at society, to consider court records as representing the society. The focus of such a study is crime, criminality or the social causation of crime. Such analyses there-fore confront a problem which is often considered insurmountable—the 'grey area' of conflict which did not appear before the courts. As George Rude writes:

> the repeated caveat voiced by other workers in the field [is that] criminal returns are hopelessly inade-quate in providing a full and total picture of crime, both because nineteenth-century authorities kept changing the rules . . . and more significantly because of the delay before full account was taken of crimes known to the police as opposed to before the court.[11]

Rude talks of 'the grey area of unreported crime' and 'the enormity of this problem'.[12] He seeks to deal with it by following Howard Zehr 'in refusing to be intimidated on the very practical grounds that half a loaf is better than no bread and because the present half a loaf will take an adequate account of all prisoners tried at assizes and quarter sessions in selected years'.[13]

Rude's approach looks at 'crime' as behaviour rather than analysing those 'changes in rules' and examining the interaction of community and court. Rude may indeed avoid the problem of 'grey areas', but he still uses court records as an indication of social behaviour.

'Crime' as behaviour was not discussed as a historiographical problem in the work of Hay, Linebaugh and others in *Albion's Fatal Tree*. It was, however, subject to a note in the preface of that book:

> It is rather easy when taking a superficial view of eighteenth-century evidence to propose two distinct kinds of offenders. There are 'good' criminals who are premature revolutionaries or reformers, forerunners of popular movements . . . this appears as social crime; and there are those who commit crime without qualification, thieves, robbers, highwaymen, forgers, arsonists and murderers.[14]

The editors of *Albion's Fatal Tree* found that 'it became less possible to sustain any tidy notion of a distinction between these two types of crime . . . we found little evidence of a morally endorsed popular culture here and a deviant subculture there'.[15]

Similarly, George Rude found in his examination of records from Sussex, Gloucestershire and London that it was impossible to delineate a separate 'criminal class', a group of people prone to petty theft, robbery or greater offences.[16] In this note by the editors of *Albion's Fatal Tree*, as in Rude's work, 'crime' is separated from notions of 'deviant persons'; but it is still defined as a social practice, a form of behaviour. 'Crime' is something that happens in society, rather than the result of the interaction of people and court.

The focus of *Albion's Fatal Tree* lay elsewhere;

> it appears as if it is not just a matter of 'crime' enlarging but equally of a property conscious oligarchy re-defining, through its legislative power, activities, use rights in common or woods, perquisites in industry, as theft or offences. For as offences appear to multiply so also do statutes—often imposing the sanction of death—which define hitherto innocent or venial activities . . . as crimes. And the ideology of the ruling oligarchy, which places a supreme value upon property, finds its visible and material embodiment above all in the ideology and practice of the law. Tyburn Tree, as William Blake well understood, stood at the heart of this ideology; and its ceremonies were at the heart of the popular culture also.[17]

Albion's Fatal Tree introduces another strand of law history, that which focuses on 'changing the rules' rather than looking through the courts at crime and social behaviour. What is examined is the structure and complexity of authority in eighteenth-century England. This analysis was continued by Brewer and Styles. The 'rule of law' was, as they write, 'central to seventeenth- and eighteenth-century Englishmen's understanding of what was special and laudable about their political system . . . [this served as] a potent fiction . . . which commanded widespread assent from both patricians and plebeians'.[18]

Albion's Fatal Tree has been criticised by John Langbein on the grounds that it misrepresents the role of law in eighteenth-century society. Langbein argues that the law served no-one's interests but the victims of crime. Prosecution was undertaken by the lower orders, who also sat on juries—juries that were likely to undervalue goods or to acquit.[19] New measures were enacted because they were reasonable: 'the discretion which characterized this system was not arbitrary and self interested, but rather turned on the good-faith consideration of factors with which ethical decision makers ought to have been concerned'.[20]

Langbein, in turn, has been criticised by Peter Linebaugh, who questioned such a mechanistic view of law. In a defence of *Albion's Fatal Tree*, Linebaugh argues that Langbein sees crime as inherent in society, and that legislators sought to deal with this crime by developing the most efficient system possible. To Linebaugh such an approach is ahistorical. It fails to see law as developing from particular social conditions and interests that were subject to change.[21] Crime is not a constant and law was not in the process of continually refining itself to deal with this 'everpresent' crime.

There is a profound difference between the approach of the legal historian and the approach of the social historian. Douglas Hay addressed the difference between approaches with a geographical analogy:

> Historians tell a modern fable about the Law Mountains. It concerns an historian geologist who asked a lawyer climber what he knew about them. The lawyer's answer was (of course) 'Because they are there'. But, persisted the historian 'How did they get there?' 'Why are some aspects so precipitous, others so gentle? What's *inside* the Law Mountains?'[22]

David Philips in 1983 made a similar point in relation to older legal historical work such as that of Radzinowicz. Philips maintained that Radzinowicz

> takes a simple linear view of reform as progress . . . there is no place . . . for any notion of reforms urged on the state and adopted by it as a means of improved social control; nor does this approach offer any analysis of how these moves by the state were seen and felt from below, by the people most affected by them'.[23]

To continue the geographical analogy, while the legal historian seeks to track the outline of the Law Mountains, the social historian seeks to understand their formation. Hay's perspective implicitly rejects Langbein's mechanistic view of law; yet Hay's work since *Albion's Fatal Tree* also suggests further complexities in the impact which common people had on the development of law. In 1982 he wrote:

> The argument that we should abandon the study of serial crime rates and seek instead to understand only 'criminal justice systems' may be logically untenable. Unless one proves that control is overwhelmingly, irresistibly determinant of indictment levels . . . then officially recorded crime must be the net result of both the behaviour of those subject to law and those controlling it.[24]

He continued:

> Until we understand popular attitudes formed at the boundary of appropriation and control, we do not understand the criminal law.[25]

In these statements Hay is still working inside the realm of social causation of 'crime', but the terrain he maps out is a useful starting point because behaviour also involved perception of law on the part of common people. These were not only perceptions of 'justice' or 'rule of law' but of what constituted an 'offence'.

Michael Ignatieff, in his review of histories of punishment, also begins to think of this terrain which is far less certain than histories of control. He writes of the prison reformers:

> The gulf between the reformer's rationalizing intentions and the institutionalized results of their work ought to make us rethink this equation of modernity and rationalization, or at least to give greater room for the idea that modernity is the site of a recurring battle between rationalizing intention and institutions, interests and communities which resist, often with persistent success.[26]

This uncertainty, or recurrent battle, also involves some perception on the part of common people which affects or influences the development of the prison. The uncertainty suggested by both Hay and Ignatieff thus provides good ground from which to question perception of law in colonial New South Wales. The nature of authority and modernity has begun to be seen as subtle and complex.

Though the work suggested by Hay and Ignatieff has not yet begun, the logic and complexity of authority has been the subject of other studies of English law. There is now recognition of localised differences.[27] Authority, though differently defined, has also been of concern in French history. Olwen Hufton in her study of eighteenth-century Languedoc discusses attitudes to authority—how much respect the common man had for *ancien régime* magistrates, tax collectors, landlords, bailiffs, bishops, priests.[28] She discovered, 'there was a sense in which public hatred was the most constant and powerful expression of community solidarity, a binding force in a society otherwise marked by private altercation and fragmentation figures of authority were often recipients of that hatred'.[29] Iain Cameron in his study of the Auvergne and Guyenne between 1720 and 1790 considered extra-legal means of solving disputes and the impression the development of policing in the French countryside made on them. He, too, finds resistance to figures of authority.[30]

While English studies stress the centrality of legal symbolism to structures of authority, these French studies suggest that the authority existing in the French countryside was centred not on law but on tested means of feuding, or assault. Authority, in the form of constables and magistrates, was rejected in favour of the authority of the vendetta. Authority need not always rest, then, on 'rule of law'.

Michael Sturma, in his study of crime and society in the colony, has considered ' "moral entrepreneurs"—those who define moral categories and have definitions enforced as public policy, [which] becomes as important as those who are treated as immoral'.[31] He also examines environmental causes of criminal offences. His identification of particularly colonial influences on crime provides an important influence in this work. Sturma's focus was on the 'creation of crime' as a definition, and the ways in which actual offences diverged from that. My own study, however, looks at the way in which the practice of law developed among the ordinary population. Therefore it does not follow the perspective set out by Sturma and should not be seen as an earlier chapter of his work. Nevertheless, his study broke ground in applying theoretical perspectives on crime to a colonial Australian environment.

Australian historians examining the late nineteenth century have concentrated on the development of policing of women, the insane, the family and public space.[32] This work is influenced by Jacques Donzolot and Michel Foucault.[33] Policing is not seen to be simply repressive: it is also considered to be productive. There were gaps in policing practice, such as the underpolicing of criminal abortion;[34] policing was also used to support parents, or to assist illegal economies.[35] In these ways, policing sustained particular social relations 'while being contested by contradictions in those social relations'.[36] Mark Finnane dates the beginning of modern policing from the mid-nineteenth century with the development of police forces.[37] While it is true that in New South Wales there were considerable disjunctions in the policing of public space in the early nineteenth century because of the convict system and the different interests of police magistrates and constables under it, we must recognise that the policing of public space became well entrenched in the colony from 1810. This was not policing of the convict, though aspects of this policing did originate in convict management, but policing of women or the vagrant ex-convict thought unwilling to work. The interests of the grand jury in opposing street vendors or those attempting to sell their labour were the interests of wealthy shopkeepers and merchants. Policing in early colonial New South Wales can also be said to be 'productive', to use Golder and Hogg's term in their essay in *Policing in Australia*; it was particularly productive of illegal economies and may be said to sustain notions of the family. The attentiveness shown to married women raped in the house, for example, meant that the court did move to sustain some aspect of women's relations to men. Unlike Judith Allen, in *Sex and Secrets*, I do not explore gaps in policing, but I do see the history of sex as central to analysis. The colonial administration divided women from men in their structuring of the convict system; the nature of this system resulted in different kinds of surveillance of public space which again delineated women from men. What was 'male' and 'female' in the early colony meant different things to administrators and to the ordinary population, but both regarded women as suspicious if they moved outside the boundaries of these different proper behaviours. Analysis of women or what it is to be 'female' is central to this book.

While I do not wish to use the term 'productive', what becomes apparent in my study of the relationship of people to law is the role of criminal law in modernising labour relations, through the actions of servants as much as of employers; and the role of law in becoming part of the wider market through accusation, informing and reward. The law, for the ordinary population, could become part of the aggressive capitalism which characterised the early economy. It was perhaps this multi-purpose nature of criminal law which gave it strength in the colony. The only serious revolt against the administration, bushranging, became caught up in the system of reward, informing and payment which characterised criminal law. So criminal law did not only protect property relations through enforcing new statutes, as it did in England; it could well become part of those property relations, when property was widely defined. The 'potent fiction' of rule of law perhaps becomes stronger when it contains so many unintended benefits.

Rather than policing producing such a situation, it is from the beginning intrinsically bound up with it. Any public space has many uses; if constables ignore some aspects of use of that space and concentrate on others, the constables in turn are ignored or concentrated on. The point for the inhabitants of colonial New South Wales is: whose world is most important? Where does real power lie? And it must be assumed that there is no neat interconnection between the two. But both administrators and the ordinary population have notions of what it is to be 'male' and 'female', and this distinction underlies all others. While notions of 'respectability' may not have appeared among the ordinary population, it is clear that the modern notions of work, payment, gender were expressed in the workings, in the practice, of criminal law and that the law, however unintentionally, did help bring them into being.

The inhabitants in early colonial New South Wales could 'take' law from the administrators and statute makers: this is the world we are to explore. It does not help to have a prior notion of criminal law as a 'mechanism', a machine-like entity which on the one hand fairly decides or on the other polices. All criminal law—for those who use it or come under its auspices—is a series of suspicions, hearsay, guilt. Eleanor Walsh, with her tracking, hoped for a conviction. It was from such outrage, real or feigned, that people were hanged. The clear disjunction between this world of formal or informal power relations and the final courtroom hearing is illustrated in Part 4. The first part of this book deals with law and the person. From the beginning of the nineteenth century and particularly in the formation of the colony of New South Wales there was a new interest in persons, their habitations and their bodies. This interest has been noted by Michel Foucault.[38] Part 1, then, considers discursive aspects of law. Part 2 deals with the crisis of bushranging; and it is here that the law as simply discursive is questioned. The offence and its policing combine to produce a culture. Part 3 deals with the use of law by constables and magistrates and administrators, and also by the ordinary population. It further explores that 'taking' of criminal law.

Despite the derivation of New South Wales from English culture and law, it does not necessarily follow that the colony would exhibit the same relations to authority which were evident in England in the eighteenth and early nineteenth century. In New South Wales the crux of legal debate of the day centred on the question, when did a criminal cease to be a criminal? As New South Wales was a colony, and a convict colony at that, how much of English 'right' should prevail? This study cannot be seen neatly to intersect with English research or as providing an earlier chapter for studies of the late nineteenth century. As stated, there is a precedent in Australian social history for the perspective that people influence institutions. There is beginning to be such a perspective in the English history of law. The slow development of analysis in England may partly be the result of the kind of evidence available. In England there has been reliance on the most available document—the indictment, or formal document of committal. The deposition is a bulkier document full of hearsay, drawings, and scraps of material. As a document it is often deemed irrelevant to a study of law.

Interpreting Available Evidence

Records surviving from early colonial New South Wales include depositions, court lists, transcripts, court records and written defences, all of which provide immense detail. The use of this raw material has been the subject of much debate. J. S. Cockburn has considered the court records as incidental information on the structure, habits, worries and recreations of local society, and David Vaissey has enlarged upon such usage: 'it is also from this sort of record that through the extraordinary behaviour of individuals which brings them to court one is afforded the common behaviour, speech patterns and even gestures of seventeenth-century people.'[39]

Though Vaissey can see the wealth of such records, he nevertheless rejects them as evidence on the same grounds as other authors. The use of depositions has often been accompanied by warnings that people, when speaking, are in court and are likely to make up information, to overstate or to underplay their roles. That this might be of significance in itself has not been considered. Court records have been seen as a distortion of social relations. That this distortion might also be part of social relations themselves has not been taken into account.

Historians of popular culture, however, have dealt with similar theoretical problems. In a response to the writings of Michel Foucault, Carlo Ginzberg has asked the question whether popular culture exists outside the act that suppresses it; he concludes that from Foucault's perspective it does not. Rather than tracking the development of discursive institutions, such as the inquisition, the prison, or the system of mental health, as writers like Foucault do, Ginzberg looks closely at the discrepancies between the questions of judges and the replies of the accused.[40] He and writers like E. P. Thompson and Natalie Davis look at contact between the religious and the popular and the worlds created by such a conflict.[41]

Such historical work owes much to anthropology and particularly to its sub-branch, ethnography. George Marcus and Michael Fischer term this approach 'the jeweller's eye view of the world'.[42] Hans Medick has used the anthropologist Clifford Geertz's work to describe the nature of ethnography. Geertz works by 'searching out and analyzing the symbolic norms—words, images, institutions, behaviours,—in terms of which in each place people actually represented themselves to themselves and to one another'.[43] What historians like Ginzberg and Davis have done is to use the methods of anthropology to see how historical change is lived. They have dealt with contradictions, subtleties and compromises in the relations of ordinary people to institutions and power. In looking at court records we are considering the relationship of people to an institution, their input into that institution and their interpretation of it: in short, how law was lived in colonial New South Wales.

Court records can be seen as representations not of social life or the attitudes of common people but of the dynamic relationship between people and law. What do ordinary people understand by guilt, suspicion, evidence, the 'offence'? What are their reference points in cases? If Henry Crane's footprints were not tracked at all and false information was given to court, it was still the snare of suspicion, and his own convictism which led to his appearance. Depositions present their own landscape; they invest particular geographical areas with significance; they describe what a culture thought should be locked, hidden, silenced or spoken of in terms of the law.

So this study deals with the realm of speech and silence: speech that is directed towards committal or acquittal, and silence with similar aims. The importance of what is said and its power has been recognised by anthropologists.[44] Oral historians also have dealt with such questions.[45] Any written record, including Hansard, is subject to question as to its authenticity. In a society where records were transcribed there was great concern for transcription as a skill. Depositions surviving from early colonial New South

Wales attest to the skill of courtroom clerks. They do not write in sentences; they note diversions, questioning and tears. The depositions, together with the badly spelt notes of prisoners, provide evidence of speech. Such an approach to speech and silence means this work cannot relate to the entire fabric of social life as the editors of *Australians 1838* have done. The approach to law followed here touches on many aspects of social life but may distort them or concentratè on particular sensitivities that do not figure largely in day-to-day life. Law in practice relates to the concerns of the everyday in peculiar ways: the arduous work of the farm may be halted by the discovery of the bloodied skin of a calf; the slow wending of the cart home from market may be brought to a jarring halt by men with coarse linen masks; the strangled body of a baby may be found in a ditch. In all of these cases people will give their versions of events: they will lie, weep, accuse and exaggerate; they will curse the court, beg forgiveness or faint at the announcement of a sentence. In that process they will describe their relationship to law and authority. It is possible to look at court records and see in them the style of life of the period. We can find, for instance, the layout of a house, the clientele of public houses, the kinds of entertainment indulged in, but this is another project. When such information intersects with the purpose of this book, note is made, for court records have uses beyond a study of law.

This book cannot comment on the debate over the origins of the convicts. The most recent contribution to such work is S. Nicholas' edited collection *Convict Workers*.[46] This collection concludes that the convict system was efficient and productive, that convicts were well fed and clothed, and that they were skilled before they arrived in the colony. In the case of women this was not recognised by the administration, and prostitution was work for these women.[47] The writers in this collection accept definitions of crime in order to refute them. They also discuss the driving mechanism of the rewards and wages of the convict system rather than the lash which was used judiciously.[48] My own study examines only the labour system as it appears before the courts. The reasons for its appearance are vastly different for town employers, country employers of different levels, and employers of convict women, as we shall see. The reluctance of large landholders to use the courts supports the finding of *Convict Workers*. So does the use of prostitution for money. However, my study sees the definition of 'work' as more difficult and also notes the divergence of theft patterns for women in the colony from those in England. Again, I begin from a perspective different to that of these authors.

Before 1824 New South Wales included Tasmania. After some examination of Tasmanian records I found that the pattern of court interactions differed so much that a separate study was warranted. The cases involving bushranging, for instance, were markedly different from the mainland.[49] I have, however, included one Tasmanian case and that is the case against Lily Mackellar for infanticide. This was for comparative purposes, cases of infanticide on the mainland being few.

During the entire period under discussion Aborigines were under sustained attack by the new society. When we consider court records, however, it is as if this is not occurring. Even reciprocal relations of trade are not mentioned.[50] There are a very few cases of massacre or charges of murder of Aborigines in the court records which I examined. They also must be the subject of a separate study, for which I am not qualified. European culture and English law include reference points readily understood by their participants. Law among Europeans, therefore, can be interpreted by the principles I have set out. Law between Aborigines and Europeans, however, is the concern of other historians: for example, those who are familiar with the history of the Dharug-speaking people, and the Blacktown region.[51] Consequently, this book is limited to an examination of the European population only.

This is a study of the dynamics of criminal law among Europeans on mainland New South Wales between 1810 and 1830. It is not a history of the entire society—which has been approached by the work of historians such as Alford, Hirst and Robinson.[52] It is concerned with the meaning of law and how it was lived in early colonial New South Wales.

The Legal Records and Their Context

The basis of this study is the 5910 remaining records of the Courts of Criminal Jurisdiction, the Quarter Sessions, the magistrates' benches and the Judge Advocate's Bench for the years 1810 to 1830. These records are mainly depositions and, where applicable, indictments. Bench proceedings were recorded by a clerk in a bound volume. The same clerks wrote out the proceedings of more serious hearings on loose sheets of paper which they folded in four, titled, and sent to the Judge Advocate's office (before 1824) or the Attorney-General or Clerk of the Quarter Sessions (in cases involving free persons after 1824). These folded records remain today. The relevant officers read the proceedings and decided if there was a case to answer; if so, an indictment was drawn up. Indictments are very formal legal statements of the charge. They state the Act under which the prisoner was charged, the name of the defendant and his or her status, whether yeoman, gentleman, labourer, single woman or wife. Such formal documents are the main surviving source for the English historian of law. In New South Wales we have the documents which provided the basis of the indictment as well as the indictment.

The records are virtually impossible to enter in a data base. This is because of the number of variables and the damage that can be done, for example, in compressing such complaints as 'Refusing to boil a kettle when asked' and 'Refusing to work before 6 a.m.' into the category 'Refusal'. Much is lost in such a compression. This does not mean that I have dealt with any less complaints than a computer could. I have examined all of the 5910 records and most of each of these contain the words of at least three informants.

I have not used a sample of the surviving records but have worked through all of them. These cases are the surviving records of the practice of a legal system which has been acknowledged by legal historians John Bennet, Alex Castles, C. H. Currey, J. A. McLaughlin and David Neal to be fraught with political tension and debate.[53] Blackstone's observation that 'colonists carry with them only so much of English law as is applicable to their new situation'[54] was at the centre of legal debate of the day. New South Wales was a convict colony, wrote Francis Forbes; 'so are the West Indies slave colonies. I never heard it contended that their measure of British right was any less because their estates are cultivated by their slaves.'[55]

The tension between penal colony and 'British right' was inherent in the structure of the courts in colonial New South Wales. Until 1824 there were two tiers in the criminal courts. Convict offences and minor offences by free persons were heard by the magistrates' benches, and in Sydney minor offences were also heard by the Judge Advocate's Bench. The latter court declined in importance from 1815 because the Judge Advocate no longer played a part in its deliberations. The second tier consisted of the Court of Criminal Jurisdiction where cases were heard by the Judge Advocate and six military officers. The Judge Advocate was both principal prosecutor and judge, and this, along with the style of a military tribunal, was the cause of complaint and petition by the Judge Advocates Bent and Wylde as well as the free population.[56] In 1824 the legal system was reformed. Courts of Quarter Sessions were established with juries which until 1829 were drawn from civilians. In that year they were replaced by military men. In 1824 the Supreme Court of Criminal Jurisdiction replaced the Court of Criminal Jurisdiction. This court included the Attorney-General as prosecutor, a judge or chief justice, sometimes sitting together, and a military jury, which nevertheless deliberated in the manner of a civilian jury. In 1824 the Colonial Secretary, Frederick Goulburn, promised that the colony would soon be 'altogether English'.[57] The legal system was becoming geared to a free population. This was a period of rapid change for criminal law in the colony.

In 1810 on Macquarie's arrival in the colony the regulation of a society based on convict labour had been reorganised. This involved surveillance of work hours, restrictions on movement, and restrictions on the economic activity which could be carried out. The policing structure was based on magistrates' benches and the Court of Criminal Jurisdiction. By 1830 the court system had undergone rapid change.

Throughout all these changes the magistrates' benches, though subject to political intrigue, remained essentially uniform in scope and action. Magistrates controlled local constables and initially heard all cases, except some murder cases which were heard by a coroner. Only a court of law could determine guilt. However, from the very beginning of a case notions of suspicion, guilt and evidence came into play. So Henry Crane was suspected, tracked, taken into custody and sent to Sydney Gaol, before the Judge Advocate decided his case warranted trial and the court found his case to warrant acquittal.

As Cynthia Herrup has written, 'the courtroom stood at the end, not at the beginning, of a complex chain of private and public actions'.[58] Herrup concentrates on the legal process from its beginnings to the court appearance in seventeenth-century East Sussex and her work is closest to the project undertaken here. Her concentration on a process limits the attention she can give to popular understandings of law. The relationship of people to law may occur inside a process, but they may stumble through that process and fail to understand its rituals, maintaining all the while that they know what is right.

Eleanor Walsh resided in the fertile Bringelly region with its mixed pattern of tenure from small farms to large estates, but she also resided in a landscape of her own perception where boundaries, suspicion and tracking were claimed by her to be important. Her involvement with the court was part of a much wider pattern of understandings of the role of law in society, and that law was to figure in her own and Henry Crane's life in different ways.

Criminal records surviving from this period have been only partly indexed. Where records come from bench books, the date of hearing provides a guide to location of cases;

this also applies to the early records of the Court of Criminal Jurisdiction until 1816. For the higher courts, records are held in boxes according to the month of trial. Thus month and year of trial will guide the reader to records. If cases did not come to trial, they are held in a box entitled 'miscellaneous' under year of trial. The different location of records accounts for the citation system used here.

The main focus of this book is the region of settlement in New South Wales known as the County of Cumberland, though settlements further afield receive attention in Chapters 4, 5 and 7. Chapter 5 examines closely records from three benches where depositions have survived, Liverpool, Goulburn and Argyle, because they provide considerable detail.

Notes

1 R. vs Henry Crane, C.C.J., September 1822, 20.
2 A. Atkinson, 'Four Patterns of Convict Protest' *Labour History*, no. 37, November 1979; M. Aveling, 'She Only Married to be Free; or Cleopatra Vindicated' *Push from the Bush*, no. 2, November 1978; M. Sturma, 'Eye of the Beholder, the stereotype of women convicts 1788–1852' *Labour History*, no. 34, May 1978; P. Robinson, *The Hatch and Brood of Time*; P. Robinson, *The Women of Botany Bay*.
3 J. B. Hirst, *Convict Society and Its Enemies*, preface.
4 D. Neal, 'Free Society, Penal Colony, Slave Society, Prison', *Historical Studies*, vol. 22, no. 89, October 1987.
5 See K. Alford, *Production or Reproduction? An Economic History of Women in Australia 1788–1850*; K. Daniels, 'Prostitution in Tasmania during transition from a penal settlement to a "civilized" society' in K. Daniels, ed., *So Much Hard Work*; A. Summers, *Damned Whores And God's Police*, Melbourne, 1976; M. Dixson, *The Real Matilda*, Melbourne, 1976.
6 P. Robinson, *The Hatch and Brood of Time*.
7 For example, S. J. Kaplan and C. J. Koepp, *Work in France*; W. H. Sewell, Jr, *Work and Revolution in France*.
8 M. Aveling and A. Atkinson, eds, *Australians 1838. Push from the Bush* (journal) Armidale, NSW.
9 See P. Bourdieu, 'The disenchantment of the world' in *Algeria 1960*; see also G. E. Marcus and M. M. J. Fischer, *Anthropology as Cultural Critique*.
10 J. Langbein, 'Albion's Fatal Flaws', *Past and Present*, no. 98, February 1983, pp. 99–101, 105–7.
11 G. Rude, *Criminal and Victim*. p. 2.
12 *ibid.*
13 *ibid.*; see also H. Zehr, *Crime and the Development of Modern Society.*
14 D. Hay, P. Linebaugh, J. Rule, E. P. Thompson, C. Winslow, *Albion's Fatal Tree*, p. 14.
15 *ibid.*
16 Rude, *Criminal And Victim*, p. 126.
17 Hay et al., *Albion's Fatal Tree*, p. 13.
18 J. Brewer and J. Styles, eds, *An Ungovernable People, The English and their Law in the Seventeenth and Eighteenth Centuries*, p. 14.
19 J. Langbein, 'Albion's Fatal Flaws', pp. 99–101, 105–7.
20 *ibid.*, p. 120.
21 P. Linebaugh, '(Marxist) Social History and (Conservative) Legal History: A Reply to Professor Langbein', in *New York University Law Review*, vol. 60, no. 2, May 1985, pp. 217-18 and 234.
22 D. Hay, 'The Criminal Prosecution in England and its Historians', *Modern Law Review*, vol. 47, no. 1, January 1984, p. 2.
23 D. Philips, 'A Just Measure of Crime, Authority, Hunters and Blue Locusts: The Revisionist Social

History of Crime and the Law in Britain' in S. Cohen and A. Scull, eds, *Social Control and the State*, p. 52. He criticises L. Radzinowicz, *A History of English Criminal Law and its Administration from 1750*, London, 1948-68.

24 D. Hay, 'War, Dearth and Theft in the Eighteenth Century: The Record of the English Courts', *Past and Present*, no. 95, May 1982, p. 158.

25 *ibid.*, p. 159.

26 M. Ignatieff, 'State, Civil Society and Total Institutions: A Critique of Recent Social Histories of Punishment', in Cohen and Scull, *Social Control and the State*, p. 83.

27 K. Wrightson, 'Two concepts of order: Justices, constables and jurymen in seventeenth century England', in Brewer and Styles, *An Ungovernable People*.

28 O. Hufton, 'Attitudes towards Authority in Eighteenth-century Languedoc', *Social History*, vol. 3, no. 3, October 1978, p. 281.

29 *ibid.*, p. 301.

30 I. Cameron, *Crime and Repression in the Auvergne and Guyenne, 1720–1790*, p. 13.

31 M. Sturma, *Vice in a Vicious Society*, St Lucia, Qld, 1983, pp. 6-8.

32 M. Finnane, *Policing in Australia: Historical Perspectives*; see also Sydney Labour History Group, *What Rough Beast*.

33 J. Donzolot, *The Policing of Families*; M. Foucault, *Discipline and Punish*.

34 J. Allen, 'Octavious Beale Reconsidered, Infanticide, Babyfarming and Abortion in N.S.W., 1880–1939' in *What Rough Beast*; see also J. Allen, *Sex and Secrets*.

35 R. Hogg and H. Golder, 'Policing Sydney' in Finnane, ed., *Policing in Australia*.

36 M. Finnane, introduction to *Policing in Australia*, p. 12.

37 *ibid.*

38 M. Foucault, *The History of Sexuality*, New York, 1980.

39 Vaissey quotes Cockburn, see D. Vaissey, 'Court Records and the social history of seventeenth-century England', *History Workshop*, 1, Spring, 1976, pp. 185, 187.

40 C. Ginzberg, *The Cheese and the Worms*; pp. xviii–xix, discussing M. Foucault, *I, Paul Rivière*, Paris, 1973.

41 E. P. Thompson, 'Rough Music, le Charivari anglaise', *Annales*, E.S.C., 1974; N. Z. Davis, 'The Reasons of Misrule: Youth Groups and Charivaris in Sixteenth-century France', *Past and Present*, no. 50, 1971.

42 G. E. Marcus and M. M. J. Fischer, *Anthropology as Cultural Critique*, p. 15.

43 H. Medick, 'Missionaries in the Row Boat: Ethnological Ways of Knowing as a Challenge to Social History', *Comparative Studies in Society and History*, vol. 29, no. 1, January 1987, p. 86.

44 For example J. Fauret-Saada, *Deadly Words*, Cambridge, 1977.

45 L. Passerini, *Fascism in Popular Memory*.

46 S. Nicholas, *Convict Workers*.

47 D. Oxley, 'Female Convicts', in *ibid.*

48 *ibid.*, p. 11.

49 Alex Castles is pursuing this work; see also R. Ward, *Finding Australia*, pp. 313–43.

50 By trade I also mean trade in labour, sexuality etc.; see L. Ryan, *The Aboriginal Tasmanians*.

51 Jim Kohan is presently involved in this work.

52 K. Alford, *Production or Reproduction?*; J. B. Hirst, *Convict Society and Its Enemies*; P. Robinson, *The Hatch and Brood of Time*.

53 C. H. Currey, 'Chapters on the Legal History of N.S.W.', LL.D. thesis, University of Sydney, 1929; C. H. Currey, *Francis Forbes*; C. H. Currey, *The Brothers Bent*; J. Bennet, *A History of the Supreme Court in N.S.W.*, Sydney 1974; J. A. McLaughlin, 'The Magistracy in N.S.W. 1788–1850', M.A. thesis, University of Sydney, 1973; D. Neal, 'The Rule of Law in a Penal Colony: Law and Politics in Early N.S.W., 1788–1840', LL.D. thesis, University of New South Wales, 1986.

54 Quoted by W. V. J. Windeyer, *Lectures in Legal History*, p. 303.
55 Francis Forbes, Private Letters to Wilmot, 6 March 1827, A1819.
56 See C. H. Currey, 'Chapters on the Legal History of N.S.W.', pp. 140–3.
57 Public notice, *Sydney Gazette*, 21 October 1824.
58 C. B. Herrup, *The Common Peace: Participation and the Criminal Law in Seventeenth-Century England*, p. 92.

PART 1

Law and the Person

'. . . her thing was her own and she
would do with it what she liked'

SOPHIA CARNE,
SERVANT TO GEORGE CHARTRES

2

LABOUR

Convict Labour in Sydney

> Bigge: How long does it take to make a London thief into a good farming man?
> Hutchinson: Two or three years.[1]

Bigge speaks here of transformation and this is the language of reform clearly under-stood by an administrator of convicts, William Hutchinson. The convict was raw material. Such language was to make an increasing appearance in the critiques of the colony of New South Wales. And it is this language which was later to influence the historiography of early colonial New South Wales. The issue of what convicts 'became' and the nature of the 'raw material' are major directions of research.[2] Alongside the language of reform was the language of commerce. This has not been fully explored by historians, except in Shaw's recognition in *Convicts and the Colonies* of the constant tension between the notion that the convict system should pay for itself and the notion that the convict should be reformed.

The language of commerce, then, is open to further exploration. It implicitly considered the encapsulation of the person of the convict—it asked the question, what was the person of the convict? Legislators and administrators were led into the difficult world of political economy. This was not undertaken in order to consider the rights of the convict; rather it was for administrators to measure, to weigh, to quantify labour, which they struggled to see as separate from the convict. Such measuring and weighing occurred alongside the transferring of numbers of convicts in the name of reform, and of a system which would 'pay for itself'.

Governor Brisbane's instructions to move convicts out of towns and out of government labour resulted from the recommendations of the Bigge Reports concerning reform and cost efficiency.[3] Brisbane's successor, Governor Darling, on the other hand, sought to have all convicts work in irons on their arrival, emphasising their status as prisoners, but was thwarted by a perceived need for labourers.[4]

Behind these conflicting expectations lay the common desire to effect the London thief's transformation into labourer, whether government or private, and his identification as worker. The concern over the meaning of labour and the ownership of the convict was precisely where the law intervened in the lives of all convicts. There were differences, however, in the intervention of the law into the life of the male convict in the town and the life of the male convict on the farm and, again, in the life of the female convict. For male convicts it is almost as if the geographical shift in placement of convicts was a shift to an older logic of labour, that of the plantation—a move back from the cash nexus to ownership of the convict's person.

The struggle over the meaning of labour is first apparent in the language of legislation, then administrators, then overseers, who came to the courts. Studies of language such as William Sewell's *Work and Revolution in France* have often shown surprising use of terminology. Sewell discovered a 'seemingly paradoxical flowering of the old regime's language in the midst of a radical revolution'.[5] Two things are apparent in language referring to convicts in the early colony: the struggle to come to terms with the dividing of labour from the person; and the seeming willingness of administrators and overseers to use the new language. Concentration on labour value was intrinsic to the regulations governing transportation. The sentence of transportation meant that the Crown obtained 'property in service' in the convicted offender. Francis Forbes, Chief Justice, wrote in 1827 to Wilmot Horton, undersecretary in the Colonial Office, 'transportation was not peculiar to New South Wales'. The language of the Transportation Act passed in the fourth year of George I is that 'in many of his majesty's colonies in America there is a great want of servants, who by their labour might be the means of improving such colonies and making them more useful to the nation'.[6]

In the American colonies servants were sold to landowners by the masters of ships, who obtained 'property in service' of the convicts they took aboard.[7] In New South Wales the convicts did not become the property of the shipowner who brought them to the colony, but were invested as the property of the governor of New South Wales by the English courts. The governor could assign the services of convicts to landholders; he could interfere in what he considered were poor conditions; and he could grant tickets-of-leave and pardons.

But the extent of the governor's power over the relationship between assignees and their convicts was unclear, at least in the eyes of Chief Justice Forbes. Forbes argued in 1827 concerning later reforms that, by the third section of Mr Peel's Act of 1824, which amended the Transportation Act,

> property is given in the service of convicted persons to the governor of the colony and his assignees for the residue of the term of the prisoner's sentence with a saving only of the King's prerogative of mercy and subject of course to the provisions of the 30th of his late Majesty, enabling the Governor to pardon the sentences of transported offenders. I have heard some strong doctrines advanced upon the clause of this Act and it is important, as recent events in the colony have shown, that there should be a clear understanding upon the real nature of the power of the governor resulting from the legal property in the services of transportees.[8]

The problem lay both in the phrase 'and his assignees' and in the lack of clarity concerning the governor's role. The Act, designed to remedy the uncertainties involving the title employers held in convict servants, had been the subject of much discussion in the colony. Forbes had heard 'strong doctrines advanced upon the clause of this Act'.[9]

He posed questions which the law seemed to beg.

> Cannot the governor then, upon the arrival of a convict ship, order as many of the prisoners as he pleases to a penal settlement, within the colony? This question may be answered by another . . . cannot any settler who is displeased with his assigned servants order them to a penal settlement?[10]

The context in which these questions were asked was that Governor Darling had been seen to overstep the boundaries of the power given to him in Peel's revision of the law. He had, for instance, removed the servants of two newspapers which had subjected him to criticism.[11] Forbes' questions were finally resolved in 1830 when British Parliament established that the governor must work with the Executive Council when he sought to intervene in assignment and it must be 'for the benefit of the convict'.[12]

This is the classic example of the clash between perceptions involving property in service, that of the relationship of labour to ownership of the person. The notion of reform of the convict was implicit in the phrase 'the benefit of the convict'. Property in service gave much more room for recognition of the convict as a person separate from his or her labour. Although the 'benefit of the convict' had not been stressed before, the sentence of transportation, with its recognition of the governor's residual power over convicts, also created a structure for authority in the colony. The relationship between master and servant in the colony was complicated by the governor's power over the servant. This power was buttressed by that of the magistrate. The employer was not able to punish his convict servants himself: he was to take them before a magistrate. This trilogy of power of governor, employer, magistrate did not change throughout the period. In Sydney, because of notions of reform, the raw material for that relationship, the convict workforce, underwent some changes.

Sydney saw three shifts in the deployment of male convicts. The procedure in operation between 1810 and 1819 on the arrival of male convicts was described by Major Druitt, Chief Engineer. After the convicts had been mustered in the gaol yard, 'they were marched to the lumberyard where they were distributed into several gangs when the Superintendent said to them "you must go to provide yourself with lodging where you can come to work when the bell rings".'[13] This organisation of the day according to time implied that convicts had time to themselves. In 1819, however, the convict barracks were opened, housing 800 convicts. Barracks convicts were able to work for themselves on Saturdays after 1 p.m. and Sundays. The third shift occurred after the arrival of Brisbane with his instructions to move convicts out of Sydney. He did this by assigning as many as possible and establishing clearing gangs to hold convicts until they were assigned. In 1825 the Colonial Secretary, Earl Bathurst, requested the breaking up of some of these clearing gangs, 'which have been solely established in consequence of a temporary relaxation in the demand for labourers'.[14] Darling further attempted to reduce the number of convicts both in Sydney and in government service because he wished gang labour to be seen as a punishment; he established ironed road gangs for that purpose.

These changing deployments of male convicts not only shifted the geographical focus of convict labour but were evidence of increasing concern on the part of colonial administrators for the management of convicts as prisoners. Yet this management did not require the building of prisons. The convict barracks did increase the surveillance of convicts. Those employed by the government were kept inside one building at night. Later, however, Governors Brisbane and Darling concentrated on the atomisation of the convict population. They were concerned with keeping convicts out of the towns, in which a convict presence was considered dangerous. Despite concerns for convicts as prisoners, both Brisbane and Darling continued to emphasise the centrality of labour in the treatment of male convicts. Male convicts were to be the responsibility of private employers who had their own methods of reward or threatened punishment to exact labour. Isolation on a farm and under an employer was meant to result in the reform of the convict.

Concerns for the hours of convict labour had long been in existence in the colony. In 1796 Governor Hunter had written that 'every labouring person whether working for public or private individuals is regulated in his hours of labour by the working hours established by government and each by this regulation has a certain proportion of time to himself during which he can let himself out to hire'.[15] The practice of convicts letting themselves out to hire was well established by the time Macquarie replaced Bligh as governor in 1810. However, the concept 'work hours' was continually undercut by the notion of taskwork, in which convicts worked on a specific task and regarded work as finished when the task was ended. Macquarie, like Hunter, attempted to end taskwork and remove the influence it had on the shortening of the working day. Macquarie was successful in orienting government work to work hours through the activities of his Chief Engineer Druitt who calculated taskwork according to hours of government labour.[16] This meant that during Macquarie's period there was strong emphasis placed on work hours and the amount of work done in them. While the sale of 'extra labour' and its measurement had been important before Macquarie's arrival, it received renewed emphasis, along with the measurement of production during the working day. For example, the superintendent of carpenters at Parramatta made regular returns of government labour. The return for 1811 from 23 February to 2 March showed that two smiths made four stock sloops for a new cart wheel for government use; this, and bullock rings, came to a total of '25 lbs of work' in the overseer's estimation of production.[17] In 1820 the magistrates at Parramatta wrote to Governor Macquarie concerning Richard Fitzgerald, superintendent of the government establishment at Emu Plains. He was 'accused of appropriating portions of the labour of many convicts amounting to the labour of one convict for 43 weeks'.[18] Robert Cartwright, questioned by Commissioner Bigge, said he believed bargains were frequently made between masters and servants for the performance of certain 'quantities of extra work' on condition of obtaining tickets-of-leave or emancipation.[19] John Morris, a sawyer employed in government work, gave evidence to Bigge concerning the subversion of government labour. 'Mr. Hutchinson promised me two years ago my ticket and that I should have it as soon as possible. I had sawed enough stuff for his first house, he pays me 8/- per hundred feet sometimes in property, sometimes in money.'[20]

The language of work was closely related to measurement of time, labour and produce. This measurement of labour was emphasised both in the language of convicts and in the language of administration in Sydney during the Macquarie period. Bigge's request for an estimation of the quantity of work done by a convict in comparison to a workman, together with his request for information as to where and how labour was measured and the value of labour, was language clearly recognised by Druitt. Druitt answered that estimations were given weekly of the number of those employed and the quantity of work done. While no estimation was made of the value of work done by government gangs, the work of other convicts was established by colonial rates.[21] So measurement of labour was closely tied to monetary value. Colonial rates had been set by Macquarie in December 1816, according to Hirst, in order to establish a standard rate of payment for convicts in private service given the introduction of sterling to the colony.[22] An earlier attempt at establishing wage levels had been made by Hunter, who set rates of payment for taskwork.[23] Druitt stated that convicts preferred work with private employers because there were greater opportunities for remuneration. This implies that wages were considered important by convicts. The 'wage', however, may have borne little relation to established rates. Before 1816 the wages given to government servants off the store (i.e. those not drawing government rations) were described by Edward Smith Hall to Darcy Wentworth:

> The magistrates up the country who by their local situation have the arranging of the agricultural wages of the colony are in the weekly habit of adjusting the wages of prisoners as follows: Messr's Cartwright and Mileham, I am credibly informed, fix the annual wages of government men at £15 currency a year, exclusive of suit of slops, Mr Marsden, at Parramatta does the same, Mr. Lowe gives his own men to my certain knowledge £20 currency p.a. and no slops.[24]

Hall added that his rate of wages was £20 and no slops; he continued:

> But as I have always made it a rule to encourage the deserving at the end of every six months I make every man that has given me satisfaction a present of £2.10 in money or clothes and . . . I contrive, if I can, that they shall receive this extra £5 a year during the winter . . . the mode I formerly adopted in regard to the time of payment was *weekly*, but I soon found that living so near to Sydney, my men generally frittered away the whole of their weekly stipends at houses of ill fame.

To prevent such behaviour he began paying them in some food and keeping the remainder of their wages at hand.[25] The above letter was passed on to Governor Macquarie, who informed Darcy Wentworth that he would call a general meeting of magistrates to discuss it.[26] These practices mean that the fixing of wages would not necessarily be adhered to and it is clear a system of rewards for labour still operated after rates had been established in 1816. Macquarie's order that convicts not be allowed to work outside their master's farm or business was not enforced by employers as Samuel Marsden, himself a magistrate, demonstrated in 1822 in the case involving his servant James Ring. Ring was allowed to work for himself and was allowed to do this as reward. Marsden's defence was that the practice was widespread.[27] Government orders, then, did not necessarily reflect the reality of master–servant relations.

Thus labour, while part of sentence of transportation, could be used to advantage by the male convict. Due to this system of rewards and payments he could in fact deal in his own labour, as both Alan Atkinson and J. B. Hirst have argued.[28] For government convicts this occurred only after work hours or, following the building of the barracks in 1819, on Saturdays and Sundays. The existence of these practices did not mean that the convict was always paid for extra work. Thomas Hughes, government flogger, said as much to Marsden when questioned by him about the flogging of three men without trial by the governor. 'I said to Mr. Marsden', submitted Hughes, 'it is some time since I have worked for you in my own time and I never got paid for it . . . he did not make any reply to this.'[29] Yet in this statement Hughes considered he should have been paid and was prepared to state it, or offer information in exchange for that payment.

Both private employers and the government used overseers, selected from well-behaved convicts, to organise work. The overseer had the responsibility to prevent absence or neglect of work for which convicts could be brought before the benches of magistrates. Druitt defined the position of overseers when he noted that 'if the task is not done I have the power of obliging the men to bring it up on Saturday under the superintendence of an overseer under whom neglect has taken place, so the punishment operates on both'.[30] For private employers, as Hirst has stressed, incentives such as extra rations, rum or monetary payments were more popular than taking the convict to court.[31] Convicts had to be punished by a magistrate, and no employer could physically punish a convict him or herself. There is some evidence to suggest that use of the court could be seen as an indication of ineffective management of convict workers. The magistrate Moore gave evidence to the Bigge Inquiry concerning an employer of servants, Dr Townson, whose servants complained against him,

> more for want of steadiness in the management of them than for any other cause. He is likewise given to notice small faults and is therefore always at variance with his men . . . he often complains of his men more than other masters, he irritates them by his manner and then they are insolent to him.[32]

The concern here is with the management of convicts as labourers, implying that reasonable management would have resulted in fewer court appearances. Such evidence suggests that there existed potential for the servant himself to be valued through his labour rather than being regarded as inherently fractious and needing to be forced to work. Thus it could be asked and understood by those persons before the Bigge Inquiry that 'convict management' varied from employer to employer and that there were 'effective' ways of managing convict labour through incentives such as food, clothing or money.

These were the possibilities for male convict servants in Sydney in the twenty years surveyed. All male convicts were labourers of some kind in the employ of either government or private employers. Their power to obtain tickets-of-leave was limited by Brisbane and Darling, but their function and role in the society remained essentially the same. Despite the colonial administration's attempts to define them further as convicts, they remained convict *labourers*.

The sentence of transportation brought with it, then, a whole series of understandings concerning time-limited work and the ability to lend, sell or buy labour. This was not necessarily present among all employers or their servants, but it was the language by which the administration referred to male convicts. It was also the language which government administrators, such as the Chief Engineer, used in their administration and which certain private employers used to exact labour from their servants.

This does not mean that a male convict's status as prisoner was obscured by his value as a labourer. Rather, the two were inseparable. Druitt's estimate of the quantity of labor to be had from a convict in comparison to a free man was one-third less.[33] This encapsulated a whole series of expectations concerning male convicts and the way their world was organised.

Convict Labourers and the Courts

The Sydney magistrates' benches are the major source for court cases involving convicts. These courts did not deal with all work-related offences. Convicts working in the lumberyard and other government work were, according to Druitt, taken directly to the governor for punishment for offences such as 'mutinous conduct and refusal to do their work, also insolence'.[34] These punishments occurred outside the boundary of summary jurisdiction, even though the corporal punishments were inflicted at the gaol. No evidence remains of those offences or punishments, when they were applied or how often. Druitt, when asked about records, replied, 'I should suppose the Gaoler files the warrants and a Black Book is kept in the Barracks.'[35] Unfortunately such a book has not survived.

We find that offences dealt with by the magistrates' benches were concerned with absence more often than with neglect of work. The availability of the alternative methods of punishment thus certainly affected the selectivity of the law in its dealings with male convicts. *Yet in terms of the relationship of people to the criminal law this very selectivity is of importance in itself.* The courts intervened in specific situations and policed a set of relationships determined by the activities of constables and overseers. The courts intervened in the lives of convicts along certain lines and according to certain understandings; it is these understandings that are of concern here. Only a few private employers brought servants before the bench, and they brought them for particular reasons. The courts protected particular relationships.

In 1820 there were 3704 male convicts in Sydney, including ticket-of-leave convicts as well as government and assigned servants.[36] In the years before 1820 the policing of convict labour was the major activity of constables both on the streets and in the dockyard, lumberyard, carters' and prisoners' barracks. After 1820, with decline in importance of government labour, the activity of constables changed. By 1828 constables were more concerned with policing runaways, often apprehending free persons and holding them until it was proved they were free when they appeared before the magistrates' bench.[37] There remain records of 874 cases dealing with conflicts between male convicts and their employers, apart from cases involving theft. These cases come from the entire records remaining for the lower courts between 1810 and 1830. A total of 159 records of theft cases survive for the lower courts of summary jurisdiction. Tables 4 and 5 set out contemporary categories of offences for male convicts and the numbers charged. Through further examination of individual cases, we can see the interaction of law and labour in the town of Sydney.

Places of work are set out in Table 1.

Table 1 Places of employment of convicts appearing before the courts, 1812–28

J.A.B.	1812	1815–16	1820–21	1824	1828
Stonecutters	Town Gang	Stonecutters	Stonemasons	Government	Iron gang
Blacksmiths	Store	Government	Hospital	Clearing Party	Road party
Lumberyard	Lumberyard	Mill	Brickmakers	Longbottom	Carters'
Wheelwrights	Dockyard	Boat Crew	Street Gang	Country Stations	Barracks
Camp Gang		Stonemasons	Shell Gang	Carters' Barracks	Grose Farm
		Gaol Gang	Carters' Barracks	Emu Plains	
		Brickmakers	Botany Road	South Head	
		Hospital	Liverpool Rd	Road Gang	
		Town Gang	Grose Farm	Woolloomooloo	
		Lane Cove	Windsor Road	Barracks	
		Gov. Bullocks	Western Road	Orphan School	
		Bricklayers	Dockyard	clearing party	
		Sawyers	Emu Plains		
		Wood Gang	Lumberyard		
		Stockkeeper	Church		
			Cockle Bay		
			Bricklayers		
			Gaol Gang		
			Longbottom		
			Lime Burners		
			Stonequarry		
			Dockyard		
			Cowpastures		
			Town Gang		
			Engineers		
			Point Gang		
			Marketwharf		

Since government work was performed in separate locations, convicts were restricted to them. Convicts were expected to work between 5 a.m. and 3 p.m. (after the opening of the barracks, until sunset); absence from work during the day was the major offence for which they appeared. This offence occurred during work time and was brought to the bench by the overseer of the work involved, or a constable at the lumberyard or barracks. Dennis Bryant, overseer at the stonequarry, appeared before the Police Magistrates' Bench in 1820 stating that 'yesterday afternoon about three I detected the two prisoners Edward Marcelle and John Merchant absent from their gang and government work without leave, they had a fire in the bush and were laying down either side of it'.[38] These prisoners had all indulgences withdrawn for three months as punishment.

It was absence during hours of work which was crucial to the appearance in court of convicts working for the government and it was their overseers or overseeing constables who reported such absence. In 1815–16 only two cases of absence were not reported by overseers or overseeing constables: one convict absent from the gaol gang was discovered by a constable swimming;[39] another, a wardsman at the hospital, was reported by a patient.[40] Only two cases of absence appeared in 1812 of government employees, both of them from the gaol gang.[41] Offenders before the Judge Advocate's Bench were either reported by overseers or sent in from country areas.[42]

The bulk of offences of absence occurred in 1820–21 when the working population of convicts was highest in Sydney. In this period the overseers were the major apprehenders of absent convicts. (See Table 2.) The importance of overseers in keeping convicts at work is clearly evident in the report of Major Druitt, who on his rounds found that five men out of the seven employed at the church were absent.[43] The overseer in this case had been negligent, the work in consequence not done.

Table 2 Officers reporting convicts absent from government work, * 1820–21

Period of Absence	Reported by:				
	Overseer, on inspection	Overseer or constable of yard	Peter Plomer, barrack clerk	Constables	Total
Overnight	3	3			6
1 hour or on absconding		4			4
1 day or afternoon		19	1	1	21
1 week or part thereof		10	4	3	17
Weeks–months		4	3		7
Sent in custody from country			10	1	11
From country			4		4
Without pass				3	3
Total	3	40	22	8	73

*18 cases involved absence from the barracks rather than from government work.

There was a blurring of distinction between runaway and absence offences before the Police Magistrates' Bench. The records for 1824 show an equal emphasis on those defined as runaway, usually from the country, and those as absent, from Sydney, usually in private employ. One prisoner in private employ was defined as absent rather than a runaway, even though he had been gone for eight months.[44] This occurs also in 1828 when runaways were persons from the country or an iron gang or road party. In 1820 and 1821 we see convicts being arrested as runaways. In the early years we find reports of absence if the servant is missed from work; through the activities of constables it became the identification of prisoners *not at work* which was important and such concerns appeared in the construction of cases. So rather than the workplace policing its own convicts, we find a development of policing of the workplace from outside. In 1826 a deposition was sent to the Sydney Quarter Sessions which presented evidence against Thomas Isaacson, free carpenter, for receiving stolen cedar from the convict servants of the sheriff. It included a map (see Figure 1) of the direction the two servants travelled

Figure 1   Map included in the Quarter Sessions case against Thomas Isaacson for receiving stolen goods, 1826
(redrawn).

when they were supposed to be fetching dung from stables belonging to Dyer. The
servants turned in to Castlereagh Street and went to the back of Isaacson's house. The
house is shown, the front of it looking on to Elizabeth Street. The other house belonged
to James and Sarah Deering who were both standing at their door when the sheriff's cart
drew up at the back of Isaacson's and eight pieces of cedar were put over the fence.[45]

The map set out the evidence presented in the depositions. Implicit in it is an understanding that the servants had gone out of their way to deliver the cedar, and were seen
to have gone out of their way by both the Deerings and the person who drew the map.
This fact formed part of the evidence for the case. The servants were meant to go directly
to Dyer's. A fellow servant, James Barnes, noticed the wood under the tailboard of the
cart and the servants said they were going to the turner's. James Barnes noted that 'they
had no time to go to the turner's'.[46] The importance of time and space apparent in this
case is also evident in the policing of workplace theft by constables and overseers. William Wilson the clerk at the Magazine at King's Wharf gave evidence that George
Johnstone, chief clerk, intimated that John Tindale employed there had 'something
hidden on his person'.[47] The clerk followed him and in a search discovered sugar. This
method of detection was also common in 1820–21. Isaac Withers, watchman in the
dockyard, gave evidence in 1821 that 'yesterday I detected the two pieces of iron now
produced on the prisoner William Ashford in the Dockyard. I saw him take them out of
his shoes and I detected them secreted under his frock.'[48]

Close scrutiny of the convict's person was also exhibited by constables patrolling the
streets during the day. They arrested convicts for absence and theft. This is further illustrated in Table 3. Constables were often precise about time of arrest. James Lane, district
constable, met the prisoners Henry Oakley and John Ratcliffe 'coming up Castlereagh

Table 3 Street arrests and charges during work hours, 1820–21

Name	Charge	Comments
Reported by Overseers		
Henry Morrissey	theft	Seen in street by overseer of Carters' Barracks at 9 o'clock in morning 'stooping over bundle'.
John Betts	absent	'Yesterday found by Superintendent of convicts in the Rocks.'
Edward Marcelle John Merchant	absent	Overseer of stonequarry 'detected prisoners yesterday about 3 with fire in bush'.
James Mitchner	absent	Overseer of stonemasons 'detected prisoner this morning standing at house in the Rocks'.
Richard Webb	absent	Overseer of Wilson's Gang 'absented half past eight without leave taken in one of the back streets with grass on his back'.
James Dowden Joseph Cox	absent and stealing peaches	Reported absent by Superintendent of Carters' Barracks 'took them into custody with a bag of peaches'.
Thos Madden	absent	Overseer of plasterers 'detected him in Castlereagh Street working at a job for himself'.
Reported by Constables		
Daniel Farrell Nicholas Hatton	runaway	'Prisoners in Sydney with false passes apprehended them between 2 and 3 pm in Pitt Street.'
John Smith	theft	'About 5.00 am prisoner passed watch house with bundle.'
William Faulkener	theft	'Yesterday afternoon between 4 & 5 o'clock I saw the prisoner sneaking about and snooping down the drain near the dockyard.'
James McNeil	suspected theft	'Yesterday at half past one I saw the prisoner in Bent Street with the white lead now produced.'
Henry Oakley John Ratcliffe	absent and theft	'The prisoners met coming up Castlereagh Street before 12 yesterday each had bundle of shingles, no gang about street.'
John Dowling John Lucas	absent	'This morning saw prisoners coming into Sydney from the Race Course, followed them up the Rocks.'
Henry Mayley	runaway	'Yesterday morning 9 o'clock met prisoner in Clarence Street.'
Thomas Paley	absent and insolence	'This morning stopped Thomas Paley in Sydney with barrow load of wood.'
Samuel Mills	disobedience	'Yesterday about 2 o'clock met prisoner in Pitt Street driving furiously up and down street . . . a state of intoxication.'
John Duiggan	absent and abuse	'Monday at 4 pm met prisoner in Clarence Street.'
William Watts	drunk and neglect	'Yesterday between 12–1 I apprehended the prisoner in George Street intoxicated, he had charge of a cart.'

Table 3 *(continued)*

Name	Charge	Comments
James Wells James Merchant	runaways	'I yesterday apprehended the prisoners, sawyers from the lumberyard.'
Edward Anderson	absence and theft	'Yesterday morn took prisoner into custody in Cockle Bay.'
William Roves	absent	'Reported absent yesterday found him on Church Hill about half past three.'
John Dunn	runaway	'Yesterday apprehended in street without pass.'
Henry Hughes	robbery	'Tuesday about 11 o'clock I saw prisoner passing my door with something in bosom.'

Street, they had each of them a bundle of Shingles under their arm and as soon as they saw me the prisoner Henry Oakley attempted to conceal those he had, there were no gangs about the streets nor had they left work for dinner'.[49] The attention given to male convicts by constables was to have implications in the policing of convicts brought forward for theft from persons who were not their employers. Work hours and place of work, as we shall see later, influenced strongly the policing of the community by constables.

Government convicts were subject to closer scrutiny than those in private employ, yet private employers also emphasised time in relation to production. In the records of the early benches, private employers usually reported the absence of their male servants much later than government overseers reported government convicts. Employers were likely to report their servants after a week of absence or repeated absence rather than part of a day, as if there was hope they would return. The length of absence is recorded only in cases from the years 1815–16, 1820–21 and 1824 and very few male servants were reported for a single overnight absence from their employers.[50] The kind of work which assigned servants were reported as leaving or neglecting was usually farm work, carting or building.[51] There was some concern with time and measurement. In 1816 John Dickson complained of his servant being frequently absent even though he paid him £6 per year for extra time.[52] Edward Smith Hall in 1820 reported his servant John Malady who

> several times refused to obey my orders to rise with the rest of the servants about 4 a.m. (except Sundays) when I require them to rise at 3 o'clock for the purpose of milking my cows . . . I never press them to any particular time I have frequently reasoned with the prisoner to no effect, his conduct is such to excite mutiny among my other men.[53]

Such consideration for the convict would have been responsible for the delays in reporting absent servants. This is not the only case in which the words 'I have reasoned with him' appear.

So the first area of conflict between servants and their employers, particularly government overseers, concerned the movement of convicts about the streets. Movement was restricted by constables and overseers who had a particular understanding concerning work hours and place of work and where or how a convict servant should have been moving. Reference points were the government hours of work and the orderly movement of carts or gangs about the streets. In effect a convict could be stopped by a constable if he was perceived *not* to be involved in these activities, if he was drunk, behaving as if he were hiding something or running, all during hours of work. Overseers would recognise a servant in the street and report him as absent or would note a servant absent during work hours. These understandings formed the basis for policing the streets for all types of theft. Policing increased with the completion of the prisoners' barracks when male convicts out at night could be regarded with suspicion. This policing of space outside work, yet defined by work hours and centring on work values, increased in the records of the benches for 1824 and 1828. Stopping of men casually in the streets or on the roads out of Sydney resulted in the capture of runaways.

Druitt described the work day of a barrack convict labourer to Bigge: 'they commence work at five in the morning in summer, work till 9 a.m. have an hour for breakfast, twelve to one for dinner, work until sunset. In winter they breakfast before they leave the barrack.'[54] The government work day was set down by Druitt according to the hour, thereby replacing the old system of taskwork. This concern with work hours was evident in the complaints of Edward Smith Hall who could not get his servants to rise at the appointed hour, and in the case involving the sheriff's carters who went out of their way in the time allotted to them. The work of town servants was centred on the activities of trade or production, and work hours could have a role in measurement of production or extra work. This could be to the advantage of the worker if he was actually paid for the extra labour he sold, and so 'hours' may have been welcome for some convicts. The work of a labourer was valued at much less than that of a skilled mechanic, yet there was a demand by townspeople for unskilled labour, especially when Macquarie kept most convicts in government service and Brisbane and Darling sent most of them to the country. For many, work still involved specific tasks, though these tasks could be quantified in terms of work hours and work after hours was characterised as extra work. In 1810 a case appeared before the Judge Advocate's Bench where a convict shaved Charles Allen, a baker, for payment in his 'spare hours'.[55] It was a task but it was linked to the 'hours' in which he could perform it. While private employment was less tied to new ideas of work hours, as we have seen, references to them do appear.

E. P. Thompson has discussed the development of the measurement of time and work discipline in England, where a work day came to be determined not by the 'rhythm of reason and labour' but by the measurement of time in monetary terms.[56] The latter most certainly governed the thinking of the Bigge Inquiry. It was also present in the expectation of overseers and constables which we have seen in absence cases. Even though employers may not have necessarily paid their labourers, the expectation was that labour was to be measured or valued in some way, whether through time or produce.

Stephen Nicholas has recently used Maxine Berg's findings to argue that such discipline may not have been new to convicts with artisan or factory backgrounds in England. Constraints on time and work existed from the 1750s.[57] However, in management of

Table 4   Offences of male convicts in government employ appearing before magistrates' benches, 1810–12

Offence	J.A.B.	1812	1815–16	1820–21	1824	1828	Total
Absent	1	2	25	91	13	53	185
Runaway	1		1	59	46	39	146
Suspected runaway						16	16
Neglect	5	2	1	11	1	1	21
Drunk and neglect				1	1		2
Drunk and absent					2		2
Abuse							
Refusal to work			7	23		4	34
Insolence				7		2	9
Assault of overseer			1	5	2		8
Using work tools for private use				6			6
Abuse of animals	1			1	2	1	5
Theft	4	5	16	60	2	3	90
Total	12	9	51	264	69	119	524

colonial labour, administrators were confronted with and emphasised this new language of measurement.

The complaints of employers, overseers and constables established the principles along which law operated. The courts exhibited concern with the measurement of labour or the production of goods within a particular time, whether weekly or daily, and this was a direct application of new ideas of political economy made important in the colony by the decisions and language of the administration. Writers like Adam Smith[58] related quantity of labour to the value of commodities; how widely they were understood, read or misread, is debatable. However, notions of quantification, of precise and exact measurement of labour, were certainly present in colonial New South Wales.

Policing heralded a wage relationship, a perception of labour as a quantity to be extracted from the servant in exchange for some kind of payment. The policing of the physical world of the male convict in Sydney worked with reference to ideas of industrial time which have been discussed by Thompson.[59]

Insolence

The most detailed study of convict insolence has been provided by Alan Atkinson's article, 'Four Patterns of Convict Protest'.[60] Convicts perceived themselves as having rights, as having access to particular kinds of treatment deemed fair. Atkinson and, later, J. B. Hirst have examined country benches. In Sydney cases of insolence and neglect demonstrate a similar perception on the part of convicts that they were able to bargain with their labour. We also find in these Sydney cases emphasis on time and place of work.

There were twenty-six different places of employment listed in court records as scenes of conflict in 1820–21. Conflicts were over matters related to work rather than the authority of the employer. The work undertaken by these various groups was described by Hutchinson and Druitt. The town gang loaded and unloaded government vessels; carters were involved in the transporting of goods; other gangs were involved in Macquarie's building projects. The shell gang was employed in collecting shells and cleaning them before they were sent to Sydney for lime burning, also to be used in building. This was difficult work, according to Druitt, because the men were often in water up to their waists and frequently dug for shells under the sand. Those in the gaol gang were undergoing punishment ordered by the courts. They cleaned away rubbish from the quarries and unloaded the coal vessels from Newcastle, working double-ironed on a single ration. The woodcutting gangs worked at Lane Cove and theirs was the heaviest employment. The government farm, Grose farm, employed fifty-seven men in 1820–21; they were mostly involved in cutting grass for government horses.[61]

There were three cases of combined action by convicts in the records of 1820–21. In October 1820 the overseer of a government work gang reported Jeremiah Buckley and Thomas Burke for refusal to work. The overseer claimed that all the gang at that time refused to work and Buckley was 'one of the leaders in encouraging them to strike their work'.[62] In 1821 the overseer for Simeon Lord's factory at Botany brought thirteen of the assigned servants before the bench for refusing to work before six o'clock, the same hours as the government men. The servants received twenty-five lashes.[63] In 1820, when five members of the stonequarry gang were ordered to work, they surrounded their overseer, abused him 'and positively refused to work'.[64] Combined action was feared by Bigge. In his questions during the inquiry he refers to the possibility of convicts combining in the barracks and wondered if the soldiers were close enough to deal with such an event.[65] These combined actions were refusals to work and did not move beyond that. In 1820, however, a number of men left the government gang at Emu Plains, taking arms and provisions.[66] This is more like bushranging than the kinds of combination we find in Sydney bench records.

Insolence and refusal to work were usually offences by single convicts or sometimes two men and were related to types of taskwork and times of commencement. Edward Hall told the overseer of the gaol gang he would be damned if he would carry any more lime for him when he was asked to do so.[67] Two government carters refused to carry a load to Woolloomooloo, taking it to the Brickfields instead.[68] Excuses of ill health were often given for refusal to work: William Harley of the gang working at Kissing Point was disbelieved by his overseer when he said he had a pain in his back and could not go to the mill.[69] James Laurence, overseer of the gaol gang, told one of his convicts, 'he was not to go to the doctor anymore'.[70] What were considered unreasonable requests made by overseers were given as the cause of assaults. Richard Wethers struck the coxswain of his government boat, saying, 'this day was a holiday given to him'.[71] Charles Wright abused his overseer in the gaol, saying he was 'a bloody niagar driver. I've never seen such a niagar driver in my life'.[72]

These same patterns persisted for convicts in private employment. Abuse and insolence resulted from specific requests for work from convicts who then refused to do what

Table 5 Offences of male convicts in private employ appearing before Police Magistrates' Benches, Sydney, 1810–28

Offence	J.A.B.	1812	1815–16	1820–21	1824	1828	Total
Absent	2		24	21	29	27	103
Absent and neglect	1	2	1				4
Runaway absent		1	3		6	28	38
Leaving master without pass					1		1
Neglect	1	1		6	2	10	20
Neglect and insolence	3		1		1		5
Neglect and drunk					5	3	8
Drunk and absent					3	3	6
Drunk			1				1
Idle			1				1
Misconduct		1	1				2
Refusal and abuse	2			4	3	4	13
Insolence			8	2	2	16	28
Insolence and drunk					9	1	10
Riot	1						1
Assault of employer	1			1	2		4
Burning huts				1			1
Abuse of animals	1				2	1	4
Destruction of tools				3			3
Spoiling work					1		1
Complaint against employer	2					10	12
Theft	12	4	15	16	10	12	69
Embezzlement	2			5			7
Apprentice complaint	6						6
Contract labour complaint			2				2
Total	34	9	57	59	76	115	350

they were asked. John Oxley's servant refused to go up to his master's house in Kirkham, was often absent and apprehended repeatedly by constables.[73] John Hutchinson brought his servant to the bench because, though he had made an agreement with him that he should lend him to John Johnstone, potter, for carrying wood and pay him four shillings per week in lieu of rations, the servant became dissatisfied and 'this morning waited on examinant to say he should not in future cart any wood anywhere in Cockle Bay'.[74] Mary Reiby directed her servant to take the bullocks up the country, offering him bread, meat and seven shillings, with which supply he refused to proceed.[75]

In 1828 of the ten complaints by servants of their masters' treatment of them, three were judged by the court to be false complaints. In 1811 James McAllister brought a complaint before the Judge Advocate's Bench stating he was ill-used by his employer, George Johnstone, saying, 'he will not employ me in my own time nor allow me to go off his farm to seek other employ'.[76] Johnstone said his servant was in the constant habit of leaving the farm without a pass and was idle. The court recommended that Johnstone should give his servant the government allowance for extra time.[77] The Judge Advocate's Bench also received complaints of apprentices which is perhaps why McAllister's complaint was so closely regarded.

All of these cases of insolence or complaint rest on expectations by servants about the type of work they should be expected to do and how they should be treated by employers and overseers. This can be related to the concern regarding 'management' of convicts which appeared in the Bigge Inquiry. Insolence occurred inside specific work conditions and as a response to them, rather than as a rejection of those work conditions. The perspective of the employer and the servant are evident in the deposition, and the point at which the servant reacted against requests is quite clear. In some of the depositions there is evidence of bargaining which had gone wrong or had been considered unacceptable by the servant. That servants did bring complaints against employers indicates that there were expectations by servants regarding the conditions of employment, however lightly the courts may have received them. The tensions presented to the courts arose from the time devoted to work and the value the convict placed on his own labour.

In 1816 Esther Hook complained that 'she requested her convict servant to light a fire as she observed it was eight o'clock, on walking towards the kitchen she heard the prisoner say: she might go asking what did she come here with her lies for and added what did she come to this country for and other abusive language.'[78] Other employers rarely repeat in such detail the insolence of their employees. It is the fact they were insolent in service after refusing work which was considered important. In Sydney there are no cases of such a total rejection of a male employer by a male servant. James Badgery's servant said his master had a very ill opinion of him and he would do nothing for him.[79] The connection between insolence and refusal and the possibility of bargaining is illustrated very well in that statement.

Neglect

Complaints of neglect of work came from a different area. Such complaints usually involved constant neglect if brought by government overseers. In 1820–21 five complaints by government overseers were of that nature. One resulted from spoilt bricks at the kiln.[80] Another three complaints were made by government officials; in these cases the chief engineer and the principal superintendent of convicts walked past a gang and observed prisoners lying down when they were supposed to be at work; respectively, the shell gang, and gangs in the dockyard and at the market wharf. Charges of neglect by private employers, however, stress the loss of property resulting from neglect by servants. Two of those charged were ticket-of-leave convicts. 'I am a loser in pigs, grain and poultry and all my farming besides',[81] complained John Thomas Campbell of his overseer. 'The duty of the Brewery to which the prisoner had so attended is totally neglected', claimed William Hutchinson of his overseer in the brewery; his ticket was cancelled and he was ordered to government employ.[82] Simeon Lord complained of his two servants, hatters, 'they have lately neglected their work to a great degree by which I am a considerable loser'.[83] There are few cases of neglect before 1820–21 and they follow the same pattern. Of three cases in 1812, two are from overseers who complain of government servants continually neglecting work. The other, brought by the private employer Gregory Blaxland, complained of Thomas Glover who had been in his employ for four years, 'during which time Glover has on many occasions misconducted himself by absenting himself and neglecting examinant's business'.[84] In 1810 William Paterson was charged by his superintendent, Isaac Nicholls, with neglect among the stone cutters. He was supposed to mark the stones, but instead he erased the marks.[85] For this he was ordered to shape five stones as extra work. The use of work as punishment by the Judge Advocate's Bench was applied also to Henry Joyce, who was ordered to work for one month for his master without the usual indulgence of hours for himself.[86]

The reasons employers gave for bringing their servants to the bench in 1824 and 1828 are difficult to discover, though the connection between neglect and drunkenness seems to suggest they follow the same pattern.[87] In 1824 the watchman of the government garden was charged with neglect. In 1828 a servant, William Frank, was charged with neglect 'of duty by which his master was robbed'.[88]

If William Paterson's rubbing of marks from stones in 1810 contains an element or suggestion of deliberate protest against what he was doing, so do complaints of maltreatment of animals, destruction of tools and spoiling of work. In 1820 Daniel Deering Matthews reported two of his farm servants as absent, complaining at the same time, 'they have been stubborn and inattentive to their duty and destroyed the tools entrusted to work with'.[89] David Maxwell, constable of Bristoe's road party, was called to witness the cruelty with which the convict Jacob Weeks was treating the government bullocks.[90] Mary Reibey's servant, who refused to take the bullocks up the country, reportedly pulled the rings out of the bullocks' noses.[91]

Cases of neglect or abuse of animals were all defined by the employer, who set the limits on what was considered neglect or abuse. The area of concern for both these offences is productivity of the workers for private employers, whereas government employers were concerned with time spent at work and constant work as well as productivity. Government-employed convicts were subject to much more surveillance while at work by overseers and officials. Private employers often reported neglect after the damage was done.

Theft

The uses to which the tools provided by employers cannot be put is demonstrated by the evidence of Peter Plomer when he reported a convict at the lumberyard 'mending the shoes now produced, in his government time, it is a constant practice with them although they have been frequently warned to the contrary'.[92] Both tools and products were stolen by government employees. Druitt said theft continued at the lumberyard until constables were set at the gate and the walls built higher.[93] There was an active trade in tools, clothing and blankets bearing the government mark.

Thefts from private employers were work-related. Isaac Nicholls had wire stolen by his cooper.[94] Embezzlement was practised by clerks or persons sent on errands. In 1821 James Fadden went to a shop and said he wanted two pounds of tobacco for Captain Piper. The shopkeeper gave evidence that he 'went down to ascertain from Captain Piper if he had sent the prisoner for tobacco and received an answer from him he had not given any such orders'.[95]

Theft by government employees was usually detected by constables or overseers. Privately employed servants were accused by a process of deduction. Jane Armytage lost four or five pounds of flour and claimed before the bench, 'no-one had access to the bakehouse between the hours of four and seven except the prisoner John Nednett who is a government servant who works in the bakehouse'.[96] He was sent to the barracks although no property had been found in his possession. Male convict servants do not seem to have been regarded with constant suspicion. In one case in 1816 E. S. Hall returned a servant because he was a 'suspicious character'.[97]

Thefts from private employers by their own servants took place within a work environment or were centred on taskwork rather than the house of the employer. It suggests the separation of these two areas for male convicts and a clear delineation of where they were able to be while in employment. They stole not from the house of the employer, but from the particular work in which they were involved, whether it was going on a message, carting, or from the workshop.

The criminal law most clearly represented the interests of the employer in cases involving convict servants but it did so along certain lines and within certain limitations, according to certain understandings. What it defended was the place of work, the time of work and productivity for government and private employers.

The responses apparent in refusal and insolence indicate that not all convicts accepted time-limited labour. However, their offences of theft, abuse or insolence did not question the whole master–servant relationship itself. They reacted according to conditions set for them which were understood to be unjust. There were expectations regarding employment and this is where the conflicts occurred: when the employer or overseer was considered to have stepped outside them by making unrealistic demands. This work relationship was one that could be bargained over, despite the fact that it could not be easily evaded.

David Galenson has written of the distinction between English servants as family and indentured servants in colonial America. He argues that because legislation governing running away existed at all in the colony, and was utilised, servants in colonial America were closer to being property.[98] When we consider the town servants in New South Wales, offences such as insolence and neglect suggest that servants saw themselves as having a role to play involving bargaining, proper conditions and rewards that implied they were workers rather than property. This was the relationship brought to court. Such attitudes of 'rights' held by convicts have already been discussed in terms of the entire convict system by Hirst and Atkinson.[99] The existing court records and the language of the administration suggest a further complexity in labour relations in the colony. The action of law validated new ideas of the management of labour, and the focus of the law was on time, production and the physical world of the workplace. The convict servant's day, work and production were the centre of the attention of the courts.

The courts and constables protected a system of imprisonment within labour and time. This was the system operational in Sydney. Many convicts passed through the town, their seven-year sentences expiring or being shortened by tickets, but the courts operated according to considerations of labour. It was part of the process of making the London thief into a good farming man.

Female Convict Servants

In 1824 Major Antill came before the Liverpool Bench of Magistrates with his servant Margaret Murphy who had 'refused to do another hand's turn in the house' because, she said, the work was too much for her health. He described her duties in the house: 'in the morning to clean the furniture and prepare the breakfast, to clean the shoes, wait at dinner, to clean the plate and lay the tea things'.[100]

There are three dimensions to this appearance of employer and servant before the bench. The first is concerned with the kind of work Margaret Murphy as a servant was expected to do; the second with the limitations of expected behaviour of a servant; and the third with her refusal to work and her opposition to her employer. Margaret Murphy continued to refuse to work and was sent to solitary confinement. Two hundred cases concerning female domestic servants survive for this period: all of them contain those three dimensions apparent in Margaret Murphy's case.

By 1810 domestic service had come to be the major employment of convict women. In that year Macquarie wrote to Viscount Castlereagh, Secretary of State for the Colonies, that 'the shameful practice of giving the female convicts indiscriminately to such who made a demand for them is very justly and properly prohibited'.[101] He wrote in 1812 that he assigned them only to married settlers as servants and assigned as many as possible in that way.[102] That Macquarie used the words 'right and proper' and 'shameful' was indicative of the new consideration of the role of women in the colony. This attitude was markedly different from that of Governor Phillip twenty-two years before.

Phillip's concern was with 'the very small proportion of females, the imbalance of the sexes'[103] and it was from this that the 'shameful practice' of assigning female convicts in an indiscriminate manner began. The division of convict labour in the colony was entirely created by the administration. The government 'gave' convicts into the employment it considered suitable for them. The need for domestic servants was clear to Phillip and the need for women for the colony was also clear, so women were distributed as labourers to those who requested them.

Hunter, in 1793, attempted to limit the numbers of female servants in the employ of officers and householders and desired employers 'would not afford protection from public labour any but such they are permitted to retain'.[104] By 1810 the kind of labour he had those women doing—spinning and picking oakum, husking corn and picking weeds—was no longer considered reasonable labour for female convicts; under Macquarie women were employed mainly in domestic service, a few in the hospital, and the remainder in the Female Factory or at the gaol settlement at Newcastle. Hunter's failed attempt at making female convicts into public labourers illustrates a marked differ-ence between the treatment of male and female convicts. Public labour was not essential to the identity of female convicts; as domestic servants in the colony, their original place was inside the house rather than in the fields.

Female convicts in New South Wales, then, were perceived mainly as domestic labourers; in this their experience differed from that of indentured female labourers in the Americas who were sold for less than male labourers but whose work was in the fields alongside men.[105] In New South Wales the situation of female convicts was not originally related to their value as transported labour. Phillip's concern for the imbalance of the sexes led him to request that more women be sent. So, originally, female convicts were defined as 'women' rather than labourers.

The method of assigning female convicts became a concern in England in 1807. Castlereagh wrote that he hoped Governor Bligh would 'endeavour to make the refor-mation of the female convict and her regular settlement by marriage a consideration superior to the saving, for any short period, the expense of maintaining her'.[106] This concern of Castlereagh's was made apparent to Macquarie, and thus his attempts to regularise assignment of female convicts were undertaken with concern for their reform and morality. Their importance to Phillip as 'women' was transferred to an importance for Macquarie as 'wives'.

Australian historiography for the early colonial period has been similarly influenced by particular valuations of the meaning of 'women'. As Michael Sturma pointed out in his article, 'Eye of the Beholder'[107] perspectives of early colonial women were shaped by the moral views of the colonial administration rather than those of women themselves. Since Sturma's article was published, and perhaps before, there has been a tendency to revalue convict women. This revaluation has followed two strands, first to revalue female morality in the early colony[108] and secondly to revalue female labour.[109] The latter has been influenced by feminist revaluing of women's work in the house. While it may now be taken for granted that women's work inside and outside the house contributes to any economy, it also must be recognised that such revaluing may blur or mask power relations operating in the colony. That is, that in reacting to the administration we are still working inside its definitions. There were particular understandings as to the meaning of 'morality' among the lower classes, and there were also particular perceptions of what it was to be 'female' and of what it was to work. Those persons who brought female convicts to court operated also on particular understandings of what was required in domestic service, what it meant to be in service. The administration saw service as a means of dealing with 'women'—that is, their sex was thought of first.

Domestic service, then, was an interval before marriage for the female convict. The assumption that domestic service was to be *the* employment of female convicts during the Macquarie period possibly came from the government's own need for servants as well as what had become the practice in the colony. Domestic service was the major employment for women in England during this period: it was natural the situation would be considered similar in a colony not devoted to the production of a staple such as tobacco.

We find, in the discussions about female convicts, not so much a concern as to what to do with them, but what to do with those *too recalcitrant* for domestic service or left over from assignment. The interest in the morality of the female convict implied in Macquarie's use of the words 'shameful' and 'right and proper' was originally an evangelical interest and it was from this quarter that the kind of domestic service built up in the colony through random assignment came under scrutiny. This helps explain why women were assigned to married settlers and families or kept in the Female Factory. Samuel Marsden had written in 1806 that 'it is much to be regretted that the settlement of New South Wales has been established for almost twenty years yet no serious attempts for the reformation of female convicts sent out here from time to time have hitherto been made'. He compiled a list of one thousand women in the colony, specifying their marital status and the number of their children.[110] His criticism no doubt reached colonial administrators in England.

The policy of both Macquarie and Brisbane was to keep as many unassigned female convicts in the Female Factory as possible, and it met with opposition in the popular press in the 1820s. The *Australian* newspaper wrote in 1825:

> had the importation of women been increased twofold in place of being diminished fourfold, had there been offered to those who might have been allowed to take helpmates to themselves, an additional few acres as an inducement to intermarry . . . we should hardly have heard of the crimes which are an indelible blot on the character of the nation.[111]

The women 'shut up in the factory' were 'a lamentable check on the growth of the colony'.[112] The *Blossom* in 1828 referred to the Female Factory as the 'convict nunnery'.[113]

Such public pressure, together with overcrowding in the Female Factory, led Brisbane to send women to the Emu Plains agricultural establishment. In an anonymous report it was 'asserted the women were selected from the factory for the express purpose of being prostituted at Emu Plains'.[114] Brisbane ordered an inquiry into the establishment which revealed that many of the women had married the male convicts and had had children by them. Despite its positive findings, no further women were transferred to Emu Plains.

Emu Plains presents a microcosm of the concerns of colonial administrators after 1810. Women were meant to be married and yet the method of arranging this was a source of distress. Darling was influenced by these reactions against the moral systems of Macquarie and Brisbane. He wrote to Bathurst that 'disposal of women in an eligible manner though most desirable is extremely perplexing and embarrassing . . . while the disproportion of the sexes is extreme, not less than 300 women are immured in the factory'.[115] Sir George Murray, Secretary of State for the Colonies, was sympathetic to Darling's predicament and wished an experiment to be carried out, 'compelling every settler to take off the hands of the government one female convict for every two or three convict men'. This would mean a considerable saving of public expense and would also mean a 'great moral improvement' in the 'unfortunate females'.[116] He relied on the good sense of the inhabitants not to abuse the system. Darling replied that he thought it would cause a great deal of additional expense and trouble as the women would be returned in a state of disease and destitution. He requested in February 1829 that no more convict women be sent to the colony for twelve months, thereby allowing him, apparently, to dispose of those in the Female Factory who would not be taken into service if any more women were sent.[117]

This was the process by which the 'female convict' came to be considered a problem. The primary consideration was the sexual value of women to a convict colony; the female convict was not regarded as a sentenced criminal serving a term of transportation irrespective of her sex. Thus 'women' were considered a separate entity to 'felons' at the same time as being considered 'unfortunate' and, by Macquarie, 'depraved'.[118]

There were two reasons why a concern with the state of the colony after 1810 should include a concern with 'the female'. The first was the original position of women in a colony run by English regiments, whose experience of women in such an environment was inevitably sexual.[119] The second was the growing concern in England by evangelical interests with reform, and the application of these ideas both to the prison and to the role of women in society.

Parallel to the measurement and quantification of male labour in New South Wales was a concern with convict women as domestic workers. This was the emphasis in the Orphan School and Eliza Darling's Female School of Industry, both of which taught domestic skills to young girls for use either in marriage or domestic service.[120]

The impetus for the involvement of Eliza Darling, Elizabeth Macquarie and women like them lay in the influence of evangelical thought on colonial administrators. That convict women were seen as reasonable subjects for 'reform' can be related to the ideas about women prevalent in England and the involvement of philanthropy in prisons which applied these ideals to lower-class women. Indeed the presence of such philanthropic ideas in the colony and the use they had in political quarrels[121] played a large part in Darling's 'embarrassment' and Macquarie's attempting to arrange marriage of these convict women without being seen as immoral.

These attitudes towards convict women do not mean they were the centre of attention for colonial administrators. There is a striking similarity in perceptions of 'women' evident in Phillip's request to 'send more women' to equalise the sexual imbalance in the colony without stating how he would deal with them when they came and Macquarie's request in 1819 to 'send no more women' because he did not know what to do with an excess of domestic labour. The similarity continues with Brisbane sending women to Emu Plains and Darling's request also to send no more women. In all of these cases women were marginal, an additional necessity or an excess to the running of the colony. Women were not seen as a crucial part of the colonial *economy*: they were superfluous to it and had to be fitted elsewhere as convicts. Where and how they were meant to be accommodated changed: in 1798 they were to be part of a simple sexual balance, whereas after 1810 they were to be wives with a moral term of conviction in domestic service behind them.

It was this administrative environment that resulted in the conditions of domestic service under which Margaret Murphy and women like her worked. The conditions of employment for a female convict were that the employer take the convict off the stores, feed and clothe her. In 1813 Macquarie established an indenture and in 1816 he set female wages at £7 p.a. In 1823 a case appeared before the governor's court where a female servant, formerly a convict, attempted to claim her wages for her service for five years. Her master, she said, had promised them to her. The *Gazette* wrote, '[she left her service] without the slightest warning . . . every attention and consideration as one of the family has been afforded her'. The court ruled that the wages stipulated in the Colonial Regulations were meant to provide 'common comforts, and necessaries beyond this stated and weekly provisions of rations'. She lost her case for wages during her servitude, and the *Gazette's* response suggests her claim was highly unusual.[122] This is in marked contrast to the attention given to male wages. Brisbane attempted to formalise relations between master and female servant in another indenture in 1823. The indenture stated that the convict should be employed for three years. He made the employer liable for the conduct of the servant and any fines she might incur.[123] The *Blossom* abhorred this last regulation and claimed it was legally unprecedented and that it was never implemented because of its impossibility to enforce.[124] The records seem to bear this out.

While domestic service was the major employment of women outside the Female Factory, it was not regulated in the same manner as male convict labour. The work of female domestic servants was centred inside the house and was crucial to its running. This work could not be limited to the hours set down by the government for male convict servants. It was repetitive rather than productive, and therefore could not be subject to measurement of time and produce. It did not result in a quantifiable amount of free time which the female servant could sell to her employer or another person. Her work, though considered crucial to the running of the household, was not *valued* in the sense that male labour was.

Offences while in domestic service were the main reasons for the appearance of female convicts before the magistrates' benches. The cases that survive show how relations between master or mistress and servants interacted with the courts. In 1813 Macquarie, noting that numbers of female convicts who were simply returned to the Female Factory with no reason given, made it requisite that the servants be brought before a magistrate and complaints made.[125] There is a dramatic difference in numbers of servants before the Police Magistrates' Bench in the year 1812 and the years 1815–16 which reflects Macquarie's 1813 decision. After 1813, then, the courts intervened and sifted relations between servant and master according to criteria of acceptable behaviour between masters and servants. Thus we see the dynamics of the household at those points at which the employers became dissatisfied with their female servants.

In many ways New South Wales presented all that had been requested by wealthy eighteenth-century employers from the legal system to control their domestic servants. Here it was possible to take a servant before the court for insolence and misconduct, absence and neglect of duty, all requested to be considered offences in England.[126] In New South Wales there existed both a central regulating body for assignment and a system of passes throughout the countryside. If an employer suspected the character of his or her servants, they could be returned. This body of legislation was created for convict labour, but employers of free persons used the same methods to bring their servants before the courts.

In New South Wales as in England there were complaints of the impossibility of getting reasonable servants. Hannibal Macarthur wrote to Nicholas Bayly in 1815:

> I . . . do most sincerely condole with you on the lamentable state your family must be in from the infamous conduct of your women servants. But you are not singularly unfortunate in this respect . . .

Those now in the factory are so bad *that though we are much annoyed Mrs. Macarthur submits rather than change.*[127]

Court cases involving domestic servants were not brought only by households such as the Macarthurs, who were wealthy by colonial standards. In Liverpool and Parramatta the majority of people who made use of the courts for their servants were wealthy land-owners, but the records of both courts include complaints from publicans, small house-holders and constables. Sydney contained, according to 1828 census records, the largest number of domestic servants. In Sydney there seems no correlation between court appearances and the employers' social standing.

Employers in New South Wales were from diverse backgrounds. The 73rd Regiment had come from India, where treatment of servants was quite different from England.[128] From discussions of poorer households in England it appears that the servant in the city was usually kin to his or her employer.[129] Lloyd Robson has illustrated that most female convicts were from servant employ in England.[130] So experience of domestic service in New South Wales in this early period was, for many people, different to their experience in England or India as servants or employers. In New South Wales also a number of women who came before the courts were not convicts but were born in the colony, though they were brought for the same reasons as convict servants, suggesting that the same principles governed both.

Cases before the magistrates' benches during this period are from the very kind of household to which Macquarie wished female servants to be assigned. Those house-holders who brought their servants before the court were 'respectable', in that there was always a mistress. The court appearances resulted from a particular environment— relatively stable households. There is only one case of a single man bringing his 'house-keeper' to court and that was when the servant had been taken by him to his house in the country and quickly absconded.[131]

However, for the domestic servant the household could not be regarded as stable. Assignment meant a reasonably rapid turnover in convict servants. A sentence of trans-portation was usually for seven years, and it could be shortened by a recommendation for a ticket-of-leave or by marriage. Before 1824 all misbehaving servants were returned to the Female Factory. In the records of the Sydney bench in 1824 and 1827 and the records of the Liverpool bench there is evidence of women being returned to their master from the Female Factory after as much as three months' imprisonment. During this time presumably another servant was procured to fill her place. Records of assignment in 1822–24 held by the Colonial Secretary also point to a rapid turnover in female domestic servants. The list of women assigned contains six women who appear in the household lists made by district constables in 1822–24. All of these women had been originally assigned to a different employer. In this list Ann Mullen was assigned three times between July 1823 and September 1824, Jane Hewson twice between May and October 1824.[132] These records suggest that service was a brief experience for the women assigned.

In the bench records surviving from 1824 there were twenty-three cases involving domestic servants. The lists made by constables in 1822–24 of household residents

Table 6 Structure of households in which female domestic servants lived, Sydney, 1822–24

Occupants of House	Status of female domestic servants					
	Convict	Born in colony, 8-18 yrs	Ticket-of-leave	Free by servitude	Came free, 8-18 yrs	Total
Husband, wife (children) and male servants	18	10	2	1	2	33
Husband, wife (children)	5	5	1	2	—	13
Male employer, male servants	4	—	2	3	2	11
Male employer	1 (2 children to him)	—	—	2	1	4
Female employer	1	3	—	1	—	5
Assigned to husband	1	—	—	—	—	1
Not resident at time of survey	1	—	—	—	1	2
Washer-woman at male orphanage	1	—	—	—	—	1
Total female servants	31	18	5	9	6	70

This survey was taken by constables who walked through the streets from house to house taking down names of residents. There were 70 female servants in 60 households.

contain sixty households with servants. (See Table 6.) Roughly, then, one-third of households with servants were affected by some kind of dispute. In 1828 there were 100 cases listed in three months while there were 267 domestic servants listed in Sydney. (See Tables 7 and 8.) This rapid turnover of servants was facilitated by the existence of the Female Factory at Parramatta. It served as a pool of labour for dissatisfied employers. The Factory reports for the half-year 1829 give the number of women returned to first class from private employment as 210 and those returned to third class as 275, due to offences while in employment.[133] The return for this one year was very high, considering the numbers of domestic servants in the colony. The report does not note this as being unusual. The Factory served as a place of exchange for employers, and the courts played a role in facilitating this exchange.

Margaret Murphy's work stretched over all hours of the day and was confined to the house. Her employer outlined her work day which began before breakfast and ended at night. Work for the women in service was often by request, and this is made plain in insolence cases. Ann Jackson was brought before the bench for 'refusing to go to her mistress when desired at 10 p.m.'.[134] The nature of female employment—cooking, cleaning and nursing—meant that the servant could not limit herself to work hours.

Free time, then, was granted by the employer at times decided by him or her. The importance and necessity of obtaining permission to leave was stressed by employers in

Table 7 Offences by domestic servants heard before Police Magistrates' Benches and country magistrates, 1810–28

Offence	J.A.B.	Police Magistrates' Bench, Sydney					Parramatta		Liverpool	Total
	1810–20	1812	1815–16	1820–21	1824	1828	1822	1824	1824–26	
Absent	1		4	2	7	26			4	44
Absent and neglect			1	2						3
Absent and drunk			3	4	3	12			1	23
Absent and insolent										
Absent and refusal			2		1	2		2		7
Absent overnight				1	2	2	1	1	1	8
Absent and misconduct									1	1
Absconding			2			2			3	7
At large						1				1
Suspected runaway						1				1
Eloping		1						3		4
Drunk			2		1	2	2		2	9
Drunk and at large						1				1
Drunk and insolent						2				2
Drunk and neglect						7				7
Insolent			5	1	1	6			2	15
Disobedience						3			2	5
Insolence and idleness			1			1				2
Misconduct					1	2			3	6
Refusal to work	1	1			1	1			3	7
Neglect			1		1					2
Insolent and disorderly						3				3
Insolent and neglect									1	1
Abuse									1	1
Sexual complaint			6	1		1				8
Useless						15				15
Suspected theft			3					1		4
Theft	1	1	5	4	3	5		1		20
Theft and drunk		1				2				3
Theft and disobedient						1			1	2
Complaint of master						2				2
Total	3	4	35	13	23	100	3	8	25	214

absence cases. This was also important for men in private employ but absence offences for them were related to work in production. There was no reference in cases involving female servants to those measurements of produce or work hours which were crucial to male labourers. 'I gave her time to go walking', said Charles Thompson of his servant.[135] This implies a different attitude to time than the concern of Simeon Lord's overseer who could not get his servants to work before six o'clock.[136]

Table 8 Distribution of female convicts, 1828

Assigned to husband	303		Institutions	
Assigned to dealer/householder	14	Female Factory		413
		Port Macquarie		14
In domestic service in Sydney	267	Lunatic Asylum		7
		Orphan Institution		5
		Moreton Bay		3
		Bathurst Gaol		2
		Sydney Gaol		2
		Liverpool Barracks		1
		Benevolent Asylum		3
		Norfolk Island		1
		Hospital Sydney		1
		Agricultural Company		1
	Country		Estates	
Parramatta	70	J. Reid, Luskingtyre		3
Windsor	17	Geo. Palmer, Pemberton Grange		5
Liverpool	10	John Jamison, Regentville		1
Other	231	Hannibal Macarthur, Vineyard Cottage		3
		William Lowe, Lovedale		4
		J. Smith, Woodville		1
		Archibald Bell, Bellmont		1
		John Blaxland, Newington		7

Female domestic servants lived in the house, so there was no necessity for them to find extra work to pay for their lodgings. It was from these living conditions that complaints of 'absence all night' originated. All of a servant's time belonged to her employer: 'absence' as an offence was not simply a denial of labour during work hours but a denial of the availability of labour at any time an employer wished for it.

Because of the proximity of employer to servant and because the nature of the work could prevent the normal functioning of the house—the dinner not cooked or served, the shoes not cleaned—the absence of a female servant was noted quickly. Sophia Carne was 'noticed absent from the kitchen' by a fellow servant of George Chartres and was brought before the bench in 1815.[137] The absence of female servants was reported because of the crucial nature of their work in the running of the house. It was 'felt differently' to the absence of male servants. Male servants were employed in groups but female servants were employed singly or in pairs. The absence of the female servants could effectively stop the running of the house. John Oxley described the effect of his servants' absence in 1816. Anne Barne 'absconded from his farm several times without leave contrary to express directions on that head, she took with her another female servant who also resides on his farm leaving the house and family deserted'.[138]

So employers brought to the courts a concern with time, with the necessity that the servant be always present in case she was needed; and they brought servants who did not see the relationship in those terms. The control an employer thought he or she should have over the servant's time also applied to her body, her sexuality.

Bridget Connell was brought before the bench in 1816 because her master Edward Eagar was informed she was 'in the habit of opening the window of a locked kitchen she slept in and getting out and spending the night with a soldier'.[139] It was not only mentioned that she got out but it was important that she had spent the night with a man. This kind of limitation was expressed by Sophia Carne, who informed a fellow servant when she was found in 'connection' with a man in her employer's house that 'her thing was her own and she would do with it what she liked'.[140] Direct complaints which relate to the servant's sexuality form one-fifth of depositions by employers to the magistrates' benches before 1824. As well as being absent, Lucy Ashton had 'a great many men around the house after her and she is continually encouraging them', complained her mistress in 1820.[141] Those employers that brought cases clearly made a distinction between themselves and their servants' behaviour.

All cases involving female servants heard before magistrates' benches were cases of complaint by the employer. Cases involving actual sexual relationship between employer and servant appear only in the criminal courts. Servants designated as 'housekeepers' to single men did not appear often before magistrates' benches. In 1818 Elizabeth Furley was apprehended on the Liverpool road by a constable. She had been engaged by Richard Hicks the same afternoon as a housekeeper and he had taken her from Sydney to Irish Town. She left with some of his property.[142] She was a free woman, born in the colony and yet bound to her employer as convict women were—by isolation and the difficulty of travelling through the countryside. What it meant to be a cohabiting housekeeper is only hinted at in wills or assignments. One housekeeper was left the entire contents of her employer's house 'for her long and faithful service as well as giving me four children'.[143]

The division of labour in the household which appears in the courts involved all the servant's time and her sexuality and thus implied the servant was bodily owned, property. What also appears important in cases is the space the servant was able to occupy in the house. This was also subject to conflict.

As we have seen, Edward Eagar, solicitor and merchant, had a female servant who slept in a locked kitchen. In property cases, it seems that if a servant did not have a room of her own she had a place where she kept her belongings—her box. Presumably brought with her into employment, the box was the place where she kept her own property but not that of her employer. Female domestic servants did not need to *take property out of the house* to be charged with theft. Ann Spinks in her written defence to the Court of Criminal Jurisdiction claimed she was working on the cloth that was found in her box when her employer searched it. She was transported for three years.[144]

Theft cases arise from a distinction made between the employer's and servant's belongings while the servant was living in the house. In 1812 Elizabeth Thompson 'purloined to her own use several articles of value'[145] belonging to her employer. Searches of the servant's box were most frequently conducted by the employer, though after 1820 employers brought constables into the house to search the servant's box.

Employers did not need material evidence of theft by a servant. It was sufficient to bring the servant before the bench and state that suspicions were held as to 'her making free with my property'.[146] All cases involving theft by domestic servants contained a strong element of suspicion. Very few domestic servants were discovered in the act of theft; rather, they were suspected for some time before their property was searched.

These divisions of property were internal household divisions and the suspicion employers held was not necessarily related to the servant being a convict—both Sarah Porter and Ann Spinks were born in the colony. The tension evident in property cases resulted from the servant being spatially restricted to an area that was regarded as her property and the consequent conflict set up between servant's and employer's property. As we shall see, female convict servants were subject to treatment similar to the English servant in the mid-nineteenth century.

These structures of time, sexuality and space in the house were the limitations imposed on domestic servants before the courts. The major offences for which women servants appeared before the courts were related to insolence, drunkenness and refusal to work. The close working conditions and constant supervision meant that insolence was more noticeable than in male servants. 'Refusing to boil a kettle but otherwise a good character' was the complaint of the employer of Margaret McRedman in 1828.[147] Requests for work were part of the servant's employment. Refusal to work was thus related to these requests, and it was from these also that complaints of insolence arose. For women these requests could occur at any time.

In the surviving records of depositions there is some evidence of statements regarded as insolent by employers. Ellen Carroll was a servant to William Cordeaux whose wife found fault with the servant and offered her good advice: 'the prisoner immediately answered I do not care a farthing for your opinion'.[148] In the records of the Liverpool Bench of Magistrates and of the Sydney Police Magistrates' Bench in 1815–16 and 1820–21, servants say to their employers that they would rather go back to the Factory or that they wish to go to the Factory. The reasons for this were often stated. Margaret Percy stated to her employer William Gore that 'she had become perfectly acquainted with the country and that all her mistress could do was to send her to the Factory from whence she could afterwards get out'.[149] Julia Bryant, servant to Isabella Curran, said her employer could return her 'as soon as she liked'.[150] Rachael Slacking told her employer, Mrs Lord, that 'she would leave my service and not live with me or Mrs Drennan but in the Factory'.[151] Such information sheds new light on recalcitrance. Rather than being only a reaction to conditions of service, it also provided a means to get out of service. The statements of most of these servants were made before the completion of the new Female Factory in 1822. Frances Oakes claimed during the Bigge Inquiry that many women married to get out of the Factory and thereby avoid what they feared would be stricter discipline in the new Factory.[152] Also, in 1824 and 1828 punishment did not consist solely of returning women to the Factory but also of solitary confinement and headshaving. Recalcitrance continued at a high level. It was possible to be assigned out of the third class of the Factory, so in effect the servant sent back to the Factory could be assigned to an employer while she was under sentence of punishment. The new Factory did not change the Factory's role as a place of exchange.

Both the Factory and marriage were means of escaping employment in domestic service. The existence of the Factory meant there was a market environment for domestic labour, except that the market existed only for the employer: the work was a necessity and was valued but the worker was not because she was so easily able to be exchanged. So the Factory, i.e. incarceration, was a central part of domestic service. This applied to women born in the colony as well as convicts: both were subject to being brought before the bench and incarcerated. The Factory did not replace the hiring fair of English practice, but it played a significant role in depersonalising labour relations. The courts were an arena for discontent on both sides, and the Factory a place for return of servants, a place of 'hire'.

That discontent could be so publicly displayed no doubt added to the incentive to use the courts. In New South Wales the female servant could easily get out of a position which did not suit her. Transitory employment could be manipulated by the servant. The Factory also provided some alternative to domestic service or at least an inkling of what time-limited, work-hour employment could be like. Women who were insolent to their employer often added that they would like to be 'on their own hands'.[153] Whether this meant self-employment—such as washing or needlework—or prostitution, the term continually recurs and indicates that was an alternative to domestic service which made the employment rest uneasily with these women.

Employers had little choice in assignment and this lack of control over who came into their household as a servant no doubt resulted in dissatisfaction and the swapping of good servants. The conflict with which the courts dealt was the expectations that the servant should belong to her employer and that leisure time should be dealt out. The beginnings of waged labour in the painstaking measurement of time and produce evident in the records involving male servants in the field and in the workplace did not apply to the female domestic servant. The house was 'safe' from this. The kind of work done by any women in the household could not be subjected to such measurement. This meant that the servant was bodily owned, her repetitive work disappearing with each day's use of the house. Such work remained unquantifiable and therefore unrewarded. At the same time, the labour of the worker herself could not become a commodity since her work was not valued. The importance of the house in the society made no difference to the way female servants came into conflict with their employers. Complaints from the military, the wealthiest class in the colony, were similar to complaints from publicans.

The policing of domestic service in Sydney assumed a servant who was bodily owned. Neither her time nor herself was a commodity, valued or traded. Yet her work was crucial to the running of the house and sorely missed, as numerous complaints of absence made so quickly after her disappearance attest. The space the servant occupied in the house was interpreted in New South Wales differently from the peasant household in France, as described by Martine Segalen, where the place which servants held in the household did not differ greatly from the place of children.[154] Lucienne Roubin in her discussion of the Provençal village writes that the village house had no room exclusively for males. 'The kitchen, which contains both the hearth and the table is to the mistress of the house what public square is to the man.'[155]

Though it is to be expected that early nineteenth-century New South Wales should bear no comparison to twentieth-century French villages, this concept of space is useful. The space a female servant was able to occupy at night in colonial New South Wales was often a kitchen. In cases brought to the courts, the servant's property was separate from that of her employer's and she was not able to use her employer's property or else she could be charged with theft. A shop or public house did not give rise to a separate group of offences. Thus the servant was not considered an equally contributing member of the household. This is where conflict appears to arise: the servant before the court was different from the rest of the household. She was perceived apart from it and occasionally regarded with enough suspicion to be returned to the government before any offence was actually committed. The relationship between servant and employer inside the house does not, from the records of the court, seem to be governed by a neatly interacting economy whereby the females work to keep the household functioning. Conflicts in the household result from the servant being considered apart from the household yet essential to it. These are not court cases resulting from quarrels between persons with close ties: rather there is a comparison to be made between the servant and the lodger in terms of the conflicts over property and space.

Yet the lodger was able to leave while the servant was bodily owned. Cissie Fairchilds has written of the development of a cash nexus between masters and servants in eighteenth-century Toulouse:

> The new independence of servants, the depersonalisation of the hiring market and the necessity of receiving into their households peoples whose backgrounds were unknown seem to have been very upsetting for the upper class of Toulouse. Finding new servants every few weeks was obviously a nuisance and might not one of these unknowns be a thief just waiting for an opportunity to make away with the family silver?[156]

The anonymity of the servants' background described by Fairchilds existed in New South Wales and this could be partly responsible for the distance the household kept between themselves and their servants that is apparent in theft cases. Leonore Davidoff, in writing of the mid-nineteenth century, also deals with similar issues. Families 'did not want their homes to be invaded by disruptive alien standards and feared theft'.[157] In colonial New South Wales, however, it was not simply the wealthy who complained of their servants.

Sex could be bought and sold in the colony and was one means for the servant to have some independence from her employer. This confronted the relationship thought to be proper between employer and servant, even if objections did not originate from religious or moral beliefs of the employer. That it was female sexuality and not labour which was valued as a commodity was clearly understood by colonial administrators in their requests regarding management of female convicts. For female servants, there were alternatives to domestic service, either in choice of marriage partners or return to the Factory. It was from this ground that Margaret Murphy 'refused to do another hand's turn in the house'. Thus conflicts arose with servants who were aware that there was something else possible for them besides service. Their expectations of 'choice' played a considerable part in the instability of domestic employment.

Domestic service, in its conditions brought before the courts, related closely to incarceration rather than waged labour. The existence of the Female Factory meant that labour was transitional, the court complaints serving also as a means to exchange servants. The conditions expected of domestic labour meant that the servant was owned by the employer and could not bargain over her labour. Relations inside the household were depersonalised, yet at the same time the control which the employer had over servants was intimate.

Conflicts in the courts give some indication of the place which the house occupied in society. In itself the court provided the conditions for this conflict by channelling recalcitrant servants back to the Factory and reassignment.

Domestic service was not regarded as productive labour either by the colonial administration or by employers who made complaint before the courts. The servant was owned by the employer and not seen as part of the household on equal terms with other members. The appearance of female servants in the courts resulted from an area of tension different to that which produced the appearance of male servants: the identity of the female servant was bound up with incarceration and the value of sexuality. The service engaged in by those convict women and free women who did appear before the courts was centred in the use of the house as a place either for the care of household members, or for entertainment, and this includes inns and public houses. The kind of relationship which the court protected was not one of 'labour' but rather the effective working of the household through the *ownership* of the servant.

Good Farming Men

'the general impression on the farm of a thousand little things better understood than explained'
John Hutton's master, Mr. Spearing.[158]

There is a marked difference between this statement by Spearing and the ordered tones of Sydney employers concerned with time and production. Implicit in Spearing's statement is both the valuing of the servant and the exasperation of long weeks of perceived offence. Farm servants, like town servants, were in an environment where production was important, but complaints against them arose from different areas of tension. Instead of time being important there was a fragility in labour relations not dissimilar to relations on a colonial plantation. Food and clothing, never mentioned in Sydney cases, appear quite often in cases before country benches.

In June 1831 the Executive Council introduced a series of regulations concerning assigned servants. They required that masters be charged for convict servants under treatment in hospitals, for the conveyance of servants from the place of assignment to the residence of their masters, for the clothing their convicts wore when it arrived from England and Ireland.

Concerning one of these regulations, Darling wrote:

I calculate its effects as very important as it issued to assigned servants a due proportion of wholesome food and comfortable clothing which I apprehend they have not received in all cases. There will consequently be less discontent—if it should furnish the means of ascertaining what persons ought to be excluded from the indulgence of receiving servants it would be a matter of little consequence . . . it is only fair to state, the settlers generally treat their servants with liberality [sic], many whom from want of means or injudicious parsimony do not supply them as they might.[159]

The political economy of assigned service in the country rested on the elements presented in the Executive Council's decision and Darling's note. Government expenditure became a matter of concern under Brisbane and Darling. There was tension between government control of assigned servants and government interest in lessening expense of those servants. Darling perceived that food and clothing were the key to good behaviour of servants at a distance from Sydney and that servants suffered because the poor circumstances of their employers made them begrudge food and clothing. These were the terms in which administration referred to convict servants in the country: the language of work time, taskwork and place of work was combined with the language of food and clothing, rations and slops.

Convicts in the country were also employed in government agricultural establishments and after 1822 in clearing land and building roads. Brisbane wrote in that year of his plans for clearing parties:

> I have a thousand men employed in clearing the country of the excess of its forest timber and brush-wood. These men fell at least an acre a week each and therefore your lordship will perceive a vast extent of country will be laid open; and this clearing system is carried on by the government on behalf of settlers by means of Convict Labourers, on the settler paying for each acre so cleared and stumped, five bushels of wheat out of his first crop into his Majesty's Stores by which means the advantage to all these parties are so nicely combined as to render them mutually beneficial to all concerned.[160]

Between 1810 and 1830 there were substantial changes made in the workings of the assignment system and in the role of magistrates mediating disputes in country areas. To obtain a balanced system of assignment which virtually paid for itself was the aim of both Brisbane and Darling. The history of the assignment system and the employment of government labourers has been analysed by A. G. L. Shaw and J. B. Hirst.[161] More recently, a collection edited by Steven Nicholas subjected convict indents to close statistical analysis.[162] The writers discovered an efficient productive labour system: convicts were well fed, worked less hours than British workers and were provided with medical care. These writers concentrated on the labour force as a whole rather than on relations between masters and servants as analysed by Hirst. All of these writers, however, emphasise a tension between rewards and punishment in extracting labour from convicts and all recount government legislation regarding wages. The notion of extra time, payment for extra work and pay levels can be briefly recapitulated here.

Shaw writes that magistrates in 1824 complained of limited power in assessing whether convicts should be recommended for a ticket-of-leave: 'They could not help a respectable and deserving convict to obtain his ticket if his master objected, protested those on the Minto bench; they needed to be able to investigate the claims of convict servants.'[163] This quotation suggests that the role of the magistrate was to mediate disputes in the convict system.

Hirst outlines the development of wages for convicts during Macquarie's administration. This is particularly relevant to farm servants. In 1816, due to the introduction of sterling, the value of convicts' wages in their spare time was drastically reduced and Macquarie called a meeting of magistrates to set new pay levels. The meeting set £10 per annum as the amount to be paid to convicts who worked in their extra time. Macquarie ordered also that persons who were assigned convicts as servants were to employ those convicts in their extra time themselves.[164] As we have seen from the inquiries of Commissioner Bigge, 'rewards' and 'wages' differed from master to master.

Hirst writes that while large landowners were willing to pay wages of £10, smaller landholders were often unable to pay and did not employ their men full time. If they paid their servants, it was not in money as ordered but in tobacco, tea, or sugar.[165]

Bigge regarded convictism and wages as contradictory concepts and subjected wages to some scrutiny. In 1823 Brisbane, following the suggestions of the Bigge Report, repeated Macquarie's 1816 wage order yet freed masters from the obligation to supply rations to their servants which were equivalent to the rations of government servants, thereby undercutting both rations and wages. In 1831 in the regulations issued by the Executive Council, Darling reinstituted an official ration for convicts in private employ.[166]

Australian historians have been concerned with weighing up rewards and punishment, to see which was more influential in convict control. There has been recognition that rewards were far more effective in managing convict labour. As we have seen, management was a consideration of landholders during their interviews before Bigge. To say that management was more effective than punishment is not to assume that management governed the convict system. It is not possible for a study of the relationship between law and labour to uncover the principles by which the convict system was governed. Rather, we can look at the points at which relationships broke down, or were perceived to have broken down. In court cases involving farm servants, employers expressed paternalistic relations towards their servants. It was not production which was important, but the authority and person of the employer. Country employers sought to have self-sufficient farms similar to slave plantations, but they also brought highly personal and violent disputes to court; this implies that they did not seek to view their servants as employees separate to themselves.

Most convicts found themselves in country areas after 1820 when Bigge's recommendations were carried into effect. When Brisbane moved the focus of the convict system to the countryside, magistrates were faced with two separate systems of employment, private and government, with two different systems of rationing, at least according to the administration.

The increase in the numbers of convicts in the countryside resulted in concern by Brisbane about the numbers of magistrates sitting on country benches. On 8 February 1825 the Legislative Council enacted 6 Geo. IV No. 5 (N.S.W.), An Act for the Summary Punishment of Any Offender in the Service of Government, which granted to magistrates sitting singly jurisdiction to deal with offences committed by convicts,

> with power to impose 'moderate punishment' (which consisted of work at the public treadmill for a period not exceeding ten days, flogging, the lashes not to exceed 50, solitary confinement on bread and water for a period not exceeding seven days, imprisonment with hard labour not exceeding six months).[167]

McLaughlin writes that such an act was in effect superfluous as Act 6 Geo. IV c 69, gave such powers to single magistrates. In 1826 Alexander McLeay, Colonial Secretary, upon

Table 9 Charges on which male convicts appeared before country magistrates' benches, 1820s

Liverpool 1824, 1826		Argyle 1826		Goulburn 1827–29	
Large Landowners					
Absent	2	Neglect	4	Absent	1
Absent 1 day	1	Neglect and absent	1	Leave farm	1
Absent intoxicated	2	Absent and drunk	1	Absconding with musket	1
Absconding	3	Threat overseer	1	Neglect	3
Runaway	4	Disobedience	1	Neglect sheep hurdles	1
Out after hours	1	False illness	1	Neglect sheep	4
Absent Sunday night	1	Insolent disrespect	2	Neglect and absconding	1
Property damage	2	Neglect and insolent	4	Neglect/insolence	1
Neglect	3	Complaint employer	2	Disobedience of orders	1
Overseer-fraud	1		17	Insolence and disobedience	3
Theft	5			Breach of trust	1
Disobeying orders	9			Disobedience and neglect	1
Insolent	3			Refusal	1
	37			Complaint	3
				Refusing message	1
					24

Total Large Landowners	78

Small Landowners					
Runaway	4	Losing property	1	Leaving family	1
Absent	3	Assault fellow servant	1	Gross neglect	2
Neglect	2		2	Neglect absconding	1
Neglect and assault	1			Neglect of duty	1
Incurring debt	1			Cattle at large	1
Drunk and riotous	3				6
Refusal to work	2				
Intoxicated and frequent abuse	3				
Improper conduct	1				
Disobedience/threat	1				
Beating employer	1				
Mutinous conduct	1				
Destroying own property	1				
Out after hours	2				
Complaint of employer	1				
Bad associations	1				
	28				

Total Small Landowners	36

Table 9 *(continued)*

Liverpool 1824, 1826		Argyle 1826		Goulburn 1827–29	
Gang Overseers					
Runaway	8	Absent 1 day	1	Robbery	1
Absent	13	Disobedience	1		1
Neglect	6	Assault of overseer	1		
Absent overnight	4	Leave without pass	2		
Refusal	8	Overseer borrowed boots	1		
Playing cards	2	Overseer not reporting and			
Intoxicated	3	allowing men to play cards	1		
Out after hours	3		7		
Losing lambs	1				
Neglect, disobedience	2				
Suspicious connections	1				
Other Government Overseers					
Insolent	1				
Beating fellow prisoners	1				
Intoxicated	2				
Runaway and violent	1				
Complaining of illness	1				
Improper use of work tools	3				
Riot	1				
Beating overseer	1				
Absent Sunday night	1				
	63				

Total Gang and Other Government Overseers	71

the advice of Francis Forbes, Chief Justice, sent a circular letter to the magistrates of the colony stating that the colonial 6 Geo. IV Act No. 5 was merged with 6th of Geo. IV 69.[168] Despite the clarification of this Act, there was still a need for more magistrates. This led to the appointment of stipendiary magistrates by Brisbane and Darling. In January 1825 Dr Donald McLeod was appointed stipendiary magistrate at Parramatta; he had already been officiating as magistrate for eighteen months. In 1828 Darling announced that he had appointed a stipendiary magistrate at Campbelltown.[169]

While there was some confusion over whether these new magistrates should sit alone or with other magistrates, either way they sat and judged all cases which came before them. The local benches were meant to undertake all punishment of convicts in private or government service.

Country benches therefore spent most of their time dealing with these complaints of masters or overseers against their servants. Shane's Park, Glenlee or Vineyard Cottage, the estates of the magistrates, were the scene of such complaints far more often than any other kind of conflict. The magistrates were more used to dealing with 'convict' law, the summary punishment of convicts for insolence, absence and neglect, than with any other kind of offence.

Bench records survive for some benches for various years throughout the 1820s. These cases appear during the administration of Brisbane and Darling and the development of conflict in these areas before the massive shift of servants made by Brisbane and Darling cannot be ascertained. So comparison with Sydney is limited by the extent of the records.

Rather than enumerating cases from all benches and comparing them to the Sydney records for 1824 and 1827–28, this section shall seek to locate differences in the areas from which cases emerged. Country benches managed disputes in different ways: the records of the Liverpool bench suggest a willingness on the part of magistrates to listen to complaints of servants and occasionally send constables out to observe the kinds of work convicts did, whereas the Goulburn bench headed by Francis Allman rigorously noted the defences of servants but took no notice whatsoever of them.

Through the records of country benches we hear the words of servants who claim their version of events. This section aims to look closely at those benches where such information is provided, Liverpool, Throsby Park or Argyle and the Goulburn bench. The different titles given to offences and the numbers charged are set out in Table 9.

Liverpool seems most liberal in its attitude to convict servants and Goulburn and Throsby Park seem harsh. As well, the records of the Court of Criminal Jurisdiction and the Supreme Court of Criminal Jurisdiction provide records of complete breakdown in master–servant relations, cases of murder, grievous assault and theft.

These benches did not only consider the offences on large farms but heard cases from small landholders with servants and overseers of government gangs. If the large landholders suggest fragility in labour relations, smaller landholders seem to have more problems, while most discipline is centred on gang convicts.

Large Landowners and Overseers

In 1824 Oxley appeared before the Liverpool bench with complaint of his overseer at Kirkham Estate, George Tate. Thomas Morgan, government servant to Oxley, said he had seen a pig delivered to George Tate's own pig yard. Robert Vance, clerk to Oxley, said he had sent the cook down for a fat working pig to kill and the cook had reported that there were none fit to kill. Oxley asked him why. Danial Leary, pigman, fed Oxley's pigs along with Tate's and reported that Tate ordered corn brought down for both. Elizabeth Neale, living in Tate's service, said, 'she has frequently seen bran and corn brought down to Mr Tate's to give to Tate's pigs . . . She has also seen a sheep killed in payment for wages . . . has also seen lambs killed and presents of same sent up to Mr Hassalls, for payment for labour she dresses [cooks] for children: ¾ of a lamb'. The case ended with the following exchange:

> by the particular desire of Mr. Tate the proceedings have been closed, Mr. Oxley not feeling desirous to proceed further the Bench declined proceedings. But the bench viewing the proceedings before them are of the opinion that George Tate's conduct in the trust that was reposed in him to be negligent and faulty and are unanimous of opinion that George Tate should be discharged from the employ and service of Mr. Oxley.[170]

This case illustrates the organisation of a large estate quite well: there was an overseer with a housekeeper and control over a large number of servants; the estate was able to feed itself; and there was a reciprocal relation of payments and gifts of wheat and meat between the overseer and nearby farms. There was opportunity through informing for four servants to be rid of their overseer. There was also confusion between the property of the overseer and the property of the employer. How much George Tate could expect in his position was clearly disputed by Tate, his fellow servants and his employer. The magistrates, however, had no doubts, which casts light on their own management of servants. To them, George Tate had been negligent and faulty in the trust reposed in him.

Overseers had virtual control of other government servants and if they appeared before the bench it was because government servants, like those of Oxley's, informed on their overseer. In 1817 when John Smith, overseer to John Blaxland, appeared before the criminal court for stealing wheat from his employer, the witnesses in the case were Richard Harris, servant to Blaxland, John Bevan, servant to Blaxland, and Bridget O'Burn who cohabited with Smith.[171]

Large farms or estates had their own power structures and economic systems in which the overseer played a crucial part in interpreting disputes for the courts. In 1824 David Paton, free, overseer to P. Murdoch esquire, appeared before the Court of Criminal Jurisdiction for a rape on Catherine Foley. The case originated in Bringelly at a farm on the Cowpastures.

Catherine Foley was employed about the house of the overseer and lived with her husband in a hut. She said:

> On Friday week last I applied to defendant for a pass to go and see my child who is at the orphan school farm. Defendant give me a pass I asked him for some tea and sugar, he replied yes, I went into the store for the purpose of getting it. After defendant had given me the tea and sugar he put out the candle and laid violent hands on me . . .

She recounted how she escaped from him, but on the following Sunday was again attacked by him:

> I called out, when he let me go my husband heard me call out. I did not tell him at first what happened but upon his threatening to beat me, I told him all about it. My husband came down to defendant and in my presence said, 'I thought you were a better man than to attempt to take a liberty with my wife', when defendant replied, 'if you caught me at it I would give you no law for it.'[172]

Patrick Foley went the next day to the overseer to ask for a pass to go to the magistrate to make complaint:

> he told me to keep my wife down at my own place, that he did not wish to have his name brought into question by the men on the farm concerning such a business, deponent then told him I should complain to the magistrate and requested a pass for the purpose which was granted to me.

Other servants gave evidence sympathetic to the overseer, Archibald McFarlane saying he had heard Foley and his wife express a wish to leave Mr Murdoch's service. Terence Hickey gave evidence that Catherine Foley had said to him that she wished to leave service, could he advise her the best way she and her husband could get away, that they had a good place to go to.

The magistrates placed their own interpretation on the case. 'I further reported she was not a married woman and was a prisoner of the crown', wrote the magistrate Lowe. The Attorney-General decided not to prosecute the case. In this case the structure of power relations on a farm meant that the overseer gave passes and allocated rations. He either gained the support of his servants or did not. If he did in fact make the statement 'I would give you no law for it', he was, in the light of the magistrates' and Attorney-General's response, correct. A rape complaint by an unmarried woman was likely to be ignored by magistrates. However, the overseer reportedly said he did not want his name brought into question by the men on the farm. Such a statement suggests that Paton's control of servants was not absolute but depended on good relations with them. The experience of Smith and Tate bear this out.

Overseers were active in bringing complaints against servants of large landholders. The bench records show that some overseers were more likely to bring complaints than others. John Bayne, overseer to Hannibal Macarthur, appeared with complaints eight times between April and December 1826. Bayne was in charge of Macarthur's concerns in the county of Argyle. He complained against Alexander Archibald who had been sent back by warrant from Sydney, saying Archibald's conduct had been disobedient and negligent to his sub-overseer.

Bayne outlined Archibald's work as nightwatchman and included the evidence that Archibald received a ration of fourteen pounds of wheat and seven pounds of meat per week. Archibald received fifty lashes.[173] On 29 April 1826 Archibald complained to the bench that at the latter end of February he received groceries of three pounds of sugar for the space of five months 'which is all the complaint he wishes to make'. He was asked what quantity of wheat or animal food he received and said seven pounds of salt meat and one peck (fifteen pounds) of wheat. He was asked how much flour could be obtained out of the wheat and said he could not say. On 29 May this complaint was judged by the magistrates '. . . to be frivolous and vexatious and without foundation' and Archibald was ordered to be worked in irons and at hard labour for one month.[174]

Alexander Archibald appeared again for refusal to work and absence. When the deputy overseer was asked if the prisoner had any authority to leave the farm, he replied, 'No he has his mess ground and everything [sic] to him'. Archibald in his defence said he had taken pigs to the place where Bayne lived and Bayne had 'fallen on him in a passion' and threatened to beat him. He also said he was barefooted, implying negligence on the part of the employer. Bayne was questioned about Archibald being barefooted. Bayne and the sub-overseer said he had shoes. This time Archibald was sentenced to three months in an iron gang.[175] Though the Argyle bench was confronted with such defences on the part of servants, they took little notice of them. When Patrick McAvoy said he did not mean to lose the sheep of his employer, David Reid esquire, and that he always did his best for his master, he was sent to an iron gang for the remainder of his sentence.[176]

Bayne's complaints dealt mainly with neglect of duty. He complained of John Middleton because he refused to work threshing wheat after being transferred from working as shepherd of Wollondilly.[177] Bayne complained of George Wiggey, who had gone into the kitchen of the sub-overseer Henry Capson to sit and plait straw. Wiggey said 'he would sooner be up a gum tree then be ordered about by any bugger'.[178] Servants refused to work and reacted abusively when they were requested to.

When overseers brought complaints against servants, their complaints were in the area of neglect or refusal to work, losing sheep, and insolence. The servants in response or as a defence claimed that they did not intend the damage or that their rations were lacking.

When wealthy employers brought their servants before the Argyle bench, they did so because of insolent and abusive language on the part of the servant. Hannibal Macarthur went before the bench in December 1826 to say:

> his proper shepherd was unwell so he asked the prisoner to work he refused with a great deal of insolent and impertinent language. He asked him where several articles of clothing were that he was not more decent and clean, the prisoner complained he could get nothing to keep himself. Hannibal Macarthur produced an allisted account of articles the prisoner received from him since June last.[179]

Thomas Evans acknowledged that he had lost his duck frock which his master had given him; it had gone to another man to whom he owed money because he had been before the bench twice in eight months. In the case he received 100 lashes and was sent to an iron gang. In January 1827 Charles Throsby brought his assigned servant Samuel Bowman before the Argyle bench because he 'refused to continue the labour assigned to him to mind the pigs, he refused to leave the premises till he'd got something to eat and went away swearing to throw stones at the pigs in a disrespectful manner and made away with five yards of Parramatta cloth'.[180]

Convicts claimed their conduct was due to inadequate provisions of food and clothing: for the master it was a case of 'disrespect', 'insolence' and 'impertinence'. Masters expected certain behaviour from their convict servants; they wanted immediate acceptance of tasks and respect for the master's position. Those servants who came to the courts were prepared to argue.

Masters also appeared to make complaint before the Liverpool bench in 1824 and 1826. John Dunn was brought before the bench in 1824 by Charles Throsby. When Throsby had asked him to get a saddle,

> he said he would be damned for it, he grumbled disrespectful language, from the insulting language deponent could not refrain from giving him one or two stripes with his whip. The prisoner had attempted to throw a stone at him previously. I came into Liverpool and heard the prisoner followed for the sake of preferring a complaint and therefore came forward.[181]

Dunn had nothing to say in his defence and received fifty lashes.

In Goulburn, as in Argyle, large landholders were likely to be absent and overseers appeared to make complaint. In all benches the notable absence of so many landowners and the constant appearance of a few such as Charles Throsby and Hannibal Macarthur can possibly be explained by the reluctance of John Jamison in one of his complaints at Goulburn. He charged James Hutchinson with 'general bad conduct' and leaving the farm without permission. Jamison said that he:

> has looked over acts of the same kind till his patience was exhausted, for two years has tried the prisoner at every sort of work and husbandry, the prisoner neglected his duty, has frequently left out sheep. Deponent has never had a man punished only now driven to this extremity by the wilful bad conduct of the prisoner.[182]

Jamison thought complaints an 'extremity' and this attitude was possibly present among other landholders. Dr Townson, in the Bigge Inquiry, was seen by other wealthy landowners as being 'unable to handle' his servants properly. It was a possible embarrassment to bring servants to the bench. Those wealthy landowners who did bring complaints appeared to have done so out of shock that their servants could speak to them with insolence.

Servants of wealthy landowners were invariably punished by the courts for their misdemeanours. Wealthy landowners and their overseers were more likely than other employers to bring cases titled 'disobedience', 'disrespect', and 'insolence'. The differences between large landowners, small landowners and overseers of gangs in their choice of charges for servants can be seen in Table 9.

Small Landowners

Small landowners also appeared before the benches to make complaint of their servants. Their cases suggest a set of relationships to the law which was different to that underlying cases brought by overseers or large landholders. Peter Stuckey of Goulburn made complaint in 1827 that his two servants, George Daniels and John Brown, absconded, 'leaving Mrs. Stuckey and her young family unprotected, they were extensively insolent'. George Daniels, Stuckey said, had been requested to sleep in an outer room for protection of the family. Daniels had replied, 'he would show them, meaning his master and mistress, that he need not stay longer than he thought proper and he would let them now see it'.[183]

In his defence Daniels said Mrs Stuckey had threatened to have him flogged because he would not grind wheat on a Sunday morning. James Brown said he had been with the Stuckeys six to seven months but during that time he never received any bedding. Both convicts received fifty lashes and were returned to their employer.

The quarrels between Daniels and Stuckey continued. In January 1828 he was brought forward for doing very little work while Stuckey was absent pursuing bushrangers. Daniels had said to Stuckey, 'how can you expect me to work without shoes and his feet were all cut for want of them'. He continued that he did not care about his conduct 'and he would sooner be hung up a tree than stop with him'. Stuckey said he gave good rations but Daniels said, 'yes, but when the wheat is cleaned it was only six quarts'. Mr Stuckey replied 'that it was the man's own fault if it was so, they had the threshing and cleaning of it themselves'. The prisoner replied '. . . he has no shoes, no quart pots or cooking utensils and they had no hut to live in'. Stuckey said since the hut fell down they had not put it up again. In court the prisoner was 'pertinent' (this word was used as the opposite of impertinent) and Peter Stuckey was reluctant to have him punished because he was principal reaper. The court decided to make an example of him if he ever appeared again.[184]

The dialogue between prisoner, employer and court went on much longer in this case between a small landowner and his servant. A week later Stuckey and Daniels again appeared: Daniels had absconded because his master did not give him a quart pot. Soon after the case on 28 January Daniels said to Stuckey, 'come down to the hut and make a muster of your quart pots, see if there is as many as you stated'.[185] Daniels was ordered to receive fifty lashes and to be sent to an iron gang for six months.

Small landowners lived without overseers and worked alongside their servants. Some of them could not meet the demands for a hut, quart pots, or flour rather than wheat. Moreover, servants meant a great deal to them, because under Brisbane and Darling it was difficult to get replacements.

In 1824 Anthony Radley and James Gogan were brought before the Liverpool bench by their employer, John Brackfield, for 'being drunk and riotous and breaking everything'. When Brackfield wanted to know where they got the spirits they had been drinking, they replied they would be flogged to the backbone before they told. The bench sentenced them to 100 lashes until they told where they had obtained spirits. Another servant, Martin Bensen, before the court appeared to say he had got rum from Stephen Jones, fencer at the Orphan School, and he had given rum to Radley and Gogan. The bench sentenced Bensen to 100 lashes for such 'barefaced falsehood'. The constable John Attwood recounted how he had arrested Gogan, who said when he returned to the farm he would make a wreck of it. Gogan and Radley were sentenced to 100 lashes, but the sentences were suspended.[186] Six months later John Brackfield was dead and his servants were charged with plotting his murder and blaming it on bushrangers.[187] They had heard from the female servant Eliza Campbell that Brackfield had money hidden away and so plotted to rob him. Martin Bensen, James Gogan, John Strole, and Anthony Radley were sentenced to death and were hanged for this offence.

Relationships between government servants and small landowners evident in cases were physically close: for instance, Brackfield's servants slept in the kitchen of his house.[188] Small landowners were also likely to be investigated for their habits of rationing their servants. William Warrham was complained of by his servants in 1826 for keeping their blankets and beds. The court ordered the blankets and beds to be sent to Mr Hely, superintendent of convicts.[189] In April 1826 Daniel Barry, government servant to Michael Henderson, appeared before the bench for being intoxicated, for disobedience of orders and for riotous conduct. He had been sent to Sydney market and returned intoxicated, saying he wanted a settlement. He struck his employer saying, 'it is very unthankful to make money for another person'.[190] The court, 'finding the evidence contradictory at the same time thinking Mr. Henderson should have given the prisoner into the constable's charge instead of taking the law into his own hands discharged the prisoner telling him to beware of such conduct in future'.

Disputes between small landholders and servants did not arise only from economic concerns for food and clothing. They arose because convict servants saw themselves in an equal position to their employer and rejected his authority, rather than simply challenging it because rations were unfair or clothing inadequate.

Gangs

The bulk of offences heard against convicts before these country benches concerned convicts from the clearing gangs during Brisbane's administration and the iron gangs or road parties during Darling's administration.

The whole gamut of convict offences—absence, running away, insolence, neglect—appeared in offences by gang convicts. The persons who brought complaints were overseers. The Liverpool bench in 1824 and 1826 heard evidence of misconduct from sixteen different clearing parties and seven road parties. Absence was the most common complaint. The overseer of McMahon's clearing party ordered his men to muster at 8 p.m., and two convicts were absent. When they returned next morning they denied being absent. The overseer said he would have them punished and they replied, 'they did not care a bugger what deponent did'.[191]

Overnight absence was a source of discontent for overseers of clearing parties. This was unlike any complaint against servants in Sydney in private employ or in public employ outside the barracks. The clearing gangs were subject to greater discipline than farm servants. In clearing gangs, however, measurement of work was also a source of complaint. The overseer of Horsley's clearing party went before the Liverpool bench in March 1824, to complain of five prisoners:

> deponent gave the prisoners their portion of work, the fifth part for the deputy overseer and himself ... Stevens objected and took the part the overseer had reserved for himself. Yesterday it worsened, they did not perform during the whole day as much work as *two* men would have completed in as many hours.[192]

Clearing was easily subject to measurement and this no doubt made country government work closer to work in Sydney, where production was considered of primary importance. Clearing parties were also suspected of theft and robbery. When Mr Church missed potatoes from his field he went to search the huts of the gang, 'having suspicion the clearing party were the depredators'.[193]

As well as offences specific to work, the morality and behaviour of government convicts was also a source of complaint. Two members of Mr Horsley's clearing party were brought before the bench for 'playing of cards'.[194] Three members of Mr Chandler's clearing party were brought for 'gambling on the Sabbath'.[195] Complaints of intoxication and drinking in public houses also appeared and these also included farm workers.

Such close surveillance of convicts resulted in attacks on overseers. The overseer of Mr Throsby's clearing party described an attack on him in June 1826:

> Hennesley asked leave to go to Mr. Chisolm's clearing party, deponent refused him and allowed Thompson. In two hours Hennesley and Davis were in a state of intoxication. Deponent mustered the gang at 7.30 p.m., both prisoners were absent. Deponent went to bed at usual time, the prisoner did not return. At 8.30 p.m. Davis reported himself said he'd been at Barne's and gotten drunk. Deponent heard himself abused and went to the hut. Hennesley threatened him. Deponent sent Foster for help to Howells the constable. [Foster] was prevented, Hennesley started kicking, deponent got a stick and struck Hennesley ... deponent went towards his hut was assaulted by Early who exclaimed 'you bugger you have got me at last but I will be your butcher this night'.[196]

The prisoners had nothing to say in their defence and were sentenced to 100 lashes and a fortnight in solitary confinement. In March 1826 fourteen members of the Orphan School clearing party were charged with 'continuing to lay down during work hours'.[197]

Clearing parties involved constant surveillance and involvement of overseers with servants. They lived in temporary buildings set up close together at the place of clearing, and this resulted in a less stable set of power relations than the productive work of farms. Close living and watching resulted in tensions similar to small farms.

The Argyle bench dealt with complaints from road gangs. Difficulties of management seem intensified in the later records. The overseer of a road gang from Mittagong was clear why he went to court: 'overseer came before the bench for the purpose of convincing the gang he is determined to do his duty although several of the men said they would not obey him'.[198]

Insolence and refusal to work were common complaints of road gangs. The overseers of road gangs were subject to surveillance themselves. Robert Fox appeared in April 1826 for two charges: on the first he was ordered to pay twelve shillings for a pair of boots borrowed from his men; on the second he was charged with not reporting a bullock driver for making away with five bushels of corn, with putting the bullock driver in gaol and taking him out again without reporting him to a magistrate, and lastly, with making false report of work said to have been done.[199] He was charged again with permitting the men to play cards. The complainant in the case was the sub-inspector, William Johnson, who said that the gang was at great distance and he had not had opportunity of visiting them often. Of the report Robert Fox 'acknowledged he is no scholar himself and did not direct the man who writes the report to conceal it'.

So the areas of tension which large landholders, small farmers and government gangs brought to the courts were quite different. Claims of inadequate food and clothing appeared only in private service and originated from both large farms and smaller holdings. This was despite the fact that larger landholders could well afford food and clothing for their servants. The concerns about free time, proper rates of payment and good conditions of work which are evident among Sydney servants do not appear in country areas. They were not a source of tension, which is surprising considering the differences among employers and the number of servants who moved from one form of employment in the countryside to another. Tensions resulted from inadequacies in conditions of living, inability to move off the farm, and insolence or impertinence to employers. These were much more basic conditions of work than the concerns of Sydney employees. In country areas there appears little evidence of bargaining with time or wages as reward in those cases brought before the benches.

Overseers of large landholders and overseers of gangs had control over the men they employed. When this was rejected it was rejected unconditionally, with no complaints on the servant's part that the overseer had let him down. In the policing of leisure and of activities at night, farm servants, particularly gang servants, had much in common with female domestic servants in the quarrels brought to court.

Convicts from gangs as well as convicts from farms were frequent visitors to public houses. During the 1820s the servants and the publican could be charged with offences related to the consumption of alcohol, the servants for drinking, the publican for allowing it. In March 1826, for example, five servants of Mr Underwood were charged with being out after hours and intoxicated: they received twelve lashes each. Daniel Tindall, publican, was charged the same day with allowing servants to drink in his home on Sunday contrary to Act of Council. He was to pay a fine of £4 and costs of 3s. 9d.[200] The complainant in the case was the constable William Meredith. Though convicts were frequently arrested in Sydney for intoxication, being out after hours and being riotous, these offences required only the presence of a convict servant in a public house. Thus there was an attempt to restrain the liberties of prisoners to walk about towns and to be involved in the commercial centre of town, the public house. The position of convicts as servants was eroded by the introduction of clearing gangs and road gangs, and the policing of them also extended to include aspects of leisure rather than work.

Small landholders and government gangs seem the weakest link in country employment of convicts and these are where murder cases emerge. In 1822 the servants of Samuel Bradley, farmer at Birchgrove, were tried for the murder of their master and mistress. One of the servants pretended to own the property in order to sell pigs and currants to the officer of the ship *Guildford*.[201] The officer was suspicious when he happened to make some remark about living in such an isolated spot. The servant appeared confused and the officer noted that his face was scratched. Other residents of Sydney became suspicious at the activity of the Bradleys' servants, which induced constables to search the lodgings of the servants in Sydney and the house belonging to the Bradleys. They found the bodies.

In 1821 the servants of Michael Minton were charged with the murder of his wife, Mary. She lived some time after she was shot and was able to explain why:

> the prisoner asked her for a pound she said she had none he said I was a damned liar went to the bedroom got a pistol shot deponent, went to my box opened it took property £9 and £5. I told him to rob the box at his peril, he replied he would take all with him. I asked him for a pillow to put under my head which he gave me, said he was sorry for what he had done.[202]

In 1819 George Jackson allegedly murdered his overseer. He did so after he had been requested to accompany a gang of men to work. When asked why he had struck his overseer with an axe he said, 'he was tired of his life'.[203]

The property of employers was as prone to destruction as in Sydney, and animals were particularly subject to abuse. In country areas direct attacks on wheat and haystacks also appeared in court records. In 1825 Dennis Kieffe was charged with burning the haystacks of Messrs Berry and Wollstonecraft at Shoalhaven. The case was accompanied by a number of letters; one from the overseer Smith reads:

> Four of my employer's servants John Flood, Thomas Bailie, William Brain and William Flannagon, a few days ago left this establishment after committing several robberies procuring almost all fire arms, six firelocks and ammunition. They have since been playing on the Shoalhaven River and lurking about continuing to commit depredations both by day and by night in a daring manner. I request your goodness to take immediate steps to secure the delinquents and protect me and my employer's property.[204]

This was what occurred when servants in the country rejected their employer outright. They absconded, became 'delinquents' and committed 'depredations'.

Overseers concerned about their employers' property and about runaway servants committing depredations were the main witnesses in theft cases against convict servants; fellow servants of the prisoners were the major informers. There were very few cases of combined action among servants in either government or private employ in the countryside.

The balance of power seems less sure in the country, less subject to measurement than in Sydney. Country quarrels suggest fragility in labour management where personalities played an important role. This has much in common with the plantation as described by Eugene Genovese. In the Southern American plantation a form of paternalism 'encouraged by close living of masters and slaves' existed. Paternalism insisted upon 'mutual obligations, duties, responsibilities and ultimately even rights'.[205] This was similar to the experience of the white indentured servant in America, though the white servant was afforded greater protection by law.[206]

While it is true that both in the American South and in New South Wales differences existed between one master and another, the relationship which the court protected in country New South Wales was paternalistic in terms of the expectations of employer and servant. As Alexander Archibald's cases demonstrate, the country courts dealt with a level of emotion, abuse and violence unknown to the Sydney benches. In the countryside the law was likely to protect absolute control of particular servants rather than ownership of the servant's time. The limitations of such use of law are shown by the reluctance of overseers to bring cases at all. Use of the law in itself could perhaps be destructive to power relations on the farm.

So male labour was brought to the courts according to two different perceptions of labour: in one the relationship was essentially paternalistic; in the other it was similar to the wage relationship in its focus on the measurement of production.

That labour was crucial to the experience of male convicts and that the courts were part of the management of labour has been a central point of colonial historiography, but examination of court records shows further complexity in the interaction of law and labour. When we consider the role of law in the labour experience we can see the interaction of new ideas of management of labour with older colonial notions of plantation labour, and the law plays a role in validating these notions of labour.

The focus of the courts on female labour was different. It too, however, was policed according to new principles—those of domestic service and household management appearing in Britain and Europe. In them the servant was separate from the rest of the household and was to be managed as if apart from familial relations. It was a situation comparable to the relationship in Toulouse, as discussed by Cissie Fairchilds, except that there were no wages in the sense of extra time or spare time involved. Employment of female servants, when it appeared before the court, was depersonalised, involved a high turnover and at the same time stressed the ownership of the servant's body rather than her time.

While these elements may have combined, or fused, in relationships on farms or in households throughout the colony, what is of importance here is the relationship of the law to convict labour. The law protected a relationship at once modern and at the same time intensely colonial. New ideas combined with patterns of labour relations specific to the colonial plantation. The servant operated according to English understandings relating to the importance of taskwork and the regard of the employer to his or her servant, but the employer before the court expressed newer relations as important.

Thus the court functioned as a point of exchange for female servants, as a part of discipline for servants in government employ and seemingly, as a 'last resort' for private employers in the towns. Country employers, if wealthy, went to court to argue for their *position*, the respect they or their orders were meant to receive. Small landholders went to gain some position as employers. The whole gamut of servant offences—from 'refusing to boil a kettle but otherwise a good servant' to 'lying down at work'—formed the bulk of the activity for *all* magistrates' benches in the colony. The central task of the magistrates' benches in the colony was to discipline labour.

As the base of all criminal procedure this placed them in a particular relationship to society. To begin with, the looseness of the terminology of offences resulted in a haphazard but extremely personal intervention in everyday life. 'Refusing to boil a kettle', 'playing at cards', 'bad associations' were all deemed offences by magistrates, as well as the more common 'absence', 'disobedience', 'neglect'. The law could keep surveillance of the sexuality of the female servant, the time of the male town servant and the consumption of the male farm servant. This capacity and the understandings it involved were to have implications for all other forms of policing.

In its treatment of labour, the law clearly operated differently for men and women: in the policing of space, the value of the labourer and the labour, and in the responses of the employee to the court. In its relationship to the person, the law in practice distinguished between the male and female person. The receptiveness of the court to any form of complaint meant that the law intervened in personal life in other ways that were sex specific. In the interaction of magistrates, constable, statute law and dispute, in the use of the household, in the role of men and women in marriage or cohabitation and in the questions asked of male and female body, the law utilised different principles for men and women.

Notes

1 Evidence of Hutchinson, Bigge Inquiry, 10 November 1819, Bonwick Transcripts (hereafter B.T.), 19, p. 11.

2 The concern as to the 'character' or to the nature of 'raw material' of convicts was first expressed by M. Clark, 'The Origins of the Convicts Transported to Eastern Australia 1787–1852', *Historical Studies*, no. 7, 1956; A. G. L. Shaw, *Convicts and the Colonies*; M. B. and C. B. Schedvin, 'The Nomadic Tribes of Urban Britain: A Prelude to Botany Bay', *Historical Studies*, no. 18, 1978, pp. 255–7. Later writers influenced by this issue are Portia Robinson, *The Hatch and Brood of Time*, and S. Nicholas, ed., *Convict Workers*.

3 According to Fletcher there was a general shortage of labour between 1810 and 1815 (B. H. Fletcher, *Landed Enterprise and Penal Society*, p. 136–7). After an influx of convicts in 1815, Macquarie maintained there was a surplus of labour but Fletcher claims a shortage still existed in skilled labour (*ibid.*, p. 162). Complaints came from landed employers, particularly Blaxland and Macarthur, during the Bigge Inquiry. Bigge himself thought it dangerous to have so many convicts centred in the town of Sydney (J. Ritchie, *Punishment and Profit*, pp. 221–2). He advised a reduction in the number of town convicts as well as ending land grants to emancipists in order to provide a labour force for landholders (B. Fitzpatrick, *British Imperialism and Australia, 1783–1833*, pp. 229–30). Brisbane's instructions to move convicts out of Sydney and into service resulted from the acceptance of Bigge's reservations (Ritchie, *Punishment and Profit*, p. 248). Darling continued the practice of assigning as many as possible.

4 Shaw, *Convicts and the Colonies*, p. 195.

5 W. H. Sewell Jr, *Work and Revolution in France*, p. 2.

6 Forbes, Private letters to Horton, Sydney, 6 March 1827, M.L., CY 760.

7 Richard Morris, *Government and Labour in Early America*, writes (p. 336) that convicts were sold by shippers in 1739–40 for £9 10s. for unskilled workers, and £25 for trained artificers.

8 Forbes to Horton, 6 March 1827, in Forbes, Private letters to Horton, p. 105; see also C. H. Currey, *Francis Forbes*, pp. 244–5, 248.

9 Forbes, *ibid*.

10 *ibid*.

11 'Darling withdrew servants from the editors of *The Australian* and *Monitor* whose ceaseless attack on administration he had for three years been trying to curb.' See Hirst, *Convict Society and Its Enemies*, p. 233.

12 Currey, *Francis Forbes*, p. 348.

13 Evidence of Major Druitt, Bigge Inquiry, 27 October 1819, B.T. 1, p. 1–99.

14 Colonial Secretary to Acting Governor, 5 December 1825, Colonial Secretary, Letters to Private and Official Persons, A.O. 4/1618.

15 Hunter to Duke of Portland, 19 August 1796, *H.R.A.* 1, II, p. 360.

16 This attack on the idea of taskwork has been well described by Hirst, who sees a process of attack on the convict's 'own time' as having been begun by Macquarie through his emphasis on work hours and the building of the barracks. Hirst, *Convict Society and Its Enemies*, p. 40.

17 Returns, Superintendent of Carpenters 1811–17, vol. 1, 1811, ML A2086. Druitt in his evidence to Bigge said he required a weekly report for every overseer. A report of work by government gangs given to the Bigge Inquiry states, 'Ambrose Ryan notwithstanding repeated solicitation persisted in not giving weekly reports of the work done upon the ground with men's names at the prisoner barracks . . . the work done is not half the usual work'. B.T. 19, p. 2977.

18 Letters submitted to Bigge Inquiry, B.T. 24, p. 4929.

19 Evidence of Cartwright to Bigge Inquiry, B.T. 24, p. 5275.

20 Evidence of John Morris to Bigge Inquiry, 27 July 1820, B.T. 1, p. 4277.

21 Evidence of Major Druitt, 27 October 1819, B.T. 1, p. 1.

22 Hirst, *Convict Society and Its Enemies*, p. 45.

23 *ibid*.

24 E. S. Hall to Darcy Wentworth, 31 May 1816, Wentworth papers, M.L. A753.

25 *ibid*.

26 Lachlan Macquarie to Darcy Wentworth, undated, *ibid*.

27 S. Marsden to Colonial Secretary, 28 January 1824, Colonial Secretary Letters from Private and Official Persons, A.O. 4/1618.

28 A. Atkinson, 'Four Patterns of Convict Protest', *Labour History*, no. 37, November 1979, pp. 38–40; Hirst, *Convict Society and Its Enemies*, pp. 40–8.

29 Evidence of Thomas Hughes to Bigge Inquiry, 5 February 1821, B.T. 2, p. 654.

30 Evidence of Druitt, p. 48.

31 Hirst, *Convict Society and Its Enemies*, pp. 69–77.

32 Evidence of Moore, 9 January 1821, Bigge Inquiry, B.T. 2, p. 736.

33 Evidence of Druitt, p. 47.

34 *ibid*.

35 *ibid*.

36 Enclosure, Macquarie to Bathurst, 28 February 1820, *H.R.A.*, 1, X, p. 287.

37 There were 21 cases of suspected runaways in 1828.

38 Edward Marcelle, John Merchant, P.M.B., 3 November 1820.

39 James Murgean, P.M.B., 12 February 1816.

40 Michael Mileham absent from the gaol gang; Morris Hickey, absent from the hospital, P.M.B.,

7 April 1812.

41 Joseph Ibberton, Joseph Lee, P.M.B., 14 May 1814, sent from Parramatta, absent from gaol gang. Garret Armstrong absent 5 days from the gaol gang, reported by overseer 24 November 1818.

42 Two cases reported (See Table 4).

43 Report, P.M.B., 24 January 1821.

44 Charles Wood, S.P.S., 1824.

45 Thomas Isaacson, Q.S., Sydney, May 1826, 20.

46 *ibid.*

47 John Tindale, P.M.B., 18 August 1815.

48 William Ashford, P.M.B., 21 March 1821.

49 Henry Oakley, P.M.B., 6 February 1821.

50 Two servants 1820–21 absent overnight.

51 Police Magistrates Bench 1820–21. Activities which male convict servants were involved in were Farmwork 12, Hatter 1, Carting 5, Assistant Cook 1, Building 2, Supervising brewery 1, Factory 1, Not stated 8, Stockman 1.

52 George Brake, P.M.B., 17 March 1816.

53 John Malady, P.M.B., 1 December 1820.

54 Evidence of Druitt, p. 27.

55 Charles Mansell, J.A.B., 8 September 1810.

56 E. P. Thompson, 'Time, Work Discipline and Industrial Capitalism' in *Past and Present*, no. 38, 1967, pp. 56–97.

57 S. Nicholas, 'Care and Feeding of Convicts' in S. Nicholas, ed., *Convict Workers*, p. 187.

58 Adam Smith, *The Wealth of Nations*, London, 1776.

59 Thompson, 'Time, Work Discipline'.

60 Alan Atkinson, 'Four Patterns of Convict Protest'. *Labour History*, 37, November 1979.

61 Evidence of Druitt, p. 49; evidence of Hutchinson to Bigge Inquiry, 10 November 1819, B.T. 1, p. 111.

62 Jeremiah Buckley, Thomas Burke, P.M.B., 14 October 1820.

63 Benjamin Helston, P.M.B., 6 January 1821.

64 William Sweeney and others, P.M.B., 25 September 1820.

65 He questioned Hutchinson who replied that he did not consider it a problem. Evidence of Hutchinson to Bigge Inquiry, p. 131.

66 J.A.B., 8 July 1820.

67 Edward Hall, P.M.B., 25 August 1820.

68 P.M.B., 28 December 1820.

69 William Harley, P.M.B., 2 February 1820. This is also discussed by Atkinson, in 'Four Patterns of Convict Protest'.

70 Patrick Mackay, P.M.B., 13 March 1821.

71 Richard Wethers, P.M.B., 19 March 1821.

72 Charles Wright, P.M.B., 4 March 1816. 'Niagar' apparently implied slave.

73 Phillip Hughes, P.M.B., 4 March 1821.

74 Moses Presser, P.M.B., 23 October 1815.

75 Edward Mason, P.M.B., 6 March 1816.

76 George Johnstone, J.A.B., 16 November 1811.

77 *ibid.*

78 John Exile, P.M.B., 8 July 1816.

79 Luke Grant, P.M.B., 17 May 1816.

80 James Leston, P.M.B., 2 November 1820. The overseer of the brickmakers left the kiln after which those employed there also left. The kiln was neglected throughout the night.

81 William Evison, P.M.B., 24 February 1821.

82 Thomas Smith, P.M.B., 4 March 1821.

83 John Canter, Isaac Bennet, P.M.B., 6 November 1820.

84 Thomas Glover, P.M.B., 22 February 1812.

85 William Paterson, J.A.B., 4 April 1810. Presumably this had something to do with counting.

86 Henry Joyce, J.A.B., 4 April 1810.

87 Only two cases in 1824 deal simply with neglect; all the others state 'drunk and neglect'.

88 William Frank, P.M.B., 1 September 1828.

89 George and William Green, P.M.B., 18 October 1820.

90 Jacob Weeks, P.M.B., 13 March 1821.

91 Edward Mason, P.M.B., 6 March 1816.

92 Patrick Burke, Hugh McLean, P.M.B., 26 January 1821.

93 Evidence of Druitt to Bigge Inquiry, p. 27.

94 Manassa Booth, P.M.B., 24 March 1812.

95 James Fadden, P.M.B., 3 March 1821.

96 John Nednett, P.M.B., 20 December 1820.

97 Richard Dennis, P.M.B., 7 May 1816.

98 D. W. Galenson, *White Servitude in Colonial America, An Economic Analysis*, p. 8.

99 Hirst, *Convict Society and Its Enemies*, pp. 70–1; Atkinson, 'Four Patterns of Convict Protest', passim.

100 Margaret Murphy, Liverpool B.M., 28 April 1824.

101 Macquarie to Castlereagh, 30 April 1810, *H.R.A.*, 1, VII, p. 252.

102 Macquarie to Liverpool, 17 November 1812, *H.R.A.*, 1, VII, p. 614.

103 Phillip to Lord Sydney, *H.R.A.*, 1, I, p. 23.

104 Hunter to Duke of Portland, 7 November 1793, *H.R.A.*, 1, II, p. 360.

105 R. Morris, *Government and Labour in Early America*, p. 517.

106 Castlereagh to Bligh, 31 December 1807, *H.R.A.*, 1, IV, p. 202.

107 M. Sturma, 'Eye of the Beholder: The Stereotype of Women Convicts 1788–1852', *Labour History*, no. 34, May 1978.

108 See M. Aveling, 'She Only Married to be Free, or Cleopatra Vindicated', *Push from the Bush*, no. 2, November 1978; see also P. Robinson, *The Hatch and Brood of Time*—two quite different perspectives on marriage and morality.

109 See K. Alford, *Production or Reproduction?*; D. Oxley, 'Female Convicts' in S. Nicholas, ed., *Convict Workers*.

110 S. Marsden, 'A few observations on the situation of Female Convicts in N.S.W.' in S. Marsden, *Essays*, M.L. MSS18.

111 Brisbane reported this in full to Bathurst, Brisbane to Bathurst, *H.R.A.*, 1, XI, pp. 598–9.

112 *ibid.*

113 *Blossom*, quarterly magazine edited by John Walker Fulton, an Australian, no. 1, 30 May 1828, M.L. 059/B.

114 Brisbane to Bathurst, 10 September 1825, *H.R.A.*, 1, XI, p. 812.

115 Darling to Bathurst, 3 September 1826, *H.R.A.*, 1, XII, p. 525.

116 Sir George Murray to Darling, 16 July 1829, *H.R.A.*, 1, XV, p. 79.

117 Darling to Murray, 18 February 1829, *H.R.A.*, 1, XV, p. 262.

118 Quoted in A. G. L. Shaw, *Convicts and the Colonies*, p. 101.

119 M. H. Ellis, *Lachlan Macquarie*, discusses concubinage and English regiments.

120 Elizabeth Windschuttle, 'Feeding the poor and sapping their strength', in E. Windschuttle, ed., *Women, Class and History*, discusses the development of such ideas in N.S.W.

121 The Ann Rumsby case, for example, where the magistrate Douglass' servant was brought before

the Parramatta bench so inquiry could be made into the relationship between master and servant. This was a deliberate attempt to discredit Douglass as a magistrate. See C. H. Currey, *Francis Forbes*, pp. 51–68.

122   *Sydney Gazette*, 16 April 1823. For wages see K. Alford, *Production or Reproduction?*, p. 207. For the indenture see Bigge Evidence, B.T. 14, p. 1237. For the indenture's establishment, Government Order, 24 July 1813, in Colonial Secretary, Copies of Proclamations, AO 5/2756.

123   Brisbane to Bathurst, 23 April 1823, *H.R.A.*, 1, XI, p. 80.

124   *Blossom*, no. 1, 30 May 1828.

125   Government Order, 24 July 1813, Colonial Secretary, Copies of Proclamations, AO 5/2756.

126   Such requests were made by many important figures. The main spokesperson in legal circles was Patrick Colquhoun in 1795 who called 'attention to the fact servants in husbandry were punishable by justices in a summary way. He recommended extending the same laws that governed them to domestic servants. Masters, he held, would be protected against the errors and improprieties as well as the crimes that the ill regulated passions of domestics often led them into, if examples could be occasionally made by inflicting slight punishments on them in the same manner as other servants for breaches of contracts': J. Jean Hecht, *The Domestic Servant Class in Eighteenth-century England*, p. 89.

127   H. Macarthur to N. Bayly, 9 October 1815, B.T. 13, p. 894.

128   Ellis, *Lachlan Macquarie*. Servants were bought and sold in India as children.

129   Laslett for the eighteenth-century and Edward Higgs for the nineteenth-century stress the importance of kin relations in servants moving from country to city. P. Laslett, *Household and Family in Past Times*; E. Higgs, 'Domestic Servants and Households in Victorian England', *Social History*, vol. 8, no. 2, May 1983, pp. 201–9.

130   L. Robson, *The Convict Settlers of Australia*, Melbourne, 1965, reprinted 1976, p. 84.

131   R. vs Elizabeth Furley, C.C.J., December 1818, 3.

132   Colonial Secretary: List of Convicts Assigned who were not mechanics, 1822, AO 4/5700.

133   Transmitting Copy Report of the Management of the Female Factory for half year December 31, 1828, Enclosures Government Despatches, M.L. A1267.

134   Ann Jackson, Liverpool Bench Magistrates, 8 October 1825.

135   Jane Clements, P.M.B., 1 April 1816.

136   Benjamin Helston and others, P.M.B., 6 January 1821.

137   Sophia Carne, P.M.B., 27 September 1815.

138   Anne Barne, P.M.B., 19 March 1816.

139   Bridget Connell, P.M.B., 21 May 1816.

140   Sophia Carne, P.M.B., 27 September 1815. 'Connection' means sexual intercourse.

141   Lucy Ashton, P.M.B., 17 October 1820.

142   R. vs Elizabeth Furley, C.C.J., December 1818, 3.

143   Judge Advocate, Register of Assignments and other legal documents, M.L. S/1113, vol. I, p. 248.

144   R. vs Ann Spinks, C.C.J., September 1822, 1.

145   Elizabeth Thompson, P.M.B., 6 November 1815.

146   Only two servants before the magistrates' bench were discovered with property on their persons: Celia Mcloughlin, P.M.B., 21 March 1816, and Catherine Jordon, P.M.B., 9 November 1815, who dropped money in her employer's presence.

147   Margaret McRedman, P.M.B., 2 September 1828.

148   Ellen Carroll, L.B.M., 13 July 1825.

149   Margaret Percy, P.M.B., 29 April 1816.

150   Julia Bryant, P.M.B., 15 August 1815.

151   Rachael Slacking, P.M.B., 5 February 1821.

152   Evidence of Francis Oakes, Bigge Inquiry, B.T., 1, p. 282.

153 Cases of Bridget Cassidy, P.M.B., 30 May 1816, Margaret Percy, P.M.B., 20 April 1816, Eleanor Meades, P.M.B., 11 March 1816, Mary Stillwell, P.M.B., 20 September 1815.

154 M. Segalen, *Love and Power in the Peasant Family,* pp. 59–62.

155 Lucienne Roubin, 'Male and Female Space in the Provençal Community', in R. Ranum and R. Orrest, *Rural Society in France,* p. 159.

156 C. Fairchilds, 'Masters and Servants in Eighteenth-century Toulouse', *Journal of Social History,* Spring 1979, vol. 12, no. 3, p. 379.

157 L. Davidoff and C. Hall, *Family Fortunes,* London, 1987, p. 389.

158 R. vs John Hutton, S.C.C.J., June 1827, 88.

159 Darling, Missing despatches, 29 June 1831, M.L. A1267 Part Four.

160 Brisbane to Bathurst, 30 August 1822, *H.R.A.,* 1, X, p. 722.

161 See Hirst, *Convict Society and Its Enemies,* pp. 28–77, and Shaw, *Convicts and the Colonies,* pp. 184–248.

162 Nicholas (ed.), *Convict Workers: Reinterpreting Australia's Past.*

163 Shaw, *Convicts and the Colonies,* p. 192.

164 Hirst, *Convict Society and Its Enemies,* p. 45.

165 *ibid.,* pp. 45–6.

166 *ibid.,* p. 46.

167 McLaughlin, 'The Magistracy in NSW', M.A. thesis, University of Sydney, 1973, pp. 267–8.

168 *ibid.,* p. 268.

169 *ibid.,* pp. 295, 296.

170 George Tate, Liverpool Bench of Magistrates (L.B.M.), 16 February 1824.

171 R. vs John Smith, C.C.J., 1817.

172 R. vs David Paton, S.C.C.J., November, 1824, Miscellaneous.

173 Alexander Archibald, Argyle Bench Magistrates, (A.B.M.), 3 April 1826.

174 Alexander Archibald, A.B.M., 29 May 1826.

175 Alexander Archibald, A.B.M., 7 August 1826.

176 Patrick McAvoy, A.B.M., 2 October 1826.

177 John Middleton, A.B.M., 3 April 1826.

178 George Wiggey, A.B.M., 3 April 1826.

179 Thomas Evans, A.B.M., 9 December 1826.

180 Samuel Bowman, A.B.M., 8 January 1827.

181 John Dunn, L.B.M., 29 March 1824.

182 James Hutchinson, Goulburn Bench of Magistrates, (G.B.M.), 11 April 1828.

183 George Daniels, John Brown, G.B.M., 13 November 1827.

184 George Daniels, G.B.M., 28 January 1828.

185 George Daniels, G.B.M., 4 February 1828.

186 Anthony Radley, James Gogan, L.B.M., 22 May 1828.

187 R. vs Eliza Campbell and others, S.C.C.J., February, 1825, 1.

188 *ibid.*

189 William Warrham, L.B.M., 8 April 1826.

190 Daniel Barry, L.B.M., 15 April 1826.

191 John McGinnis, Isaac Radford, L.B.M., 28 February 1824.

192 James Stevens and others, L.B.M., 6 March 1824.

193 James Dowler, L.B.M., 19 June 1824.

194 Peter Martin, Thomas Caine, L.B.M., 10 July 1824.

195 John Eustace and others, L.B.M., 10 July 1824.

196 Thomas Davis, Charles Hennesley, James Early, L.B.M., 3 June 1824.

197 James Eglerton and others, L.B.M., 14 March 1826.

198 James Heanes, A.B.M., 26 October 1826.
199 Robert Fox, A.B.M., 3 April 1826.
200 Jeremiah Kennedy and others, L.B.M., 20 March 1826. Daniel Tindall, L.B.M., 20 March 1826.
201 R. vs Thomas Barry, William Barry, Dennis Lamb, John Cochrant, Bridget Howell, C.C.J., September 1822, 18.
202 R. vs Daniel Rogan, William Swift, C.C.J., August 1821, 66.
203 R. vs George Frederick Jackson, C.C.J., 1819, 17.
204 R. vs Dennis Kieffe, S.C.C.J., March 1825, 1.
205 E. D. Genovese, *Roll Jordan Roll. The World the Slaves Made*, pp. 5–6.
206 D. Galenson, *White Servitude in Colonial America*, pp. 172–3.

3

THE HOUSE

Property

In 1815 James Clarkson, baker of Clarence Street, Sydney, made out a deed of gift to Ann Eaton 'by whom I have had four children as well as her long and faithful service'. He gave her all his household goods which were set out in a schedule. It read:

> One camp bedstead one feather bed, one flock bed, two pair of blankets, one coverlet, eleven chairs, two tables, one iron, one shop counter, two iron pots, one copper kettle, three hot irons, eight china plates, six china pint mugs, one plated teapot, one cream jug, two pairs of scales, one set of brass weights, three bread troughs.[1]

These were the entire contents of the house which he felt were important enough to give to Ann Eaton.

The value of household property can be markedly different from culture to culture. 'Turn now to the area of mental and emotional connections', John Demos writes of household sieves, 'and consider that in the seventeenth century they were also used by conjurors and magicians in obscure ceremonies of fortune telling.'[2] If the way in which objects were considered differs from one culture to another, divisions of personal property and responsibility for property in the household also differ. Disputes over these divisions were brought to the courtroom. In this sense, the law, as in cases of convict servants, had access to particular areas and not to others. This is influenced by the attentions of constables and differing uses of the courts by different groups. In colonial New South Wales, because of the convict system, constable attention during the day concentrated on men. Also, women made use of the courts for personal disputes. The familiarity of women with the court does not necessarily imply familiarity with statute law. It has been argued that complainants in criminal cases in England were sometimes familiar with statute law and claimed property was stolen when it was not, over or undervalued stolen property, or claimed houses were locked when they were not.[3] While this may have occurred in some cases, such tendencies would not have resulted in the overall pattern of complaint we find in early colonial New South Wales. There is a marked difference between male and female complainants and defendants. Women brought complaints from a more personal arena than men and they seemed more familiar with the idea of going to court. The bulk of male theft was anonymous and these people were detected by constables. It was the actions of constables and of women which shaped how much the law intervened in the house.

To discuss the house is to discuss an arena which was out of the sight of the colonial administration. The house could be seen as being on the fringes of the convict system, yet it was the house that was most often before the courts. Theft was the major offence in New South Wales during this period, with theft from a dwelling house the principal form. The house, then, was the centre of criminal activity for both men and women. According to the records of the benches and criminal courts, men usually stole anonymously. They were apprehended for thefts either after the event by constables or at the scene by persons they did not know. The victim was not present when the property was stolen. For women, the situation was nearly the opposite. Most women were apprehended for stealing from persons they had been drinking, sleeping or living with. (See Tables 10, 11, 12.) Court appearances by men for theft were brought often, therefore, by persons wealthier than themselves. Women were brought by a close neighbour, a friend, or a person they had been socialising with.

Theft from houses was legally classified into a number of categories. Burglary required that the house be broken into:

> there must be actual breaking of some part of the house, or a breaking in law . . . an actual breaking may be by making a hole in the wall, by forcing open the door, by putting back picking or opening the lock with a false key, by breaking the window . . . the turning of the key when the door is locked on the outside or unloosing any other fastening which the owner has provided will amount to a breaking . . . the time must be in the night for in the day time there can be no burglary.[4]

Larceny from a dwelling house meant virtually any other kind of theft from an empty house, in the day time, without breaking and entry. The Court of Criminal Jurisdiction was involved if the goods were valued above five shillings: 'every person who shall be convicted of feloniously taking away in the day time any money or goods of the value of 5s in any dwelling house or outlivery thereunto belonging and used to and with the same although no person be therein shall be guilty of a felony.'[5] In 1827 this distinction was abolished and 'every larceny whatever be the value of the property stolen is of the same nature and subject to the same incidents in all respects as Grand Larceny'.[6] Robbery in a dwelling house was always heard before the criminal courts, the prerequisite being, as with all robbery, that the inhabitants had to be put in fear.[7]

Through depositions by complainants and constables we can obtain a view of what was considered theft and how the stolen property was regarded. Theft cases fell into two groups, those by women being mainly from acquaintances and those by men being mainly anonymous. Consequently the cases demonstrate two different areas of concern with property—conflict over the relatively anonymous world of missing property, and

Table 10 Relation of accused to victim in cases of house theft* appearing before benches and criminal courts, 1812–30

Court	Male accused				Female accused				Total
	Stealing from acquaintance or friend		Stealing anonymously		Stealing from acquaintance or friend		Stealing anonymously		
	n	%	n	%	n	%	n	%	
Judge Advocate's Bench									
	21	22	51	53	15	16	9	9	96
Police Magistrates' Bench									
1812	7	12	33	55	15	25	5	8	60
1815–16	20	22	61	66	9	10	3	3	93
1820–21	14	12	84	73	11	10	6	5	115
Court of Criminal Jurisdiction									
1810–15	14	24	30	51	8	14	7	12	59
1816–24	44	20	150	69	16	7	9	4	219
Supreme Court of Criminal Jurisdiction									
1824–30	41	21	134	68	18	9	5	2	198
Total	161	19	543	65	92	11	44	5	840

*Servant theft and bushranging are not included.

Table 11 Cases appearing before the Quarter Sessions of theft from houses and public houses, Sydney, 1824–30*

Status of accused	1824		1825		1826		1827		1828		1829		1830	
	M	F	M	F	M	F	M	F	M	F	M	F	M	F
Caught in act	1	2	23	1	15	1	15		12	1	5		10	3
Neighbour			2	2			1	1		1				1
Anonymous	3	1	11		15	2	4	2	5		5		3	
Lodger			2				9	2	4	2			2	
Slept at house			1				2							
Visiting			2			3	3	4	2					
Friend				2	1	2	1	1				1		
Begging					3						1			
Seduction				1		3		3				1		2
Washing					1									
Drinking					1		2							
Taking care of house						2	1	1						
Total	4	3	41	6	36	13	38	14	23	4	11	2	15	6

*Country Quarter Sessions cases concentrate on neighbours and suspicion of them. They will be dealt with in Chapter 7.

Table 12   Relationship of accused to victim in theft cases appearing before magistrates' benches, Sydney, 1810–21

Relationship of accused to victim	Judge Advocate's Bench	1812	1815–16	1820–21	Total	%
Female accused						
Caught in act		2		2	4	8
Female friend	5	3	1	2	11	22
Female neighbour	2	2	1		5	10
Male neighbour	2				2	4
Male cohabitant	1	2			3	6
Husband	1				1	2
Woman seduces victim	1	3	3	4	11	22
Woman she was visiting			3		3	6
Woman she was living with		1			1	2
Brother		1			1	2
Woman she was washing for				1	1	2
Woman she was drinking with				1	1	2
Glass from publican			1	1	2	4
Shopkeeper	3	1			4	8
Total	15	15	9	11	50	
Male accused						
Fellow traveller on ship			1		1	2
Caught in act, recognised	14	2	5	2	23	37
Man he was begging from			2		2	3
Person whose house he was in charge of	1		2	1	4	6
Fellow convict in barrack				2	2	3
Male friend	1				1	2
Male he was asking for				1	1	2
Fellow patient in hospital			1	1	2	3
Male he was drinking with		1	1	1	3	5
Attempt to embezzle	1			1	2	3
Former employer	1			1	2	3
Female friend	1			1	2	3
Public house	1	2	2	1	6	10
Male neighbour		1			1	2
Former landlord			2	1	3	5
Lodger		1	3	1	5	8
Washerwoman	1		1		2	3
Total	21	7	20	14	62	

conflict over the emotive world of relations between occupants and visitors, the world of giving and taking.

In 1822–24, 28 per cent of households in Sydney were claimed to contain simply a couple or nuclear family, that is, a couple with children. In those years the Sydney constables walked around the streets, going into every house and taking down the names of the residents. This was the means by which all census data was gathered. Though the collection was a long time in completion and it is by no means accurate nor to be regarded as such, the constables seemed to be diligent. They noted when a house was empty and the inhabitant could not be found. They surveyed 670 households and listed 190 households as containing a family or couple, and 480 containing families with lodgers, families with servants or relatives, adults sharing a house or single persons. (See Table 13.) These dimensions of household structure, even though taken over time, clearly divide lodgers from

Table 13 Structure of Sydney households, 1822–24

Type of household	Number
Nuclear family	190
Nuclear family and servants	121
Nuclear family, servants and apprentice	10
Nuclear family, servants and lodger	30
Nuclear family and relative	2
Nuclear family, relatives and servants	2
Nuclear family and lodger	81
Nuclear family, lodger and children	2
Single person and servant	20
Single person and lodger	9
Single woman and children	18
Single man and children	2
Single person	20
Single person and apprentice	1
Single person and family	5
Single person, servant and servant's wife	1
Single man, servant and children	1
Two families	6
Two families and lodger	1
Adults sharing	118
Adults sharing and family	2
Adults sharing and lodger	2
Adults sharing and children	3
Adults sharing and servant	3
Widow and servant	6
Widower/Widow and child	7
Widow and lodger	7
Total	670

This information was taken down by constables walking through the streets of Sydney. The nuclear family refers to 1 man, 1 woman and children.

owners and suggest that property ownership in houses was diverse. Houses were often small, containing two rooms with a skillion, which was a back section or lean-to used as another dwelling or kitchen. Renting in Sydney was much more common than ownership. The survey in the same year suggested that the pattern in Parramatta was very similar though it is reasonable to assume that previous to the survey the town had contained a larger number of female lodgers, due to the necessity for Factory women to rent accommodation. The Parramatta Female Factory was opened in 1821. Houses in the countryside were not surveyed. However, in 1827 the constables at Prospect, Castle Hill, Seven Hills, the Field of Mars and Kissing Point gave details of the inhabitants of their districts to Darcy Wentworth, Police Magistrate. The constables at Prospect listed thirty-four people as householders, four of them being tenants.[8]

The layout of houses is difficult to ascertain, though written descriptions give some indication of how rooms were used. In the Liverpool case concerning the murder of John Brackfield in 1824 the layout of the house was described (see Figure 2). In the case against James Kirton for assault and having a disorderly house, the plan of his house in Parramatta is included (see Figure 3). There was a separate bedroom for his male servants, and his own door opened to the shop rather than to the rest of the house.[9] In the case of the murder of Mary Rowe, two houses are described in some detail (see Figure 4).

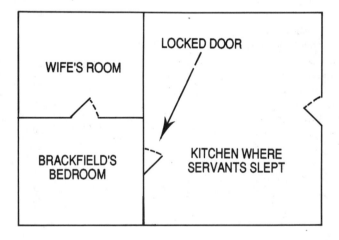

Figure 2 Plan of John Brackfield's house included in the murder case against his servants, 1824 (redrawn).

In this case Ann Wilson described the sorting of stolen property wherein 'the prisoner took a bench and set it before the fire they all sat on the ground around the bench'.[10] This was a much smaller house and seems to have possessed only moveable furniture or very little furniture at all. Yet they drank coffee and were owed money by Owen Martin of Seven Hills, so it was not a poor household.[11] It was not uncommon for several people to sleep in the same room; this occurred in cases involving servants and lodgers in Sydney. Servants slept before the fire while the master lay in bed or lodgers slept in kitchens.

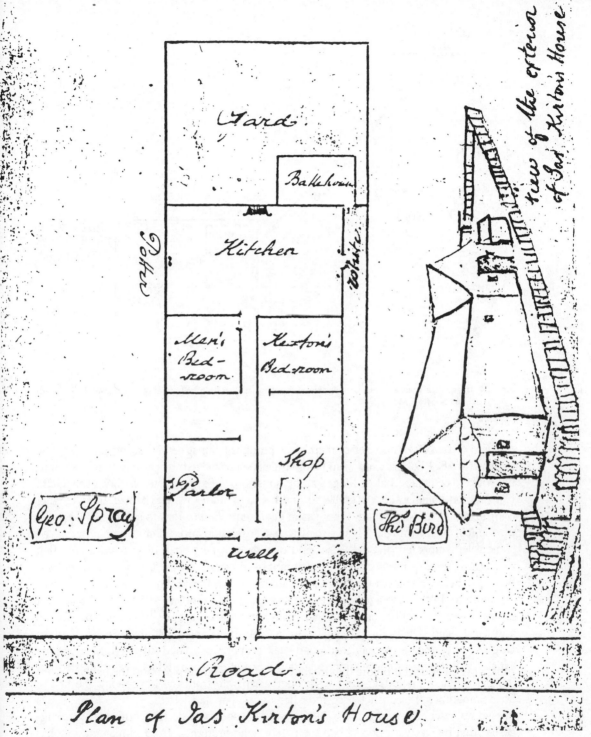

Figure 3   Plan of James Kirton's house included in the case against him for assault and having a disorderly house, 1821.

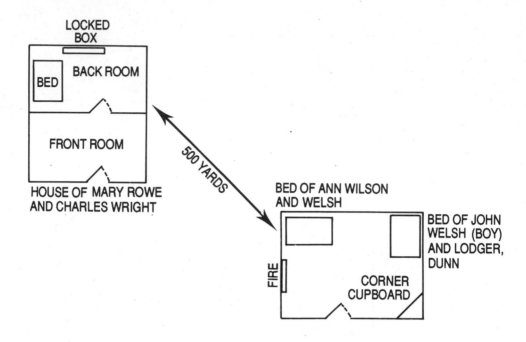

Figure 4   Plan of two houses included in the case against Thomas Welsh for the murder of Mary Rowe, 1811 (drawn from description).

There were a large number of theft cases brought against servants, but fewer against lodgers. In 1821 Robert Cole went before the bench of magistrates and then to the criminal court to complain that he lodged at the house of Mr Barber rented by one Monaghan. He returned home on 25 December to find his bag cut and his waistcoats, handkerchief and razors taken. Monaghan, who was in gaol, sent word to him to say he would make up the loss of the things.[12] This two-way power relationship, where bargaining played some role, is apparent in such cases and may explain why such disputes did not often reach the courts. As many cases were brought by lodgers as by those who let part of their house. Robert Cole stated only that his bag was cut open and did not say his room was broken into. In the case against Ann Frances and James Goff, in 1814, the complainant James Dogherty said he lodged in their house and missed articles from his box. Frances and Goff 'said it was best to go before a magistrate and clear themselves of it' so Dogherty obtained a constable and had their property searched, thereby retrieving the articles.[13] In the cases concerning lodgers it was not the room which was contested but the place where the lodger kept his property separate from the household, the bag or box. Sometimes the conflict occurred after the lodger had left the house. Mary Lewis missed a shawl after James Lillywhite left her house where he had lodged. It was suggested that he was very poor when the person who brought it from him stated, 'he has only received a loaf of bread in payment for it'.[14]

There were disputes over property between cohabiting couples and between husbands and wives. These were concerned with the entire contents of the house after one partner had left. Catherine Murphy was brought before the Judge Advocate's Bench in 1812 for theft of wearing apparel and bed linen, the property of the man she had cohabited with for several years.[15] Henry Henry returned to the house of Elizabeth Henry in 1820; she stated he was drunk, abusing and assaulting her claiming the house was his and she should leave it.[16] Such disputes arose after the relationship had broken down, and property was one aspect of the dispute.

For women complainants, the main offenders against household property were not lodgers or servants but acquaintances of the same class. In 1821 Ann Benjamin, free, of Castlereagh Street brought Jane McCoy before the Police Magistrate in Sydney:

> three months ago I lent the prisoner Jane McCoy a flat iron which she had never returned and on Monday evening last a blanket was stolen from my back premises. The prisoner Jane McCoy the following morning showed me the blanket over the paling I had in half in my hands when she pulled it out and afterwards denied having it.[17]

Kettles, teacups, spoons, gowns and petticoats were lost in such a manner to neighbours.

If the thief was not immediately caught, neighbours were quickly suspected. In 1820 Eleanor Skulthorpe returned to her house to find it robbed. Jane Mitchell, a neighbour, came to her a week later to ask if she suspected another neighbour, Mrs Harris. Skulthorpe said she did. Mitchell said 'I have seen the things and Mrs. Harris did not rob you'; Skulthorpe told her 'if she would bring the worse article amongst the things to convince her Mary Harris did not rob her she would make her any recompense in her power'.[18] Jane Mitchell was subsequently charged with the theft. This does not mean that there were no cases involving suspicion of close neighbours by men, but they were much fewer and more reason seems to have been given. Isaac Wise, a Sydney saddler, in 1823 was possessed of 211 Spanish dollars. He quarrelled with his wife who wanted the money to go away with, and he decided to bury the money in the garden. The next morning he proceeded to the hole and found it gone. He saw William Gwillin standing in his own premises and asked if he had taken the bundle out of the hole. Gwillin 'went away remarking in a laughing manner that there was no person there but himself'.[19] Wise mentioned his suspicions to the chief constable who told him to keep silent until he could trace the property. For both men and women, those persons represented in the courts as 'suspected' were close neighbours with a clear view of the house of the victim. When Thomas Fuller was robbed in 1814, he suspected Elizabeth O'Bryan who lived opposite—'nobody knew the house as well as she did'.[20] Rather than being the last person he would suspect she was the first, because of her proximity.

It was in this context that friends and acquaintances were accused of theft. Catherine Leeson was drinking with Margaret Woodyer in her shop when Woodyer noticed tobacco missing. Leeson was taken before the bench.[21] Ann Faulkner gave evidence to the criminal court in 1822 that Martha Young was 'in the habit of coming to my house in Princes Street, three petticoats were in my box, it had no key, the property was stolen'.[22] Elizabeth Henry in her testimony against Catherine Fitzgerald in 1813 gave evidence 'on Sunday week I was in gaol under sentence of assault Catherine Fitzgerald was there on the same day in consequence of having taken things clandestinely from my house, I prosecuted her'.[23] Clara Ward in 1812 accused Maria Jones who 'came into my bedroom in the pretext of getting a pipe to smoke' of stealing her tortoiseshell hair comb.[24] These cases did not always result in conviction because of the necessity that stolen goods be actually carried away, but they were deemed an offence by women themselves.

It is with this closeness in mind that Eliza Nuttal wrote in her defence when she was charged with stealing a gown from Sarah Erwin:

> the prosecutrix is a woman of bad character I hope you will examine her very minutely, she is capable of swearing anything . . . she had been drinking in a public house kept by Flood and was beastly drunk. I asked her to pay me (for washing) she said to take the old gown. She was a woman in the market wearing the gown and said take off my gown which the woman did. I said to her 'did you not give it to me?' she said 'yes, but I did not think you would have sold it'. She flew into a passion and sent for a constable.[25]

Passion was what brought this kind of property theft to the courts. The thefts were often discovered inside the house—a spoon hidden in a dress, a glass concealed. If they were not discovered in such a manner, the complainant, looking out the doors or windows of the house, would suspect the neighbour or the last person who left the house. Ownership of an article of property cut through friendship or charitable relations and brought a case to the courts. Theft by women was mainly restricted to this emotive world of giving or taking; in the pattern of their policing of each other, women of the same class fitted the society's view of where they were meant to be. In these cases the area of conflict was not the walls of the house with unwanted or anonymous thieves interfering, but some part of it where property was threatened: the bag of a lodger, the box of a servant, or a teacup.

The willingness of the courts to hear all complaints before them combined with the focus of theft policing by constables to produce this pattern of theft offences. Though women's theft is relegated by this process to the personal arena, it is not comparable to women's theft in pre-industrial England as discussed by J. M. Beattie. Female theft in New South Wales did not involve food. It was not centred on subsistence, therefore does not fit the pattern of Beattie's female rural theft. At the same time female theft in the colony does not merge with patterns of male theft as it did in London and other cities.[26] In New South Wales policing of theft did not focus on the female as suspect. Women may indeed have robbed wildly from shops or stores, but they were not suspected or detected in the same manner as men. Such a gap in policing of women does not explain fully the character of female theft. Women also brought markedly personal cases before the courts. The defendant and complainant were of the same status. For women the courts formed an arena for personal dispute. They were seen as accessible by the women who used them. The courts seem to have been less attractive to, or less open to, men.

The use of the courts as a weapon by women is perhaps comparable to the use of the courts by female domestic servants. By rejecting the employer and appearing in court the female servant could be returned to the Female Factory where she was closer to being 'on her own hands'. An examination of property cases also shows the shaping of law to different roles for men and women.

Property cases also reveal sensitivities over divisions of property inside the house. An examination of what was stolen and where it was stolen from shows further tensions over personal property.

Thomas George appeared before the Court of Criminal Jurisdiction in 1816 for attempted theft and breaking and entering. He was found opening the door to a butcher shop with a key that had gone missing some weeks previously.[27] Burglary as an offence depended upon a house being broken into at night and property being taken out of it. Cases of burglary therefore contain reference to the house being locked and broken into. Elizabeth Glade gave such evidence in 1818: 'last night at 8 p.m. I returned to my house. When I went out I left the doors and windows secured on my return I found the house had been entered by the window of the bedroom being forced open by some instrument.'[28] Cases such as these contain reference also to keys, to houses being padlocked and windows secured by string. William Thompson appeared before the Police Magistrates' Bench in 1820 to say his house had been robbed. Some person 'entered my house by the back door which I had incautiously left open'.[29]

If houses were kept locked up, so were their contents. Houses such as William Thompson's had locked trunks and boxes broken into and their contents taken. This occurred sometimes while the victim was in another room. Thus Martin Brummingen had his box broken open when he lodged at Mrs Kennedy's in Clarence Street.[30] Boxes contained articles of clothing, property of value and occasionally food, and they were also kept locked. The boxes in the house of Thomas Reese, who cohabited with Maria Thomas, contained the following: 24 shirts, 24 neck handkerchiefs, 12 silk handkerchiefs, 6 waistcoats, 6 silver teaspoons, 3 silver tablespoons, 5 pair cotton stockings, 1 silver nutmeg grater, 1 silver corkscrew, 1 snuff box, 1 black cloth coat, 2 blue coats, 1 dark coloured great coat, 1 black silk vest, 1 table cloth, 6 hand towels, 2 pair of sheets, 1 gold pearl set pin, 6 pocket handkerchiefs, 1 gold ring and 8 silver dollars, both household and personal property.[31] Brackfield's box, robbed by his servants, contained 'apparel, cash, seeds, papers, a fowling piece and a watch'.[32] Matilda Jones, indicted for receiving in the same case, kept tea in her box, she said: good Lyson tea rather than ordinary green which she did not lock up.[33] The locking of boxes occurred not only in Sydney with its close population and numerous lodgers, but also on isolated farms. John Matthews, servant on a farm in the lower Hawkesbury, kept the key to his box on a string tied to his trousers.[34] In the case of the murder of John Brackfield at Liverpool by his servant, it was carefully noted that the female servant had left the back door unlocked and that his box had been broken open.[35]

The box was also the location of the property of the lodger or servant. These people lived transitory lives, yet we find cohabiting women and wives with similar methods of keeping property. Money could be made from hiring out a room or part of a room for a night or for some time, and this kind of activity split up property in the house. Numbers of people sleeping in a house complicated the disposition of personal property and its significance.

The activity of constables in searching houses also reflected this perception of property. John Russell, constable, described his search of the house of William Marley:

at nine o'clock last night Lawrence Butler called at my residence and informed me he had suspicion some property of which he had been robbed lay at the house of William Marley, I thereupon, accompanied by Thomas Dunn, District Constable after receiving necessary instructions repaired to the house of William Marley, entered, found Mr. Parker a gentleman who lodges there, the prisoner Marley, James Larder who also lodged there, James Wright and also Jane Evans . . . who co-habits with Marley and then was in bed . . . I proceeded to search the house took from out of the pocket of a jacket which was hanging on the wall in an inside room and which was claimed by Larder, the roll of ribbon now produced. I found on a table near Jane Evans, the other bundle of ribbon now produced claimed to be her property. I searched the person of Marley and found the key now produced. I took them into custody.[36]

People were deemed to be in possession of stolen property if it was found either on their persons or in close proximity to them.

Constables searching houses often had a clear idea of who was suspected and proceeded to search the room or box of that suspect. William Dunn, constable, gave evidence in 1820:

I searched the house of Margaret McKennel Phillip Street, I had an order from the magistrate to search the house, she asked what I wanted, I replied I was not at liberty to tell but if I saw the articles I was in search of I would know them—I opened the box in her bedroom and found the articles now produced: silk work, 1 box of Wellington Victories, five gilt snaps, pearl earrings, brooches and a black necklace.[37]

Margaret McKennel's lodger also gave evidence against her.

The typical house in theft cases was locked when the inhabitants were absent, though when they were at home it was frequently full of visitors, sometimes not on good terms with the owners. The house was spatially divided not into rooms but into areas of ownership, boxes or bags kept locked which contained the personal possessions of members of the household. These possessions were regarded highly: they were more important than friendship or household relations. It is to this value that we shall now turn.

It is very rarely that we hear of any kind of food at all being stolen. The meat from slaughtered and stolen cattle is an exception, being often found among the clothing of the suspects. However, meat or food is not stolen from the house. Household utensils were much less important than clothing as items valued by thieves and they are reported much more often in cases of theft between friends. It was more common for clothing to be stolen. (See Tables 14 and 15.) Sarah Alloby, wife of the drummer of the 48th Regiment, lost five gowns, three petticoats and two shifts when her house was broken into in 1817 and this type of clothing was commonly listed in informations as stolen property. In the country theft of tea was more likely to be noted, followed by sugar and soap; all these articles were difficult to buy and given value by their importance to convict servants. Clothing was stolen also from lines where it had been hung out to dry and from yards where it was spread out to bleach.

Clothing was not stolen for the thief to wear. Dresses are not often found on the backs of the woman who stole them, nor shirts on the men. Theft cases bring with them large numbers of people listed as receivers and it was these people who wore or resold the clothes, but not for money. Clothing itself was currency. We have seen how Eliza Nuttal received a dress from Sarah Erwin in exchange for washing, how James Lillywhite gave a shawl for a loaf of bread. These were not gifts, but currency. Clothing was hoarded,

Table 14 Property stolen from houses and public houses by persons other than servants, 1816–29

Property	Number of cases
Court of Criminal Jurisdiction, 1816–24	
Blankets, bedding, sheets	15
Bedding and clothing	3
Government clothes, bedding, tools	7
Clothes	103
Clothes and money	9
Wheat	2
Watches, jewellery	15
Teaspoons	2
Food	4
Fowls	3
Dog and clothes	1
Rum, tobacco, tea and soap	6
Rum, tobacco, tea, soap and clothes	1
Seeds	2
Household utensils	36
Quantities of stores	12
Money or notes	10
Pistols	1
Food and clothing	1
Total	233
Supreme Court of Criminal Jurisdiction, 1824–29	
Blankets, bedding	6
Bedding and clothing	1
Government clothes	2
Clothes	93
Clothes and money	22
Wheat	2
Watches, jewellery	12
Rum, tea, soap and clothes	1
Household utensils	4
Quantities of stores	14
Money or notes	10
Pistols	1
Food and clothing	1
Fowls	2
Teaspoons	1
Total	172

measured out and kept much as money would be, had it been as available. Payment in kind was common in the colony, yet clothes also had a cultural significance. Beverly Lemire has written of the thriving trade in secondhand clothing in England in

Table 15 Property stolen by women in cases of theft appearing before magistrates' benches and criminal courts, 1810–29

Property	J.A.B.	1812	1815–16	1820	C.C.J. 1810–15	C.C.J. 1816–24	S.C.C.J. 1824–29	Total
Crockery	1		1			1		3
Clothes/print	10	10	4	4	10	13	17	68
Household utensils	1	1	1	1	1	1		6
Blankets, bedding	2			2	1	6		11
Furniture						1		1
Jewellery/watch	2	3	2	1		2	1	11
Wheat						1		1
Turkey/fowls/geese			1	3				4
Money	4	6	3	3	2		4	22
Tobacco	3							3
Spoons	1							1
Total	24	20	12	14	14	25	22	131

the eighteenth and nineteenth centuries and the taste for higher fashion that accompanied such a market. The exchange of clothes for other property is also noted.[38] Christine Stansell in *City of Women* writes of the Bowery girl and notes the importance of barter in clothes and other goods in early nineteenth-century New York.[39] Household possessions were important in the colony: they were not only signs of wealth but wealth itself.

Sensitivity over personal property is perhaps to be expected in a colony where the economy was closely tied to barter of property in place of money. In such an environment the actual value of property could be subject to dispute. Thus 'an old gown' such as that given to Eliza Nuttal for labour could have renewed importance if it was sold again. In such cases the courts were sought out and the dispute presented.

In cases involving convict labour and in theft cases it is possible to see the processes by which law in practice was made. The passion of the woman wronged by her neighbour, the affronted wealthy employer, the recalcitrant female servant, all have some input into the shaping of law in the colony. In the statute books the definition of theft was set out much more clearly than servant offences were set out in colonial regulation, but such statutes do not deal with the importance of an old gown, a teaspoon, the box, the strings that held the windows of the colony secure. Yet all of these issues were brought into court.

We can see the law in practice operating in two different realms. The house, as a scene of offences, was represented to the courts differently according to the gender of the defendant. Property cases dealt with areas of ownership and disputes over them. Cases concerning violence, however, dealt with the emotions. In these cases we will find the courts beginning to ask different questions of men and women and to be met, often, with silence.

Domestic Violence

In 1825 at Liverpool an inquest was heard into the death of the wife of an innkeeper. It was stated that the innkeeper, John Clegg, had arrived at his house with a friend at 8 p.m. His wife seemed intoxicated and his friend unwisely 'used some expression as to her husband having engrossed the society of "four females at Liverpool"'. The wife 'abused generally the natives'. Her husband recommended her to be quiet and not offend her customers, which of late she had been much in the habit of doing. A violent quarrel followed, in which the wife 'staggering, struck her head against the chimney part of the wall'. The jury at the coroner's inquest were uncertain how this could have happened and asked the witness to 'state to the court how she struck her head, whether the back part or part of the head and how she got round to the end of the table to the opposite side she was sitting on'. A plan of the kitchen was included in the case (see Figure 5). The friend answered 'in her passion she somehow got round'.

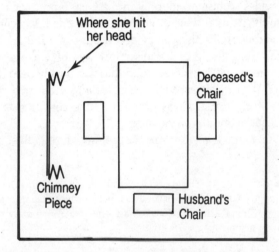

Figure 5   Plan of kitchen included in the case against John Clegg for murder of his wife, 1825 (redrawn).

The questions asked by the jury throughout the coroner's inquiry suggested the husband's guilt. 'How did you get your new straw hat?' the innkeeper's friend was asked. An assigned servant to the innkeeper who spoke for him was asked 'who gave you the money for the hat and handkerchief?' and 'what change were you able to keep?' The case heard before the coroner was passed on to the Supreme Court, the jury being unanimously of the opinion that the deceased came by her death 'in consequence of blows and a fall received from her husband caused by [her husband's friend] who was present during such blows and a fall'.[40]

In drawing up the indictments, William Henry Moore was uncertain whether the defendant should be tried for murder or manslaughter.[41] He decided, as he wrote in an undated letter to the Attorney-General, that murder should be the charge, as 'it appears to me if he is indicted for manslaughter he could not be found guilty, there do not seem to be any circumstances (suppose the woman to have died from blows she received) to reduce the offence beneath that of murder'.[42] The defendant was tried on 25 May 1825 and adjudged by the military jury to be not guilty.[43]

Court records provide us with several insights into domestic violence and legal responses to it in early colonial New South Wales. The case was created at the inquest before being legally defined as manslaughter or murder under which it was tried. Inquests were concerned with minute descriptions by neighbours or witnesses.

Violence in the household also appeared through the complaints of individuals before the magistrates' benches concerning assaults. All evidence given before the courts was heard within certain legal understandings, channelled by the procedures of the court. As the coroner's inquests or initial investigations by the magistrates both included and sought all evidence possible, the initial inquiries into these deaths contain a lot of evidence which may have not appeared in the criminal court: hearsay, questions by coroner's jurors, perhaps irrelevant accounts of what people thought or were doing at the time. This material provides an insight not only into a legal process or a process of legal understanding but also the point at which the courts intervened. Violence was different to theft in that it required not only physical evidence but some statement relating to its cause. Ordinary people were aware of permissible levels of violence with justifiable causes; this awareness intersected, in a case, with what was legally permitted to be heard before a criminal court. We can dissect violence cases into those two components and focus on the point at which violence was brought to the courts. It is first necessary, however, to state the legal definition of violence.

Richard Burn, in the main legal text of the colony during this period, defined assault as:

> an attempt to offer with force, and violence to do corporal hurt to another, striking at him with or without a weapon, presenting a gun at him at such a distance to which the gun will carry, pointing a pitchfork at him standing within reach of it or by holding one's fist at him or by any such like done in an angry or threatening manner.

So assault included not only the act but also the intent to commit it. Battery was defined as 'when any injury whatsoever be it ever so small is actually done to the person of a man, in an angry or revengeful or rude manner, by spitting in his face or in any way touching him in anger or violently jostling him out of the way and the like'. Assault could be justified in defence of the person or his wife, master, parent or child. It was also justified in defence of possessions: 'if a person comes into my house and will not go out I may justify laying hold of him and turning him out'.

Manslaughter was to be understood as such killing 'as happens either in a sudden quarrel or in the commission of an unlawful act without any deliberate intention of doing any mischief at all'. Burn continued, 'there is no difference between murder and manslaughter but that murder is upon malice forethought and manslaughter on sudden occasion'. Malice was in two forms. The first, malice expressed, was 'a deliberate intention of doing bodily harm to another whereunto by law a person is not authorised . . . the circumstances of such malice must arise from external circumstances discovering that inward intention as lying in wait, menacings antecedent, former grudges, deliberate compassings and the like which are various according to a variety of circumstances'. Malice implied was when 'one voluntarily kills another, without any provocation; for in this case the law presumes it to be malicious and that he is a public enemy of mankind'.[44]

So inquiry in assault cases centred not only on the act of assault but on the intent to assault; inquiry in murder and manslaughter cases dealt with intent also, and malice in committing the act. Cases of assault or murder were heard in different courts. Assault cases before 1824 were heard before the magistrates' benches, for which we have records mainly from Sydney. After 1824 they were heard before the various benches of Quarter Sessions, in Sydney, Liverpool and later Campbelltown, Parramatta, Windsor and Bathurst. These were heard before a jury but, unlike cases before the magistrates' benches, Quarter Sessions assaults were heard some time after the event. Thus we find many requests for a stay of the hearing. In the time before the case was heard there was opportunity for defendant and prosecutor to come to agreement or to receive or deliver threats. The courts could be seen as ineffectual in solving disputes because they gave this opportunity; the delay became typical in assault cases and only those determined to bring cases did so.

Murder and manslaughter cases were initially heard before a coroner and his jury. These were held near the scene of the murder if not at it; the body was presented and a surgeon gave evidence as to the cause of death. Occasionally cases of murder were heard before a magistrate rather than the coroner, but reasons are rarely given for this. In the case against Eliza Campbell for the murder of John Brackfield, the magistrates openly intervened in a coroner's inquiry, resulting in a violent quarrel between coroner and constables.[45] Such incidents would normally appear in evidence and as they do not appear in other cases, it is safe to assume that the functions of coroner were interchangeable with a magistrate's duties.[46]

Cases of household violence are relatively few in comparison to cases involving street assaults and violence between neighbours. The point at which such violence was brought to the courts, then, becomes interesting: we must look at how quickly cases were brought and the reasons given for bringing them.

Cases of assault in houses were the results of disputes between husband and wife or cohabiting couples rather than disputes between lodgers and people renting houses. Complaints which were most successful were those heard before the Police Magistrate's Bench where judgment was handed down immediately and there was no time either to resolve a case or for threats to the prosecutor to be made. Mary Trainer of Gloucester Street appeared before the Police Magistrates' Bench on 18 June 1812, saying that at 3 p.m. the previous day at the race course her husband had struck her violently on different parts of the body. She had given him no provocation and 'from frequent ill treatment and abuse she apprehends serious injury, she craving the peace'. The constable to whom she ran for assistance, John Burgess, was also attacked by her husband.[47] Both she and the other complainant in 1812, Jane Carter, who cohabited with William Henry and had done so for eleven years, made statements to the effect that they had suffered *frequent* abuse.[48] They had come to the court not at the first attack but after some time. This pattern continues throughout the records of the Police Magistrates' Bench and the Quarter Sessions. Women appeared either alone or with witnesses and claimed they had been subjected to frequent abuse or continued ill-use rather than one violent attack. All of the reported attacks were very violent in comparison with the single blow struck against neighbours and constables in the street: for example Hannah Field reported in 1820 that Thomas Ball 'assaulted me with a hewing knife and poured a pot of barley water off the fire and threw it over my body'.[49]

In cases heard before the magistrates' benches early in the period, the woman, like most complainants in assault cases, wanted her husband bound to keep the peace rather than imprisoned. Such a request for sureties to keep the peace was invariably granted. The man was bound to keep the peace or forfeit up to £40. We rarely hear of the husband or cohabiting man *breaking the bond*. In 1820 Richard Dalton, constable, said of Henry Henry, who had attacked his wife, 'I reminded him that he had promised the magistrate not to go near the house again.' Henry Henry then abused the constable. His sentence was 'three months' gaol, at the expiration of which to find sufficient sureties to keep the peace for twelve calendar months being a notorious vagrant'.[50] Elizabeth Mumford's case in 1819 and the case against Henry Kettle in 1829 both mentioned that the men had been before the courts previously. Henry Kettle was brought before the Supreme Court for failing to appear on a summons for assault of his wife. The case was dismissed.[51]

Requests that the husband be bound were not made in cases that reached the Quarter Sessions. These cases were most likely to be listed as 'settled' or 'not prosecuted' because of the time spent waiting for the case to be heard. At the July sessions in 1828, however, the grand jury noted a circumstance which concerned it:

> The Grand Jurors cannot separate without noticing to the Court of General Quarter Sessions that in the course of investigations issuing out of the numerous Bills of Indictment a large number of cases were for assaults of the pettiest character which have generally arisen from the system of unlicensed sellers of spirits.[52]

Following this announcement, three cases of domestic violence were rejected by the grand jury, the cases being 'not found', that is, not deemed suitable for a legal case to be made. This pattern of discouragement continued and the preliminary 'not found' occurred frequently in the records where it had not been so extensively used before. There were, then, legal factors mitigating against the hearing of a domestic violence case, and against a woman bringing a case at all.

Later cases before the Quarter Sessions seem muted because of discouragement or the time spent waiting for a case to come up; but they appeared as frequently as before the Police Magistrates' Bench and there are other elements they have in common with the earlier cases.

The first is that accounts of extreme violence were often accompanied by accounts of damage to property or clothing. Eleanor Holmes saw her husband 'burning up all her wearing apparel and bed linen'.[53] These attacks on property were stressed by the women and were, apparently, directed at specific property. The importance of clothing or personal property can be compared with its place in theft cases, and shows the value of clothing as currency as well as the separateness of property inside the house. Samuel Horner tore his wife's clothes off her back and made their elder child burn them before her face.[54] Either Esther Horner fabricated this evidence because she thought it would carry great weight, which is possible, or the attack was made and was deemed important. In either circumstances, property formed a significant link between husband and wife or cohabitants.

Very few cases detail the cause of violence and fewer still locate it in disputes over property. Though property was not a direct cause of conflict in most cases, it was a source of grievance in some. Elizabeth Mumford stated of Michael Cassidy in 1819:

> I am most crippled and black and blue all over my body . . . he has made away with my property and has left myself and four children destitute. We were married during Usurped Government which has since been declared void, thereby he has no power or authority over me.[55]

Eleanor Holmes in 1828 stated her husband was 'regularly settling into habits of drunkenness . . . he sold every description of property except one bed, with the proceeds of which he continued his state of drunkenness'.[56]

For these women their concern was an economic relationship that had failed them, as well as the violence encountered from their husbands. For Elizabeth Mumford marriage involved a control that was not present in cohabitation. For other women this economic relationship was important enough to delay bringing a case or to request that a case be dropped. Eleanor Holmes also said:

> I have often been requested to bring him [her husband] to the Police Office but refrained from so doing in the hope infant children and deponent's remonstrances restrained his cruelties, even his children, without means of subsistence and now driven from their home by his conduct makes any impression on him [sic].[57]

Property, then, was both a cause of conflict and a contributing factor to keeping that conflict out of court. It was mentioned in cases alongside beatings, and women implied that their husbands had failed them. Such complaints mainly occurred in cases involving married women, though it appears questionable whether women using two names, such as Mary Biggs who is also referred to as Mary Jennings, were actually married even if they represented themselves as such. 'Married' women, that is those that referred to the man they were complaining of as 'my husband', formed three-quarters of complainants of domestic violence, though women who were cohabiting were not given less credence by the magistrates' benches or the Courts of Quarter Sessions. Overall it appears they received similar treatment and the complaints they made, apart from this concern with property ownership, were similar.

Drunkenness was one reason given for the man's violence. One-fifth of cases said the husband or cohabiting man was drunk at the time of the assault. In these cases the husband 'came home drunk'. In other cases little reason is given for the assault or continuing assault. Mary Wright claimed in 1815 that her husband was 'actuated to such measures from motives of amusement'.[58] The husbands do not speak at all in these cases, so their reasons for violence rarely appear. The ritual of assault cases involved the prosecutor stating that no provocation was given and this continues in the cases involving husband and wife or cohabitants.

Only one written defence by a man brought before the courts for such violence has survived. This is by Patrick Moore, whose wife followed him to New South Wales when he was transported as a convict. Ellen Moore claimed she had been subject to barbarous treatment ever since she arrived to live with him. He had, the night before she appeared in court, beaten her with a spade. He wrote in his defence:

> My wife and I have been married 21 years, we have six children. She had for a great length of time conducted herself with the greatest impropriety following every vice that can be named particularly drunkenness and whoredom. In the present case I am fortunate enough to have witnesses. I can prove she was the aggressor, no man endowed with the greatest patience could have restrained from the same source of proceeding as I followed and which was guided by every attention to moderation. I humbly beg leave to throw myself upon your mercy and leniency.[59]

He does not complain of a neglected household or neglected children, but of his wife's sexual behaviour. Whether this was calculated to appeal to the jury or whether he actually felt such a concern is irrelevant. This is the issue he brings to the court. It is her sexuality on which his defence rests.

The husband and wife, or the cohabiting couple, were not the only participants in a case of domestic violence. Four-fifths of cases had other participants, such as John Bagley who made the first complaint of Abraham Kemp. Without such participants, many cases would not have been heard at all. Many of them were constables. Mary Trainer, according to John Burgess, constable, in 1812, 'came running up to examinant and Donnely for protection'. Samuel Horner in 1828 was seen by a constable to be beating his wife. The constable intervened.

There were other people to give evidence, to reinforce the woman's statements and to state the situation themselves. Thus women claimed they had been rescued from the violence of their husbands. Hannah Roberts was 'released from the outrages of her husband by the interference of three men'.[60] Neighbours intervened, either at the request of the wife or because of their own concern, in four cases in 1828, one in 1821 and one in 1822.

Domestic violence did not appear in court at the sole instigation of the wife. It was a public offence in the sense that it usually involved other people. The circumstances of their involvement, however, are interesting. Many of the women bringing cases claimed they had been consistently beaten by the men, and yet neighbours, constables and passers-by intervened only when there was extreme violence, when the woman was 'covered in blood'. When the concern of outsiders, the woman's request for assistance, and extreme violence interlocked, a domestic violence case was brought.

The circumstances working against a case being heard were quite extensive. Domestic violence cases were very rarely completed in the Quarter Sessions. They do not seem solid legal cases. So many factors intervened even before complaints were made. Economic dependence, the possibility of further violence or threats, the slowness of the legal system, all combined to prevent a case actually being heard. Domestic violence cases, in comparison with assault cases between members of the community, are very hazy. That is their character. There is, however, another side to them that has already partly been dealt with. This is, what women *invoke* in their cases. Women rarely wished to see their husbands criminally charged; rather, they wanted them bound to keep the peace.

In 1827 and 1828 we find two women claiming that the man's conduct towards them was 'unmanly', or that the treatment they had received was 'unmanly'.[61] It is interesting that 'manly' behaviour precludes violence. In the cases against Samuel Horner and John Holmes it is implied that the man had neglected his responsibilities. There is only one other case where such responsibilities are brought into the open and this is a case heard before a country bench of Quarter Sessions at Windsor in 1827.[62]

Ann Douglass was a native, aged seventeen, who had just given birth to her first child. She claimed she had been left alone in labour and had begged her husband to send for her mother, which he finally did. When she was confined her husband gave her very little food and while she was at her mother's her husband came and took the baby from her and returned home with it. Her husband received a sentence of hard labour for two years. It was implied that the husband had neglected his wife and that his behaviour should have been quite different from what it was. Male responsibilities in this case went beyond simply providing.

These ideas of what a man should be appear in cases in the late 1820s, but are foreshadowed in earlier cases concerning destruction of property and disputes over control of property. As well as extreme violence, what is invoked by these women is the idea of what a man's behaviour should be in the society.

A domestic violence case then was unlikely to appear before a court unless there were interlocking factors of extreme violence, repeated violence, witnesses or persons who intervened. When it did appear it was highly likely in the 1820s that it would be 'not prosecuted' or 'settled'. However, when it did appear, through all the obstacles, it was not only the woman's body, her bleeding and bruising, that were sources of complaint but often also the behaviour of the man apart from violence, his attitude towards property and the household. This is what is apparent in the evidence given by women, in the image they presented to the court. We hear very little but abuse from the men, and from the neighbours or other members of the community we hear nothing but descriptions of extreme violence and little reference to it having occurred repeatedly. Generally the response of magistrates in cases was in the woman's favour and women were possibly aware of this when they brought their cases.

As well as women's own perspective of what was wrong in domestic violence cases, these cases also involved members of the community. They seem to have been drawn in only in the direst of circumstances: a woman covered in blood or thrown into a fire.

While there were numbers of complaints by women of domestic violence, there were two cases of domestic violence where the woman was defendant. One was in 1820 where a gaoler brought a woman before the bench for being a common prostitute and added 'she uses her husband who is a helpless old man, very badly'.[63] Another involved Catherine Martin, a native. John Newbury stated of her:

> last night I went home with the prisoner whom I have lived with four years, she abused me and deponent gave her a blow, she fell down with the chair. The deponent went out and the prisoner fastened the door the deponent burst it open and the prisoner took a knife in her hand or some sharp instrument and gave him wounds to the head.[64]

This case was heard before the Supreme Court in 1825 and Catherine Martin was acquitted. She was charged with cutting and maiming with intent to slay. In this case details were given of violence on both sides, and the husband in his evidence explained his actions as if they were matter of fact. His provocation probably lost him the case of assault. Assaults of men by men inside the house do not appear before the courts. When we consider cases involving theft and lodgers it is possible to understand why. Men had other ways of resolving household disputes than going to the magistrate. As we shall see, assaults of men by men are related to disputes between neighbours or to social festivities.

Violence in the household occasionally became murder and these murder cases provide further evidence of reactions to household violence. Murder cases contain whole series of images of what the court could hear or would want to hear. These images reveal community attitudes to violence within households. In murder cases, therefore, we are not concerned with the interests of the inquisitor or the judge or jury in establishing innocence from guilt. Rather we will consider how the accused and the victim were construed in the evidence.

There were nine killings by cohabiting men of women during this period and five of men by the women they were cohabiting with, the latter being considerably more than assaults. These cases of murder or manslaughter were markedly different in form. This was not necessarily a result of the act of violence itself but of the questions that were asked and the assumptions made by the court, the jury, deponents and judge. The rate of acquittals for murder was reasonably high. Legally such acquittals rested on lack of evidence. The courtroom, however, was not where most of the activity surrounding the case took place. The inquest, held at the scene of the murder, heard evidence which may have been unacceptable in court.

These inquests present pictures of the accused and the victim and of the circumstances surrounding the death through the eyes of neighbours, friends, surgeons, constables. Cases fell into two patterns; the first where violence was instantaneous and resulted from beatings or arguments; the second where there was evidence of plotting, or long-term plans. Cases where a man was defendant follow the former pattern except for one. Cases where a woman was defendant follow the latter.

In the case of John Clegg, the surgeon William Walker was called and he examined the body of the deceased soon after her death. William Ikin, chief constable, gave evidence that:

> on Thursday evening last upon the closing of the business of the inquest this deponent had a conversation with William Walker who had been called on to administer to the deceased who said to deponent, my dear friend, supposing you and me had words and I was to give you a clink and you was to give me a clink, we must consider the poor family, why must we hurt anybody, thereby implying to deponent's belief that it was in consequence of his evidence a decision was come to by the jury and that the evidence he had sworn was not strictly to the truth.[65]

Ikin may not have been entirely correct in his assertion that Walker had influenced the jury, but this evidence captures well the atmosphere of an inquest. What was said can never be an accurate portrayal of what happened between accused and victim, but such statements form the perimeters of a case. On the ground of Walker's 'who clinked who' or rather who initiated violence, these cases of murder or manslaughter of women were fought out.

Was Mrs Clegg intoxicated? Was she subject to fits? There were questions asked by the inquest jury in that case. We develop a double picture of her: on the one hand an intoxicated woman angry at the suggestion of her husband's infidelity to her who possibly went into a fit and struck her head; on the other hand a woman subjected to extreme violence by her husband. Four days before her death she had been beaten so badly that she was covered with blood.

The question of intoxication was frequently brought up in cases of murder of women. Ann Gamble was in 'a sober state', according to witnesses in the inquest involving her death. Her husband, John, was also seen to be sober.[66] William Venables was said to be sober on the night of his wife's death by one witness and not sober by another. John Coghill esquire went to the house of Venables who opened the door and said, 'this is all owing to the devil' and pointed to the keg saying, 'the keg is the cause of all this'.[67] This did not amount to a confession; he claimed his wife had fallen out of bed. Intoxication of one partner did not sway the case, but if both were intoxicated and the injuries could be ascribed to a fall in a quarrel the man could be acquitted. William Venables, despite his intoxication, was charged with wilful murder.

William Henry Moore wrote to the clerk of the criminal court to 'draw an indictment against Clegg for the murder of his wife by beating according to the precedent of 231 in Archbold'.[68] The evidence of a surgeon in murder cases was important as they could relate cause of death to reasons other than beating. Darcy Wentworth in the case against Thomas Fenlon found 'a large contusion behind and below the left ear, the skull had been fractured and a suffusion of blood . . . extended down the base of the brain'. When he was asked if the injuries causing the death of the deceased had been inflicted by a heavy stick, he replied 'they might'.[69] At the inquest into the death of the wife of Arthur Hughes, William Richardson, surgeon, said he examined the body and found 'a severe contusion in the thigh and groin, the small intestines bore marks of inflammation, the parts inflamed correspond with external marks of violence, drinking might bring an inflammation'.[70] John Dalhunty, surgeon, examined the body of Ann Gamble: there were 'no marks of violence except a blow on the face appears to be caused by a fall, cannot state the actual cause'.[71]

The complaint by Ikin against William Walker was that he gave evidence to have the accused acquitted, but it cannot be assumed that this was the concern of all surgeons. Beating as a cause of death was the most difficult to prove and the connection between outside bruising and internal injury was a controversial one. If no internal injury (i.e. an infusion of blood) could be ascertained or was physically evident, then it was impossible to establish that this was the cause of death.

Intertwined in establishing cause of death was a judgment on the condition of the victim. Indeed the type of woman the victim was, was also of some importance to witnesses. The *Sydney Gazette* reported on the trial of Terence Fleming for the murder of Catherine Kennedy that 'from the evidence that came out in the trial it appeared the prisoner and deceased co-habited together; that the deceased was occasionally a drunken and intemperate woman and the prisoner a sober and industrious man'.[72] This comment reflects newspaper reporting of trials at the time. Yet such comments appeared also in the trial themselves, with the temper of the woman being discussed. Joseph Smith gave evidence at the inquest into the death of Elizabeth Massey that 'the deceased was a passionate and abuseful kind of woman I never knew the prisoner in any way spiteful or malicious'. John Ryley gave evidence at the inquest into the death of Mrs Hughes that he lived in the back part of their house and 'on Thursday the deceased and her husband had words and husband left the house he could not pacify his wife, she went out and threw stones and bricks at him'.

In such evidence the woman was portrayed as the aggressor and this point is associated with her drunkenness and her husband's sobriety. John Jones admitted to the stabbing of Elizabeth Massey, saying they were quarrelling about family matters and 'she had something in her hand coming up with intent to strike him, he had a knife in his hand— whether it was in kicking her off or how it was he could not tell . . .'. His was the only case which included a confession and this confession presented the image of an aggressive woman.

Elizabeth Massey lived some time after the stabbing, yet she refused to implicate John Jones. She begged the surgeon, Evans, to 'cure her privately otherwise Jack might get into trouble'. Mary Barter, though, gave evidence: 'I asked her the reason she did not send for anybody . . . she said he was gone for the doctor, she said this is what he did'. In Catherine Kennedy's case also some of the witnesses gave evidence that she said she had been kicked by a cow. Margaret Daily, however, said in evidence, 'I enquired if Terry had not been beating her, she hesitated, Terry acknowledged he had, she said yes the brute he did, never ask me about it in front of him'. Such responses were comparable to cases of assault by husbands or cohabiting men where women either protected their husbands or did not appear in court to give evidence against them.

Witnesses also made general comments on the state of the relationship. Walter Birmingham lodged with Terence Fleming and Catherine Kennedy, where 'there was no quarrelling', he stated. All witnesses in John Jones' case, except Mary Barter, stated that they thought the defendant a quiet man. William Fisher gave evidence at the inquest into the death of Margaret Venables that 'all was harmony and good humour . . . this deponent had every opportunity of ascertaining that as he was shown into the inner apartment by the husband of the deceased in order to display the care he had taken to provide for the winter in tea, sugar, wheat etc.' John Vernall said of the Venables that he 'always considered them a happy couple—has heard the deceased express herself in the highest terms of her husband being a careful and excellent provider for his family'.

An unfortunate incident; harmony interrupted by a sudden quarrel; intoxication; a woman subject to fits of temper: these were elements of cases of domestic violence where the woman was the victim. Another element—consistent beating by a violent man—appears also, but this is related to the cause of death, not to motivation.

Domestic violence cases which involved numbers of witnesses occurred mainly in Sydney. Country cases were more isolated. The Venables lived in a farmhouse with only their children, as did the Gambles. Arthur Hughes and his wife lived in the town of Windsor. Two of the witnesses, John and Ann Ryley, a married couple who lived at the back of the Hughes' house, gave evidence as to Mrs Hughes' 'strange behaviour' two days before her death; they said that she had tried to strangle herself with a handkerchief, and claimed they saw no violence. It was George Stubbs who heard a noise and went to the gate of Hughes' yard and saw Mrs Hughes being dragged by the hair and kicked by her husband, and James McConnel, a visitor, who saw Hughes give his wife a violent kick to the belly.

Evidence of intoxication, of aggressive women and quiet men, comes from the inner circle of friends of the accused: neighbours, lodgers and servants. Friends of the deceased often give evidence strikingly different to that of other witnesses. Terence Fleming's cow was 'perfectly quiet', according to Margaret Daily, implying that it would not have kicked Catherine Kennedy in the stomach. Lucy Clegg was 'a very healthy young woman' whose close friend Ann Morgan never saw her drunk.

Legally, for most of these cases, there was not enough evidence to convict the accused of murder. The jury returned to the court and acquitted Terence Fleming but the Judge Advocate 'announced to the prisoner that it was doubt and doubt alone that [saved] him from the ignominious destiny which otherwise would have inevitably awaited him'.[73] John Clegg was found not guilty. Arthur Hughes was found guilty of manslaughter. Wilful murder was the verdict for William Venables. Ann Gamble's death was not brought to court. John Jones was judged not guilty of murdering Elizabeth Massey but guilty of feloniously killing and slaying her. He was imprisoned for six months and paid a fine of £5.

This violence seems to be, in part, an extension of domestic arguments. It results from a quarrel gone wrong, or from extreme violence in the haste of the moment. Intoxication plays some role. It is important, though, that amongst these cases of sudden murders or killings, there is only one confession and this portrays the defendant in a position of protecting himself by violence to his wife. This, then, is the image of most cases of domestic violence where the man is the defendant. The issue is 'who hit whom' and the questioning rests there. The surgeon's opinion was important and the cause of death contested. There is a geographical difference in the nature of cases, Sydney murder cases being much more linked to the 'public', as were domestic violence cases. The silence of the countryside seems to be not only in the isolation of houses but the unwillingness of lodgers or servants to become involved in quarrels and the absence of the passive observer, the passer-by, who played such a crucial role in the town. The community, to a certain extent, and the household seem to play a protective role in relation to the defendant: it is not that they hide guilt or do not give evidence, but that they limit the terms of reference for these cases. Surgeons are complicit in this. The woman, the type of person she was and how she carried on her relationship were as much under question as the death through beating itself.

There is one case of attempted murder which does not fit a pattern similar to cases of beating. This is the case against Edward Hoar for conspiring with Peter Cooke to administer corrosive medicine to take the life of Sarah Hoar who was pregnant. The principal witness in this case was Peter Cooke, 'having apparently acceded to the design of the said Edward Hoar with the permission of [magistrate] Brabyn in order to further the ends of justice'. Edward Hoar wished to give his wife corrosive sublimate, little by little, 'so that it might appear she died of consumption'. Not realising he was victim of a counter plot by Brabyn and Cooke, Edward Hoar was stopped by a constable who found the secretly marked packets of poison. Hoar had been quite clear to Cooke as to why he wanted to poison his wife: 'I want to get shot of the whole concern for her family who had lately made [me] pay 11/- sixpence for court fees.' He also expressed his love for Elizabeth Charleston and carried a lock of her hair.[74] He was gaoled before he could begin to poison his wife. The element of plotting was more common in the murder of men by women and the Hoar case has two other points in common with murder of men by women—love and debt.

When we turn to murder of men by women, the cases rarely involve single defendants. The cases concerned Charlotte Dunn in 1825, Mary Ann Bradney in 1824, Mary Minton in 1824, Eliza Campbell in 1824 and Harriet Purcell in 1827. Where women were accused of murdering men, the cases were seen in much blacker terms by the press and the magistrates. 'There was never a more bloody deed perpetuated in the land' claimed the *Sydney Gazette* of the murder of Michael Minton.[75] 'In truth a more terrible transaction I have never yet heard of', wrote Charles Throsby to Saxe Bannister concerning the Eliza Campbell case.[76] The Windsor magistrates wrote to Saxe Bannister concerning the case involving Charlotte Dunn, 'we are of the opinion and such is the public feeling that the parties are guilty but not in the decided manner they were in the Minton case'.[77] The *Gazette* wrote of Mary Ann Bradney, 'the peculiar heinousness of this crime was pathetically depicted by the Attorney General at the opening of the trial'.[78]

These trials were marked by public interest. The defendants were, except in the case of Mary Ann Bradney, groups of people. The hangings that did result were well reported. All these trials involved a plot. What they also have in common is the kind of environment in which the crime was said to occur.

Michael Minton was murdered at night on an isolated farm on the Nepean River. Half a mile away were the houses of Mary Peckham, William Langhan, John Abbeth and Samuel Levy. The Nepean River was the area where small settlers took up land after the Hawkesbury River and the South Creek became too densely settled. John Brackfield was murdered at night, also in a farmhouse, on the South Creek. The Dunns lived at the small settlement of Pitt Town, also in a farmhouse. The Purcells lived in Windsor, the Bradneys at Port Macquarie, both in relatively isolated farmhouses.

The murders are markedly similar in character, as if the perpetrators copied one another, taking note of the pitfalls of earlier cases. In 1817 John Castles and Harriet Purcell were charged with cutting John Redmond Byrne with intent to murder him or John Purcell. It was argued in the case that Byrne was struck because Castles believed him to be Purcell. Christopher Malone, a servant of Mr Fulton, went to see Harriet Purcell the Friday before the attack on Byrne:

> she said she was going to dissolution between the acts of her husband she wished somebody would break his neck or kill him she would do anything she could for witness if he would kill Mr. Purcell she would get some [gun] powder from Sydney and give him Purcell's own gun to murder him with and it should be done immediately as Mr. Purcell was so involved in debt that he would soon be taken.[79]

In August 1824 Michael Minton was killed. James Stack, a servant, made a confession in the inquest which was not admitted to court, having being given under promise of acquittal.[80] Stack said, 'his mistress Mary Minton told him she would give him 50 pounds to kill Minton and afterwards make him her overseer and give him twenty pounds a year'.[81]

Eliza Campbell was servant to Brackfield at the South Creek. The magistrate Throsby wrote to Saxe Bannister:

> it appears the unfortunate man had quarrelled with his woman servant (who perhaps was admitted to too much familiarity) she thought he had a considerable quantity of money and had planned with the men to rob him for which purpose she left the back door unfastened . . .[82]

The charge against Mary Ann Bradney in 1824 was of poisoning her husband. When he was taken to hospital, a surgeon ordered she not be allowed near him and no food she sent should be given him.[83] Stephen Dunn drowned in 1825. His wife Charlotte Dunn, according to witnesses, was involved with a neighbour, John Hanabus, and had often wished her husband dead.[84]

These descriptions of the women identify them as the main instigator of the crime. In contrast, however, Mary Ann Bradney and Mary Minton had favourable reports given at the inquest and trial of their character as wives and mothers.[85] The judge commented in the trial against Mary Minton that it was difficult to find a motive for her involvement in her husband's death.[86] The women were not seen in a negative light throughout their trial though the construction of their guilt in pre-trial depositions rested on points closer to suspicion and community disapproval than material evidence.

Cause of death in these cases was of minor concern and surgeons played a minimal role in the cases except for that of Mary Ann Bradney. Stephen Dunn had drowned despite the fact he was a good swimmer. Michael Minton's throat was cut. John Brackfield was strangled with a black silk handkerchief. John Byrne, in the Purcell case of attempted murder, was struck on the head from behind. These cases were handled differently to cases against men who were charged with the murder of women.

Thomas Tibbut of Windsor was on his way to Sydney shortly after the murder of Stephen Dunn when he put up at the Talbot inn where he usually stopped. The innkeeper's wife, Mrs White, remarked to Tibbut: 'What a business Mrs. Dunn had been doing.' She added that Mrs Dunn must have had this in contemplation some time as the last time she was in Sydney she bought mourning. Tibbut asked her if she knew where Mrs Dunn had bought it. Mrs White answered that she bought it at Mr Blaxland's. Next day at dinner time Tibbut entered again into conversation on the subject of mourning. Mrs White said her daughter had been with Mrs Dunn when she bought eight yards of love ribbon. Tibbut asked Mrs White if it were not unusual for a person to wear that kind of ribbon except on occasion of a female going into mourning for her husband. Mrs White continued that Mrs Dunn had purchased a hat. She showed it to Mrs White, who, supposing it was purchased for Mrs Dunn's husband, objected that the hat was very ugly. Finding Mrs Dunn displeased at her remarks and John Hanabus being present, Mrs White did not wish to offend them, because they were customers of hers. She then 'altered her tune' and said it was very fashionable hat, one many people liked, but she did not like hats of that shape herself.

Thomas Tibbut gave all of this evidence before the magistrate Cox on 8 January 1825 at Windsor. The ribbon, the hat, all were deemed relevant by Tibbut to the death of Stephen Dunn. Thomas Bulgar, a servant of Dunn's, gave evidence that 'their quarrels were always about John Hanabus who sleeps with his mistress when they can find an opportunity'. He noted also that when he was on his way to the barn to sleep on the night of Dunn's disappearance, the door was locked on the outside. Someone other than Mrs Dunn must have locked the door, because she was inside.

When Patrick Dooling, employed by Dunn, stacking and reaping, saw Hanabus crossing a field towards Dunn's, he said, 'there goes the fancy man'. Dooling's wife, Euphenia, was in the house of Dunn on the night he disappeared. She saw he was too drunk to walk. Mary Mackenzie, a neighbour, asked Thomas Jones, who was a servant of Dunn's and later charged with complicity in his murder, if they had searched the creek after the master's disappearance; 'on this question being put to him he looked down and appeared confused'. When Jones left her house she remarked to her husband that it had a very bad look and she would not wonder if they put him in the creek.

When the body of Stephen Dunn was found, it bore no marks of violence. The surgeon, Major West, could not say if it was immersed in water before or after death. John McDonald of Pitt Town, foreman at the inquest, made the statement that where the body was found the pond was very narrow. There were no signs of anyone falling down the bank. Another witness, Charlotte Capp of Windsor, served at the inn. After Dunn had disappeared Charlotte Dunn came and called for a glass of spirits, 'very unusual for her'. She said she did not care if Dunn was dead.

James Floyd of Parramatta was travelling to Parramatta. He had instructions from Mrs Dunn to purchase mourning and she had given him sixteen bushels of wheat to pay for it. He said she knew the prices of most of the articles. Those who gave evidence which could be seen to be in favour of John Hanabus and Charlotte Dunn were Robert Rose, servant to Gilderthorpe, and John Gunning of Pitt Town, who both said Stephen Dunn kept a bottle of rum in the reeds near the creek and that he had fallen in the creek once and found it very difficult to get out.[87]

Charlotte Dunn, John Hanabus and Thomas Jones were to wait eight months before they were tried. They were acquitted.[88] The Windsor magistrates had written to Saxe Bannister in March:

> you suggest in yours as to the propriety of detaining the parties in prison or discharging them on bail or otherwise and you call our attention to the most eligible of these modes to be adopted, which we from our experience or from the feelings of the country would recommend. We are of the opinion and such is the public feeling that the parties are guilty but not in the decided manner that they were in the Minton case.[89]

The evidence to make a case came at the end of July. Patrick Dooling made a voluntary confession. He and his wife Euphenia had gone to bed in Dunn's barn. Dooling had to get up during the night and saw Hanabus carrying a large bundle like a child (equal to Dunn who was a small man). Hanabus walked as fast as he could to the water, and

Charlotte Dunn followed. Dooling was asked why he had not given this evidence before. He said he was afraid of his life from Hanabus and his connections. He had no house to go to and Charlotte Dunn owed him a considerable sum for his labour. Henry Green, sawyer, had been at work on the harvest with Dooling when Dooling had said to him that 'if Dunn was found convenient to the house he would hang Mrs. Dunn if there were not another woman on earth'. Green was positive that on the night of Dunn's disappearance Dunn had been too drunk to walk.

At the closing of the trial the Chief Justice addressed the prisoners:

> although the evidence did not appear to the Jury sufficient, direct and positive for them to ground a verdict of Guilty, still a considerable impression existed in the mind of the Court as to their knowledge of the crime with which they were charged, that a considerable degree of criminal intimacy appeared to have existed between them, which he seriously admonished them to break off, and so to conduct their lives in future, as that suspicion of the murder should not again fall on them.[90]

The judge's suggestion that suspicion had brought the defendants before the court is apparent both in the statements of magistrates and the evidence of witnesses. 'We are of the opinion the accused are guilty', 'such is the public feeling that the defendants are guilty' say the magistrates. 'What a business Mrs. Dunn has been doing'; 'What have you done with Dunn. Amongst you, you have done away with him' say the deponents. This opinion far outweighs any material evidence and months are spent waiting for it. The construction of guilt in this case is related to what is obvious to the local community: Charlotte Dunn and John Hanabus, her neighbour, were intimate; she had often wished her husband out of the way; he disappears. Love ribbon, knowing the cost of mourning, drinking a glass of spirits which was unusual, all of these were carefully noted by deponents. Her behaviour is carefully scrutinised. All of it was deemed useful to the court by deponents.

Similar suspicions appear in other cases. The principal deponent in the case against Mary Minton was Thomas Jones, an assigned servant to Minton, who claimed that Mary Minton had sent him out of the house with calico at 11 p.m. to the house of Mary Peckham, a neighbour. While at Mary Peckham's he heard a gunshot; as he was returning to the house he saw Mary Minton and Stack in deep conversation walking towards the creek.[91] He returned to the house to find Stack saying, 'My God, my God, my master is killed'. Stack said five men had entered the house and killed the master. Mary Minton did not disagree. The judge pointed this out and detailed the discrepancy in her story of five men breaking into the house. The five, later in her evidence, included Stack and Hand. The evidence that the murder was committed by household members was that no money was taken, and that all the murder implements, the gun, axe and the knife 'belonged to the household' and were found outside in the drain. Stack and Hand were found guilty and Mary Minton, not guilty.[92]

The *Sydney Gazette* reported on the hanging: 'How satisfactory how congenial, would it have been to popular feeling, had Stack only cleared up the point which implicated *the woman* [sic] that was seen on the way with him, to the drain? But no, not a syllable! As the wretched creatures lived the enemies of man, probably it was systematic for them to die in sullen and marked contempt with mankind.'[93]

Suspicious behaviour also played some role in the beginnings of a case against Eliza Campbell and her fellow servants. They too claimed a group of men, a banditti, had burst into the house and killed their master Brackfield. Lewis Solomon, Liverpool publican, gave evidence:

> On Sunday 14 he proceeded to the farm and requested to be shown the body which being in a bad state required more assistance than his own to place the corpse in a coffin. Deponent enquired for a female to assist in putting the shroud on the body. Eliza Campbell came into the deponent. On being asked to assist in putting on the shroud she replied she had never done anything of the kind. From circumstances deponent had a strong suspicion she was implicated in the murder of the master which induced deponent particularly to examine the door.[94]

He found the door broken open on one side.

In the case against Harriet Purcell and John Castles, neighbours and servants had their suspicions. William Parry said he had overheard a conversation between Mrs Purcell and her maid Sally, in which the servant accused Harriet Purcell of having Castles in bed all night when John Purcell was in Sydney. 'Mrs. Purcell wished everything bad to befall Mr. Purcell.' Christopher Malone gave evidence that Mrs Purcell had requested him to murder her husband. She also said, 'she had prostituted herself repeatedly for her husband's benefit and had often paid money for him, he was aware how she had obtained it ... that she would do as she pleased for her own pleasure ...' Two of the servants claimed they had seen Castles and Mrs Purcell in bed together.[95]

In the case against Mary Ann Bradney, the surgeon's suspicions played a major role. He suspected her of poisoning her husband after his symptoms did not abate. He removed the man to hospital, giving an order that no provisions were to be sent by his wife. Witnesses seem to be equally divided, those who believed she showed no remorse at the death of her husband and had sent soup to the hospital, and those who said she ate some of that soup herself.[96] The *Gazette* reported the judge's comments: 'it would be essential for the ends of justice, in the first place to ascertain that the deceased came to his death by poison: to which Dr. Moran and several other gentlemen of the Faculty could come to no conclusion; and in the second instance, it must be proved that the poison was administered by the prisoner, which in no stage of the evidence, had been developed'. Mary Ann Bradney was found by the jury to be not guilty. In the course of the trial, according to the *Gazette*, 'it was attempted to be proved that there was an illicit intercourse maintained between the prisoner and one James Duff: but only one interview, that had the blush of criminality, was manifested throughout the whole trial'.[97]

This 'blush of criminality' was particularly important in cases involving women and the death of their husbands or cohabitants. The element of plotting, indeed the kinds of murders they were, meant that the questions were asked of them were different to those asked in cases of death by beating. There were questions of motivation, of other interest, that may have suggested a reason for the killing of husbands or cohabiting men. These motivations were presumed to be sexual. An involvement with a man outside marriage was made much of.

The motives discerned by deponents in cases of murder of men by women are money, and wanting to live with another man. There are no such reasons given for the murder of women by men except in one case. The 'cause of violence' in cases where men are defendants was largely the activity of the woman herself, her temper, her spite, her intoxication. There is some protectiveness by the community of the men whose wives are found beaten to death.

Shooting, strangling and axing were much more obviously 'horrifying' and the murder of men by women involved accomplices, but in these cases it is the role of the women which is under scrutiny. Their behaviour makes them subject to suspicion.

The acquittals and judgments of 'not guilty' were often a result of inadequate evidence to convict. On the other hand, where these cases involving domestic violence emerge, they do so from perceptions of women's role in the society. Masculine violence in the household could be extreme before anyone intervened and it became a 'public offence'. Acceptance of this level of violence probably led to tolerance of death by beating of women. Murder of men by women was much more offensive to 'the public feeling'.

In cases of domestic violence women set out their reasons for finally resorting to law; they include references to property and to the expected behaviour of men. There were, however, mitigating circumstances of property, threats or unwillingness which worked against the court hearing a case. The nature of domestic murder mean that murders by women were judged by different criteria to men's. Plotting and intent were the issues argued in murder cases, whereas temperament was at issue in manslaughter cases. The shaping of these cases was not only determined by the legal requirements for a case. Surgeons and witnesses created a frame of reference for cases of domestic murder. The quiet man driven to violence was an image often presented by witnesses. Surgeons found it difficult to identify the cause of death in examining the body of a woman killed by beating. In comparison, and though accomplices were involved in the murder of husbands or cohabiting men and women, the community clamoured to give all relevant evidence concerning the sexuality of the woman. Mary Minton, Eliza Campbell and Charlotte Dunn figured large in hearsay, in suspicion and in public interpretations of the crime, while their male accomplices did not.

Like domestic assault, murder of men by men did not occur in the house apart from the cases listed above. Male violence occurred in the streets, on farms or in public houses and in those cases the dispute is clearly set out or the sudden killing easily explained by onlookers. Domestic murders emerge out of intimate relations between man and woman. In such cases the law clearly reacts differently to the 'male' and the 'female'. We cannot easily dissociate the requirements of law from the perspectives presented to it by witnesses. Both create the texture of law in the colony. Women figure differently in this convergence of local cultures and law. These differences will be further set out through an examination of cases involving male and female sexuality.

Notes

1 Judge Advocate, Register of Assignment and other legal documents, M.L. 5/1113, Vol. 1, p. 248.

2 John Demos, *Family Life in Plymouth Colony*, pp. 21–2.

3 J. M. Beattie, *Crime and the Courts in England 1660–1880*, pp. 181–3.

4 J. H. Plunkett, *The Australian Magistrate: A Guide to the Duties of Justice of Peace*, Sydney, 1835, p. 42.

5 R. Burn, *The Justice of the Peace and Parish Officer*, 7th edn, vol. 1, 1762, p. 360.
6 Plunkett, *The Australian Magistrate*, p. 213.
7 *ibid.*, p. 345.
8 Darcy Wentworth, Police Reports and Accounts, 1810–27, M.L., D1.
9 R. vs James Kirton, C.C.J., 1821, 57.
10 R. vs Thomas Welsh, C.C.J., 11 October 1811.
11 *ibid.*
12 R. vs Alexander Monaghan, C.C.J., August 1821, 46.
13 R. vs Ann Frances and James Goff, C.C.J., March 1814.
14 R. vs James Lillywhite, C.C.J., February 1818.
15 Catherine Murphy, J.A.B., 2 May 1812.
16 Henry Henry, P.M.B., 20 October 1820.
17 Jane McCoy, P.M.B., 24 March 1821.
18 R. vs Thomas Waite, Jane Mitchell, Parramatta, C.C.J., May 1820, 374.
19 R. vs William Gwillin, C.C.J., September 1823, 9.
20 R. vs Elizabeth O'Bryan, C.C.J., March 1814.
21 R. vs Catherine Leeson, C.C.J., 30 October 1813.
22 R. vs Martha Young, C.C.J., October 1822, 11.
23 R. vs Catherine Fitzgerald, C.C.J., 16 March 1813.
24 Maria Jones, P.M.B., 8 January 1812.
25 R. vs Eliza Nuttal, C.C.J., March 1822, 16.
26 J. Beattie, 'The Criminality of Women in Eighteenth Century England', *Journal of Social History*, vol. 8, no. 4, (Summer 1975), p. 108.
27 R. vs Thomas George, C.C.J., December 1816, 16.
28 R. vs William Oliver, C.C.J., March 1818, 395.
29 William Russell, P.M.B., 26 December 1820.
30 R. vs James Rotten, C.C.J., September 1822, 9.
31 R. vs William Blaxcell, William Tripp, C.C.J., October 1816.
32 R. vs Eliza Campbell, S.C.C.J., February 1825, 1.
33 *ibid.*
34 R. vs Richard Holloway, C.C.J., May 1822, 10.
35 R. vs Eliza Campbell.
36 R. vs William Marley, James Larder, Jane Evans, C.C.J., November 1816.
37 R. vs Thomas Delworth, William Smith, Margaret McKennel, C.C.J., December 1820, 230.
38 B. Lemire, 'Consumerism in Pre-industrial and Early Industrial England: the Trade in Secondhand Clothes', *Journal of British Studies*, vol. 27, no. 1, January 1988.
39 C. Stansell, *City of Women: Sex and Class in New York 1789–1860*, pp. 90–1.
40 R. vs John Clegg, S.C.C.J., May 1825, 20.
41 *ibid.*, Informations and other papers, Letter W. H. Moore to Mr Wood, 18 May 1825.
42 *ibid.*, Letter W. H. Moore to Attorney-General.
43 *ibid.*
44 Richard Burn, *The Justice of the Peace and Parish Officer*, 7th edn, vol. 1, 1762, p. 94.
45 R. vs Eliza Campbell and others, S.C.C.J., February 1825, 1.
46 This has been suggested by A. Castles, *An Australian Legal History*, p. 69.
47 Mary Trainer, P.M.B., 18 June 1812.
48 William Henry, P.M.B., 24 June 1812.
49 Thomas Ball, P.M.B., 17 October 1820.
50 Henry Henry, P.M.B., 20 October 1820.
51 R. vs Henry Kettle, S.C.C.J., 1829, Miscellaneous.

52 Quarter Sessions, Grand Jury Presentment, Sydney Q.S., July 1828.
53 John Holmes, Sydney Q.S., July 1828, 62.
54 Samuel Horner, Sydney Q.S., December 1828.
55 R. vs Michael Cassidy, C.C.J., June 1819, 131. (The point about the status of her marriage was her own perception. Macquarie did not declare all former contracts void in 1810.)
56 John Holmes, Sydney Q.S., July 1828.
57 *ibid.*
58 George Wright, P.M.B., 21 October 1815.
59 Patrick Moore, Sydney Q.S., January 1828, 55.
60 George Roberts, Sydney Q.S., April 1828, 46.
61 James Stuart, Sydney Q.S., April 1827, 49; John Holmes, Sydney Q.S., July 1828, 62.
62 Philip Douglas, Windsor Q.S., April 1827, 17.
63 Jane Marcus, P.M.B., 6 September 1820.
64 R. vs Catherine Martin, S.C.C.J., November 1825, 165.
65 R. vs Clegg.
66 Inquest papers included S.C.C.J., 1829 Miscellaneous.
67 R. vs William Venables, S.C.C.J., June 1829, 101.
68 R. vs Clegg, Informations, 1825, 77.
69 R. vs Thomas Fenlon/Finland, C.C.J., April 1817, 6.
70 R. vs Arthur Hughes, S.C.C.J., March 1829, 132.
71 Inquest papers, death of Ann Gamble, S.C.C.J., 1829, Miscellaneous.
72 *Sydney Gazette*, 2 January 1823.
73 *ibid.*
74 R. vs Edward Hoar, C.C.J., December 1823, 55.
75 *Sydney Gazette*, 19 August 1824.
76 R. vs Campbell and others.
77 Letter included, R. vs Charlotte Dunn, Thomas Jones, John Hanabus, S.C.C.J., September 1825, 140.
78 *Sydney Gazette*, 12 August 1824.
79 R. vs Harriet Purcell and John Castles, C.C.J., September 1817, 34.
80 *Sydney Gazette*, 24 September 1824.
81 R. vs James Stack and John Hand, R. vs Mary Minton, S.C.C.J., August 1824, 66.
82 R. vs Campbell and others, Throsby to Saxe Bannister, 27 November 1824.
83 *Sydney Gazette*, 12 August 1824.
84 R. vs Dunn, Jones, Hanabus, S.C.C.J., January 1825, 140.
85 *Sydney Gazette*, 12 and 19 August, 24 September 1824.
86 *ibid.*, 24 September 1824.
87 R. vs Dunn, Jones, Hanabus.
88 Supreme Court Returns, X727.
89 R. vs Dunn, Jones, Hanabus, letter included Cox, Brabyn, Bell to Saxe Bannister, 22 March 1825.
90 R. vs Dunn, Jones, Hanabus.
91 R. vs Stack, Hand, Minton.
92 *Sydney Gazette*, 23 August 1824.
93 *ibid.*, 30 August 1824.
94 R. vs Campbell and others.
95 R. vs Purcell, Castles.
96 *Sydney Gazette*, 19 August 1824.
97 *ibid.*

4

THE BODY

Sexuality was subjected to scrutiny in cases concerned with sodomy, bestiality, rape and murder. These cases dealt differently with male and female sexuality. Statute law required that there be different sets of questions asked of defendants and complainants. However, like cases of domestic violence, the appearance of such cases at all also resulted from a complex interaction of understandings of acceptable behaviour and unacceptable violence by witnesses, victims and the authorities. In the colony cases concerning such direct scrutiny of sexuality are few and therefore their construction was unusual. What makes a rape case, for example, will show us nothing of the extent of rape in the colony; but it will show us the interpretations which local communities, surgeons and magistrates placed on the female body at such times of crisis. So, in this chapter, we are asking how the body figured in criminal cases: what kinds of affront were claimed and what questions were asked of the evidence presented.

Cases concerning the body, like those concerning household violence, come from the population rather than from constables. In them we find another subtle net of power relations resembling the more direct control of the convict's body. This is the net of suspicion or expectation of proper modes of behaviour, a sensitivity to gesture and speech which was sex specific. Like the administration, popular attitudes held clear notions of male and female roles, and what was female was subject to more scrutiny than what was male.

The Male Body

In January 1812 Daniel Dacey went before the Sydney Police Magistrates' Bench to say he saw a man 'driving some asses and in commission of an unnatural crime with one of them'. He then saw him taking peaches. Dacey went to a neighbour, Elinor Cooper, and told her only that a man was stealing peaches from a garden. He suggested they should take him into custody by surrounding him. Dacey went back to the garden and confronted the man, asking him, did he know what he was at before he came to that garden, to which the man replied 'at what'; whereupon Dacey 'told him he ought to be hanged and burned'. Dacey turned to Elinor Cooper and the owner of the garden and asked who the man was; 'they made no reply but almost instantly Elinor Cooper's husband came up and examinant [then] asked them if they knew who the prisoner was, some of them informed examinant he was one of the Brickgang but did not mention his name . . .'. Dacey continued, 'examinant did not wish to have any hand in it himself after having seen all parties disparate'. Dacey did not wish to bring the case alone, and the other persons in the garden seemed reluctant to become involved. But one of the Brickgang was standing nearby. He told Dacey the prisoner was 'rather extraordinary and in the same gang with him'.[1] The next day Dacey went to Sydney and mentioned the circumstances to Robert McAllister, constable, who consequently took the prisoner into custody. This case was dismissed; Dacey had possibly been aware that he needed another witness when he went in search of Elinor Cooper.

The offence that Dacey claimed to witness would have been prosecuted under the 1533 Act of Henry VIII, the sentence for such an act of buggery being, as Dacey understood, death. The offence involving an animal required two witnesses and Dacey could not produce another. The offence of sodomy could be proved by medical verification; this verification was generally unforthcoming, Jeffrey Weekes writes, so the usual charge in England was attempted sodomy. For attempted sodomy the punishment was to stand in the pillory, be imprisoned for ten months and pay a fine.[2] Most of the offences relating to buggery in early colonial New South Wales fell into this lesser area of punishment, whether they involved bestiality or sodomy.

The association of tropical climates with sexual practices deemed perverse was common in eighteenth- and nineteenth-century literature.[3] This did not result in any precise expression of fear on the part of colonial administrators for the effect of the colonial environment on the convicts transported. The primary identification of convict men as transported labour was just beginning to merge with concepts of incarceration, and the initial focus of such concerns about sexuality was not men, but women. Discussions of sexuality and policing centred on women; the press, as well as the government, saw women as a problem in the colony.

Cases of sodomy, attempted unnatural intercourse and bestiality were heard before both lower and criminal courts. The uncertainties involved were expressed in the titles given to cases by magistrates. In 1812 a free man was charged with 'having attempted carnal knowledge of a bitch' before the Judge Advocate's Bench. He was found guilty, sentenced to 100 lashes and exposed in the pillory, after which he was put to hard labour for three years.[4] In the same month three persons, two prisoners and one free man, were charged with 'attempting to commit an unnatural crime, one with the other, brutal grossly indecent conduct in violation of good morals and the disgrace of society [sic]'.[5] Both of these types of offences were heard before the criminal courts and the cases were not returned to the benches or deemed unsuitable for hearing. Why is not clear. Cases kept in the lower courts were often described as 'misdemeanours'.

If there was a lack of clarity in determining where cases were to be heard, there was also no expressed interest on the part of constables or magistrates in policing these offences. Charges of sodomy and bestiality did not emerge from the policing of convicts in penal settlements, or from surveillance by constables or magistrates, but resulted rather from persons like Daniel Dacey who thought the offence was severe enough to hang and burn the culprit. Buggery cases originated from passers-by or observers or persons who were attacked themselves.

Inns were the most common site of unnatural assault. Travellers often were required by the innkeeper to share a bed and assaults were reported the next morning to the constable or innkeeper. The attacks occurred after some drinking and the victims do not report leaving the bed but make complaint the next day. Intoxication was made an issue in a case in the Quarter Sessions in November 1826 when the complainant, Thomas Rogers, reported that he was assaulted by two men he was sleeping with. He was asked, 'When you gave evidence before Captain Rossi were you sober?' and replied, 'I was not—I had been drinking rum and was not quite sober—I drank the greater part of a quantity of rum while I was in the Rocks in the morning.'[6]

The deponents in this case were the complainant, a constable called to the scene, and a witness. The case was greatly aided by the constable's evidence that one of the defendants had offered money to a man who was present in the public house so that he would not say the attack had occurred.[7] In fact the man had not been present when the attack occurred. The defendant was found guilty and sentenced to stand in the pillory, to be imprisoned for two years and fined £20.[8] This pattern continues for other cases, and it is in stark contrast to the evidence required for rape cases where the sobriety and reputation of the victim were questioned. There was enough basis for a trial in the complaint itself in unnatural assault cases.

Not surprisingly, this left cases open for false accusation and false swearing. A successful defence in one case was that the complainant was well known for making such complaints.[9]

Complaints made by passers-by or observers required witnesses, and those persons who made the complaint were, like Daniel Dacey, quite willing to find a witness. In 1828 the assistant cook at Government House, Thomas Kinger, called the butler when he heard suspicious conversation between the head cook and the sentry. The head cook and sentry were consequently charged with 'indecently, unnaturally exposing their persons to each other'. The under cook waited some time before making the complaint. His reason was that, 'being a prisoner, deponent was informed his testimony would not be credited'. The butler's evidence was that the sentry entreated him not to make complaint. The case was not heard; according to the Attorney-General, 'no indictment can be supported'.[10] In 1812 George Jubbe saw two men in criminal connection. He went out and called John Anson who was working nearby, and John Stanton, a passer-by, and all three of them crept back to the place where the two prisoners were seen.[11] This case has no recorded judgment.

The derivation of these cases links them to community concerns about assault, theft and neighbourly relations. These cases could well be constructed as related to other disputes, but the courts do not subject them to such questioning. While cases were heard at Quarter Sessions, magistrates' benches and criminal courts, the sentencing for such offences was similar; public humiliation in the pillory, a term of imprisonment or transportation, and the lash.

In comparison to rape, unnatural assault was a relatively easy complaint to make, bestiality or sodomy were easily witnessed. The courts were quite receptive to these complaints; if evidence sufficed, these cases invariably resulted in harsh sentences. These cases originated within the community. They reveal community assumptions about 'acceptable behaviour'. There was little recourse to a defence for those persons accused and the complainant was not subject to either physical examination or interrogation. Those persons charged, then, were quite easily falsely accused of committing abominable crimes. It was the community which subjected male sexuality to surveillance. The complainants were not only persons from wealthy backgrounds: convicts, labourers and employers all made complaint. The ease with which cases were presented and proved suggests that reasons for initiating a case may have been subject to considerations other than affront, shock or disgust.

False accusation combined with the harsh sentences involved make such accusations effective and devastating for the accused. When we look at rape cases, however, the scrutiny of the law is most definitely on the female body. It is not vague, indiscriminate or 'unspeakable' as is the attempt at scrutiny of the male body.

The Female Body

The colonial administration saw women's sex as a different and difficult quantity. Administration took careful note of the numbers of women in the colony and expressed a need for more of them or less, depending on their view of women's sex. Local communities as well had their own views of women's sex, and the importance of it in maintaining the stability of the community. All of the conflicts involving women's sexuality were expressed in the courts through cases of theft, assault, disorderly conduct and rape. What was thought to be possible and what was thought to be illegal appeared in the courts, and particular assumptions about women's bodies were implicit in this. The law dealt with women's own use of their bodies as it did with men's labour. Underlying all of this was a particular view of the female anatomy and it is this view which we shall subject to scrutiny.

Two groups of persons appeared as victims of rape in the colony: old, married or pregnant women; and young girls aged between five and ten. A rape case was described in Burn's book, *The Justice of the Peace*, as one of the most difficult cases to judge.

> On the whole, rape, it is true, is a most detestable crime, and therefore ought severely and impartially to be punished with death, but it must be remembered that it is an accusation easily to be made, harder to be proved and harder to be defended by the party accused tho' never so innocent . . .

The description of the offence continued, 'The party ravished was able to give evidence on oath and is in law a competent witness, but the creditability of her testimony and how far forth she is to be believed must be left to the jury.' This belief was to depend on whether the witness was of good fame; if she made pursuit; if she showed circumstances of injury; if the offender fled; or if there were other witnesses.[12] Built into the law were questions to be asked and cynicism about the woman's claim. The law regarding rape of children had been reformed during the reign of Elizabeth; before that it had been doubted whether a child could be raped. The reform set out 'a plain declaration of law if any person shall unlawfully carnally know and abuse any child under the age of ten years every such unlawful and carnal knowledge shall be felony'. For a child above the age of ten felonious rape could not occur unless it was against her consent. Deflowering a child between ten and twelve was a misdemeanour.[13] Neither a woman nor a child had to prove emission: it was enough for them to hint to the magistrate that emission had taken place.[14] Children could be sworn to give evidence if they understood the nature of an oath. For the child under ten what was at issue was penetration; for the woman, consent. The law essentially structured the kinds of questions asked in court.

'It is with extreme regret', wrote Windsor magistrate Archibald Bell to Saxe Bannister in 1826, 'that I have to inform you a number of children in these districts are labouring under gonorrhea . . . which disease has been imparted to them by men of the description of the prisoner—I find several parents for the credit of their families have generally withheld these circumstances.'[15] For children the evidence for rape cases could rest also on transmission of a sexual disease. The rape was discovered when the child was seen to have difficulty in walking or her linen was soiled. The child was questioned and brought before a magistrate where her evidence and the evidence of her parents was heard. The parents would give evidence that the child did not know the meaning of an oath and the evidence of the child would be heard without her being sworn.

In the colony in cases concerning girl children, surgeons played a major role. The opinion of surgeons was needed to establish penetration and their opinions differed. When Harriet Smith's case was heard in 1826, Major West gave information that he was positive no penetration had taken place: 'there might have been an attempt but he was positive no penetration had taken place, the child may have tumbled on a stick'.[16] Mr Kiernan, assistant surgeon, examined the child and 'thought from the inflamed state of the parts . . . that the hymen was ruptured and that the blood produced was from frequent friction'.[17] When Ambrose Burnsides reported the rape of his daughter by a soldier, he stated the surgeon had said to him there were marks of violence. Surgeon West said before the magistrate that he could see no marks of violence.[18]

In determining penetration or violence, consent became of concern regardless of statute law. In 1822 in the case of the rape of Mary Ann McGreevey, aged seven years, the magistrate at Newcastle wrote to the Attorney-General:

> it does not appear to me from the evidence . . . that there was any attempt at rape as it seems it was perfectly with the child's consent, yet as the girl is under ten years of age I suspect it is amenable as an assault I therefore think it necessary to send him up for your decision as he is a prisoner and has been discharged from his master's service in consequence of the affair.[19]

There is a vast difference between the attitude of this Newcastle magistrate and the concern of the Windsor magistrate for children in his local area afflicted with venereal disease. In the letter which dealt with venereal disease the Windsor magistrate wrote concerning Dr West:

In transmitting these papers to you I feel it incumbent on me also to forward an affidavit sworn by the father of the children relative to the extraordinary conduct of Dr. West in anticipating the acquittal of such a villain as Cunningham and wishing to introduce a man into his service whose conduct should be the abhorrence of everyone.[20]

West had offered a rape defendant work in the expectation that he would be found not guilty, while he himself provided part of the prosecution.

Children gave evidence in court and were sworn if it was indicated they understood the nature of an oath. If they did not, they gave evidence without swearing. The uncertain perception of children understanding legal procedure is comparable to the issue of consent. When did a child consent knowingly to sexual intercourse? The answer of the colonial courts was surely sometimes they did and sometimes they didn't, depending on the circumstances. When consent was considered by magistrates, they saw a child as a grown woman with comparable control of the use of her sex. The proof of consent was as difficult medically to ascertain as penetration or 'falling on a stick'.

The abhorrence referred to by the Windsor magistrate also appeared in the evidence of deponents. When Robert Lane, government servant to William Palmer, in 1818 'saw a soldier in a field obviously to do with a female he was horrified it was such a small girl'.[21] Ann Bayliss heard Mrs Smith, mother of Harriet, cry out, 'her child was ruined' after she heard of her rape.[22] In 1816 when Margaret Holmes, eight years old, returned to her mother's from service with venereal disease, the family she had been staying with was concerned not with consent but with the child having had the disease when she went to service: it was suggested she was born with it.[23] Wiliam Holmes, her father, stated 'sure enough my child is ruined, she has got the bad disorder'.[24] The attitude of deponents was protective of childhood and virginity. William Holmes thought it could be valued: he stated he expected some compensation and redress.[25]

Parents brought the case of child rape, though it was magistrates who perceived that such cases could involve consent. This was not the view presented by either witnesses or defendants in cases of child rape; there was a clear distinction between child and woman. Even if the child was seen as being 'ruined', she did not ruin herself: she was innocent.

Magistrates considered rape, unlike other assaults, could involve false swearing on the part of the woman. This suspicion determined their management of rape cases involving adult women. There was a marked predominance of married women bringing cases of rape: single women did not appear at all and domestic servants appeared very rarely. Either single women did not bring cases or they were not believed at magisterial level.

Rape of adult women also required penetration. If it had not been achieved, the case could be brought under 'assault with attempt to rape'. Eleanor Nemio, a married woman, went in May 1823 to obtain a government servant for her husband in Windsor. She lost her way and was attacked. Thomas Smith, Windsor constable, gave evidence that he came upon a woman lying on the ground surrounded by four men. He was accompanied by Thomas Newton, who saw a man getting off the woman. The man said 'damn her eyes I could not open her thighs'. Newton asked the woman if they had had connection with her. The men said they had done their best, one of them saying 'he had work to open her thighs so let fly about her backside'.[26] The defendants were brought forward to the Supreme Court for 'assault with intent to rape', a charge of which they were acquitted. Heavily underlined by the Attorney-General was the constable Smith's statement that before he came upon them he heard 'a woman speaking very low'.[27] Such evidence threw into doubt her testimony that she was attacked.

These then were the reference points for rape of an adult woman: penetration and an obvious wish not to participate in intercourse. This could be partly determined by how quickly the woman reported the attack. When Elizabeth Maloney gave evidence concerning an attack on her by her husband's servant, she claimed that she went back to her house and put her bonnet on to go to her neighbours'. The defendant came in and said 'she should go to bed and do the best for herself as she was pregnant'. She barred the door when he left and went the next morning to the neighbours'.[28] When Isabella Gamble brought a case against her employer, she said she did not tell his wife 'as she was apprehensive she would by such disclosure have been detained longer at Mittagong and thereby be prevented from making the earliest report to her parents'.[29] The alacrity with which these women included an explanation for the delay in their reports suggests that they were aware of the tenuous nature of their complaint or knew that the law included reference to delay being suspicious. They too assumed the possibility of complicity in the attack on them.

The method by which consent on the part of the woman could be established was through the evidence of neighbours or others as to her reputation. When in 1813 a woman was violently gang-raped by a group of twenty soldiers in her house in the presence of her husband, Samuel Marsden felt it necessary to add in giving evidence on her behalf that she had once been a loose woman but was no longer one.[30] When Elizabeth Maloney was raped in 1827, the defendant told her husband that it was her fault as she had made him drunk.[31]

The cases concerning rapes of adult women did not contain a great deal of physical information concerning the woman, nor did they involve medical viewpoints as in child rape. The women did not recount the physical details of the rape, despite the fact that for rape to occur it was necessary to prove ejaculation as well as penetration. It was difficult for women to say 'he achieved his purpose'. Thus the *word* of the woman was the crucial point in the case. Though medical proof was not necessary, there was a preoccupation with the question of consent. The underlinings, the asterisks, all emphasised points brought up by deponents. Elements such as talking in a low voice or intoxication were crucial in establishing a case. The women themselves assumed they would be questioned on such points.

Rape was an offence punishable by death. In 1829 when Elizabeth Baker complained that Robert Taylor had raped her in her house he, according to John Smith, 'looked like man half hanged'.[32] Yet it was Taylor who first went to the court saying that Elizabeth Baker 'has been saying that he had committed a rape upon her and as such a charge effects complainant's character—he prays the Bench to enquire into the complaint'.[33] Men were much more likely to be hanged for rape than for child rape, so this step of Robert Taylor's is an interesting one. He felt a complaint to the bench was preferable to the continuing aspersions on his character. He admitted to one deponent that he had connection with her but that it was with her consent. Complaints of rape were not taken lightly by members of the community, no matter at what level they had to be proved.

But in the cases themselves there are several levels of power relations operating. Of these, 'reputation' and the gossip and speculation surrounding that were the most important. This was where a woman was suspected.

In all the information presented, the reference points show also particular cultural understandings of the role of women held by deponents. This is particularly evident in cases concerning rape on the roads. And it is in these cases and cases of murder of women that we find intense scrutiny of female movements and demeanour among members of the local population. One can only guess at the real situation behind manipulations of evidence and suspicion.

The women who brought these rape cases gave clear accounts of where they were going and why. Sarah Fletcher was going to a miller's to have wheat ground when, she claimed, she was attacked shortly after dusk in 1825. She was walking along the road between her neighbour's and the miller's.[34] Abigail McLucas was travelling on the road to Liverpool in her cart at night when, she said, three men forcibly stopped the cart, robbed it, took her son from the road and forcibly had carnal connection with her.[35] Sarah Gibberd on a Friday morning 'had occasion to come to Sydney'[36] from Eliza Point and on her return at 2 or 3 p.m. was met by Patrick Morgan who, she stated, raped her.

These women present either a dependence on the persons they travelled with or a need to stay on the roads when attacked. None of them say that they ran into the bush. This is further graphically illustrated in the 1810 case of Ann Tibbut. She lived at the Hawkesbury with her husband. On 17 March 1817 she had gone to Humphry Tailor's with a bundle of shoes. On her return she stopped at the house of one Dunstan. While she was there Michael Bryant came in and asked her to drink, but she refused. About twenty minutes before sunset she left Dunstan's. It was three miles from Dunstan's to her house by a much frequented footpath. Ten minutes after she left, she said, Bryant overtook her. He said he was going her way and before he went any further he must have 'a bit of a sport',[37] knocked her down and raped her. 'He threatened me if I told, I said I would not. He walked with me a quarter of a mile. He threw me down again . . . I was stronger than him.'[38] They walked side by side for some time again and he again attempted to rape her. A woman passed close by but Ann Tibbut could not speak. They walked together to the house of Dudley Harrogan and Ann Tibbut requested him to walk with her to her house.

Ann Tibbut continued to walk on the footpath, she claimed, despite the fact her attacker was close beside her. This pattern of reliance on footpaths and roads no matter what is evident in other cases. The attackers leave the women on the road or follow them, but there is no pursuit through the bush. Ann Tibbut implied that she was safe when she stated it was a well-used footpath. Her walking with her attacker was not a crucial part of the prosecution and neither the magistrates nor the Judge Advocate commented on it. Nor did they ask other victims why they stayed on the road.

What were the reactions of fellow travellers, witnesses and people who saw the victim after the attack? What image of the victim did they present to the court? Even if the deponent was sympathetic to the man being tried, he or she presented the events making the case in a certain way. Fellow travellers, perhaps unintentionally, provided evidence not always sympathetic to the woman. In the case brought by Rose McCullen in December 1825, she travelled with the driver of Mr Ogilvie's dray on her way to Captain Pike's. They went into a hut with five men and soon after the driver of the dray left. The evidence of the driver was that:

> we picked up the woman and had our supper in the middle hut . . . I heard the man offer the woman a bed just as I was leaving the huts to go to my dray I heard nothing more . . . as we were coming up she said several men had offered her to live with them. When I enquired for her the next morning the men could not tell me where she was gone. I tracked the woman on the road back again so I'd thought she'd gone to live with one of the men she mentioned.[39]

The assumptions evident in the driver's statement would have spoken volumes to the listening magistrate and possibly endangered her chances of obtaining a conviction. It could well have been what the driver wished the court to hear, but in either case he disappears from the scene, he is of no help to the woman, his relation to her is unimportant to him.

In 1829 Harriot Gilbert related how she walked with her friend's husband William Sadler, towards her master's house. She claimed Sadler disappeared, and his account reads:

> about half way to the Prosecutrix's house the prisoner [John McGrath] desired me to bid the prosecutrix good night but she desired me not to leave her just then, the prisoner on her saying struck the prosecutrix on the side of the head . . . the prisoner urged me to bid the prosecutrix good night which I refused to do unless it was her wish, the prisoner told me he wanted to speak to her privately and that I might stand a few yards off and if there was anything improper she would screech out and I would hear it—the prisoner and prosecutrix went aside and I waited nearly a quarter of an hour . . . they left me having hold of each other's hand . . . On a sudden I lost sight of them . . . I went to the spot not seeing them. I went quickly up to her master's house I saw the manservant sitting outside the door I asked him if Harriot had come home, he said no but expected her any moment . . . I bid him good night.[40]

This evidence clearly resulted in the case being not heard at all. Quite a different picture was presented of the relationship between what is called the 'prosecutrix' and the defendant. 'The prisoner and prosecutrix went aside' was heavily underlined by the Attorney-General. A legal case could not be presented on such evidence.

The presentation of a woman's case depended upon the statements made either by witnesses or by the persons from whom she sought help. Because their evidence was deemed relevant, it is possible to ask what kind of help a woman could expect either initially or before the court.

Eleanor Nemio was assaulted at night by three men in the streets of Windsor. She said:

> she called for assistance, a constable came to her and enquired the cause of her crying out and having told of the treatment she experienced the constable said he was a single man otherwise he would take her to his lodgings and take care of her till morning, after the constable left the prisoner came again . . .[41]

Thomas Smith, the constable, said that he had gone to get help. The logic of this case is intriguing, as both Eleanor Nemio and Thomas Smith portray the constable as leaving her in the street, where she was soon attacked again.

If it was difficult to obtain immediate help unless the defendant was caught in the act of rape, the reports of people who saw the woman afterwards often seriously jarred with the complaint of the woman herself. Thomas Calligan, in the case brought by Abigail McLucas, said that she had called at his house at 8.30 p.m. and said she had been robbed. She seemed much intoxicated. Calligan added that she had had black eyes when she went to Sydney.[42] Ann Bowler supported this.[43] In the case brought by Ann Tibbut in 1810, Dudley Harrogan gave evidence: 'I did not see her clothes torn—she appeared to be a little frightened . . . she was sober.'

What makes a successful case is the strong evidence of another witness, a constable or passer-by, immediately after the attack. Ann Tibbut had her husband. He said 'when my wife came home she complained of a violent blow on the head, her clothes were much tumbled and full of cow itch. She had violent retchings and was ill for several days.' He went searching for Michael Bryant and took him before the magistrate.[44] At the Court of Criminal Jurisdiction in Sydney Bryant was found guilty, confined to hard labour in His Majesty's gaol at Sydney for twelve calendar months and was bound £50 for good behaviour.[45] Sarah Fletcher in 1825 clearly felt she could not tell her husband because of his ill temper.[46] John Butler, the accused, was acquitted.

It was not that the magistrates were necessarily unsympathetic: in Abigail McLucas' case the magistrate Moore wrote: 'Although I have no doubt in my mind as to the guilt of the three men, I could not but commit them on the positive oath of the woman.'[47]

It was only her evidence that could convict, the other evidence being doubtful. The possibility of the court accepting her evidence was greatly aided by the defendants' pleading guilty.[48] This occurred on 22 June but on 31 July the court, in consequence of 'some information received by the Judge Advocate', revoked their decision of guilty and entered not guilty.[49]

The assessment of guilt in these rape cases was closely related to various cultural understandings of the role of woman in colonial society. The truth of the testimony had to be ascertained and the statement had to be backed up by travellers, witnesses or constables. The point is that it was very likely it would not be backed up and a contrary picture of events or of the woman would be presented. Exactly why this occurred is related to the perceptions of women travelling, their sexuality and their likely behaviour. In comparison to street assault, very few rape cases were brought to the magistrate and this was a direct result of the matter of belief. The question of who would believe Abigail McLucas, Ann Tibbut, Eleanor Nemio, for instance depended upon their ability to convince people they had in fact been raped, that they were not intoxicated and did not deliberately go with the man. The magistrates passed all complaints on, but the Judge Advocate or, later, the Attorney-General, picked up the legal discrepancies which were also essentially moral discrepancies, and underlined them or asterisked them before he decided if there would be a case.

On 7 October 1826 Archibald Bell, magistrate at Windsor, wrote to Saxe Bannister:

An aged woman of the name of Catherine Conner came before me and complained of being violently ravished by her servant man . . . At first I deemed it violent rape, I am satisfied that she has been guilty of the most shocking species of wanton perjury that has ever come under my notice.[50]

Bell related this unusual case where everyone who gave evidence spoke for the defendant and against the complainant, saying she had been involved in a long-term relationship with the defendant.[51] Rather than seeing this as an unusual case, which Bell did, we
should see it in terms of the depositions as an extreme. Assumptions of 'wanton perjury'
lurk behind the treatment of every case heard by magistrates concerning rape on the
roads. They are presented in that way by magistrates, by the Judge Advocate or Attorney-
General and by the deponents, including the victim herself in her denials or qualifi-
cations. These cases appear only because of the tenacity of these old, married or
pregnant women.

By contrast, the evidence of women who were raped in their own houses was more
solidly supported by witnesses. Isabella Gamble in her complaint against her employer
was supported by Eliza Lilly, a former servant, who lived close by. Lilly's husband also
gave evidence:

> deponent's wife [Eliza Lilly] asked her [Isabella Gamble] why she was not contented where she was,
> she replied it was in consequence of the ill treatment she had received from Mr. Cutter, deponent's
> wife asked her to describe the ill treatment, she replied she would not then nor until after she had left
> the premises and seen her father who would be very much offended at it, deponent's wife then said
> I guess Mr. Cutter has been trying the same trick with you that he did with me, upon which Isabella
> Gamble blushed very much threw her arms about deponent's wife's neck and began crying.[52]

The questioning in this case centred on Eliza Lilly's 'skylarking', why the complaint
was not made immediately after the attack, and suggestions by another former female
servant that Isabella Gamble had made up the whole of the evidence.[53]

In a charge of rape the role of women in the stability of the community was defined. It
is in this sense we perhaps can understand the idea of 'ruin' of girl children, or the
reason why Sarah Fletcher brought a case of rape after a doctor began to think ill of her
husband. Yet rape appears so rarely in criminal cases, and when it does is fraught with
such suspicion of the woman that it must be stated this is a particular type of rape we are
dealing with. Where the concerns of women themselves, the interest of the community
and the legal system coalesced, they produced a 'rape case'.

What view, then, is presented by the courts in their consideration of the female body?
It was characteristic of English law to see the woman's sex as the property of her father or
her husband.[54] Through the questions asked of deponents and the views of deponents
themselves we can obtain a cultural view of women's bodies and their place in legal
understanding.

The courts were automatically suspicious of women's use of their bodies. Immorality
was a concern of magistrates. For the courts, adult women's bodies were assumed to be
immoral and were to be proved innocent. Ordinary people were also concerned about
the use to which women might put their sexuality: they were concerned about the
disturbance it created.

This concern about disturbance is also apparent in the evidence given in cases where
women were found dead on the roads. In June 1826 George Henley, government servant
to George McGiannis of Wilberforce, gave evidence before the Windsor magistrate,
Bell, that on 23 May he was returning by boat to his master's dwelling when he saw

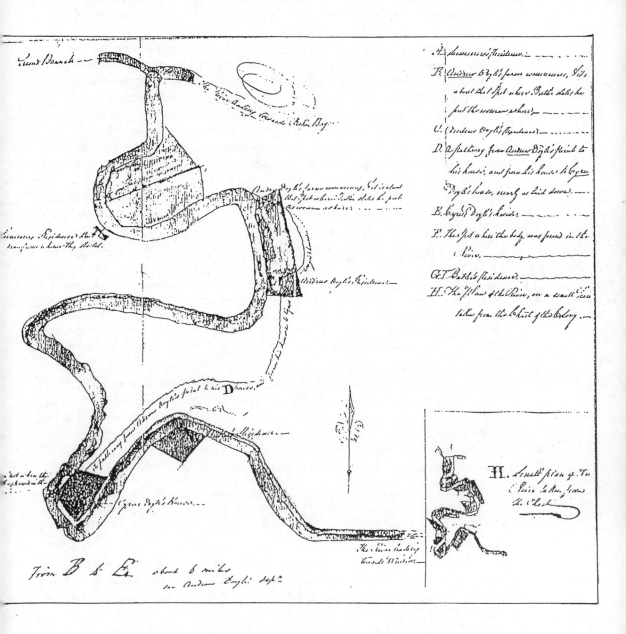

Figure 6   A map of the area in which Kitty Carmen's body was found, included in the case against Charles Butler for her murder, 1826 (drawn from description).

something floating in the water. Perceiving 'it had a cap on it', he immediately pulled towards it and discovered it was the dead body of a female. It was the body of Catherine Collins, known locally as 'Kitty Carmen'.

The Hawkesbury River was a principal highway and boats travelled up and down its length for commercial and social purposes. Kitty Carmen resided at the house of the Butler family which was close to Windsor. She had travelled up the river with Charles Butler to visit James Clarke who resided at Sommers'. Butler was going to pick up a load of corn and as Kitty Carmen had formerly resided with Clarke she went with him, hearing that Clarke had hurt his shoulder. After the visit Clarke tried to persuade her to stay the night 'as it was late and she could go away in the morning'. She would not stay and he gave her money as she climbed into the boat.[55] Clarke arranged to travel down the river to see her the next morning.

Clarke did travel down the river the next day; he visited the Evans family and they persuaded him to stay overnight. He arrived at the Butlers' house the day after Whitsunday and the following conversation ensued:

> Mrs. Butler enquired 'Where's Kitty?' 'Why do you ask me' said deponent 'for you know . . . I suppose she's here'. 'No she's not' said Mrs. Butler 'Why do you say so, she left Sommers' with Charlie [Butler] on Saturday night'—then answered Mrs. Butler 'Why Charlie never told me so!' . . . Charles Butler came into the house after some little conversation deponent said 'Charlie, where's Kitty?' Butler answered 'I don't know'. 'Damn it' said deponent, 'you don't know that be hanged'. Butler said 'I landed her at Doyle's Point in the lower end of Mr. Doyle's farm'. Deponent observed 'what in the name of God did you land her there for, had it been me I wouldn't have landed her there'.

The next day Clarke decided to return to Sommers': he thought Kitty Carmen might have gone there to see him because he had not visited her on Whitsunday as promised. He travelled up the river with Butler. On arrival he discovered she had not gone there. Sommers said, too, that he had been over the river to a house where there were some persons drinking and if she had been on that side of the river it would have been known.

George Evans of Portland Head gave evidence that

> he knew the spot represented by Butler, has seen it and has been upon it, deponent says it is scarcely possible by a man in broad day, much more by a woman at night and it's not the road to Doyles' house it's ¾ of a mile from Doyles' house, or thereabouts, Doyles' wharf is on the water's edge only about 12 rods from the house.

Andrew Doyle gave evidence that the body was found at a place some distance from where Butler said he let her off. She would have needed to pass by his house to get there and he had several dogs who would have given alarm. A map was supplied in the case to support this.

Kitty Carmen always had a pair of scissors tied to her waist and these had been left in the boat; the Butler household used them for some time after the night of her disappearance. Her body was examined by Thomas Allen, surgeon. There was a large wound on the left side of her face and another on the left side of the neck. There were wounds on her arm and one on her shoulder which might have been an old sore; he could not tell because of the decomposition of the body. The wounds were not sufficient to cause immediate death, but the resultant loss of blood would have made her unconscious for some time.

The case and the construction of the guilt of Charles Butler centred on the solitary movement of Kitty Carmen across the Windsor riverscape. She was well regarded by the local community. It was unlike her to leave her scissors in the boat as she always wore them. There must have been a struggle. Doyles' Point was such difficult terrain she could not possibly have wanted to get out there. Then, her body was found so distant from that spot that she would have to get out of the boat and walk close to Doyle's house: his dogs would surely have made some alarm.

The case exhibits a clear understanding of the local area by its inhabitants. What was possible to do at night was stated clearly. A man could not have got through the scrub at Doyles' Point, let alone a woman at night. The deponents were asked constantly whether they had seen her. It would have been known if she was on the other side of the river, from the people drinking at the house. The visibility of Kitty Carmen and the expectations surrounding her behaviour resulted from her sex. When she did not arrive at Butlers' it was thought unusual—why hadn't Charlie Butler mentioned it to his wife? But the case did not eventuate until the evidence of her body was found. Her disappearance worried James Clarke but not enough to make him frantically search for her. When he and Butler arrived back at Sommers' they jokingly asked, 'Have you seen a strayed woman?', and Clarke left the area soon after to find work at the Five Islands. This 'sudden' leaving made the magistrates suspicious. Clarke, however, was not tried. He supposed, he said, that Kitty Carmen had gone to Sydney. There is a clash here between the magistrates' understanding of what a woman could do and that of the local population.

The sensitivity of local residents to her movements, her expected behaviour and the unusual report that Butler gave provide us with the substance of the case. But the ease of her disappearance was related to her constant travelling, the expectation of invitations to stay overnight and the assumption that if she was not at home she was safe somewhere else. The case provides us with an interesting illumination of Clarke's relationship to her: he gave her money and stated that it was a sign of affection and that he did not care when he got it back; yet he left for the Five Islands presuming she had gone to Sydney. It is not the relationship with Clarke that is the centre of the case. Her *travelling* is. This is what is described to us.

Sensitivity to the movements of women about the colony is evident in other cases where bodies are found and suppositions are made concerning the death. Mary Yardley was found dead in the woods twenty miles below Windsor in October 1818. The first person to give evidence was Hannah Hardcastle. She said that Mary Yardley had 'passed by her house on her way home she spoke to her as she passed by and appeared to be in good health but agitated'. Her son-in-law Richard Heyman had passed by a few minutes before and a person who passed by 'asked the way to Kelly's about noon'.[56] She implied Yardley and Heyman were arguing. Jane Darrington gave further evidence that Mary Yardley had called at her house and her son-in-law Richard Heyman had been there just before. Darrington tried to get Mary Yardley to stay but Yardley said she feared Heyman would ill-use her daughter. Other deponents in the case gave evidence of

Heyman calling on them and expressing his dislike of his mother-in-law, saying he knew how his wife and her mother could be separated. Richard Heyman was found not guilty and there was no further inquiry into the death of Mary Yardley. She had been killed by a blow to the back of the head, stated the surgeon Tristram.[57]

In 1820 Susan Hackett's body was found in a terribly mangled state, naked as far up as her loins. She was found beside the road in the District of Cooke. There were two arguments put in this case. We will examine the first, which related to her movements on the day of her death and the knowledge of animosity between herself and Mary Pinkerton. John O'Brien, Mary Pinkerton and Eleanor Grant were tried for her murder.

The first person to give evidence was James Hackett. He said his wife went to Mr Hook's farm on Thursday for rum and did not return, but he did not go in search of her that day. This point was underlined by the Judge Advocate in a manner suggesting a comparison with the view of the magistrates in the case of Kitty Carmen that Clarke should not have left the district. But Hackett was quite clear why he didn't search for his wife. He thought she might be at Chartres', the neighbouring house. On Friday Mr Everett came to Hackett's and when asked said he had not seen Susan Hackett. Eleanor Grant was present and told Hackett that his wife had been in Hassall's kitchen late Thursday night. Everett said he was there and she was not.[58]

James Hackett then went to Mary Pinkerton's and asked had his wife been there. She had been and had borrowed a gown and left a wrapper. She had papers with her. A search began for Susan Hackett. John Pearsal, a servant to Hassall, was in the bush with cattle and he saw a woman pass. He was asked was it the sawyer's wife, another woman, and he said no, he would have recognised her, so it must have been Susan Hackett. John Spaely, a government servant to Campbell, saw a woman pass Campbell's at two o'clock.

When the body was found, discussion allegedly began as to who could have murdered Susan Hackett. Mary Ann East reported that Polly (Mary) Pinkerton had said she would be avenged on Susan Hackett by day or night; she had said that Mr Pinkerton had been in the habit of visiting and giving things to Susan Hackett and she would be avenged by taking Susan Hackett's life. There were frequent arguments between wife and husband in the Pinkertons' hut on Hooks' farm.

The jury of the inquest decided to search Pinkertons' hut after this important information concerning disputes had been given. They found tools concealed in a pond, a bucket with a frying pan, teapot and broad-handled knife which was covered with a quantity of congealed blood. John O'Brien's blue jacket was found in the Pinkertons' hut.

Robert Biddle, a servant to Hassall, said O'Brien had left his sheep on the afternoon of Susan Hackett's death, and he did not return. He was seen later coming out of Mary Pinkerton's hut.

Mary Pinkerton was called to appear before the inquest. She related how eleven or twelve o'clock on Thursday Susan Hackett came and borrowed a gown and handkerchief and took some papers from her bosom. Mary Pinkerton said you have a plant [i.e., something hidden] there. Hackett said she had some money and a bottle for some rum. In brackets is the jury's note that there had been no bottle found among the possessions of the deceased. Mary Pinkerton was asked questions as to when her mother Eleanor Grant had left and she stated it was Saturday morning. Did Mary Pinkerton dress (i.e. cook) dinner that day? No, she did not.

John Young, servant of Lowes, appeared. He had seen Eleanor Grant crossing Lowes' on *Friday* and, he related, she was walking very fast with something in her apron. Jane Everett appeared and said that at twelve o'clock on Friday Eleanor Grant was at Lowes' and that Samuel Blackman would prove the same.

William Bouch gave evidence that he knew the Pinkertons and lived in O'Brien's hut. O'Brien was in the habit of visiting Mrs Pinkerton in the absence of her husband. He slept in the hut for her protection. Cornelius Hughes gave evidence that at ten o'clock on Thursday he had seen Susan Hackett pass, then at two o'clock O'Brien had come and said he wanted a knife to bleed sheep at Hassall's. He did not go there but said later he was prevented by Eleanor Grant. On Saturday, Hughes continued, O'Brien asked for £1 saying he would give Hughes tea and sugar for it. The money was for Mrs Pinkerton to go to Sydney in search of her husband. O'Brien said Mrs Pinkerton had lent the deceased a gown but later O'Brien denied it.

Stories did not match; people had been seen where they said they were not: Mary Pinkerton, Eleanor Grant and John O'Brien were to be tried for the murder of Susan Hackett. Mary Pinkerton wrote a letter to the Judge Advocate stating her innocence. She introduces the second argument. For her evidence she was to call Patrick Hart who saw Aborigines on the road where the murder was done, Richard Evelin who saw Eleanor Grant travelling on Saturday morning, James Everett who also saw Aborigines, and James Connor who said the blacks had been outrageous that day at Mr Oxley's farm at the Cowpastures. Patrick Martin was to give evidence that Susan Hackett lived at McCarty's farm; he knew that 'some of the blacks appeared to take improper liberties with the deceased'. He thought her a very abandoned woman, a loose woman.

The body of the deceased was discussed. Jane Everett said she saw the position of the body and after being in the colony thirty years she was certain the natives were the perpetrators of the death of Susan Hackett, and that they were likely to have carnal connection after death. She 'saw two black natives on the spot where the deceased was murdered'. Sarah Collet from the Nepean river area said the deceased had the appearance of being abused by intercourse. Samuel Blackman, foreman of the inquest, said that several persons had sexual connections with the deceased previous to the body being discovered. From the situation of the corpse, he was certain the blacks were the transgressors.

Phillip Hughes had spoken to the blacks at Oxley's farm: 'on one of them being charged he said it was not him, it was another tribe who committed the murder and drank rum'. On 3 January more evidence was received by the Judge Advocate. Charles Kent said Eleanor Grant had returned to her home at 9 a.m. on Saturday. Thomas Parsmore supported this, Eleanor Grant having called at his house. But the most interesting piece of evidence was given by Felix McCoy who was at Dunn the boatman's and spoke to Mary East with whom Dunn cohabited. As we have seen, Mary Ann East had given evidence against Mary Pinkerton. McCoy said he had asked about her willingness to prosecute Mary Pinkerton. Mary Ann East had said:

she did not know or care [if Pinkerton was guilty]—she had no right to turn me out of her house and right or wrong I will swear her life away, she [East] would get £1 for going down £1 for coming up and 3/9 per day while she was there and, moreover, she could get £2 for prostitution.[59]

These cases were some of the few genuine mysteries in the murder cases of the early colony. We are left with the bodies of these three women, one having bled to death or drowned after stab wounds, another dying from head injuries, and another raped and murdered by stabbing. Their fates befell them by travelling along the rivers and roads of the colony.

What is important, besides their fates, is the way in which the cases are represented to us by the deponents and the juries of the inquests or the magistrates. 'Was she a loose woman?', 'Did you dress dinner?', 'What seems suspicious is that she left her scissors, which she always carried by her waist': these are all questions or assumptions about women's expected behaviour by magistrates or coroners who had specific understandings of what was suspicious or unusual behaviour for women.

This occasionally clashes with the suspicions of the local community, who do not find it unusual that Clarke should leave the district to look for work without finding out where the woman he had lived with had gone. The local community do not find it suspicious that James Hackett did not go immediately searching for his wife, as they understood he assumed she was somewhere else.

The focus of deponents is on travelling itself, who saw the woman, how she seemed, what she carried and what she said or asked for. They were aware of the conflict that existed, trying to prevent Mary Yardley from following too closely behind her son-in-law; they are aware also of Mary Pinkerton's feelings regarding her husband's lover, to whom he gave things. The complexity of local relations which they present centre on the women defendants and deceased, who are invested with jealousy, anger and immorality.

Behaviour is recognised also as suspicious. Eleanor Grant was walking very quickly across the paddock and she carried something suspicious. Mary Yardley was seen climbing the rocks so closely behind her son-in-law only because she seemed so anxious when she left Jane Darrington's house.

The attitudes evident in these murder cases also appear in rape cases. The magistrates in these three cases clearly perceived a 'proper' relationship of man to woman. The women should have been around the house a great deal more than they were. Magistrates had set assumptions about travelling that were not reflected in the evidence of deponents. In Susan Hackett's case there was clearly a realignment of the community around the idea that she was a loose woman involved with blacks. James and Jane Everett gave a different perspective from their earlier evidence.

The community also expresses ideals of the proper role of women. Their sexual relations could cause considerable violence and disturbance in their area. Marriage was not the key to such a role, but cohabitation and fidelity did have meaning. This compares with tensions revealed in evidence by witnesses in cases of domestic murder. What was suspicious or a sure sign of guilt was behaviour which had no meaning in terms of legal evidence.

In comparison to the importance to female sexuality in determining both male and female guilt in cases of rape and murder, the attention given to male sexuality in sodomy and murder cases was quite different. The questions surrounding the discovery of a male body were entirely different to those surrounding the discovery of a female body.

The bodies of men who had been murdered were not discovered for some time after their disappearance. The men were noticed absent from work, not tending sheep or not returned from a task on which they were sent. The deponents in the case against Thomas Ryan, accused of murdering a fellow servant, had not seen the deceased passing and were not expecting dire consequences to follow an argument which he had had. They were his employer, the employer's wife, and the fellow servant, along with the seven-year-old son of the employer who had discovered the body.[60] The evidence consisted of descriptions of the work the servants were sent to, and of poor relations between the deceased and the accused man; thus it was centred not on community relations or morality, but on the life of the farm. When economic life was disturbed, the farmer began to wonder where the servant was. After some weeks and following the persistence of the boy the body was found. This case was similar to the trial of Samuel Withnall, accused of murdering a boy who had to pass through the farm where he worked. The absence of the deceased was noticed when it affected the economy of the farm. The boy had been sent with a bag of corn to the mill. Evidence against the prisoner consisted of the amount of food he had at the time and the clear knowledge of all the deponents that he was very hungry, was constantly asking for food, and that he was seen with a bag of corn when he was meant to have none.[61] In the case against Matthew Finnegan, the sheep of the deceased were seen to be wandering about and all of the deponents recounted the violence Finnegan had expressed about any sheep that would enter his corn.[62] Finnegan had confessed to giving the man a beating. Men did inhabit a different economic landscape in the colony. Their patterns of work, and the value given to the work they did, meant they were missed from this work, their farms or their role on the farm. The networks of suspicion and of questioning were quite different when it is a female body that was found.

Colonial law in practice operated differently for men and women. It intervened in the lives of men and women in different ways and was utilised by them for different purposes. The convict system of labour organisation had great influence on this practice of law. Under the ill-defined convict regulations, very slight arguments between employer and servant could be brought to the courts. Such power gave the courts a wide scope of activity, and definitions of an offence were very flexible. The court could oversee an area of intimate social relations that, in a society which was not convict, they would have had no access to. However, rather than mounting a full-scale onslaught on the most intimate lives of all convicts, the courts in practice operated according to notions of the value of labour. For male convicts, the courts operated according to a peculiar logic of the management of wage labour alongside the paternalism of plantation labour. For female convicts, the courts essentially acted according to the understanding that, while female labour was anonymous and not part of the family, it was also valueless. These ideas of labour were just beginning to develop in England and they were highlighted and referred to by the colonial administration. Law validates them further. So, curiously, in providing the discipline for the convict system, the law helps to bring about modern ideas of labour management.

Women and men also participate separately in creating such a system of law in that they use the courts differently and are perceived differently by the courts. For the magistrates marriage, and legal marriage at that, was extremely important in judging female guilt and truthfulness in giving evidence. In contrast, popular perceptions of the proper role of men and women did not appear to place great value on marriage but rather on the capacity of women to misuse their sex. It is such misuse which determined signs of guilt and evidence in cases of murder and rape. Questions asked of the male and female body were different not only because of statute law but also because of the way cultural understandings of the role of women locked into that law.

That there were two concepts of morality operating in the colony, one held by the administration and the other held by the lower classes, has been suggested by Michael Sturma.[63] Criminal cases show how both perceptions clash and also work together to isolate women in constructions of guilt.

This chapter has considered the realm of social activity which underlies all others: what it meant to be convict or to be male and female in terms of the law. Law hardly intervened in the person in a systematic or complete way. When it intervened in the house it opened up an arena of female dispute; when it intervened in the body it subjected the female body, dead or alive, to far greater scrutiny than the male body. Similarly, different questions were asked of the male convict offender and the female convict offender. An examination of law and the person gives a much clearer picture of the female person than of the male, precisely because law concentrated on what was female to a much higher degree.

But this intervention is facilitated not only by the willingness of magistrates to hear all complaints against convicts, or to hear the complaints of women, but also by the actions and complaints of all sections of the population.

The legal system in practice in the colony was made by the intermeshing of statute law, magisterial power and popular attitudes. This law was flexible in its intervention because of the location of that legal system, the penal colony and the labour practices it involved. Such flexibility introduces another question: how far can law be shaped by the colonial environment? A close look at the major crisis of the period—the bushranging crisis—will begin to answer such a question.

Notes

1 John Linton, Sydney P.M.B., 21 January 1821.

2 J. Weekes, *Sex, Politics and Society*, p. 21.

3 R. Trumbach, 'London's Sodomites: Homosexual Behaviour and Western Culture in the Eighteenth Century', *Journal of Social History*, vol. 2, 1977–8, p. 21.

4 Daniel Gilmore, J.A.B., 22 February 1812.

5 Richard Bayley and others, J.A.B., 18 January 1812.

6 William Taylor, Thomas McClear, Sydney Q.S., November 1826, 57.

7 *ibid.*

8 *ibid.*

9 R. vs Caleb Wilson, C.C.J., 28 March 1814.

10 William Williams, Thomas Hoto, S.C.C.J., 1828, Miscellaneous.

11 Richard Bayley, P.M.B., 23 January 1812.

12 Burn, *The Justice of the Peace and Parish Officer*, vol. III, p. 200.

13 *ibid*, p. 476.

14 *ibid*.

15 R. vs William Cunningham, S.C.C.J., January 1826, Miscellaneous.

16 *ibid*.

17 *ibid*.

18 R. vs Michael Murphy, C.C.J., December 1818, 365.

19 Letter in R. vs John McCook, C.C.J., November 1822, 23 and 24.

20 R. vs Cunningham.

21 R. vs Murphy.

22 R. vs Cunningham.

23 R. vs John Bayliss, Windsor, C.C.J., November 1817, 438.

24 *ibid*.

25 *ibid*.

26 R. vs James Butler, Edward Manalty, Thomas Smith, C.C.J., October 1823, 51.

27 *ibid*.

28 R. vs Dennis Lynch, S.C.C.J., January 1827, 17.

29 R. vs George Cutter, S.C.C.J., February 1828, 30.

30 R. vs James Blackstock, C.C.J., March 1814, p. 178.

31 R. vs Lynch.

32 R. vs Robert Taylor, S.C.C.J., February 1829, 53.

33 *ibid*.

34 R. vs John Butler, S.C.C.J., September 1825, 176.

35 R. vs Thomas Sackbury and others, C.C.J., July 1820, 168.

36 R. vs Patrick Morgan, C.C.J., April 1817, 10.

37 R. vs Michael Bryant, C.C.J., May 1810.

38 *ibid*.

39 R. vs James Fordham and others, S.C.C.J., January 1826.

40 John McGrath, S.C.C.J., 1829, Miscellaneous.

41 R. vs Thomas Smith and others, C.C.J., October 1823, 51.

42 R. vs Thomas Sackbury.

43 *ibid*.

44 R. vs Michael Bryant.

45 *ibid*.

46 R. vs John Butler.

47 R. vs Thomas Sackbury.

48 *ibid*.

49 *ibid*. Unfortunately this information remains unclear. The McLucas family received a considerable amount of attention from the constables of the Liverpool region—the information given could relate to this.

50 R. vs Catherine Conner, S.C.C.J., November 1826, 175.

51 *ibid*.

52 R. vs George Cutter, S.C.C.J., February 1828, 30.

53 *ibid*.

54 N. Bashar, 'Rape in England between 1550–1700', *The Sexual Dynamics of History*, ed. London Feminist History Group, London, 1983.

55 R. vs Charles Butler, S.C.C.J., July 1826, 109.
56 R. vs Richard Heyman, C.C.J., December 1818, 235.
57 *ibid.*
58 R. vs John O'Brien, Mary Pinkerton, C.C.J., December 1820, 42.
59 *ibid.*
60 R. vs Thomas Ryan, S.C.C.J., 1828, 48.
61 R. vs Samuel Withnall, C.C.J., January 1818, 17.
62 R. vs Matthew Finnegan, C.C.J., May 1819, 1.
63 M. Sturma, 'Eye of the Beholder', *Labour History*, no. 34, May 1978.

PART 2

Offence in the Wilderness

'Dooley put a coarse linen bag over his face
and the inside around the eyes was blacked'

GEORGE FULLER
DESCRIBING THE DRESS OF A BUSHRANGER

5

THE CREATION OF BUSHRANGING

Women who brought close acquaintances to courts shaped the law to their own purposes. In rape cases there was considerable resistance to the woman being heard. This was due partly to the requirements of statute law, the attitudes of magistrates and the opinions of local populations. We can see, then, both this shaping of law to local purposes and resistance to it. Such a relationship to law is even more apparent in the offence of bushranging. This offence was created both by local perceptions and by the interpretations of these by the administration. It was a crisis which was to provide opportunity for the administration to react strongly without regard for 'freedom' and its connotations. The response to this policing created its own culture.

Thomas Scott, superintendent of the sugar plantations at Port Macquarie, appeared before the Port Macquarie Bench of Magistrates on 13 June 1826. He claimed that on the night of 2 June he was asleep in his house when his servant woke him. Three men were in the house. They requested a light and when the servant was slow about it, one of them stood over him with a cutlass in a menacing attitude. The men took flour, hemp, knives and government property. In leaving the house they said they had a great party to join from the plains and they intended to murder Keegan, one of the plantation overseers, and Charm, the overseer of the agricultural establishment. On the same night, John Cozener, overseer of the plantation, was going from his hut to let the men out of the barracks. He was intercepted and surrounded by men with knives. They robbed his hut and went down to the river, where they gave three cheers and shouted 'Death or Liberty!' On 4 June the party returned again in increased numbers and stripped Scott's house of all they could find.[1]

In 1835 John Jamison gave evidence to the Legislative Council's committee on police: he said of convict runaways that by 'taking to the bush the prisoner cannot be expected to have any honest means of support in the wilderness'.[2] His description of unsettled land as 'wilderness' is an image that recurs in the records of the criminal courts. The only places for a runaway convict to find food or money were settlers' houses or servants' huts through charity, bargaining, or theft. From such activities came the criminal offence of 'bushranging'. In some circumstances it is a description of an activity in itself. In others, it is an added description of a person by a magistrate in his transferral of cases to the criminal court; as in: 'a bushranger charged with robbing a dwelling house'.[3] A term used both loosely and to describe an offence, it was also used by defendants to describe themselves. 'We have been in the country three weeks and since then we have been bushrangers', a free husband and his convict wife described themselves before the Argyle bench in 1826.[4] There has been considerable work done already in Australian history on the subject of bushranging, the most recent being by Jennifer McKinnon.[5] This work considers bushranging as a social phenomenon, and concludes with statements as to its nature and impact on the society. Bushranging, however, had considerable influence on policing in the countryside in the years 1810–31 and it is the crucial part it played in *policing* that will be considered in this chapter. The reality might well have been that bushrangers were desperate, hungry, runaway convicts but the *image* presented of them in the court is quite different. It is this image which established court reactions and to a certain extent the culture of bushranging itself.

Bushranging was of most concern to magistrates, the Legislative Council and the governor when it described gangs of persons banded together, who were armed and plundered carts and houses. Such 'banditti' armed with 'carbines',[6] wearing masks or with their faces blacked, became major sources of concern for the government in 1825 and in 1830–31. This activity had been evident in Van Diemen's Land during the Macquarie period,[7] but became of concern on the mainland towards the end of Macquarie's term and in the 1820s under Brisbane and Darling. In 1830 the Legislative Council, together with magistrates, decided upon a plan to march constables, disguised, in groups of three across the countryside, arresting all persons who could give no reasonable identification. As an offence 'bushranging' had considerable impact on the policing of the countryside. The Legislative Council's policing initiative in 1830–31 was simply an escalation of the existing activities of the Mounted Police and ordinary constables. They had pursued bushrangers, been involved in sieges, and searched for stolen property in houses suspected of receiving since 1815. It was an extension of their activities in the apprehending of runaway convicts. There is apparent in depositions a confusion on the part of small farmers as to the identity of strange men bursting in their doors carrying firearms. 'I thought they were constables',[8] say many persons in depositions given concerning robberies in their houses. Bushranging carried with it a web of harbourers and receivers. It also carried a much wider web of suspicion as to who these people were. This suspicion was activated by other factors than simply the capture of bushrangers, however: it was the existence of the offence of bushranging which created an atmosphere in which these suspicions could be pursued.

The Offence

The term 'bushranging' carried with it a number of images presented to the court by constables, defendants and deponents. What kinds of understandings led to such a cry as

Table 16 Number of bushranging cases sent to trial before criminal courts by committing benches, 1816–31

Place	1816	1817	1818	1819	1820	1821	1822	1823	1824	1825	1826	1827	1828	1829	1830	1831	Total
Parramatta	1				1	4	10		1	4	3	4		4	5	1	38
Sydney							1	1		2	3		1	4	1	2	15
Argyle										2		1	1	4	3	1	12
Bringelly			1	1					1		3		2		1		9
Minto						1		1									2
Liverpool		1			1			1		1	1	4	2	2		1	14
Bathurst							2			1	1	2	1	2	3	1	13
Penrith	1								1	1	2	1		3	1	1	11
Windsor	1	1		1	2	1	2			2		3	2	3			18
Campbelltown												1	2	5	3		11
Cooke												1					1
Wollongong												1	1			1	3
Wallis Plains										2		1		2	1		6
Cawdor										1							1
Newcastle										1	1		1				3
Port Macquarie										1				2		1	4
Goulburn										1				1	1		3
Durham										1						1	2
Patrick Plains													1	2			3
Sutton Forest													1				1
Cox's River													3	1			4
Stone Quarry												1					1
Maitland															1	2	3
Mount Elmington															1		1
Portland Head														1	1	1	3
Total	3	2	2	2	4	6	15	4	3	20	14	20	18	36	22	13	182

'Death or Liberty' in New South Wales in 1826, nearly twenty-two years after its use in the Irish rebellion, and what kinds of dissatisfaction appear in these cases?

Bushrangers, whether alone or in gangs, concentrated on robbing carts and travellers or plundering houses or servants' huts. Individual gangs rarely committed a single offence; their attacks more often numbered ten or more. One case often represents a number of attacks or complaints related to attacks. For the years 1816–31 there survive 182 cases concerning bushranging. (See Table 16.) These are exclusive of robberies committed by convicts who were absent overnight. Bushranging gangs numbered up to twelve persons but most often consisted of four or five.

Up to 1824 those whose houses were raided and plundered by bushranging gangs divide quite evenly into those who knew their assailants and those who did not. Recognition sometimes came from notoriety, as in the case of William Geary in 1821 who was called 'Captain' and his gang was known as 'Gurrey's Gang'.[9] Recognition could also come from acquaintance. This was possibly one reason for blackened faces, masks, handkerchiefs or crepe around faces and disguised voices. Recognition was more common during the early period when bushrangers were more likely to be local servants, or servants of someone familiar, than runaways from clearing gangs or road gangs or from the agricultural establishments at Emu Plains or Port Macquarie, all of which were established as a result of the distribution policies of Brisbane and Darling. In the years after 1825 policing was more intensive and constables circulated descriptions of bushrangers. Most bushrangers were runaway convicts rather than free persons. Their status if specified is set out in Table 17. Some cases sent to the Criminal Court had no defendants listed. Magistrates took depositions hoping a defendant would be caught, and other bushrangers were indicted for a number of attacks. So 132 cases are recorded here.

Some cases give descriptions of runaways' feelings toward their former employers and overseers. In the case related at the beginning of the chapter there were threats to former overseers. In another case a servant claimed he did not need to go with the bushrangers as his master was good to him. In a letter to Major Ovens, the chief engineer, the magistrate Fennel wrote that the attack on Thomson's house by a gang calling themselves the Stoney Ridge boys in 1825 occurred because Thomson was considered, along with the magistrate Rankin, 'a bad master'. In the depositions, he was referred to as a 'bad man'; his house was burned.[10]

In 1822 an approver before the court at Windsor gave evidence of the reason for a bushranging attack on McKewsie, a settler, by a gang of free men:

> Linegan first mentioned about McKewsie two months since, he said he had £200 no doubt of their being able to get it, it would make men of them as long as they lived . . . he turned . . . and said 'this old man had a stockman he turned off to get his certificate and sent him to Sydney with never a penny of money in his pocket and scarce a rag to his back, he was forced to beg so he could get his certificate' . . . we must mention if he did not give his stockman one of his best cows he, meaning McKewsie, would be killed.[11]

It is interesting to note in this case the importance placed on the ill-treatment of a former stockman. But this case was unusual: there were not any large-scale attacks on former employers apart from Thomson, and references to any such attacks were few. Revenge,

Table 17 Status of bushrangers in criminal cases, 1810–31

Year	Runaway servants	Runaway gangs	Servants	Gangs	Free	Not stated
1816	1					
1817					2	1
1818			2		2	
1819	1					
1820	1					
1821	1					
1822	3	7	1		2	
1823	2	2				
1824	1	1				
1825	10	7	1	2	1	1
1826	3	4			3	
1827	2	4		1	2	
1828	5	3	1		3	
1829	8	15		2	3	1
1830	2	7	1	2	1	
1831	3	3	1			
Total	43	53	7	7	19	3

as we shall see, was usually directed against informers, constables or magistrates. If we look at all the cases we do not often find bushrangers seeking justice from former employers or necessarily seeing themselves in a relationship that had been crossed and should be righted. The reason usually given for bushranging was the attractions of an easy life with no masters or overseers. In three cases the hope of leaving the country was stated as the reason for joining a gang. Thomas Blazey's gang left their several employs in Sydney to go to Timor.[12] Geary was going with his gang on a six-month voyage.[13] Thomas Peacock said he only went with the bushrangers because William Poole told him he would get him out of the country.[14] William Poole also stated he could lead others to a new settlement he called 'Finan'.[15] As we progress through the 1820s, however, bushrangers seem poorer and more desperate and they were less likely to speak except to request food and guns. There were more sieges and fewer informers or approvers (i.e. those who gave evidence in order to escape prosecution).

The offence of bushranging, in the majority of cases, was perpetrated by the absconding convict, so it was a reaction against the conditions of convict labour, the gang, or the restrictions of life as a farm servant. The cases suggesting plans to leave the country and the notable absence of attacks on former employers indicate that the bushranger did not see himself as a former employee. The inequalities which they claimed to address, as we shall see, come, it seems, from a much wider definition of the part they were said to have played in the colony.

For the victims of the bushranging attack, the characteristic of a bushranger was the clothing of the attackers. Muston wore a 'red cape with a wide black belt on which there was a dagger in the shape of a half moon'.[16] John Brown had 'a dark coloured jacket, and a white hat with a green ribbon round it'.[17] Patient had 'a long white coat'.[18] Clothing was extremely important in the colony and a sign of status. Convicts had particular dress after 1820, and settlers were distinguishable as well. The extravagant dress adopted by some bushrangers was also apparently worn by constables. The difficulty of distinguishing between the two, as we have seen, was stated by settlers in reports of robberies. Even when the armed men were still inside the house and had begun to search, settlers reported that they still thought they were constables. James Shadray, when his house was robbed, stated that 'they were well dressed, I took them for constables'.[19] One runaway servant was approached on the road by a constable and asked if he was a bushranger. The servant replied, 'so are you'. The constable took advantage of the misunderstanding until they came close to the watchhouse where he took the servant into custody.[20] Alternatively, later in the period, poorly dressed men with no shoes, or possibly no trousers, were considered bushrangers because they were so inadequately dressed. Flamboyance and the wearing of distinctive or brightly coloured clothes was evident, however, throughout the period by those bushrangers who successfully robbed carts or houses. Thus while it is true some bushrangers were desperate or hungry men, badly dressed, it is clear that some pride or self-gratification could be gained from the pursuit. The offence was also characterised by certain reported attitudes and behaviour.

Eight groups of bushrangers during this period gained access to a house by claiming they were constables, an employer, the Mounted Police or travellers. When the door was opened they rushed in and confronted the inhabitants. Some approaches to houses were theatrical. Joseph Morley gained access to a hut by knocking at the door and stating that 'your master is here and has got in liquor, open the door quickly for we have a great work to get him home'. The servant heard the act of vomiting and so opened the door and weapons were thrust in.[21] Thomas Maher in 1831 heard knocking at the door and asked who it was; the answer came they were the military. Maher said the military would not be out so late; they replied they were in search of strangers; he opened the door and the bushrangers gained access.[22] In 1828 Mary Kelly of North Rocks heard a knock at the door and asked who was there. 'We'll let you know when we get in', one of them replied.[23]

It was this last response which was more common as bushrangers burst in the door and confronted the inhabitants of houses. These men were usually armed with muskets, fowling pieces, pistols or bayonets. However, very few cases resulted in any violence to the inhabitants of the houses. There were ten cases in which the inhabitants of houses were injured, one involving a rape, and two cases in which people were shot. John Suddis was shot when he attempted to climb through a window while bushrangers were in the house.[24] The other shooting occurred in Bathurst when a man refused to join a gang of fifty who were collecting all the farm servants in the area.[25] Violence was much more likely on the roads than in houses.

In some cases it is suggested that the gangs were structured. William Evans, settler at Paterson's Plains, gave evidence when his house was attacked that 'Clynch seemed to be the ringleader'.[26] James Ryan in 1828 gave evidence at Goulburn of the bushrangers who plundered his house, describing them as 'one tall, six foot, brown hair, deeply pockmarked, seemed to take an active part, another, the leader, five foot seven or eight, pockmarked, fair hair, blue jacket and blue trousers of very good quality'.[27] William Geary was clearly the leader of his gang in cases concerning him in 1821.[28]

Bushrangers controlled the inhabitants of houses through threats, such as threatening to 'blow the brains out' of anyone who crossed them. The inhabitants were tied up, made to lie in bed with blankets over their faces or stood facing the wall. Most bushrangers were masked, and their faces blackened. George Fuller described a mask in 1816: 'Dooley put a coarse linen bag over his face and the inside around the eyes was blacked'.[29] William Geary, most successful and notorious, was not disguised and was recognised by his victims.[30] Violence resulted when bushrangers were crossed: when a door in a house was not opened for them, or they were told there was no property in the house or they were refused food. In some cases one bushranger intervened in the violence of another: 'If you shoot him I'll shoot you', stated one of the bushrangers robbing William Guthrie's hut in 1830. He added that 'young life shall not be taken'.[31]

Property stolen was primarily clothing, money, food or firearms: 'where are all your fine things?' asked the bushrangers of Eleanor Clowers in 1827.[32] When Daniel Leary robbed the house of Benjamin Grainger, he said that 'Grainger used to have plenty of money, how was it he had none then'.[33] The most likely subjects of bushranging attacks were small settlers, possibly because the houses of larger settlers were well guarded and difficult to attack without rousing the servants. Small settlers lost property in attacks. In one attack Timothy Beard, Liverpool publican, lost thirty-five gowns, ten shirts, one fivepence and two blue jackets.[34] Both the existence of leaders and the frequency with which money or clothing of some value was obtained seem to indicate that the robberies were well planned, and there was some knowledge of the wealth of the settlers robbed.

In all of these cases involving houses or huts, food was taken or even eaten during the robbery. Some houses were robbed simply for food available in them. The concern with food echoes the interest of farm servants in receiving fair rations. William Geary broke into Thomas Thompson's house at Pennant Hills and told him not to be frightened, that they would not hurt them, they only wanted something to eat.[35] John Tors, a servant to P. Simpson esquire, was approached by three men in his hut, who said 'they must have something . . . they were in the bush they must have something'.[36] Orders were given to the women of the house to cook, to 'bake a cake' which was made of flour and cooked in the ashes and eaten with butter. When bushrangers raided the huts of Leslie Duguid at Wallis Plains in 1828 they ordered the servant to kill a sheep and cook it and they made the servants eat some of it for their breakfast.[37] When John Lynch's gang raided the house of Mary Marshall at the Nepean they took all her food and ate it; when she asked them to leave bread for her children they refused and desired her children to go to hell.[38]

The theft of food was very rare in New South Wales outside these cases and yet the settlers recall all of what was eaten and taken. Mary Marshall implied in her case that food was scarce. Obtaining food was a large part of the relationship between bushrangers and their harbourers. In these cases also the generosity of these people was noted afterwards by precise recall of what was eaten or given. These bushrangers were from ironed gangs or agricultural establishments and some had been farm servants. Rations were much more important to country than to town servants and formed the basis of complaints after Brisbane ruled that they need to be accounted for. For bushrangers without kangaroo dogs (and the use of dogs seems to have occurred only at Newcastle where convicts would leave the settlement for some time and live off kangaroo caught by their dogs),[39] it was the necessity for food which tied them to settled areas and perhaps kept them in a cycle of robbery and receiving and a tenuous relationship of harbouring in spite of their hopes to leave for Timor, or for a new settlement called 'Finan'. Thomas Blazey and his gang had 100 pounds of biscuit and 100 pounds of salt meat for their venture and this was gained through theft and stockpiling over some time. If we can discover a purpose behind bushranging as an offence, it was not tied to the clothing bushrangers stole but to the need to be free and the need to eat.

Despite the obvious relationship of bushranging and survival, we find in the cases a distinction between rich and poor made by bushrangers themselves and a perception of bushranging in relationship to such a distinction. As I have written, it was not the employer–servant world which was the concern of the bushrangers, for they had left that behind; but they did see themselves in terms of rich and poor, as is evident in the cases of highway robbery. It was by highway robbery that convicts came into contact with the wealthy of the colony and this, partly, I would argue, was the reason for the strong reaction in 1830–31 by the magistrates and Legislative Council. Attacks on wealthy landowners increased late in the period (see Table 18), and the reaction was fierce. Aron Murphy was driving a cart with provisions for Mr Bowen in 1830 when he was stopped by three bushrangers who first asked whose cart it was and then robbed it of gunpowder and ammunition. They told Murphy, 'they were not intending to distress him as Bowen could well afford it'.[40] Jesse Coalman, a servant to William Bingle, was stopped by John Alexander and John McConnor who robbed the cart he was driving. McConnor gave his compliments to Mr Bingle and said to tell him to consider it a present and if he could not meet him on the road he would pay him a visit in his house.[41] The magistrate Dalhunty was stopped in 1830 and robbed of all his clothing.[42]

Bushrangers seem to have made a distinction in their treatment of rich and poor. On two occasions bushrangers returned the property of poor persons they had robbed on the roads. When William Reilly, a dealer, was stopped and robbed by bushrangers in 1831, he complained he had no money to pay the toll to Parramatta; they gave some coppers back. One bushranger wanted O'Reilly's shoes, but another said no shoes were to be taken.[43] Catherine Roley was on her way to Sydney from Liverpool when her cart was robbed. She was told, 'Don't blame us for what we have done, but to thank the governor.'[44]

The distinction we find between rich and poor in highway robberies appears also in house robberies. Geary stated he robbed from the rich and gave to the poor. When he said this, he was in the house of people who were free by servitude where he and his gang had gone to get food.[45] What he meant by rich and poor is difficult to discover, however, as the persons he robbed were not wealthy landowners. The question can possibly be answered by Patrick Clynch, who said of himself when captured that he 'intended to give himself up to his excellency [the governor] in person but that he had been apprehended', stating further that the gang had never more than £5 at a time, and

Table 18 Status of victims of bushranging in criminal cases, 1816–31

Year	Cart robbery			House robbery		
	Servants of wealthy persons	Small settlers	Wealthy persons	Servants' huts of wealthy persons	Small settlers	Wealthy persons
1816		1			1	
1817	1				1	
1818						
1819						
1820				1	1	1
1821					11	
1822		1	2	2	6	1
1823				2	2	
1824				2	2	1
1825	3	3	1	7	9	3
1826	2	2		4	5	
1827	4			3	10	
1828	2	3	2	5	14	1
1829	5	5	4	15	13	9
1830	3	5	5	5	9	3
1831	1	3		7	6	8
Total	21	23	14	53	90	27

'what cash they took they give to the government servants and other poor people they met'.[46] Even if this statement was calculated to appeal, he still identifies the poor primarily as government servants. Small settlers with 25 acres lived a markedly different style of life to government workers, and government workers formed a large part of the population of the countryside. In terms of the colony small settlers may have been poor but compared to a government servant they were considerably better off. Bushrangers, in speaking of rich and poor, placed themselves outside both. They were able to see past the distinction between rich or poor and considered themselves not as representative poor but as being a particular relationship to the poor—they were capable of giving back part of stolen property and distinguishing between a wealthy victim and one less able to pay. Yet they were more likely to give to the landless than the small settler.

According to depositions, once a bushranger had left employment he no longer saw himself in terms of that relationship. He existed outside it. This is borne out by the identity of those persons whom bushrangers thought were deserving of revenge and whom they threatened in the presence of others. When Robert Hawkins was involved in a shooting between bushrangers and his master's servants and he lay on the floor bleeding, one of the bushrangers came in 'kissed him and said he did not think to shoot him but that old bugger Cunning who had been the death of many a one'.[47] Informers and constables bore the brunt of threats by bushrangers.

Persons mentioned as subjects for revenge were informers, constables, scourgers and magistrates. All of these people were involved in the legal process of committal, trial and execution. This process was, of course, of direct interest to bushrangers, yet the fact is that it was revenge, rather than any other aspect of life in the countryside—such as inequitable rations, unfair employers and the difficulties of renting land—that was central to their attacks. This is crucial. Bushrangers as represented in the courts not only lived in fear of being captured: it was this capture and the likelihood of it that was central to their behaviour. To live outside a system was possible but to live off it meant that the threat of capture was always there. It was a legal world of informers, constables and magistrates which the bushranger inhabited. This was the limit of his horizon and so his behaviour was limited also.

The forms which revenge took also bore relation to the legal process. When the magistrate Dalhunty was stopped on the road by bushrangers, one of them asked if he was not the man responsible for Muston's death (Muston had been sentenced to death for bushranging in 1826). Dalhunty said he was not, but the bushranger said he was the man responsible for the ironed gang and sentenced him to be flogged.[48] Such sentencing occurs in other cases where an informer is formally sentenced to be flogged and the sentence ordered to be carried out. In 1826 James Farrell, acting constable and hut keeper to Rossi's cattle station, was visited by four bushrangers who told him to get on his knees for they were to take his life in fifteen minutes. One of the bushrangers stripped himself and showed marks of a shot at the back of his neck and said Farrell had shot him. The bushranger then said they would give Farrell a boy's flogging. They tied him up to a post, stripped him, and ordered one of the bushrangers to give Farrell fifty lashes saying, 'mind boatswain do your duty'.[49] In cases like this we can see the appeal of the pretence to be constables. This imitation is not far from the custom of English charivari, street processions in fancy dress, where the pretence to be figures of authority was a mechanism by which complaints were heard.[50] It is perhaps in this context that we find Geary in 1821 writing a petition to the governor and the claim from the bushrangers who robbed Roley's cart that it was the fault of the governor the cart was robbed, not the fault of the robbers.[51]

The appearance of bushrangers with their masks, blackened faces and threats also brought particular references to religion. Victims were ordered to kneel and say their prayers or made to swear on the Bible that they would not disclose the identity of bushrangers. Blazey's gang took an oath of allegiance before they joined to go to Timor.[52] To swear was an important part of the criminal case, as well as bearing reference to religion. It was the centre of attention on the part of judges or magistrates. At this point people giving evidence broke down or refused to swear. To swear was binding possibly because it was on the Bible, and so we find bushrangers as well as persons in criminal cases placing great weight on the act of swearing. This was possibly imitation again, but swearing was taken seriously: it was part of legal culture and popular culture at once.

Despite the imitation of magistrates' sentencing and the emphasis on swearing, bushrangers did not seem to have any illusions about the legal process. We find frequent references to death. Donohue and his gang referred to themselves as 'a box of dead meat already'.[53] When another bushranger was asked if he had anything to say in response to the deposition of one of his victims, he stated, 'all he wished was to be out of the world' as quickly as possible'.[54] When Daniel Leary went to the house of Benjamin Grainger, he said, 'don't ask me where I am going or what I am doing I am a dead man taken where I will these two months'.[55] This concern with death stresses again their relationship to the society. They were both outside it and tied to it by plundering for survival. Yet bushranging does seem to be regarded as a better life; the plans to leave the colony were utopian; what lay in giving oneself up was the threat of a death sentence. It was indeed a case of 'Death or Liberty'. Despite its isolation, its seeming hopelessness, it was in itself a movement against the whole structure of the society, not a cry for justice, or a wish to see things righted. In this sense it bears much more relation to Irish peasant movements described by Paul Roberts. 'Small farmers and rural labourers in pre-famine Ireland thought of themselves as one distinct class—"the poor" ', he writes.[56] His description of the Caravats who wore blackface, used the sawn-off shotgun and had millenarian hopes of creating an alternative society[57] bears some relation to the behaviour of bushrangers in New South Wales. Bushrangers were not runaway servants, in their own view, but a different group altogether.

The term bushranging was used by bushrangers themselves to describe their activities. It also becomes clear that large and successful bushranging gangs obtained notoriety not only among the people but with each other. Members of John Donohue's gang refer to both Geary and Muston, as do other bushrangers. There was a consciousness of being engaged in an activity which had a past and which could be continued. Clothing, sentiments, theatricality all gave bushranging an image which could be aspired to. Yet it was not a popular uprising. Despite the fact that the Bathurst bushrangers Entwhistle, Graham and Webster went from farm to farm and recruited and the servants went with them,[58] they left most of them in a barn and ten or eleven proceeded by themselves. The bushranging phenomenon was a movement of small gangs, not necessarily bearing any relation to each other, who sometimes most successfully survived and at other times did not.

This was the image of the bushranger presented in the criminal court by deponents. It was the image that was presented to the court and judged. It is agreed to by the confessions of bushrangers themselves and it is this image which was partly responsible for the various Legislative Council decisions regarding bushranging, the establishment of the Mounted Police and the intensification of policing in the countryside.

Two of the most notorious gangs of the period, those of William Geary alias Gurrey, and John Donohue, had members who became approvers after the gangs were apprehended. Thomas Jeffreys of Geary's gang in 1822 and John Walmesly of Donohue's both gave elaborate accounts of the persons who received stolen property and harboured them. These gangs were most successful, Geary's remaining at large while committing robberies for two years and Donohue's for three. The methods by which they were harboured are typical of patterns of harbouring throughout the period.

Thomas Jeffreys gave evidence that the gang was harboured at Peisley's farm at Prospect in the servants' huts in March 1822. Two, John Muston, free, and John Sharp, convict, were servants to Mr Peisley. The bushrangers tore off the markings of a shirt and striped dungaree and gave it to them; they gave Sharp a book and a tin pot; to William Seville, free, of the Hawkesbury Road, who was working for Peisley, they gave a shirt also. Muston, Sharp and Seville were arrested after this information was given and the property was found in their possession.[59] The bushrangers went to the hut of Marsden's servants and gave nankeen trousers to William Craig, servant to Marsden, 'as a remuneration for provision he supplied'.[60] The trousers they had stolen from Mary Carney's house on 9 January 1822. Constables searched Craig's hut and found the trousers. While the bushrangers were at Peisley's, William Bell, convict and servant to Mrs Shelley, came there and bought a print from them. He also informed them of the property to be found on Mrs Shelley's farm, including a pistol and a double-barrelled fowling piece. Jeffreys said William Bell appeared to be dirty for want of a clean shirt and gave him a sky-blue jacket, a waistcoat and a shirt.[61]

The bushrangers left Peisley's farm at Prospect and went to the house of Joseph and Mary Charington, free settlers at the Dogtraps. Joseph Charington was absent in Sydney. Mary Charington took some material and tore off the makings of two skirts for herself, and one for her daughter; Jeffreys gave her a pair of half boots. He was given rum and mutton.[62]

From Parramatta to Prospect, Geary's gang was aided by both convicts and free settlers. This aid, though, was dependent upon exchange or payment: it was not a relationship of charity or generosity. Nearly ten years later, we find John Donohue's gang operating by the same principles.

John Walmesly gave evidence against two families, those of Edward Chalker and of Michael O'Brien at the Seven Hills. The first time the gang went to Chalkers' was before Christmas in 1829. Edward, free born, Daniel, free born and Mrs Chalker, free by servitude, were there. Mrs Chalker got them supper; they left and robbed Mr Bowman on the road and returned to Chalkers' where they gave the family '50/- for friendship and provisions'. The bushrangers left and stayed in Mr Cox's paddock. A week later Chalker came and told them where the constables and soldiers were, in what number and direction. The bushrangers 'went very much to Chalker's until the constables suspected the place'; then they camped half a mile from it and Chalker went to sit and drink with them. This relationship went on for some time. They gave £5 to Chalker to buy gunpowder and tobacco. As Walmesly described it, 'he gave us no change . . . we did not request it'. While Walmesly was in Cox's paddock some time before this, two servants of Mr Cox went to see him and gave him provisions. Walmesly said he had escaped from gaol and had nothing but 'he would make amends'.[63]

When the gang first went to see the free settlers, the O'Briens, they went there because they heard O'Brien had harboured Geary. They told him they were bushrangers and the girls and the old woman asked them to 'bring some presents'.[64] They returned to O'Briens' many times, always bringing them property from the robberies they had committed (see Figure 7). To a son of O'Brien's they gave a watch 'out of friendship'.[65]

The relationship between bushrangers and their harbourers was a material one, a friendship measured in material exchange. Some loyalty was shown bushrangers by convict servants. When Jonathan Blaxland's overseer asked his servant where a missing sheep was, he said, 'the devil a know, he knew where they were'. The overseer charged him with giving sheep to the bushrangers and was answered, 'he had done no such thing but the poor fellows ought to have something'. The overseer informed him that if

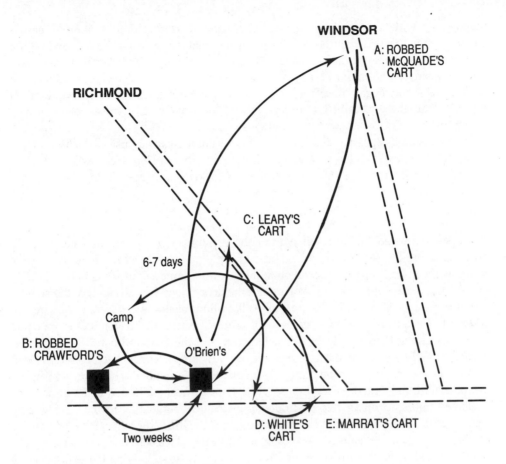

Figure 7   Activity of John Donohue's gang, 1829.

he told where the bushrangers were he should take the reward for apprehension. He said he would not tell even if he knew where a thousand were.[66]

Donohue's gang returned to O'Briens' a second time and they stayed in the house for five days, sleeping in the kitchen at night and sitting in the girls' bedroom, which was very small, during the day. When two butchers came and bought meat from Mrs O'Brien, the bushrangers hid in the girls' bedroom all evening until they could make an escape into the orchard.[67] The dependence on the house for such a long period is interesting. Donohue stopped visiting Chalkers' only when the constables began to suspect them. At this time movement through the countryside was difficult because of the activities of the Mounted Police, yet ten years before we find Geary equally dependent on the house of Robert Allan at Pennant Hills[68] and on Peisley's servants' huts. Geary returned to Allan's because he lost his way at night. Bushrangers do not seem to be any more familiar than the military or the Mounted Police with the landscape, and all were dependent on Aboriginal people to get from place to place. Bushrangers seem more dependent on local shepherds who were reluctant to give information to the police. Though Geary plundered a wide area of the countryside, he seemed to have done this only because when arrested the first time he escaped from the boat transporting him to Sydney for trial. Most bushranging gangs remained localised, even though their members may have originally run away from Port Macquarie, Newcastle or Bathurst. They headed directly to settled areas and began their robberies and did not move much further until their capture. Thus the houses of harbourers and receivers were safe houses to be used to the utmost.

The localisation is possibly the reason we find William Evans' house at Wallis Plains so frequently attacked. His house was on a direct route inland from Newcastle and south through the hills from Port Macquarie. It was attacked four times during the period.

Policing

The cases discussed so far resulted from the capture of bushrangers either through informants, by the searches of constables, or by pursuit and siege. These cases were heard by the magistrates and passed on to the Court of Criminal Jurisdiction before 1824 and the Supreme Court after 1824. Through the depositions we can observe the activity of the constables in a particular area, as well as how bushrangers were either shot or taken into custody. In passing on cases to the criminal courts, the magistrates often wrote letters discussing the character of the defendants and the level of bushranging in their particular area, and from these letters and the amount of concern expressed we can gauge the response to the offence. The reactions to bushranging were expressed in the creation of the Mounted Police in 1825, the appointment of troops in 1826 and the combined police action against bushranging in 1830—culminating in the Bushranging Act of 1830. 'This provided that any person could be arrested on suspicion of being a convict runaway and the onus was on him to prove it.'[69] This activity had been engaged in by constables and magistrates at bench level for some time. In 1832 Governor Bourke wrote to Viscount Goderich, Secretary of State for the Colonies, concerning renewal of the Act:

> It was passed in 1830 when the roads were infested by bushrangers and it was Unsafe to proceed even a short distance from Sydney without an escort or being well armed and in company. Burglaries had become common and I am informed there was an absolute want of security for life and property within the best peopled parts of the colony. Certainly a less alarming state of Society would not have justified the passing of a law which Subjects all persons to be arrested on Suspicion without a warrant and empowers a Justice of the Peace to detain any person in custody or to send him from any distance to Sydney. Unless he can prove to the Satisfaction of the justice that he is not a transported felon, and further enables Justices to issue general Search Warrants to be executed by day or Night.

Bourke added that the colony 'is very different—Highway Robberies and Housebreaking are now by no means frequent and the roads are traversed at all seasons without greater precaution than is frequently used in England'.[70]

For its part, the Legislative Council, which had unanimously introduced a renewal of the Act of 1830, 'expressed apprehension of renewal of the outrage'.[71] Early in 1825 Governor Brisbane made a proclamation of an amnesty for all those at large in the bush. He wrote in March, 'Finding they did not avail themselves of my late Proclamation which expired on 20th inst. I have ordered an increased number of constables for the present with soldiers and aborigines to accompany them with a reward of £5 for every bushranger.'[72]

Bushranging did result in an extensive reaction by magistrates and the Legislative Council and was perceived by both Brisbane and Darling as a threat to the colony. It made such an impression on Viscount Goderich that he asked Darling in 1831 to check the dispersion of settlers and promote the concentration of the inhabitants of the colony.[73] He wrote:

> I think it will require the utmost vigilance on your part to guard against the danger, which I apprehend and which is the more serious, as it cannot be doubted that should these Bands increase in strength they will direct their efforts to the release of the chain gangs, by a union with whom they would enable to threaten the very existence of the constituted Authorities.[74]

How then did the constituted authorities regard bushrangers?

The apprehension of bushrangers was based on a reward system: both constables and their informers received money. In 1813 constables Martin Swiney and John Brown received £30 for apprehending the bushrangers James Cobb, Isaac Walker and Angelo le Rose.[75] In 1822 in search for Michael Doras, Mr Campbell's stockman 'stated he could take them any time provided there was a warrant offered for them but he had not heard of any reward being offered'.[76] In 1826 after the bushranger Patient was captured; the governor offered rewards for information leading to the apprehending of receivers, noting that 'the inducements to Plunder, which leads to murder and other atrocities, would be diminished were the receivers of Stolen goods prevented from pursuing their nefarious traffic'.[77] Bushranging included receiving. With such a reward system it had its own economy: money changed hands both between bushrangers and their harbourers and receivers and between constables and their informers. There was money to be made from it. However, this reward system did not work successfully and so pursuit as a means of capture was adopted.

James Macarthur wrote to Governor Macquarie in 1819 describing Lieutenant Close's search for bushrangers:

> the neighbourhood of the Stonequarry was diligently searched without success there is no trace of the Bushrangers even being seen ... there is a probability of falling in with the object of the search tomorrow or the next day on the banks of the rivers ... But should he not be so fortunate any further search at present must be of little avail the Banditti without doubt have received information of the measures that have been taken for their apprehension ... from the circumstance of their being no mark of Cattle killed I should think the natives must have exaggerated the report of the number. A strong party, has however without doubt been very lately in the Cowpastures and constables say 18 men with 14 dogs.[78]

Such was the pattern of all pursuits: interminable searching, wrong information and an inflated view of the numbers involved.

It is apparent from the letters between magistrates and officials, and between the governor and the Colonial Secretary, that the views bushrangers held of themselves as being a formidable threat (such as those on the sugar plantation who planned to join the great party from the plains) were accepted by the authorities. When Launcelot, Legget and

Dixon, the Stoney Ridge boys, burned Mr Thomson's house at Bathurst,[79] the magistrate Major Fennel wrote to Major Ovens that,

> having been apprized of the present and ultimate plans of the armed gangs by one of their party the statement being fully corroborated from another source induced me to detail it for government information . . . it is nearly a year since Mr. Rankin's and Mr. Thomson's men formed a plot for getting out of the colony . . . after obtaining the powder they were to be joined by more of Mr. Rankin's men being thus formidable 60 in number they were to attempt Mr. Rankin's life, force his wife and servant girl and take the latter with them, his premises they were to set on fire and with those of other individuals whom they term bad masters . . . they were to take cattle until five miles above Wellington Valley and be joined by men of that establishment and then make the best of their way to the sea which they expected to reach in four months, on their arrival put the seeds in and wait until they met with a vessel . . . it is reported some runaways from Wellington Valley have founded a settlement not far from that establishment and got in several acres of wheat, also some stock.[80]

The magistrate E. C. Close wrote to Ovens in 1825 concerning Newcastle:

> I make no apology for urging what we with great respect conceive the only means left of putting down the increasing and I say increasing for also after the desperate acts committed by these misguided men few seem disposed openly to join their party yet there is scarcely a farm where they have not well fed adherents and there is decidedly a strong party of the free emancipated population aiding their efforts by succoring them in various ways . . . they are confederated with all the thieves in Newcastle those who do not join them seem little disposed to resist.[81]

In 1826 after Dr Dalhunty's house was attacked, Darling issued a government notice:

> His excellency cannot permit the events of Saturday night at Burwood the Residence of Dr. Dalhunty to pass without expressing his admiration of the spirited conduct of that gentleman and his family . . . the result would be highly important if only in providing how much may be effected by a cool and determined resistance against them, even of the most desperate characters.[82]

Saxe Bannister wrote quickly to him that it was important not to confound a crime with prejudice.[83] Brisbane wrote to Earl Bathurst, Secretary of State for the Colonies, in 1825 concerning the necessity for mounted police:

> In a country like this, where a thin population is scattered over a large tract of country, the temptations to plunder are increased by the facilities of escape; and once Bushranging has become sufficiently concocted to have its ramifications and connections in different parts of the Colony nothing short of Military movements will be sufficient to put it down.[84]

On 12 December Acting Governor Stewart wrote to Bathurst:

> At the united request of Sir Thomas Brisbane and the Members of Council I have some time since carefully selected and equipped as light cavalry 1 officers 2 sergeants and 22 rank and file from the regiment under my command to act as mounted police.[85]

In March 1826 Darling ordered the distribution of troops throughout the country areas: 'the officers employed will immediately put themselves in communication with the magistrates of the neighbourhood with whom the Lieutenant General desires they will be pleased to co-operate to the utmost of their power'.[86]

In 1830 a series of confidential letters passed between the magistrates and the governor; all were marked 'secret and confidential', a sign of the urgency of the matter. A letter from the Colonial Secretary on 17 April 1830 stated that

> small parties of troops will be placed at each of the stations, named in the margin . . . for the purpose of scouring the country accompanied by constables under the direction of magistrates . . . furnished with bush clothing for disguise as you recommend will take their rations for four or five days [the action will be] instantaneous be prepared for commencing on Wednesday by which time the troops will be in readiness.[87]

What kind of views of bushranging resulted in such action? Firstly, magistrates, the governor, Legislative Council and the military credited the bushrangers with a great deal of cunning and capability of organising and with intentions wider than simply robbery or survival. It was the elaborate plans of Patient and Launcelot that they discovered and thought possible. What concerned magistrates most were their connections: 'all the thieves in Newcastle', wrote E. C. Close.[88] Their suspicions developed on the small emancipated settlers and ticket-of-leave holders recently increased in number under Macquarie. These people were most likely to be receivers. In Patient's case, Darling remarked that all of the receivers were *free*. The emancipists and ticket-of-leave holders had long been a source of concern. Thus the Bushranging Act provided that their houses could be searched at any time of the day or night and that ticket-of-leave holders were to stay in one district and not move out of it. The Bushranging Act was as much directed against the ticket-of-leave holders and emancipists as against bushrangers themselves.

Pursuit and Suspicion

When we look at the dreams of the bushrangers to escape the settlement and the reactions of people in authority to them, it seems that myth played an important role. With this point in mind we shall approach the method by which bushrangers were taken, and examine the related cases of harbouring and false accusation.

Bushrangers were apprehended in a number of ways: though informants, through the activities of individual constables, through an approver—one of the gang going to a magistrate—and through pursuit by the Mounted Police, a group of constables, soldiers or a landowner with his servants. In 1819 for example the magistrate Cox ordered two constables and three soldiers to go in pursuit of the gang of Richard Chapman and James Blackman. The constable at Richmond described the pursuit, in which he was ordered

> to proceed to Mulgoa cross the river there in search of bushrangers, the next day witness sent . . . five natives to look out for the bushrangers. The natives returned at midday saying they had discovered the tracks of four men, three of whom had crossed the river the fourth had returned.[89]

The constable and soldiers crossed the river and proceeded for a distance of five miles following the tracks till dark and discovered the two prisoners. The bushrangers shot at them but their guns misfired and they were seized. This pursuit had lasted for three days and was successful. Though this arrest occurred relatively quickly, this was the pattern of most pursuits, and they became much more numerous after 1825. The Mounted Police were often out for weeks in pursuit of bushrangers generally, rather than any particular gang.

In all of these cases the constables or Mounted Police were armed, and so we find bushrangers in their attacks on houses searching for weapons and gunpowder in order to defend themselves. Donohue successfully fought off two pursuits by the Mounted Police until he was finally shot in 1830. Thomas Quoley, corporal of the Mounted Police, described his pursuit in 1831, beginning at Maitland:

> on the first of September I was ordered by Aubin to proceed with the Mounted Police to the upper district of the Hunter to apprehend an armed banditti, using any exertion to capture them. We arrived at Dulwich received information a party of men was seen at Dartbrook, we proceeded to Liverpool plains and found several robberies had been committed and of Mr. Jones at Goulburn River a mill and horses had been taken. On the fifteenth of September we received reinforcements, at Goulburn we procured two natives, we camped at the Warrumbungle Mountains and split the party into two after which the other party came upon the bushrangers.[90]

The use of the Mounted Police in such an extensive way meant that sieges became more violent and bushrangers more willing to fight. Up to 1828 we find bushrangers were likely to be on foot but because the police were mounted there was incentive also for bushrangers to be on horseback. Mounted Police were stationed in all country areas and were under the command of the local magistrates. They were not unlike soldiers and the countryside became more militarised by their activities. They were used not only in the search for bushrangers but also in searching houses of suspected harbourers. The familiarity of settlers with them enabled bushrangers to pretend to be police.

Nearly all cases of sieges involved tracking by Aborigines. Their co-operation was gained by the exchange of clothing for services, in much the same way that bushrangers 'paid' their harbourers and receivers. The use of their services shows that the Mounted Police were unfamiliar with the landscape; this was also evident in bushrangers themselves. Tracking as a practice was quickly learned by settlers and we find cases of them tracking stolen goods to their place of concealment, across country; we find the Mounted Police still using trackers in 1830.

The existence of informers was encouraged by the reward system. It came into operation after the arrest of the bushrangers, and rewards were given to receivers or informers who gave information of the whereabouts of bushrangers when they were seen at a neighbour's or a fellow servant's house. All of this information was denied by the receivers; some cases were acquitted and bear all the signs of false accusation. In 1826 a case between neighbours occurred where a settler, Hefferman, was accused by his neighbour Caroline Williams of being one of a party that robbed her house. It was discovered that she was considerably in debt to him and would do anything to relieve herself of that debt.[91]

Approvers gave information about receivers or the whereabouts of the gang. When Michael Kelly came forward and gave evidence in 1818, he stated that 'the others gave me nothing for my share'.[92] Since an approver was acquitted of all charges if he gave evidence against his gang, there was some incentive to do so. The keenness of magistrates to gain information concerning harbourers and receivers suggests that strong persuasion was used. After Walmesly of Donohue's gang gave information concerning the receivers O'Brien and Chalker, George Savays wrote to the Attorney-General:

Having attended most of the examinations for harbouring bushrangers or receiving their plunder I am apprehensive that in a legal point of view there is not sufficient evidence to commit many of the most guilty of them. Walmesly's testimony may not be deemed sufficient by a jury, though I believe every word of it.[93]

We can see in this the determination of magistrates to have persons convicted for receiving. The magistrates had the power both to order the Mounted Police to search and to commit persons for trial. In many cases the suspicions of magistrates and constables came into play. In 1827 Edward White, town constable of Windsor, went with a number of constables in pursuit of the bushrangers George Kilroy, John Donohue and William Smith. He gave evidence that 'we searched several houses in the neighbourhood without success'.[94] John Eckford and the Mounted Police at Wallis Plains searched several houses in their pursuit of Richard Lowe in 1824.[95] In 1826 servants of Darcy Wentworth were taken into custody for suspicion of stealing a heifer. A military party from the 40th Regiment were in pursuit of bushrangers when they went to the estate of Darcy Wentworth. John Robinson gave evidence that

we went up to the farm and enquired how many belonged to it, a stranger said he was free I demanded to look at his freedom. We walked to the creek and saw Neale with a bucket following us having some suspicion on my mind regarding the prisoner I took him into custody.[96]

The servants were acquitted by the Supreme Court. When Patrick Cawell was robbed by a group of men on the Liverpool road in May 1826, his suspicions fell immediately on Thomas Cawell, ticket-of-leave, who lived near the place where Patrick Cawell was robbed.[97] In one case in 1820 we find the house of Jeremiah Buffy being searched for bushrangers and an hour later for stolen property.[98]

Such suspicions rested on status, and constables were likely to suspect ticket-of-leave holders and government servants as well as poorer emancipists. In 1817 Benjamin Carver, constable, noticed a man by the name of Gilbert with other people, selling a quantity of Lyson tea in the neighbourhood of Parramatta. He 'knew none of the persons were possessed of property' and so became suspicious about where they had obtained it.[99] People moving through the countryside and regarded as strangers were likely to be arrested because they looked suspicious. In 1829 Joseph Kerr, a Parramatta constable, went to the house of Richard Newhouse at Prospect and said, 'if there are any people here that I don't like, meaning suspicious people, I shall take them with me'.[100] Small settlers themselves gave information regarding strangers. In August 1828 William Meredith, Liverpool Road constable, received information that there were 'three suspicious characters in a hut in Salt Pan Creek'.[101] In 1829 four persons were committed to the Court of Criminal Jurisdiction for absconding: William Ashton who was free was committed for having nothing to show for his liberty in June, six months before the Bushranging Act was passed.[102] It is clear from cases such as these that 1829 was not only the peak of a period of magisterial reaction to bushranging but also the year in which the Mounted Police and regiments were active in crossing and re-crossing the countryside in pursuit, not knowing precisely which gang they were pursuing but following rumour and suspicion and their trackers until they came upon a group of men in the bush.

Though the bushranger may well have been a starving man, sitting in the bush dressed in rags with no thought in his mind except of 'cake' and where he could obtain it, he was in the eyes of the law a Donohue. The bushranger was presented as a man who dramatised his role. In a luxurious costume he would commit acts of poetic daring and in his very existence would challenge the order existing in the colony. It was certainly not new in English law of the eighteenth century to perceive a crisis and to create new legislation to deal with it,[103] but both the offence of bushranging and its policing were to create something new in the colony. An offence created partially by the magistrates and partly by bushrangers themselves produced a particular type of policing, and particular kinds of behaviour bound up with what was considered legal or illegal. For the magistrates, this behaviour was winnowed down until it no longer rested on the act of bushranging, but on the act of being suspicious. And this suspicion did not centre on the bushranger but on his connections. The whole sweep of the countryside inhabited by the freed population was thought to be bristling with the exchange of stolen goods, the feeding of these bushrangers and the wanton rejection of authority. To deal with such practices the authorities set up a particular economy of rewards or payments for information and a net of policing which could have the doors of the settlers opened at any time of the day or night and the houses searched. This was intensive policing of a group which through ticket-of-leave or emancipation existed outside servitude. As we shall see, magistrates and constables always had considerable difficulty in regarding these people as other than convict, so it is not surprising that suspicion fell on them.

Bushranging possessed an economy and freed persons were an essential part of it. The exchange of property for food or as a sign of gratitude involved careful measurement, and it appears to be a great compliment for a receiver if the bushranger stated he did not 'care about the change'. The free population participated in both the economy of bushranging and the economy of capture. The offence of bushranging, then, seems to have had a culture of its own. Such an interplay of popular participation and magisterial reaction in this culture suggests that law had particular uses in community relations. The connections between those uses and the policing of public life outside servitude will now be considered.

Notes

1 R. vs John Gough and others, S.C.C.J., December 1825, 190.

2 Minutes of Evidence, Committee on Police, 10 June 1835, Legislative Council, *Votes and Proceedings*, p. 396.

3 Such descriptions are common from 1822, e.g. R. vs Will Bull, C.C.J., March 1822, 36.

4 William Webb and Sarah Webb, Argyle Bench of Magistrates, 3 April 1826.

5 J. McKinnon, 'Convict Bushrangers in N.S.W., 1824–34', M.A. thesis, La Trobe University, 1979.

6 The term banditti was used more often in the early period than the term bushranger. A carbine was a musket sawn off.

7 This phenomenon in Van Diemen's Land was markedly different to what later occurred in N.S.W. It is in Van Diemen's Land we find George Hillier cutting off the bushranger Peter Sefton's head to bring it in for reward: both were runaways.

8 This statement appears in eight robberies.

9 R. vs William Geary, C.C.J., June 1821, 85.
10 R. vs Will Poole and others, C.C.J., October 1822, 27; Fennel to Ovens, Bathurst, 22 August 1825, Brisbane letter book, A1559; R. vs Launcelot, Legget, Hindustan, S.C.C.J., 1825, Miscellaneous.
11 R. vs Thomas Roach, William Varley, John Maloney, C.C.J., 1822, 103.
12 R. vs Thomas Blazey and others, C.C.J., March 1820, 90.
13 R. vs William Geary.
14 R. vs William Poole.
15 ibid.
16 R. vs Thomas Muston and others, S.C.C.J., November 1826, 150–2.
17 R. vs John Brown, David Connor, S.C.C.J., February 1827, 11–12.
18 R. vs Charles Patient and others, S.C.C.J., 1825, Miscellaneous.
19 R. vs Brown.
20 R. vs Patrick Burke, S.C.C.J., August 1830, 196.
21 R. vs Joseph Morley, S.C.C.J., February 1830, 33.
22 R. vs Lawrence Moore, S.C.C.J., May 1831, 64.
23 R. vs Charles Connor, S.C.C.J., February 1828, 21.
24 R. vs John Walker, Ralph Pearson, Elizabeth Pearson, C.C.J., July 1817, 31.
25 R. vs Ralph Entwhistle, S.C.C.J., September 1830, 281.
26 R. vs Riley, Cleary, Price, Clynch, S.C.C.J., November 1825, 177.
27 Deposition only, no defendants, S.C.C.J., 1828, Miscellaneous.
28 R. vs William Geary.
29 R. vs Colin Hunter, Michael Ryan, Thomas Dooley, C.C.J., 1816.
30 R. vs William Geary.
31 R. vs John Thomas, Lawrence Fraine, S.C.C.J., June 1830, 151.
32 R. vs Michael Callaghan, S.C.C.J., January 1827, 7.
33 R. vs Daniel Leary, S.C.C.J., November 1825, 187.
34 R. vs John Weaver, Will Moir, Florence Henly, S.C.C.J., January 1825, 19.
35 R. vs William Geary.
36 R. vs Charles Jordan, George Byfort, John Older, S.C.C.J., February 1831, 39–40.
37 R. vs Peter Riley, Will Bouman, Joseph Turner, S.C.C.J., March 1829, 6 & 29.
38 R. vs John Lynch and others, S.C.C.J., November 1825, 177.
39 Evidence of John Evans, Superintendent of Government Works at Newcastle, 18 January 1819, Bigge Appendix B.T. 18, p. 2402.
40 R. vs Richard McCann, George Toalman, Joseph Turage, S.C.C.J., March 1830, 35.
41 R. vs John Alexander, John McConnor, S.C.C.J., December 1827, 121.
42 R. vs William Dalton, S.C.C.J., June 1830, 166–7.
43 R. vs Lawrence Sullivan and others, S.C.C.J., June 1831, 103.
44 R. vs Edward Lee, Francis Muller, Will Dalton, Henry Wheeler, S.C.C.J., June 1830, 166–7.
45 R. vs Will Baker, Peter Hilson, C.C.J., June 1821, 86.
46 R. vs Patrick Clynch, S.C.C.J., 1825, Miscellaneous.
47 R. vs Will Baxter and others, C.C.J., October 1822, 47.
48 R. vs William Dalton.
49 R. vs John Tennant, S.C.C.J., June 1825.
50 As discussed by E. P. Thompson: 'Rough music, Le charivari anglaise', Annales, E.S.C., 27, March–April 1972.
51 R. vs Geary.
52 R. vs Thomas Blazey.
53 Donohue's thefts are reported in R. vs O'Brien, S.C.C.J., June 1831, 197.
54 ibid.

55 R. vs Daniel Leary.

56 Paul E. L. Roberts, 'Caravats and Shanaveste. Whiteboyism and Faction fighting in West Munster, 1802–11', in S. Clarke and J. S. Donnelly, eds, *Irish Peasants, Violence and Political Unrest, 1780–1914*, p. 64.

57 *ibid.*

58 R. vs Ralph Entwhistle, Will Graham, Robert Webster. There is some confusion over this. Jennifer McKinnon and Hirst both maintained none of the men would go unless threatened. However, the bushranger John Ward said that before they came to Evendon's farm all the men got ready to go with them, despite the threatening mentioned by Thomas Mack.

59 R. vs William Seville, John Muston, John Sharp, C.C.J., February 1822, 72.

60 R. vs William Craig, C.C.J., March 1822, 72.

61 R. vs William Bell, C.C.J., December 1822, 72.

62 R. vs Joseph Charington, Mary Charington, C.C.J., March 1822, 72.

63 R. vs Edward Chalker, Elizabeth Chalker and others, S.C.C.J., June 1831, 99.

64 R. vs Michael O'Brien and others, S.C.C.J., June 1831, 197.

65 *ibid.*

66 R. vs Owen Malone, S.C.C.J., December 1826, 185.

67 R. vs O'Brien.

68 R. vs Robert Allan, C.C.J., March 1821, 39.

69 Hirst, *Convict Society and Its Enemies*, p. 125.

70 Bourke to Viscount Goderich, 19 March 1832, *H.R.A.*, 1 XVI, pp. 364–5.

71 *ibid.*

72 Brisbane to Horton, 24 March 1825, *H.R.A.*, 1, XI, p. 553.

73 Viscount Goderich to Darling, 22 March 1831, *H.R.A.*, 1, XVI, p. 115.

74 *ibid.*

75 Accounts, Police Fund, Wentworth papers, D1.

76 R. vs Michael Doras, C.C.J., September 1822, 53.

77 Gov. order, Col. Secretary's Office, 6 March 1826, *H.R.A.*, 1, XII, p. 209.

78 James Macarthur to Macquarie, 21 May 1819, Macarthur papers, M.L. A2920.

79 R. vs Launcelot, Legget.

80 Fennel to Ovens, Bathurst, 22 August 1825, Brisbane letter book, M.L. A1559–1.

81 E. C. Close to Ovens, Newcastle, 1 September 1825, in *ibid.*

82 Gov. Notice, 29 September 1826, A1267–10, Gov. Despatches, M.L. A1267–10.

83 Letter included in *ibid.*

84 Brisbane to Bathurst 95, 8 November 1825, *H.R.A.*, 1, XI, p. 897.

85 Acting Gov. Stewart to Bathurst, 12 December 1825, *H.R.A.*, 1, XII, p. 85.

86 Gov. Order, 21 March 1826, *H.R.A.*, 1, XII, p. 265.

87 Confidential letters Apprehension of Bushrangers, 1830–31, Col. Secretary Special Bundles AO 4/7090.

88 E. C. Close to Ovens, 1 September 1825, Brisbane Letter Book.

89 R. vs Richard Chapman, C.C.J., April 1819, 23.

90 R. vs Edward Brown, Charles Reisbery, John Mason, Hugh Duffy, Patrick Leary, Maitland, S.C.C.J., June 1831, 73.

91 R. vs Caroline Williams, S.C.C.J., December 1826, 66.

92 R. vs Hugh Duffy, C.C.J., April 1818, 13.

93 Savays to Att.-General, 2 March 1831, Confidential letters, Apprehension of bushrangers.

94 R. vs George Kilroy and others, S.C.C.J., December 1828, 4.

95 R. vs Richard Lowe, John Conroy, S.C.C.J., 1827, Miscellaneous.

96 R. vs Robert Nesbit and others, S.C.C.J., March 1826, 97.

97 R. vs Joshua Lockett, S.C.C.J., June 1826, 98.
98 R. vs Jeremiah Buffy, Mary Buffy, C.C.J., June 1820, 645.
99 R. vs John Walker, Ralph Pearson, Elizabeth Pearson, C.C.J., July 1817, 31.
100 R. vs Joseph Kerr, S.C.C.J., 1829, Miscellaneous.
101 R. vs Patrick Kegeny, S.C.C.J., 1828, Miscellaneous.
102 R. vs William Ashton, S.C.C.J., 1829, Miscellaneous.
103 E. P. Thompson, *Whigs and Hunters, The Origin of the Black Act.*

PART 3

Suspicious Characters: Police and People

'... you bugger I am a free man'

JAMES BRYANT
IN HIS ASSAULT ON CONSTABLE JONATHON DAVID

6

THE STRUCTURE AND STYLE OF POLICING

The convict system sought to regulate the person of the convict and his or her movement around the town. The administration also sought to regulate and control the free or freed person. This was met with considerable resistance in the form of skirmishes between constables and local people. Controls over the person developed not only from the administration but also from local populations. As we have seen, these local populations had their own uses for law and their own means of dealing with defendants and complainants. Thus policing combined with resistance and popular use of law to create the restrictions and freedoms of the colonial population, to create what was possible. As with bushranging, policing regulations do not reflect the reality of policing. In colonial New South Wales constables had their own interests and magistrates had their own interpretations of statute law.

In 1810 Governor Macquarie established a system of policing for the town of Sydney. This began a structure of street surveillance and house searching which was intended to make an impact on the social and economic lives of the inhabitants of the town. In many ways it was a fledgling and ineffective system. However, the focus of this policing and of the reformed system introduced by Francis Rossi in 1825 demonstrates an attempt to create a method of policing that was unknown in England.

The capacity of colonial administrators to develop new modes of policing in an untrammelled environment has been well recognised by legal historians.[1] Historians of the early nineteenth century in England have stressed that the concept of a police force was unpopular in English public debate. The 'rights and liberties of Englishmen' were seen to be under attack from French notions of policing.[2] In England local constables were under the control of magistrates and the concept of a metropolitan police force was to be accepted only after considerable debate.[3] In New South Wales there were no such reactions to the introduction of street policing or to those new 'French notions' of policing.

The manner in which people were arrested and their reactions throughout the period show the convergence of convict policing with the policing of a free or freed population. Both entailed attempts at curtailing the use of social space, buying and selling and related sexual activity. Attempts by constables to police were often met with violent reactions. Underneath such clear confrontations lay the economic world of the free and freed population of the town which had its own uses for law. The propensity for the colonial population to play a part in rape and murder cases had already been observed but there was also present in the colony a creative and often ingenious use of law in disputes between competing individuals or groups. We have seen how women were more likely to bring personal quarrels to the courtroom and played an important role in establishing the presence of household disputes in the courts. Such a propensity for dispute extended to the economic and social life of the wider town, and to relations between households as well as inside them.

The country magistrates' benches also possessed a policing apparatus. The methods of each of these benches in arresting, searching and suspecting differed and this was to affect local use of law as well. To begin we shall consider the policing system in operation in the colony and then closely examine the use of law by the ordinary population.

Sydney

On 1 January 1811 Macquarie's policing regulations came into force. The town was divided into numbered districts. Each district had a watchhouse 'for the reception of such persons who will be found in the streets, idle disorderly or suspicious',[4] one district constable and six other constables. The orders stated that

> at 7 a.m. every morning the District constable shall receive the reports of the night constables of the respective districts and carry the same signed with their several hands to the chief constable as soon afterwards as possible. District constables shall be under the orders of the chief constable and shall convey prisoners before the superintendent of Police. Night constables shall receive and take down the names and places of abode of such persons as may be brought into the watchhouse during the night. Ordinary constables shall come on duty precisely at the hour appointed and remain there until relieved . . . each will be armed with a cutlass and a rattle for the purpose of giving alarm, they shall strictly stop every prisoner or other suspicious person being about the streets after the hour of nine o'clock and take them immediately to the watchhouse of the district where they shall leave them in the charge of the constable at night . . . if at any time during the night any fray or riot or disturbance shall take place they shall do their utmost to restore order.[5]

The chief constable was to take before the superintendent all persons 'who have no apparent means of obtaining a livelihood that they may be dealt with according to the law . . . they shall watch narrowly all prisoners and suspected persons and make enquiry as to the different modes of employing their hours'.[6]

Such orders gave constables wide powers over both convict and free persons, as the term 'suspicious' could include virtually anyone. It was applied to those people without visible means of supporting themselves throughout the period 1810–30, free or freed. Policing in Sydney underwent two changes in the period. The first resulted from the construction of the Hyde Park Barracks in 1819 which took 800 convicts out of the town of Sydney. Convicts no longer resided in the town as tenants or owners of small houses, unless they were well behaved and had obtained exemption from the barracks. Convicts also wore distinctive dress. Constables thus began to police both absence from the barracks and the trade in this distinctive clothing. In 1825 when Captain Rossi replaced Darcy Wentworth as Police Magistrate he set about reorganising the police of Sydney. An age qualification was introduced: no-one younger than twenty-two or older than forty-five was to become a constable. The language of policing also changed with Rossi: police districts became 'wards', chief constables, 'wardsmen' and constables, 'conductors'. This change in language was self-conscious and reflected the amount of administrative atten-tion given to the new ideas of policing. The threat of bushranging, or the eventuality of convicts 'coming to Sydney to obtain their tickets of freedom', meant, said Rossi, that 'the streets of Sydney were crowded with [persons who were] loose, disorderly, desperate in character, idle and profligate'.[7] Rossi recommended a Vagrancy Act. The attention given by constables to these returning ex-convicts increased and this was aided by both the Bushranging Act (1830) and Rossi's early introduction of a reward system for the capture of runaway convicts.[8]

Consequently, the particular emphasis on policing the streets changed during this period in Sydney. So, too, did the wages of constables. Constables were initially paid wages in much the same way as convicts, in clothing, spirits, tea and sugar. These wages were a constant source of complaint by constables and Police Magistrates. In 1816 Darcy Wentworth passed a request on to Macquarie from five district constables and one constable requesting a 'trifling increase of salary'. The discontinuance of payment in spirits had resulted in their wages being reduced by half.[9] In 1820 Judge Advocate John Wylde wrote to Macquarie:

> It appears that at the first formation of the establishment in 1811 every constable with an occasional grant of spirits received four pairs of shoes, a waistcoat, two sets of slops. He was also allowed a full ration and half if single and if married himself only a ration, half a ration in many cases being taken away but his wife and two children stays at the usual ration—a diminution which seems reasonably stated renders it impossible to derive even a common subsistence from the situation.[10]

Wylde requested that the wage be fixed for a district constable at £20 p.a. and for an ordinary constable at £10 p.a. This was granted, but we still find Rossi complaining in 1826 of the low rates of pay for constables. He stated that until better pay was offered he did not expect to be able to recruit an efficient police force. 'Constables', he said, 'should be placed above want and should then be above temptation.'[11] He recommended their wages were to be for a chief constable £150 p.a., for a police officer £183, for a wardsman £72, for a conductor £60, for a patrolman £82, and for a night constable £25. An increase was granted by the Legislative Council after its consideration of the report, of amounts only slightly less than what was recommended.

If the financial status of the police officer improved, the apparent quality of the officers did not. During the inquiry by Commissioner Bigge, the activities of constables were a matter of concern. They were, stated chief constable Redman, frequently dismissed for misconduct.[12] So, apparently, wage increases did not place them above temptation. Pecuniary rewards for policing were much wider than simply wages. Rossi introduced a system of rewards which became £1 for offences not capital and £5 for capital charges. Such a system of rewards had existed during the Macquarie period. The fines for selling spirits without a licence and for selling lightweight bread went to the constable and his informers;[13] for runaway sailors constables received £2 payable to those who apprehended them and '18p' per night for those that remained in gaol.[14] For any offence for which there was a fine a constable seems to have received a fair proportion, if not all of it. Thus the lists of fines paid presented to the Bigge Inquiry exhibit consistent policing by constables of those who sold spirits without licences or who distilled spirits. We are concerned here with the policing of other activities, such as thefts, assaults and riot, yet the policing of the former offences must have made the constables more zealous in pursuing the latter.

Police activities on the street resulted from their own direct arrests, calls from other persons and the activities of informers. The Police Magistrates' Bench is the most likely source of information on direct arrests, since the suspects were held overnight and appeared before the Police Magistrate the next morning. After 1824, free persons arrested in such a manner were brought before the Quarter Sessions, i.e. they were indicted, they paid recognisances and then were bound to appear before the next sessions. These cases were originally heard before a Police Magistrate and then passed on, and in the period after 1826, some convict cases were also passed on in this manner.

The records of the Sydney magistrates' benches, the Petty Sessions and the Quarter Sessions show three developing tendencies in the policing of the streets of Sydney by constables. The first concerns the constables' attentiveness to the man carrying property in the streets during government hours of work. It was regarded as suspicious in 1812 that James Hargreave was wheeling a barrow through the streets, that Thomas Dalton was carrying a pot through the streets and that John Baker walked down George Street between 12 and 2 p.m. with a bulk under his shirt.[15] Between 1812 and 1821 those persons arrested were mainly convicts and so we can see constables making assumptions concerning what property a convict man should be carrying, how he should be carrying it and when. In the mentality of street policing the convict was closely tied to the workplace. Neither James Hargreave, Thomas Dalton or John Baker had obtained their property from their place of work. The barrow came from outside the house of Simeon Lord, the pot had disappeared from the house of Ellen Cooper in Pitt Street and the meat hidden under John Baker's shirt came from the military mess house. Nevertheless, the policing of these men was tied to work hours and place of work.

In 1820–21 such attentions extended to the night; constable arrests are set out in Figure 8. Policing of men's movements at night developed because convicts were meant to be inside the barracks at night and a convict outside them could be regarded with suspicion, especially if he was carrying property in the streets. George Rolley, constable, saw Joseph Brand in Cambridge Street between 9 and 10 p.m. with two hats; Richard Rochford was seen carrying a pair of shoes.[16]

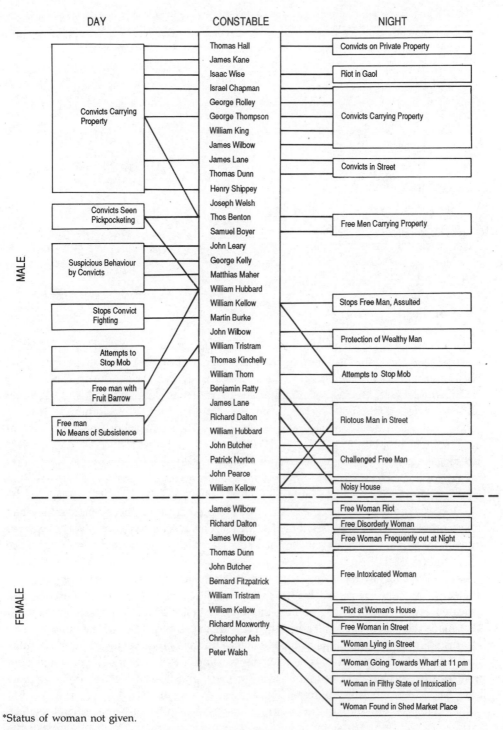

DAY   CONSTABLE   NIGHT

Convicts on Private Property

Thomas Hall
James Kane
Isaac Wise   Riot in Gaol
Israel Chapman
George Rolley
George Thompson   Convicts Carrying Property
William King
James Wilbow
James Lane   Convicts in Street
Thomas Dunn
Henry Shippey
Joseph Welsh
Thos Benton   Free Men Carrying Property
Samuel Boyer
John Leary
George Kelly
Matthias Maher
William Hubbard
William Kellow   Stops Free Man, Assulted
Martin Burke
John Wilbow   Protection of Wealthy Man
William Tristram
Thomas Kinchelly
William Thorn   Attempts to Stop Mob
Benjamin Ratty
James Lane
Richard Dalton   Riotous Man in Street
William Hubbard
John Butcher
Patrick Norton   Challenged Free Man
John Pearce
William Kellow   Noisy House

Convicts Carrying Property

Convicts Seen Pickpocketing

Suspicious Behaviour by Convicts

Stops Convict Fighting

Attempts to Stop Mob

Free man with Fruit Barrow

Free man No Means of Subsistence

MALE

FEMALE

James Wilbow   Free Woman Riot
Richard Dalton   Free Disorderly Woman
James Wilbow   Free Woman Frequently out at Night
Thomas Dunn
John Butcher
Bernard Fitzpatrick   Free Intoxicated Woman
William Tristram
William Kellow   *Riot at Woman's House
Richard Moxworthy   Free Woman in Street
Christopher Ash   *Woman Lying in Street
Peter Walsh   *Woman Going Towards Wharf at 11 pm
    *Woman in Filthy State of Intoxication
    *Woman Found in Shed Market Place

*Status of woman not given.

Figure 8 Reasons given for arrests by constables, 1820–21.

Table 19 Street arrests by constables in cases appearing before the Quarter Sessions, 1825–30

Charge	1825	1826	1827	1828	1829	1830	Total
Theft							
Male	14	11	4	24	9	8	70
Female			1				1
Riot							
Male	5	2	2				9
Female	2						2
Assault on constable							
Male	1	7	17	29	2	5	61
Female				1			1
Attempted Theft							
Male	1	1					2
Female							
Obstructing constable							
Male				1			1
Female							
Total	23	21	24	55	11	13	147

Such methods of policing extended to the free population. The records of the Quarter Sessions show constables suspecting free men seen carrying property, both during the day and at night. The numbers of Quarter Sessions arrests are set out in Table 19. In 1825 George Brown, free, was stopped on the Parramatta road between 8 and 9 p.m. by John Bryan, constable, who searched him and found a bundle of clothing.[17] Thomas Connor was seen by Thomas Brown, constable, with a blue cloth under his arm in Market Street between 5 and 6 p.m. He was asked by Brown where he had got it.[18] Arrests were also made during the day: for instance, George Jilkes, constable, saw James Callaghan 'this morning in King Street' with something under his arm; he was asked to hand it over and it proved to be a tea kettle.[19] Theft cases required that evidence be produced and so the only people we find before the bench are those who actually had stolen property in their possession. As with runaway charges, we have no way of knowing how many people were stopped and searched or questioned and no evidence was found.

A change in the law regarding larceny in 1827 resulted in a ruling that every larceny, whatever the value, be heard before the criminal court.[20] Theft cases, however, still appeared before the Quarter Sessions, though constables began to be very exact about what made them suspicious. 'I passed the prisoner in George Street with a bundle under his arm [I] knew he had no means of subsistence but by petty thieving so I apprehended him', said William Hamilton, conductor, in the April 1828 sessions.[21] Challenging for proof of freedom led directly to an arrest for theft, and this kind of reasoning is more likely to be found in later Supreme Court cases.

The constables' attention to men was originally governed by the same principles which operated in the convict system: time of work, place of work and theft of articles from

Table 20   Street arrests of free persons for offences other than theft appearing before magistrates' benches, 1820s

Year	Title of Offence			
	Male		Female	
1820–21	'With fruit barrow in street'	1	'Noise'	3
	'No means of subsistence'	1	'Disorderly conduct'	1
	'Challenged'	1	'Drunk'	5
	'Landed boat wrong place'	1	'Riotous'	2
	'Assault of constable'	1	'Drunk and riot'	2
			'Noise and prostitute'	1
			'Lying in street'	1
			'In street'	1
1824	'Assault of constable'	2	'Riotous'	1
	'Riot, disorderly'	1	'Pest'	1
	'Riotous assembly'	1	'Drunk and riot'	2
	'Firing gun'	1	'Drunk and leaving husband'	1
	'Drunk and out after hours'	1	'Drunk and disorderly in street,	
	'Abuse of constable'	1	indecent language'	2
			'Drunk, disorderly'	3
			'Drunk prostitute'	1
1828	'Riot'	4	'Prostitute'	4
	'Disorderly conduct'	1	'Drunk'	32
	'Drunkenness'	72	'Riotous'	4
	'Assault of constable'	1	'Notorious prostitute'	8
	'Abuse of constable'	2	'Rogue and vagabond'	2
	'Idle vagabond'	6	'Drunk and indecent conduct'	1
	'Incorrigible, dangerous'	1	'Absent from husband'	1
	'Insane pauper'	1	'Living in a state of adultery'	1
	'Rogue and vagabond'	1		
	'Drunk, indecent conduct'	1		
	'Riot, assault of constable'	4		

work. This mentality of policing extended to free men, incorporating them in an essentially convict-orientated definition of suspicion.

By contrast, the surveillance of women was from the beginning centred on their movements in the street at night. In 1812 Ann Ward was a 'common vagrant and prostitute around the town'.[22] Ann Doyle was heard to be making a great noise between 8 and 9 p.m.[23] Ann Chapman was much intoxicated and heard to be making a great noise in Gloucester Street.[24] In 1820 such policing began to include men. There are repeated references to constables challenging people they met late at night. William Quinn was arrested at 10.30 p.m. on Saturday 'in the streets of Sydney contrary to government and general orders'.[25] A free man was arrested for having no means of maintaining himself.[26] Robert Williams was termed 'a common pest to society having no visible means of subsistence'.[27] He was the only male to whom the term 'common pest' was ascribed. The term was applied in court to eleven women[28] and to another eleven were applied the terms 'common prostitute'[29] and 'infamous',[30] 'vagrant'[31] and 'common nuisance'.[32] Twenty-one women were charged with this type of conduct and only four men were charged with being intoxicated in the street. All of these arrests occurred at night.

By the late 1820s men were being included further in the policing of vagrancy and the development of descriptions of street offences is set out in Table 20. The records of 1827 for 16 January and 1828 for the month of February and from July to September provide the same kind of information as for 1824. However, even for this short period the records are markedly different from previous years. The highest number of street arrests are of free men for drunkenness, for which there was a five-shilling fine. Seventy-two free men and thirty-two women were arrested on this charge. Only eight women were charged with prostitution, though two were charged with being rogues and vagabonds. This new definition is comparable to other new charges listed: one man was charged with being an 'insane pauper in the streets', and free men were being charged with being idle vagabonds. In Rossi's report in 1826 specific reference was made to the Vagrant Act:

> A number of persons who daily become free by the expiration of their sentences are in the habit of coming to Sydney to obtain their certificates of freedom, and being generally of loose dissolute and frequently of a desperate description of character abandoned to idleness and profligacy, they remain in Sydney where they can with greater facility commit robberies ... these evils must necessarily increase as persons become free; and nothing short of the strict operations of the Vagrant Act, aided by a strong and active police, will check the progress of such dangerous combinations.[33]

Brisbane noted in 1825 that Macquarie's Police Regulations requiring registration of all households in the town 'would be intolerable at present', but that in a colony which had six times the crime rate of England 'a vagrant law of greater rigour is needed'.[34]

The records of 1827–28 seem to follow that initiative of new attention to free persons suggested by both Brisbane and Rossi. Male vagrancy and drunkenness were concerns which did not dominate in earlier cases before the benches. Constables stood to make money out of the fining system and this incentive probably accounted for their diligence in pursuing free, drunken men.

The reports by the grand juries made at the beginning of each Quarter Session often mention the type of offences found on the streets and the concerns of the wealthy populace. The first sitting in 1824 resulted in the following statement: 'we beg leave to call to your attention the low inhuman, and frequent practice of cockfighting—this barbarous amusement, being usually accompanied with disorder and idleness, drunkenness and common swearing is likely to be very hurtful to the moral habits of younger people'.[35] This report referred also to the numbers of petty dealers in tea, tobacco and soap and suggested that petty larceny could be reduced considerably by the police restricting the numbers of petty dealers.[36] The grand jury was concerned mainly with preventing the offences it saw before it. It requested in 1827 that street lamps be provided for the protection of property,[37] and it made note of the 'disorderly, idle and dishonest men at the King's Wharf under the character of Porters and labourers'.[38]

In October 1827 the grand jury regretted 'the increasing practice of erecting and removing a low description of wooden building on wheels into the most public places of the town, multiplying a very doubtful class of dealers already too numerous in Sydney of great injury to the respectable shopkeepers and to the disgrace of public thoroughfares'.[39]

By the 1820s two strands of policing practice—the surveillance of the convict and of the vagrant—had begun to converge. According to Rossi and the grand juries, the focus of street policing was to be the idle disorderly ex-convict. Policing of vagrancy had begun with women; who could be arrested for simply being in the street; these women were not policed according to the requirements of the convict system but according to the requirements of morality. The policing of the vagrant women pre-dated the policing of the vagrant man. However, the notion of vagrant for both men and women supposed proper places of work and leisure and proper kinds of economic activity.

In England the policing of vagrancy was under considerable debate during the 1820s. The law was reformed in 1824 to combat magisterial excesses following the Act of 1822.[40] Michael Roberts considers that despite such refinements the direction of law had already been sealed. As he writes, 'the move to enforce tighter and more uniform standards of external behaviour on urban populations was clearly under way'.[41] Such concerns about external behaviour appear in the colony as a direct result of what was considered to be the character of the population. It was not necessarily a case of what the lower orders were doing with public space, but who they were. The key to such anxiety on the part of magistrates and grand juries was what was understood as freedom. The convict population was becoming more tightly controlled, and freed convicts were also becoming subject to regulation. The 'vagrant' in the colonial environment was therefore closely tied to the 'convict'.

The third aspect of street policing in Sydney was that it was met with considerable resistance, which extended to direct assaults on constables. In 1812 Mary Barker stood outside the house of William Redmond, constable, and abused him.[42] In 1816 William Spears, constable, heard in Harrington Street a cry of murder and saw on the other side of the street a dispute between some seamen and a woman, but before he could interfere he was struck by a stone on the left cheek.[43] The term riot as description of an offence or an exact charge appears in 1820–21. There were references to mobs. William Thorn, constable, saw a mob of 200 people on the Rocks.[44] Mobs of people were seen in the vicinity of the King's Wharf. Thomas Kinchelly saw a mob attack a sailor there at three in the afternoon.[45] At six at night William Fellow saw a mob there and a fight began.[46]

Resistance to arrest was much more common in 1820–21 than it had ever been in earlier years for which cases remain. Jeremiah Monday was stopped near Sussex Street with a bundle by Thomas Barton, constable, and was asked what he had there and where he was going. 'He would not tell me but told me to ask my arse, he would not satisfy any of us kind of gentlemen and if he did satisfy anyone it should be our master.'[47] William Kellow arrested William Murphy for rioting 'in a most violent way he called me a blood sucking rascal and he stood in defiance of any damned rascals like us he said he was a freeman'.[48] Patrick Berry, when he was stopped by Samuel Boyer, said he was 'a free man'.[49] Freedom, then, was used by these people to defend themselves from constables who were looking for and policing a convict population.

In Quarter Sessions records there are cases involving assaults of constables and fighting in the streets. For 1825 alone there were several cases involving assault of constables. The Quarter Sessions records refer to constables 'challenging' people. Assault cases show what could happen when constables challenged groups of people. Thomas Welsh, constable, saw Thomas Sparkes, free, and two other men 'near the Emu Inn' one Saturday in November 1825. 'They made use of gross language and ran, I pursued him and found them in a skillern [skillion] on the Brickfield Hill.'[50] Sparkes struck him, the 'man of the place' called for a chopper and said he would chop Welsh's head off. Two other constables came and they managed to arrest Sparkes, but the others escaped.[51]

Constables began to appear themselves as defendants in assault cases, and attacks on them in the streets also increased. In August 1826 John McCooke, constable, saw two men, Smith and Parsons, fighting at the market and took them into custody. Smith told McCooke that he must either carry or drag him there; he then struck the constable and lay down in the privy, refusing to get up. A mob gathered and stones were thrown at the constable; then the mob rushed at him and he fell against the wheels of a cart, bleeding badly.[52] This was at two in the afternoon, unlike earlier cases of mob violence which were usually at night. Lying down in the street was used by Richard Nugent, also in August 1826, when he assaulted William Hamilton, constable.[53] There were four other assaults of constables heard in this session and one of these involved an attack on constables by a mob on a Saturday night between eleven and twelve.[54]

In October 1827 definite reasons were given by James Bryant for his assault of Jonathon David, constable. David gave evidence that at 6 p.m. a large mob had assembled in Pitt Street, and Bryant and another man were amusing them by play-acting. The constable laid hold of Bryant and ordered him to the barracks. Bryant said 'you bugger I am a free man' and struck the constable.[55]

This pattern of assaults continued. Assaults by constables were generally related to public houses and searches, but assaults on constables occurred also in the streets. Throughout this period it was common for a constable to attempt arrest, meet resistance, and then be attacked either by an individual or a mob. The attempted dispersal of 'assemblages' is also frequently reported by constables. There were five cases in January 1828 where assemblages were reported and constables attempted to deal with them. In one, William Hamilton, constable, confessed he was afraid to continue his duty because of the size of the mob.[56]

Such events had increased during this period. It is true the freed population in Sydney also increased and this resulted in the response of the grand juries. However, the juries saw the behaviour of a freed population as an irritation and sought its cause in cockfights or the activities of small vendors and spirit retailers. What happened in the policing of the streets of Sydney is quite clear—along with increased court appearances of people charged with drunkenness were increasing references to assemblages, to mobs. From a concern with policing convicts, the constables had become interested in a freed population, and that freed population in its own statements showed some signs of exercising its freedom.

House Searching

Sydney constables searched houses either on warrants obtained from the magistrate by the victim of a theft, or in the case of convicts by 'instructions' from a magistrate. They also initiated house searches themselves in which no mention of warrants or instructions were made. Constables were also active in quelling noise from disorderly houses, and this gave them free access to houses which they considered too noisy. Early in the period these warrants seem unimportant to constables or soldiers, but by the mid-1820s regular reference was made to the obtaining of warrants in theft cases. The numbers of searches reported in remaining records and the reasons given by constables to gain access are set out in Tables 21 and 22.

Table 21   Reasons given for house searches in cases appearing before Sydney magistrates' benches, 1810–21

Reasons for search	J.A.B. 1810–20	P.M.B. 1812	P.M.B. 1815-16	P.M.B. 1820–21
Information received, consequent search	5	8	1	16
By military	1			
Search for still	1			
Search warrant	1			1
Called to search	1	1	1	1
Search for convicts				1
Sent by magistrates to search	1	1	5	4
Disorderly house	2			2
Noisy house		3		1
Attempted to search				3
Total	12	13	7	29

The unimportance of warrants in 1810 is demonstrated by the case against Barbara Sutherland in August 1810. Elizabeth Cassidy gave evidence:

> I live at the Rocks, on Thursday evening I missed a great quantity of clothes out of my bedroom from a washing pan. The prisoner lives next door but one. I had reason to suspect her. The patrol came by at this time, I asked Marlborough the captain to search, he did I was with him. She was in the bed. We found nothing in the bedroom. We made her get up and went into the kitchen. The first thing I saw was a shift and a bed gown lying on a chair, they were mine . . .[57]

This patrol was military; no reference was made to obtaining permission or any knocking or request to enter. The absence of these elements was not mentioned by the Judge Advocate's Bench or the criminal court, which sentenced her to twelve months' hard labour in the Female Factory.[58]

Cases from late 1810 show the chief constable, Redman, participating in house searches himself. He reported searches 'in consequence of information received'.[59] No mention of a warrant was made. In the 1812 Police Magistrates' Bench records there was

Table 22 House searches by constables in cases appearing before the criminal courts, 1816–30

Type of search	1816	1817	1818	1819	1820	1821	1822	1823	1824	1825	1826	1827	1828	1829	1830	Total
Search warrant																
Sydney	2	1	2	1	1	4	3	3	1	3	4	2	1	7	6	41
Parramatta	1				2	4	2	1	1			1			1	13
Windsor			2	2	3	1	5		2	1		2			2	20
Liverpool		1					1	2	1	2	1	1		1		10
Other areas							1	1	1		2	2	3	1	2	12
Search on information																
Sydney	1	13*	5	2	2	9	11	9	5	2	6	1	4	8	7	85
Parramatta	1				1	1	9	1	1	1	1	1		1		17
Windsor					1	1	1	1							4	8
Liverpool		1	1					2		1		1	2		3	14
Other areas							2	2		2	2	6			6	16
Called for																
Sydney	1	2	2			3	2	1	1	1				5		17
Parramatta	1					1	1					1				5
Windsor		1	1				1	2			1					6
Liverpool						1	1	1		2		1				5
Other areas			1				1	1								2
Search on suspicion																
Sydney	1					1		1		1		1	2	2		8
Parramatta			1		1		2				1					5
Windsor							1				1		1	2		5
Liverpool					1		1				1		1		2	5
Other areas			1							1	1		1			3
By direction of magistrates																
Sydney		1	2	1	1	1		1					1			7
Parramatta		1	1	1	1											3
Windsor	1						1					1				3
Liverpool								1								1
Other areas			1				1									2
Total	8	21	18	6	13	26	46	27	13	17	20	21	16	28	33	313

also reference to constables initiating searches because of information given. House searches were closely related to the illegal selling or distillation of spirits. Four cases involve this search for spirits. In May Aaron Peckham, constable, 'in consequence of information received, he, accompanied by other persons, went to a house in Rush Cutting Bay'.[60] He found a keg in the house but its ownership was denied by the two residents, who claimed the keg belonged to soldiers. The two inhabitants of the house were not charged.[61]

It is not until the records of 1815–16 that we find constables referring to 'proceeding due to instructions', meaning they had obtained permission from a magistrate. In the case against Charles Wright and George New, William Donnelly, constable, was careful to note that, although he searched the house in the absence of the prisoners, he had permission from its owner.[62]

From this period on we find reference to 'the necessary instructions' in court cases and by 1820 there was a reference to obtaining a search warrant. Thomas Dunn in March 1821 reported, 'I received directions from the Principal Superintendent to search the house of the prisoner Hughes . . . on entering the house I told Hughes I had a warrant and proceeded to do so in company with William Thorn and James William, district constable'.[63] Dunn also added that he did not tell Hughes what he was searching for.[64] Constables still reported searching houses without warrants, usually in cases against convicts. Constables also reported opposition to their searches. In 1821 Francis Wild, constable, reported that he heard that James Gates, prisoner of the Crown, harboured a bushranger, 'and last night observed a man go to the prisoner's house, I attempted to enter the house when the prisoner slammed the door in my face and after a short time he opened the door and said I was welcome to search the house'.[65] Charles Linton, a constable of the prisoners' barracks, reported in January 1821 how he went to the house of Mrs Arkell in Pitt Street: 'I went to the door and enquired if Mrs. Storer was there but [she] was engaged I said I wanted to see the company she was with as well as her and he [Thomas Nickery] slammed the door in my face.'[66] Thomas Nickery lost his ticket-of-leave for such refusal to let a constable into a house.[67] In 1820 John Leary, constable, said he was prevented from searching a house, 'not having a search warrant'.[68]

Constables were extremely active in cases which involved persons selling spirits without a licence, and closely related to this was the policing of disorderly houses. In 1812 Samuel Champell, constable of District No. 5, heard noise emanating from a house, recording that 'it was not a proper hour of the night . . . examinant called and desired they should be quiet it was not a proper hour of the night to be making such a disturbance'.[69] In 1821 a William Kellow, constable, reported that Elizabeth Burne kept a very disorderly house and 'there is scarcely a night I am on duty but I am compelled to go there and quell some riot, I have often warned her to alter her conduct'.[70] She received a sentence of twelve months in the Female Factory.[71] The methods of reporting disorderly houses did not change throughout the period but the numbers of households described as disorderly steadily increased. In 1821 Thomas Dunn, chief constable, went to the house of Mr Walker on the Rocks in company with other constables:

> after I had entered the house I heard several voices in the inner room, I went into the room and found the prisoner James Moon, ticket of leave, Thomas Davidson, ticket of leave, Benjamin Darlington,

ticket of leave, and John Wilson, ticket of leave, sitting at a table playing cards, I took the cards and Cribbage now produced from them and took the whole of them into custody.[72]

For such an offence these men had their ticket-of-leave cancelled. The policing of disorderly houses automatically drew in free, freed and ticket-of-leave persons: no warrant was required and arrests for drunken behaviour could be made. Free persons refused to be arrested without a warrant as early as 1817. When James Lane, constable, was taking a disorderly woman into custody, 'we were interrupted by Archibald Wood who desired the woman not to go with me unless I had a warrant and she was a free person who had no right to be confined without one'.[73] Rejection of constables without a warrant, and abuse, became important factors in constables' activity after 1824 when the Quarter Sessions were established.

In these years tensions seem to centre on the streets rather than on house searches. Nevertheless, searches continued: they were a major means of obtaining property or evidence in theft cases, and appear regularly in court records. Constable surveillance of disorderly houses increased. In 1826 Thomas Sutland, conductor, gave evidence that he and other constables 'went to the house of Mrs. Waterhall as they knew it to be a house of ill-fame they proceeded to search of runaways and suspicious characters and found Thomas Turner and Henry Sutur in the yard—at which time Campbell had the two female prisoners in custody'.[74] These constables had gone to the house, according to their evidence, without hearing any unusual noises or seeing crowds about the streets. It was this kind of policing which we also find evident on the streets in the late 1820s. Constables initiated arrests according to their own suspicions.

Sydney was at the forefront of the development of new methods of policing. The convict system seems to have governed many aspects of the policing of the free population, despite the specific attention given to the development of new methods of surveillance for freed convicts. What made the man in the streets of Sydney worthy of suspicion was that he was an ex-convict, an idle, disorderly and useless character. There is a clear struggle in Sydney to define the limits of freedom. The constables, the grand jury and the magistrates seek to curtail the economic and social activity which free and freed persons attempt to make for themselves. They are resisted actively by persons claiming that they are 'free', meaning that they should not be treated as if they were convict. The latter refer to the legal system they expect should exist. Sydney presents a clear distinction between authority and its subjects: we can see two perspectives of law in the town. Country benches and their constables, however, were highly individual in their modes of policing. In them a distinction between authority and ordinary people begins to blur.

Parramatta

Policing methods in the country were diverse. This can be partly explained by the structure of English legal practice which, being dependent on local magistrates, automatically resulted in diversity of policing rather than uniformity. Local magistrates had considerable control in the way they chose to exercise the law.[75] This diversity was reflected in the establishment of the office of Justice of the Peace in early colonial New South Wales, whereby magistrates were given parochial powers and exercised these powers in various manners.[76]

In the New South Wales countryside this diversity was also apparent in the responsibilities given to local constables by magistrates, and in the diligence or lack of diligence with which the constables approached their work. These local constables had local interests and consequent 'styles' of policing which were vastly different. For Francis Rossi such local interests seriously affected the quality of policing; the country constables, he said in 1826, 'were mostly individuals so mixed up by connection with the inhabitants that from private interest receivers are safe and the actual thieves allowed to escape'.[77]

Rossi wished effectively to centralise policing of the mainland colony, and to establish adequate communication between magistrates so that wanted persons could be more effectively dealt with. Rossi's complaints were responded to quite readily by the Legislative Council and the governor in both 1826 and 1830. But the provision of an assistant and a clerk in 1830 was halted by the Colonial Office in London, which saw such a measure as unnecessary.[78] Consequently, because of the amount of time needed to deal with local duties, Rossi's attentions continued to be restricted to Sydney.[79]

If centralisation was not to come about bureaucratically, as Rossi wished, it was achieved in a minor way through the establishment of Quarter Sessions in 1824. There was considerable crossover in duties between magistrates' benches and Petty Sessions during Quarter Sessions. McLaughlin writes that the distinction between these separate responsibilities was never clear:

> the distinction between magistrates sitting as a mere Bench of Magistrates, or as they were commonly referred to, in Petty Sessions, and the same magistrate constituting a court of General or Quarter Sessions was, in practice, throughout the late 1820's not entirely clear, especially since 6 Geo. IV c 69 enabled certain powers of the Courts of Quarter Sessions to be exercised by one or more Justice of the Peace.[80]

McLaughlin suggests that local magistrates could effectively control both Quarter Sessions and Petty Sessions. As well as the opportunity for use of such power, there appears in court records a considerable interrelationship between the Justice of one area and the Justices of another in the hearing of Quarter Sessions cases. For instance, from 1824 to 1830 cases heard originally before the Parramatta Bench of Magistrates would be transferred to the Campbelltown or Liverpool Quarter Sessions. The reasons for such practices were considerations concerning the timing of sessions or relevance to a particular area, or it was considered that a conviction would be more likely if a case was heard in another area. Such practices produced a kind of cross-referencing between magistrates' benches and thus some uniformity in the country regions, making the magistrates' benches less parochial in their activities.

The country magistracy were criticised, not for policing methods but for the kinds of punishment they ordered. In April 1820 Macquarie sent out a circular requiring that they no longer transport offenders for minor offences:

> 1st: No convict or prisoner of the Crown is to be transported to Newcastle or elsewhere otherwise than by the sentences of the Criminal Court or by a Bench of Magistrates which must always consist

of two J.P.'s . . . the term of such transportation is on no account to be left open . . . for the governor's pleasure.

2nd: No magistrate is to grant any convict whatever to retire from assigned service unless on a well founded complaint of ill usage. No magistrate is to grant a ticket of leave.[81]

The magistrates had been interfering in, and modifying, the sentence of transportation. Quarrels during the Macquarie period particularly were to centre on this legal point of the status of convict and the right of the governor, as opposed to the magistrate, to intervene in this status. But the magistrates were, it appeared, uncertain who was convict and who was free. Rossi's concern was to make the laws of vagrancy relevant to a *newly freed* population because its specific character, comprised of ex-convicts, required this. The magistrates, according to the Legislative Council's report in 1828, had great difficulty in distinguishing between convict and free and in determining the appropriate modes of punishment and trial.

> The magistrates were here placed in circumstances of much risk and hardship to which no parallel existed in England, because of the great multitudes of crimes and misdemeanours brought under their cognizance through the vicious character of the population. Their summary jurisdiction being applicable to one part of the community and to none besides became in its administration a subject of much perplexity. In discriminating between the persons who were amenable to that jurisdiction and those who were within the ordinary jurisdiction of the law, the most careful and experienced judgement was liable to err. Cut off from the possibility of mutual consultation in consequence of the thinly peopled state of the country, few of them enjoyed the advantage of being able to rectify their own first impressions by reference to the opinions of others.[82]

Both this comment and Rossi's in 1826 and 1830 were directly related to the character of the population. Throughout the long struggles of the Parramatta magistracy and the appointment of the first stipendiary magistrate to that bench in 1826, the mechanisms of arrest, suspicion, hearing and committal were continuing.

Parramatta has been recognised as the most economically stable area in the colony.[83] By contrast the Parramatta magistracy played a far from stable role in the political life of the colony. Samuel Marsden refused to sit as a magistrate after Macquarie attempted to appoint emancipists to the bench. The consequent struggle between Marsden and Macquarie has been described[84] but the struggle between the Parramatta magistrates and the governor also continued. The most crucial argument between the governor and the established powers on the bench was the controversy surrounding the appointment of Henry Grattan Douglass to the Parramatta magistracy by Brisbane. The use of the bench in political quarrels has been described by C. H. Currey in his discussion of the James Ring case and the Ann Rumsby case.[85] In the first, Marsden was to be brought before the bench in 1822 for allowing his convict servant to work for himself. In the second, Douglass was to appear before the bench so that it could inquire into the nature of his relations with his female servant.

For legal historians, and indeed for legal debate of the day[86] such quarrels raised specific questions of the legality of appointments to the bench, the relationship of the governor to legal institutions, and the rights of convicts under the law. It is doubtful if any of these issues were of concern to the Parramatta magistrates.

By 1824 animosity towards Douglass was such that a former judge of New South Wales, Barron Field, wrote from England to Samuel Marsden:

> In pursuance of the enclosed letters Captain King and I dined slept and breakfasted at Wilberforces. Captain King told him the whole story of Ann Rumsby in his accurate manner and I read aloud and commented on your last letter to Mr. Wilberforce on Mr. Douglass. The instance of his tyranny in torturing that convict to confess his crime had great effect and has produced such an impression on John Smith the Chairman of the Australian Company that he says if Douglass gets the place he will bring it before Parliament.[87]

It is necessary to see this letter in relation to the struggles over land and the establishment of the Executive Council. The contents of Marsden's letter about the Rumsby case and torture resulted in considerable discussion in England. In New South Wales the Council set up an inquiry into illegal punishments and Brisbane felt it necessary to order that any criminal proceedings against a magistrate for a sentence passed before the New South Wales Act, 4 Geo. IV c. 96, should be stayed.[88] He considered that the magistrates' position was unclear before this Act.

In 1825 the Legislative Council examined the records of all benches which were available. The inquiry discovered that torture or corporal punishment to obtain confession had been adopted on principle by the Parramatta bench as early as 1815. It also discovered that 'since the institution of regular courts [the practice] has been discontinued altogether'.[89] Douglass was not solely responsible, but the incidence of torture increased after his appointment. He was, however, always accompanied by one of the other magistrates who was jointly responsible for the sentence.[90]

They discovered similar practices in other country benches. Although flogging did not necessarily relate to confession, it appeared to be used to obtain information as to the whereabouts of stolen property.[91] Such practices are comparable to seventeenth-century England where Langbein finds torture used 'to identify accomplices and forestall future sedition'.[92] Langbein documents a decline in the use of torture in England with a decline in treason.[93] Its appearance in New South Wales must be related to assumptions of criminality and guilt in a convict population.

Throughout the period magistrates experienced great difficulty discerning who was to be tried and in what manner. The records of the benches, particularly the Parramatta bench, seem to work to a system which the magistrates themselves desired rather than according to the legal requirements for passing a case on to a higher court.

The evidence for the activity of the Parramatta bench comes primarily from lists made for other purposes than the bench's own use. The Bigge Inquiry provides the records for the years 1815–17, from which Bigge deduced that Marsden was a harsh magistrate.[94] After 1820 it was required that every magistrates' bench provide returns for the Colonial Secretary of cases tried in its courts. There remain the records of the years 1822, 1824 and 1826. For 1822 there are records for March–May and June–August; for 1824, July–December; and for 1826, January–March.

These do not appear to be the same as the 'books of records' included in the report of the Legislative Council's inquiry into alleged illegal punishments. Of them Council writes:

In explanation the Council consider it proper to state that the cases they have consulted have been partly taken from the books of records, partly from the Warrants of Execution preserved in the Gaol or Convict Barracks. The books of records of latter years are not entirely to be relied on as they appear to have been made up from the minutes of the clerk after the cases had occurred that it is probably that many errors may be found in them.[95]

The Council does not explain how they could ascertain unreliability or how the books of records could 'appear to be made up'. This statement, though, has been adopted by historians.[96] The records we have which were supplied to the Colonial Secretary do not seem inconsistent in terms of the numbers of convict and free persons arrested in those years. It would have been difficult for a clerk to reproduce such a pattern. The books of records reproduced in the Legislative Council's report and compared by them to warrants of execution show that some cases were left out of the record books and this is possibly where they established a discrepancy. Nevertheless there survive 311 records of street arrests for the years 1815–16, 1822, 1824, and 1826, contained in the Colonial Secretary's records as well as the early Bigge records. Combined with the records of the Quarter Sessions, these are sufficient to establish policing methods in the Parramatta area. The charges and the numbers arrested and brought before the magistrates' benches are set out in Table 23.

The obvious difference between the Sydney bench records and the Parramatta records is the presence in Parramatta of the Sabbath offences: 'Driving a cart on Sunday', 'Breach of the Sabbath' and 'Drunkenness on Sunday' all appear as offences in 1815–17. Sunday offences account for eight street arrests in 1822 records, two in 1824 and six in 1826. The Sabbath offences were introduced by Macquarie in May 1810. Persons walking about the town during divine service were to be committed to gaol if they could not give satisfactory account of themselves.[97] In November 1810 it was ordered that ticket-of-leave men must be mustered on Sunday and marched to church.[98] In the Police Regulations of 1 January 1811 it was ordered that constables apprehend any persons 'profaning the Sabbath'.[99] None of these regulations appear to have resulted in offences in Sydney, but notice was taken of them in Parramatta.

Policing in Parramatta focused on the areas of drunkenness, disorderliness and vagrancy. Parramatta was similar to Sydney in the policing of women. Despite the existence of the Parramatta Female Factory, it was mainly free women who were arrested in the town. These arrests were not as sexually based as arrests in Sydney. The term prostitute appears only twice in the records of the period and this is in the offence 'notorious prostitute', applied to only two women. The policing of free women centred on the offences of riot, riotous conduct, disorderliness and drunkenness. Convict women assigned to their husbands were also arrested on these charges. In 1822 Ann Kelly, a convict who lived off the store assigned to her husband, was charged with being 'an incorrigible vagabond' and was consequently ordered into the Female Factory for twelve months.[100] In 1822 also, Ann Birkin, a convict assigned to her husband, was 'found dead drunk in the streets of Parramatta'; she was admonished and discharged to her husband.[101] The distinction between convict and free was made by the sentencing magistrate rather than the arresting constable. Mary Hutchinson, free, was charged with drunken disorderly conduct for which she was to be exposed in the stocks or pay five

Table 23 Titles of offences in street arrests, Parramatta Bench of Magistrates, 1815–26

Title of offence	1815–17		1822 June–August						1824 September–December						1826 March					
	Male	Female	Male			Female			Male			Female			Male			Female		
			F	T/L	B	F	T/L	B	F	T/L	B	F	T/L	B	F	T/L	B	F	T/L	B
Riot	7	1																		
Riotous conduct	2	6			1	1														
Riot and drunkenness	2	2	3		11	2		1					4				1	2		
Assault and riot	1																			
Disorderly	3	6																		
Drunk and disorderly	1	1	6	1	8	7		3			4	7	9				5	6		
Drunk and vagrant	1	1																		
Vagrant	2	1																		
Drunk	4	7			2						1									
Incorrigible vagrant	1																			
Bad characters		1																		
Absconded husband		1																		
Notorious prostitute		1																		
Found in streets intoxicated	1											1								
Drunk on Sunday	3				7												1			
Breach of Sabbath	1																			
Driving cart on Sunday	2				1		1													
In Parramatta without pass	8										1						1			
Riding in cart	4																			
Abuse of constable	1																			

Table 23 (continued)

Title of offence	1815–17		1822 June–August						1824 September–December						1826 March					
	Male	Female	Male			Female			Male			Female			Male			Female		
			F	T/L	B	F	T/L	B	F	T/L	B	F	T/L	B	F	T/L	B	F	T/L	B
Assault of constable	2									3	3	3								
Resisting constable	2																			
Constable drunk and assaulted	1																			
Away from lodgings					16	1														
Away from barrack					4												2			
Absent from gang					5															
No pass					14															
Drunk after hours				5			1				1									
Intoxication late hours					3			1												
Late hours					2	1					3									
Drunk lodgings					2															
Nuisance in streets					1															
Away from employer, intoxicated					1															
Incorrigible vagabond								1												
Drunk constable					1															
Gambling in street					1															
Driving furiously			1																	
Making escape from new factory and attempt to stab constable						1														
False certificate					1															
Incorrigible character					1	1														

Table 23 (*continued*)

Title of offence	1815–17		1822 June-August						1824 September-December						1826 March			
	Male	Female	Male			Female			Male			Female			Male			Female
			F	T/L	B	F	T/L	B	F	T/L	B	F	T/L	B	F	T/L	B	F
Leaving cart on road				1														
Insolent to constable					4													
Fighting in street				2	2													
Attempted robbery					2													
Drunk without pass											1							
Violent breach of peace												1						
Away from gang, improper hours											2							
In streets in gross state of intoxication												1						
Out of house, improper hours													2					
Having a fish on person											1							
Asleep in cart through street										1	1							
Drunk on Sabbath without pass											1							
Rioting on the road										1	2							
Drunk in town										1								
Taken up with her mistress's clothes at improper hours of the night and improper intercourse													1					
Taken up in street, runaway																1		
Gross insolence constable																		
Drunk and riot in town late at night and assault of female																		1
Repeated drunkenness in town																		1
Pair trousers could not account for																	2	

Table 23 (continued)

Title of offence	1815–17		1822 June-August						1824 September-December						1826 March			
	Male	Female	Male			Female			Male			Female			Male			Female
			F	T/L	B	F	T/L	B	F	T/L	B	F	T/L	B	F	T/L	B	F
Eloping from barracks																	2	
Runaway from factory														2				
Continued drunkenness																		3
Gross intoxication in town																1		
Absent and tippling																	1	
Shawl could not account for																		1
Riot Sunday																	2	
Drunk, lying in street														1			3	
Gross intoxication on Sunday																	1	2
Improperly at large																	2	
Drunk, riot, assault on constable												1			1	1		
Insolent conduct on Sabbath															2			
Going up and down the country—no residence, no authority to be at large												1						
Abuse of constable, common vagrant												1			1			
Out of hours, insolent												1			1		1	

F = free; T/L = ticket-of-leave; B = bond.

shillings. She was exposed.[102] For the arresting constable, however, the status of the woman was either not apparent or not important.

The offence of vagrancy appears in Parramatta much earlier than Sydney and is applied to women and men. In 1815–17 two men and one woman were listed as vagrant. The most common offence was 'drunken conduct in the town' which applied to both men and women, convict or free.

While Sydney constables took possession of unattended animals, Parramatta constables arrested people for careless driving,[103] for riding in their carts in the street, and for being asleep in their carts while they were going through the streets.[104] Night policing of men and women seems much more common in Parramatta than in Sydney. Beginning in 1824, 'late hours' are taken into account in arrests. Male convicts were arrested for being out of their lodgings or being found out late at night.

As with the later Sydney benches, it is difficult to discover how property theft was ascertained, but there are some street arrests which indicate that Parramatta constables were as attentive to appearance as Sydney constables. George Hibbard was arrested in 1826 for carrying a shawl he could not account for.[105] Samuel Hughes and Joseph Piggot were charged with having 'a fish on their person': Hughes was discharged and Piggot received a hundred lashes, he 'being a most incorrigible character'.[106]

Though the policing of women remains constant, constables move from policing a male convict population to policing a free or freed male population for offences such as drunkenness and riot. In 1826 arrests of free men were almost equal to arrests of convict men and this is a considerable increase in the percentage of arrests from 1824 records. This is similar to Sydney and parallels Rossi's attempts to cope with a newly freed population. The Parramatta magistrates seemed wary of freed persons as early as 1820. In his comments to the Bigge Inquiry Samuel Marsden gave negative reports on prospects for ex-convicts.[107] On 1 January 1820 a proclamation from the courthouse at Parramatta suggested serious discrepancies between the attitudes of these magistrates and their chief constable, Francis Oakes.

Mr. Macarthur states that Mr. Oakes had of late affected great scrupulousness in taking up free men. He had stated in a public court room that in his opinion it would be unlawful to apprehend free men by the orders of the magistrate and that he should not be justified in obeying them.[108]

The conflict between Oakes and the magistrate Macarthur had developed over Oakes' support of Macquarie.[109] Oakes was accused of encouraging complaints by the gaoler, Beale, and planning to share with the gaoler a fine imposed on the keeper of the tollgates for selling spirits without a licence. Oakes said he regarded Macarthur's charge against him as 'calculated to create a feeling decidedly inimical to the governor'.[110]

When we consider the arrest patterns evident in the records of the Police Magistrates' Bench, its seems from the early appearance of vagrancy and related offences that Parramatta constables were as attentive to free persons as Sydney constables and there seems no reluctance to arrest free persons, at least for street offences. Local political quarrels bore little relationship to the reality of street policing. At the same time assault of constables appears to be rare in Parramatta Magistrates' Bench records.

The records of the criminal courts and Quarter Sessions provide us with detailed information on the methods of policing and the responses of the population to them. The criminal court records contain several statements by constables on the nature of their work. Five constables give accounts of direct arrests. These are Francis Oakes, Benjamin Ratty, William Potter, John Thorn and James Cook. Oakes in 1818 reported to the bench how he found a cart with a bullock in George Street. When John Clue, a free man, came by, Oakes asked him why his cart did not have a name on it and received 'no satisfactory answer'.[111] He noted that the bullock was branded with the Orphan School brand and, 'knowing Clue to be a notorious character, he having been reported two months ago as a runaway from Liverpool Gaol', Oakes took him in charge.[112] In another case in 1817 Oakes worked according to his knowledge of the defendant's character. He reported in September of that year that he had stopped Benjamin Metcalfe who was walking down the street, searched him and found stolen property on his person.[113] John Thorn, the chief constable who took Oakes' position, seemed to work on a similar principle to Oakes. In 1823 he reported that on a Wednesday at 7 p.m. he saw a man pass on the street; he stopped him to know who he was and then perceived something rolled up in his jacket. He took it out and found part of an iron axle tree.[114]

William Potter, district constable, described himself in two cases in 1821 as 'patrolling the town'.[115] In one case he and the constable Riley fell in with six men whom they challenged. In the other, a month before, he described himself as patrolling the town with Burke and other constables 'at 11 p.m. when they saw a number of people around Jones' beer house'. He reported that 'on seeing the constables a number made their escape'.[116]

The activities of constables in groups is more apparent in bushranging cases. The Mounted Police were particularly attentive to lone travellers. William Ashton was arrested in June 1829 by a patrol for having nothing to show for his liberty.[117] As early as 1822 in two reports of robberies constables went for arms and assistance before proceeding along the road.[118] This group policing is possibly the reason for the low numbers of court appearances for assault on constables. Unlike Sydney, Parramatta experiences no escalation of assaults on constables. Parramatta records do not evince the same kind of outright hostility evident in those of Sydney. In one example, Peter Rush reported in 1822 his assault by John Burrell, free. Burrell was galloping violently through the streets and went through the toll bar. Rush followed him to ascertain the number of the cart, and then returned to the courthouse. Burrell sought him out and assaulted him.[119] In another case John Thorn, chief constable, attempted to break up a fight between a soldier and his brother and was consequently assaulted.[120] Neither of these cases were judged in the criminal court: Brown's was returned to the magistrates, and Burrell was released from prosecution.

Detection and Warrants

Opposition to constables arose in their main area of activity: this was the searching of houses and the detection of stolen property, receivers and thieves. The jurisdiction of country constables extended to the activities of the local road gangs. These groups were seen by the grand jury of the Parramatta Quarter Sessions as a threat to travellers. The jury recommended in 1826 that the gangs be kept in portable prisons and that their rations be increased so they would have no desire to steal.[121] Richard Cross, constable at Longbottom, reported in 1822 how he, hearing of a robbery on the road between Long-bottom and Williams' Halfway House, went to muster Fords' road gang to see if the defendants were among them.[122] The searching of the huts of government servants required no warrant because the inhabitants were not free. Regular searches were carried out in cases of highway robbery: the convicts were mustered and the victim of the robbery told to identify the defendant.

The suspicion of road gangs extended to small settlers. In 1824 John Thorn 'in conse-quence of suspicions entertained proceeded to the house of Joseph Bridges to search for stolen property'.[123] Constables were successful in their search at this house and were not opposed. Other Quarter Sessions depositions suggest that constables regularly searched the houses of small settlers: they often found nothing and were frequently opposed. In December 1824 three constables went to the house of Richard Newham where they accosted a servant of Newham's for a government shirt he wore. The constables left the house and Richard Newham came after them 'putting himself in a boxing attitude . . . he demanded why deponent insulted his man'.[124] Constable Hugh Taylor recorded William Wells' reaction: 'he showed him his staff and with a pistol in his hand told the prisoner he would shoot him if he struck deponent'.[125]

The Parramatta constables had weapons in order to pursue bushrangers; the Newham case suggests they carried them always, even in their duties about the town. Benjamin Ratty in 1826 recorded how he was accidentally shot by William Wells: he

> proceeded in company with Chief Constable Thorn and William Wells on the night of the 23rd pursuant of runaways said to be near the tollgate deponent volunteered to take a pillow tied up and a handkerchief and proceed along the road while the others waited in the bush.[126]

A bushranger stopped Ratty and was consequently shot. Wells and Thorn then mistook Ratty for a bushranger and shot him. 'Mr. Thorn came up and was going to strike deponent with a cutlass, deponent cried out "don't strike me, Mr. Thorn".'[127] The house of Richard Newham was the scene of a shooting incident also. In 1829 Joseph Kerr, constable, went to the door of the house and asked for suspicious persons; he asked how the household could account for them. Kerr left the doorway 'walked up to the window and immediately shot deponent'.[128]

The Parramatta constables' arms no doubt made them formidable. James Bailey described his reaction to the appearance of five constables in his house: 'when there are five constables inside with firearms it is time to look out for one's own preservation'.[129]

The shooting of Benjamin Ratty by his fellow constables resulted from his partici-pation in a stakeout for the purpose of capturing bushrangers. This kind of detection was not uncommon and Parramatta constables showed great ingenuity in their methods of arresting receivers or thieves.

In January 1826 Edward White and Samuel Horn, constable, went to the house of Margaret Haslam, publican, on the Sydney road. White, who was not a constable, went inside and intimated he wished to buy a watch. Margaret Haslam 'said I can sell you two. Deponent said perhaps they are prigged [stolen]. She smiled and said maybe they are and said I can give you a fob if I thought I could trust you.' White went out and informed Samuel Horn, who obtained a search warrant and searched the house and the person of Margaret Haslam. The watch was found and the Quarter Sessions sentenced Margaret Haslam to a fine of £100 and to be imprisoned until it was paid.[130]

The case against George Yeates demonstrates the behaviour of Parramatta constables when on patrol. John Thorn, chief constable, was in February 1826 patrolling the town of Parramatta with two other constables. Thorn heard a fiddle in Payton's public house, 'knowing that one of the men there was a prisoner some time ago in Parramatta [George Yeates] he directed the constables to demand who he was. Constable Walker did so, the prisoner told him to ask who he was, Walker told him he was a prisoner.' The confrontation resulted in a fight with 'seventy people around the house who aided the prisoners'.[131] Yeates was a free man and yet as a former prisoner excited suspicion. This case as well as the case involving setting up arrests in 1826 resulted from circumstances where the constables worked around the distinction between convict and free: the constables did not have a warrant but engineered a situation whereby they would be certain of arrest.

In 1821 a violent conflict occurred over the issue of warrants and freedom. William Potter on 23 April at 1 p.m. was patrolling with Wells. Someone told them of a 'great quantity of people leaving the house of James Kirton'. Potter went to the house and stationed one constable at the back door, himself and another constable at the windows. Potter looked in and saw one man he knew to be a prisoner, so he knocked at the door and told Kirton to send the man out or let the constables in. Kirton said 'no constable should come there, they were free persons'. Potter related, 'he called the constables all the thieves and robbers he could, how dare they come to rob him, he was a free man'. Potter said loudly he would send next door for Sherwin, the chief constable. The door opened at the mention of Sherwin's name and Kirton asked to see a warrant. Potter said his staff was his warrant, whereupon Kirton made a blow at Potter with an axe. The constables searched the house, finding government clothing and runaway convicts. Frederick Garling, solicitor for Kirton, questioned Potter as to the cause of the search: did he know if the convicts were allowed to sleep out of the barracks? Potter did not. Garling asked William Wells, 'How long have you been a constable?' Wells answered six months. Garling asked, 'Have you not had orders to watch Kirton's house?' Wells replied yes.[132]

Kirton's house was watched by constables for suspicious activity. Kirton, like Newham and Bridges, was suspected of illegal activity. When Richard Edwards' woman, Susan Macdonald, passed a bad banknote at the shop of the chief constable, Francis Oakes, in 1818, Samuel Marsden wrote to Wylde concerning forgery in the town:

> some persons a little time back stole one of the bedpans belonging to the hospital, soon . . . dumps were circulated made out of pewter. We searched a suspected house and found the bedpan melted down with a man who was reported to be a maker of bad money.[133]

The presence of so many informants and the consequent reputations which people developed, combined with magisterial suspicion of ex-convicts, meant that Parramatta policing was based on the policing of suspected houses as well as the streets.

It was searching or approaching houses that produced most of the violent assaults on constables. John Brown, constable, in 1820 heard one morning at 2 or 3 a.m. the cry of 'murder' in Hunter Street, Parramatta. He discovered James Smith beating his wife Jemina. Brown demanded peace and attempted to make an arrest. 'Smith said he was a free man . . . he said he would not go unless he was dragged.'[134] The clerk of the police office was also present. Brown and another constable, Lynch, asked if they 'would be justified in taking all people out of the house, deponent said certainly'.[135] Brown's approach in this case was more subtle than the approach of Potter in Kirton's case, yet they both received the same answer from the inhabitants of the house. Brown hesitated before his arrest. Potter did not.

The constable armed had considerable authority. Either in a legitimate search or in a search with ulterior personal motives, the constables could obtain virtually whatever they wanted through brute force. That this possibility was open to all constables meant that the authority of constables in the Parramatta region was in practice unlimited, although superficially it was within legal bounds, in that requests for warrants were made.

The court records for the Parramatta region give us only vague notions of the locations of suspected houses. The constable of the small township of Prospect, cases from which were heard at the Parramatta bench, was rigorous in his completion of the survey for the 1828 census. John Roley, district constable of Prospect, listed thirty-eight residents and householders of the town. He wrote of Mary Cleaver, 'Tenant. Free by servitude, this woman permits drinking in her house and is a general harbourer of bushrangers.' Of William Beames he wrote, 'Householder, free by servitude allows drinking in his house having no licence.' Of William Haggerly, 'Householder, free by servitude residing on Government land, this man also allows drinking in his house having no licence.'[136] These remarks became part of the official documentation for the census. Samuel James, district constable of Castle Hill, wrote of John Connor, a landholder and free by servitude, 'I beg leave to state Mr. George Sutter [has] laid a complaint to me respecting one John Connor . . . for keeping a Disorderly house. I have not been able to detect them but I believe it to be true.'[137]

Constables in the Parramatta region acted either on complaint or because they believed something to be true and consequently searched or watched the houses of suspected persons.

These activities occurred despite the fact that Parramatta constables lived among the community they policed. Their arrest rates were not inordinately high but the arrests they did make were of free persons whom they suspected and of convicts who were not meant to be out at certain hours or were seen to be carrying property. Constables were set apart from the rest of the Parramatta population: with their guns, staffs and waddies they resembled soldiers.

These constables, working in groups and also involved in the pursuit of bushrangers, did not work closely with the local magistrates. This is different from Sydney where Rossi was Police Magistrate and this difference possibly results from Oakes' disagreement with the Parramatta magistrates in 1820. The constables did not oppose the magistrates but they seem to have been autonomous; they relied on the directions of the extremely active chief constables, rather than the orders of the magistrates.

Parramatta consequently had consistent tight policing. There seemed to be little room for the unorthodox, and the police definitely held power in any dispute. The Parramatta populace, like that of Sydney, argued freedom and demanded to see a warrant; generally the constables took note of such arguments. They worked carefully to obtain an arrest; they claimed to have warrants, even if they had not.

Policing in Parramatta, as in Sydney, was influenced by considerations of public space. In Parramatta there was also intensive policing of places of leisure, the public houses, but there seemed to be less regard by constables for freed persons and a level of harassment by constables that did not appear in Sydney. Parramatta constables seemed more aggressive in their policing tactics. The resistance shown to them came from persons protecting their houses from the constables' intervention, rather than street fighting and abuse.

Liverpool

The town of Liverpool was established in 1811 by Macquarie. He hoped to grant land in the surrounding area to a number of emancipists in the expectation that they would clear land and cultivate it.[138] In 1832 James Raymond described walking into the town of Liverpool. He passed through 'a number of small grants ... Irish town, indicated by many bark huts and some houses'.[139] He advised that after crossing the bridge at Cabramatta Creek the traveller would:

> enter the town of Liverpool; the hospital is a large building and the church a neat structure ... we reach the middle of Liverpool, there are many neat cottages but none particularly worthy of notice except that of Mr. Moore J.P. The town has a straggling appearance but is, upon the whole, very clean and pleasant ... there are several inns in the town, the Union kept by Forbes is a very commodious one ...[140]

The records that survive from the Liverpool Bench of Magistrates are very sparse: one year, 1824, for February to June; another, 1826, for February to June. The Liverpool Quarter Sessions records, however, are reasonably complete from 1824 to 1828. The Quarter Sessions heard cases from Bankstown, Cabramatta, Minto, Upper Minto, Airds, Appin, Holsworthy, Cooke and Bringelly. In 1828 the Quarter Sessions for that area were transferred to Campbelltown. Both the Quarter Sessions records and the Supreme Court records contain cases originating from smaller benches for which no records remain. William Howe, for instance, heard cases from Bringelly at his house Glenlee from 1820. Appin cases were heard by William Broughton; Robert Lowe heard cases at Bringelly and Minto. Campbelltown cases were heard by Thomas Reddall and Richard Brooks. All of these magistrates would occasionally preside together at Liverpool or Campbelltown or smaller centres. The Liverpool magistrates were Henry Colden Antill, Thomas Moore and Charles Throsby. The area over which all of these magistrates presided had a population in 1825 of 4500.

Liverpool bench records for 1824 and 1826 are in the form of depositions and so a great deal of information is given concerning time and circumstances of arrest. These cases reveal that policing in the Liverpool region was markedly different to either Sydney or Parramatta. Arrests made in the streets by constables concentrated on servants in 1826 and less so in 1824. Constable arrest patterns do not move from a convict to a freed population. Also the Liverpool constables were most affected by the emergence of bush-ranging in the late 1820s. It was this offence that increased their involvement in house searches. There were two chief constables in the 1820s: William Ikin, appointed in 1821, and his successor Frederick Meredith in 1826. The attitudes of these two men largely shaped Liverpool policing.

On 19 February 1824 the Liverpool bench questioned William Ikin, 'to know whether he had direct or indirect interest arising from the sale of spirits or beer at the Ship Inn, Liverpool'. He assured the bench and was willing to assert on oath that he had no interest other than the receipts of rent—he rented the house to George Browne on licence.[141] The concern of the Liverpool magistrates arose from the main focus of Ikin's police activity: the policing of public houses in competition with George Browne's. A week before this questioning by the bench, the Parramatta constables Benjamin Ratty and William Wells explained how they had arrested Lowe, the publican. They reported they took some coppers to Ikin and he gave them a bottle, they proceeded to the house of Lowe and he gave them some beer which they took back to Ikin. The bottle was presented in the court as evidence of an illegal transaction. However, the Liverpool magistrates, Moore, Throsby and Antill, considered the case to be insufficiently made out and so dismissed it.[142]

The magistrates quite clearly did not agree with the chief constable's interpretation of the evidence. However, barely a month later, Ikin, McNamara and Attwood, constables, used tactics similar to the Lowe case on Lewis Solomon, publican. Ikin said:

> Thursday evening last McNamara and James Attwood in company with Joseph Watts, brought to deponent's house half a pint of rum they said was purchased at Solomon's giving him two dumps and a shilling. Deponent being hard of the belief that after numerous assertions made by Lewis Solomon that he would never venture to sell spirits, deponent sent in George Greenhill and Alexander Maraghan giving them one dump and one penny to purchase spirits.[143]

Ikin was careful to state that he was 'hard of the belief' that Solomon would not sell spirits, so he implied he did not expect Solomon to be caught out. Ikin is saying here he did not plant the spirits on Solomon. In court, under Solomon's questioning, an elaborate plan by the constables was revealed. Watts was disguised as a traveller, carrying a bundle filled with grass. He was asked by the constables to go to Solomon's, so disguised. In the case Solomon suggested that Watts brought the rum with him.[144] The bench also dismissed this case as insubstantial. During the next two months there were two cases brought by Ikin concerned with the consumption of spirits. In May he charged John Quigley with going into the house of George Browne and calling for spirits which he had no money to pay for.[145] In June, Ikin, Thomas White and Bishop Toft, constables, raided the house of Solomon because they believed him to be involved in suspicious activities. Solomon threatened the constables and so was bound to keep the peace by the magistrates.[146] On 28 June 1824 Solomon brought a case against McNamara, constable, for harassing his household. At between eleven and twelve o'clock at night McNamara demanded entrance to Solomon's house and said that because he was a constable, 'he had a right to enter the house, he had been called out of bed and informed there was improper persons concealed in the house'.[147]

The bench censured the constable for his conduct, 'as it does not come under the jurisdiction of the peace officer to disturb the inhabitants at such improper hours'. The constable was ordered to pay the costs of the two summons that were carried out.[148] In February 1826 William Ikin, chief constable, was charged himself with selling spirituous liquor without a licence. The charge was brought by the publicans Klensendorffe and Solomon. Ikin was fined £100.[149] From that time on Ikin is no longer referred to as 'chief constable' but as 'publican'. Frederick Meredith replaced him.

A major part of the time of the Liverpool bench was taken up with disputes between publicans. Ikin quite obviously used his powers as a constable to protect his position as retailer of spirits. His other arrests evident in the bench records were closely associated with alcohol. He arrested persons who were intoxicated in the streets.[150] In June 1824 he found James Williams, convict, 'lurking about'.[151] He also arrested convict servants he found drinking in a public house.[152] The records of the criminal courts present further accounts of Ikin's policing. In 1824 he wrote a letter to the Judge Advocate explaining his role in the case against Daniel McLucas for theft of wool from the magistrate Howe: 'On 21 January 1824 I was returning from Sydney to Liverpool and fell in with Daniel McLucas. I took the opportunity of questioning him respecting Mr. Howe's wool. I obtained from him only that Lewis and Ferguson were at the stealing of same.'[153]

Under Ikin's authority, policing in Liverpool combined these aspects of detection with a focus on alcohol. For instance, George Greenhill arrested a man lying drunk on the ground,[154] and William Crisp arrested Richard Barnes for allowing convict servants to drink.[155] There were also arrests of suspicious characters, McNamara arresting a man he had seen advertised in the Sydney *Gazette*[156] and Frederick Meredith apprehending a man he suspected to be a bushranger.[157] In June James Noland was arrested because he was suspected of being involved with Thomas Madden, described by the court as a 'robber, a bushranger'.[158]

The policing of publicans suspected of selling spirits without a licence carried over to the policing of the free population. Suspicion was intrinsic to the arrests which constables made. Richard Hicks, constable, saw Peter Geage walking very fast and had him arrested.[159] Warrants were obtained for farms where stolen property was suspected to be held.[160] It was in this atmosphere that the next chief constable, Frederick Meredith, took office. On 29 May 1824 Meredith exhibited a rigour which was to become the style of his policing. He apprehended the driver of a cart for driving on Sunday. The magistrates dismissed the case because Meredith could not produce the number of the cart.[161] This is the only record of Sabbath policing in Liverpool which survives, and its lack of success suggests that Liverpool was dissimilar to Parramatta.

Meredith's style is evident in that attempted Sabbath policing, he was not involved in the liquor trade and arrests for that activity declined dramatically after he became chief constable in 1826. Arrests of runaways and of convicts out after hours began to appear in the record books. On 4 February 1826 Thomas Bennet was forwarded to Sydney by warrant on suspicion of being a bushranger.[162] Government servants were arrested for drinking in public houses, for being out after hours, and for being intoxicated and riotous.[163] In March Charles Somerfield was arrested for being in Liverpool without a pass.[164]

On 3 March 1826 William Meredith, son of Frederick, made his appearance in Liverpool as a 'Sydney constable'.[165] His method of policing was in some ways an extension of his father's activities but it also closely resembled the pattern of policing present in Sydney during the early 1820s. He made five arrests in one week of servants found in public houses, of men who would not work, of convicts out after hours, of prisoners coming out of Mr Forbes' tap room.[166] His activities in the criminal court were of the same nature. He paid particular attention to suspicious characters.[167] In the criminal court he was classified as a road constable and his employment at that task changed the structure and emphasis of Liverpool policing.

Liverpool constables in the late 1820s concentrated on bushranging and related offences. The word 'suspicion' appears commonly as cause of investigations. Robert Wellings, constable, heard of a highway robbery and suspected the Bridge Road gang; he had them mustered and searched for stolen property.[168] In 1830 William Crisp, district constable for Lower Minto, suspected Samuel Shaw and consequently arrested him on suspicion.[169] The arrests made in the Liverpool region were no more numerous than in other areas, but as in Sydney the style of policing indicates that numbers of people were approached and challenged by constables in pursuit of bushrangers.

The relationship of the constables to the Bench of Magistrates was different to both Sydney and Parramatta. In those towns arrests by constables seem to have been accepted by the magistrate or police magistrate and very few cases were dismissed as irregular or illegal. Oakes' conflict with the Parramatta magistrates rested on the point that he refused to arrest free persons—that he did not arrest *enough* people—rather than that his methods were undesirable. Sydney constables were assured of a response by magistrates and few cases were dismissed.

By contrast, in the lower courts Liverpool constables seemed autonomous but were not seen by the magistrates to be entirely correct in their arrests. The Liverpool bench was far more stable than the Parramatta bench. No political quarrels disrupted the benches in the area. The involvement of the Liverpool magistrates, however, went beyond judgment of a case. As early as 1824 they ordered constables to check the workloads of convicts brought forward for neglect.[170] The content of their covering letters to the Quarter Sessions and Supreme Court suggests their involvement in cases.

In 1826 four letters were sent to the Parramatta bench from the Liverpool magistrates. Two concerned the case of Joshua Suttleby, who was charged with stealing a spade, and Michael Ryan, who was charged with receiving stolen property. The first letter outlined the case and said that Suttleby would be tried before the bench and Ryan, because he was free, would be sent to the Quarter Sessions. A postscript added that the magistrate Howe had realised that there was only one magistrate on the bench and that since the cases were so intertwined Suttleby should be tried at the Quarter Sessions along with Ryan. The second note was quickly scribbled during the bench hearings:

> Suttleby was detected whilst on the way to Ryan's house with the stolen articles and was taken from the treadmill (where he was sent for six weeks) to be tried for the other robbery of the spade . . . It seems and *we know* that Michael Ryan has been a *long time* receiver general to Suttleby (a horrid villain). Mr. Howe requests that Mr. Garling would have the goodness to communicate these circumstances privately (if not publicly) to the Chairman of the Court as mere matter of information for the truth of which Mr. Howe is responsible.[171]

The third letter apologised for the first two. The magistrate Howe wrote:

> I beg leave to enclose you the two *irregular* memoranda written in great haste to make such use of as you may deem proper. You may see that my only object is public good. Suttleby is a most awful thief at last detected through old practice in greater matters and Michael Ryan is a receiver that will take all that comes his way.[172]

The Parramatta bench sentenced Suttleby to 100 lashes.[173]

The fourth letter concerned the case of John Murphy. Howe wrote on 4 April 1826 to Garling, Clerk of the Peace:

> John Murphy is a most turbulent and dangerous character at the head of a party of bigoted Irish men and a terror to the neighbourhood through his great influence with this set of men and has been committed to the Sessions for the last meetings at Liverpool for dangerous assaults and got off by pleading guilty and buying out the claimants who had not been (unfavourably) bound to prosecute. In fact the parties were afraid to prosecute. I trust that this third time John Murphy may be made a severe example of *Pro Bono publico*.[174]

In the case against Eliza Campbell and others for the murder of John Brackfield, the main responsibility for the case rested with Charles Throsby. He was suspicious of the story of servants who claimed bushrangers had murdered their master, and ordered chief constable Ikin to interfere in a coroner's inquest and arrest all of the servants.[175] Throsby wrote to Saxe Bannister concerning the case against Chittendon and Jones, receivers of property stolen after the murder:

> In my last I wrote my letter on the subject of ticket of leave men and regret to find no steps taken respecting them to the present mode of permitting that class of men to roam without control which together with the want of more strict regulations respecting public houses is the cause of a long list of bushrangers and a melancholy calendar of culprits for trial.[176]

It was 'this class of men', ticket-of-leave holders and also small settlers, which were the objects of suspicion by magistrates. Liverpool constables were under greater surveillance themselves by magistrates. Their work was subject to scrutiny: Ikin was asked what were his links with public houses; Meredith was told his evidence was insufficient for a Sunday offence. Such control did not mean that the magistrates favoured the local populace over the constables, but there was greater involvement by the magistrates in criminal cases.

The magistrate Howe became directly associated in a case which involved theft of wool from his premises. He stated before the Liverpool bench in 1824, 'deponent suspected Daniel McLucas, bearing a bad character, in consequence rode to McLucas' house and met McLucas in a cart with Andrew Ferguson, Ferguson was a notorious character and I suspected him'.[177] There began a large investigation into the case, which the magistrates admitted was difficult; then Ferguson said he would make a confession. They wrote, 'we consented to hear what Ferguson had to say, Ferguson was the most correct—we cannot but be of the opinion that had he refused his admission of the fact we should not have had sufficient to send the parties (with the prospect of their being committed) before a criminal court'.[178]

The magistrate Howe worked according to his understandings of character, while the Liverpool bench were certain of guilt before they could prove it. They were not content with providing the prerequisites for a bill of indictment but wished to be assured of conviction. In 1827 one case suggests that they considered which court would most likely provide the conviction they wanted. In the case of John Lucas, charged with sending a challenge to a shopkeeper, Shadford, the Liverpool magistrates wrote to McLeay:

> concerning the conduct of Lucas we wish the utmost punishment we can impose. We request you will favour us by requiring the acting Attorney General to give opinion if we are not justified in sending Lucas to be sent before the Supreme Court for promoting and encouraging riot and disorder in the town after the unwarranted insult to Mr. Shadford in the execution of his duty.[179]

The Liverpool and district magistrates, like the Parramatta magistrates in their use of torture, saw the later courts as something to be successfully used rather than as impartial tribunals. It is not surprising that such attitudes were found also in constables who assumed guilt in their arrest of suspicious characters.

In the case against James Pretty in 1831, Peter Callahan, a constable of Kemps Creek, reported how he went with a party to a house in Irish Town which was suspected, searched it and then went to search the Bridge party.[180] Callahan mentions a general search of houses in the area rather than a warrant to search a particular house. Though this search resulted from the requirements of the Bushranging Act, such attitudes were evident earlier. In 1822 William Hill, a district constable of Bringelly, said he was out in quest of some person who had robbed a cart and he had a strong suspicion of a person named Henry McAllister who rented a piece of ground. Hill did not mention possessing a warrant. When there was no-one in McAllister's hut he waited for McAllister. He found none of the property from the cart but found a turkey for which he arrested McAllister.[181] In 1825 William Ikin searched the house of Mrs Moore which he knew a suspect frequented.[182]

Despite the ability of Liverpool constables to act according to their suspicions, they did not receive as much opposition from the population as Parramatta constables. Few persons questioned the lack of a warrant. One case where that did happen was against Daniel McLucas and his family. James Niel, a servant to Oxley, had reason to believe a stolen cart was on the premises of Daniel McLucas. Henry Bradley, a constable, was sent with a search warrant. McLucas said to him, 'no bloody whore's bastard should have the cart for it was in the shed touch it at your peril. "What are you" he asked the deponent "a prisoner or a free man." Deponent said it was of no consequence, he had a warrant.'[183] A fight followed and the constable left the farm. In 1826 Frederick Meredith was called to the Sign of the Hope Inn to prevent a fight. George Bedford, being riotous, was admonished by Meredith. Bedford replied, 'it was no business of his as he was free and deponent ought to mind his duty'.[184] In May 1826 Andrew Lumm, constable at Bringelly, went to the house of Patrick Callahan and a man came in with a bundle. The man, James Butterworth, said to Lumm, 'I am a free man' and showed him a certificate and requested to be allowed to stay all night.[185]

Small settlers were most affected by the range of offences associated with bushrangers and were most subject to the methods of constables to prove a case. Their houses were searched and their property taken to the courts to be examined. Frederick Meredith, chief constable, reported in March 1826 how he suspected Jonathon Madden of harbouring a prisoner who had absconded from the courthouse. He watched the house for three days. 'On Monday evening having secreted himself with John Strutt, ordinary constable, deponent saw a man crawling by the side of the fence when he got to the gate he threw some stones which deponent took to be a signal.'[186] Meredith took the man and Madden into custody. His watching the house for three days was reminiscent of Ikin's elaborate plans for raiding public houses.

Liverpool street arrests were proportionally far lower than in Parramatta, but there is some evidence of riot and street disturbance in other records. In December 1825 constable Robert Smith reported an 'assemblage of persons making a disturbance' in Campbelltown.[187] In 1824 on 26 December the Reverend Thomas Reddall J.P. reported profanation of the Sabbath by William Winn and John Russ. It occurred in the paddock in front of Reddall's house where the defendants were singing. He ordered them into custody. Winn said he would not go without a warrant. In the dispute that followed Reddall was struck.[188] Street disturbances in Liverpool do not appear but this is not necessarily due to the vigilance of constables or their being armed. In 1827 two constables were charged with neglect of duty. Richard Weavers was charged with allowing a prisoner to escape. He had been sent to Parramatta with four prisoners. One of them, Sarah Milligan, returned to Frederick Meredith to say that 'they were not any further advanced than Colligan's public house'. Weavers was charged with allowing her to escape,[189] and imprisoned for six calendar months. Bishop Toft was sent in 1827 with a warrant to apprehend Michael Cooke. Toft was found lying drunk in a cart and the prisoner was found walking around the town.[190]

These two constables received six months in the house of correction.[191] Their sentences were not for negligence in duty about the town but for specific tasks they were given, which is perhaps why they were apprehended. Street policing in Liverpool only seriously began with the work of William Meredith. Liverpool constables concentrated on the policing of serious cases. They did not work through terror or through immediate confrontation but through assumption. In the case of Ikin this gave them some opportunity for corruption. Liverpool constables and constables of the surrounding areas worked in the area of suspicion and then settled on their peers, the ticket-of-leave holders or small free settlers. Their use of warrants was erratic and 'freedom' was unimportant in dealing with them. It was the offence of bushranging that consolidated the methods of these constables and gave them the ability to conduct searches in pursuit of runaways or stolen property. Bushranging shaped the later policing of the Merediths and constables in the surrounding areas.

In a sense Liverpool was in the foreground of the policing of bushranging, and the inconsistencies that it produced. Policing intensified in the late 1820s and the Liverpool road was regarded as particularly dangerous for highway robberies. The kind of policing that developed in Liverpool was a result of the presence of small settlers in the area and the dangers they were thought to represent. It was now a town where the convict population was deemed as important as the receiver and harbourer of convicts. It was from such fears that profit could be made and power exercised.

Windsor

There are two remaining sources for the activities of the Windsor Bench of Magistrates. These are the records of fines imposed on free persons from 1811 to 1818 given to the Bigge Inquiry,[192] which are set out in Table 24, and the letter book of the Windsor Police Magistrates for July to December 1828.[193] These records by no means give full account of the activities of the constables of Windsor and surrounding areas. Those of the free population who were not fined are not listed and only a few of the convict population appear in the records for 1828.

Table 24 Fines imposed on free persons by the Windsor Bench of Magistrates, 1811–19

Title of offence	1811	1812	1813	1814	1815	1816	1817	1818	1819
Riot	1								1
Opposing the civil power		3							
Working on the Sabbath		1		37	8	1		2	1
Opposing man on road		1							
Opposing constable		1							
Breach of the peace		1	1						
Travelling on Sabbath			2	8				4	2
Profanation of Sabbath			1						
Cart with no board							1		
Assault of constable					1				1
Drunk on Sabbath					1				
Obstructing constable								1	
Abuse of constable								1	
Total	1	7	4	45	10	1	1	8	5

The nature of the surviving records limits this study to the policing of the free population. The Quarter Sessions records and the criminal court records are very detailed and so provide some means of piecing together the activities of constables in relation to free persons.

The Windsor Quarter Sessions were instituted in 1824 to hear cases originating in the area of Greenhills, including the town of Windsor, the areas of Upper Nelson, Meehan, Castlereagh, Kurry Jong, Evan including the town of Castlereagh, Richmond, Bathurst and Phillip including the town of Wilberforce. The Supreme Court and criminal court records contain records from all of the benches in this area.

In 1820 John Howe, chief constable of Windsor, gave evidence to Bigge that there were six constables in 1812 in Windsor and fifteen in 1820.[194] They acted as watchmen in the town and one was stationed near Howe's house in case accidents happened or assistance was wanted.[195] In 1830 there were thirty-four constables listed for Windsor and surrounding areas, twenty-seven for the town itself.[196]

In 1820 Howe said that the constables were free and possessed property and were settlers or old inhabitants.[197] Bigge added that upon inquiry he found only one constable held a ticket-of-leave and it was thought at the time of his appointment that he was free, he having been recommended by the inhabitants of Windsor for that situation.[198] In 1830 a list of constables for the Windsor region includes nine constables as holding a ticket-of-leave, two as convicts and one as holding a 'ticket of exemption'.[199] The latter is unexplained but the term 'exemption' is related to government work. Though this appears in 1830 it is possible the magistrate Bell initiated the ticket himself, thus continuing a practice criticised by the colonial administration.

The population policed by these constables consisted of large numbers of small farmers, mainly emancipists. The region had been settled much longer than Liverpool and small farmers were moving further up the Hawkesbury River in search of suitable ground for settling or leasing. These small farms concentrated on wheat and corn and the accompanying fattening of pigs.

Richard Cartwright gave evidence before Bigge concerning the nature of the Windsor population. Asked if the several classes of inhabitants had shown a disposition to attend religious worship on Sundays, he said, 'from the backwardness of the free people who in general have been convicts and from their association with men of bad character they have acquired the habit of profaning the Sabbath'. He was asked which was the most respectable class: the emancipated convict living on thirty acres of land, the more opulent of that class, or the free settlers from England. He answered that the free settlers from England were the most morally respectable and the native-born were also moral; as to the other two classes, 'there are but few exceptions in favour of their morality'. He thought these two classes were much addicted to swearing and 'use the most horrid kind of oaths'.[200]

The Reverend Richard Cartwright was a magistrate on the Windsor bench from 1811 to 1818 and the kinds of cases which survive for that bench suggest that it did police the Sabbath and swearing, particularly swearing in court. Sixty-eight Sabbath offences appear in the records of fines for 1810–20. These were for travelling on the Sabbath, working on the Sabbath, selling goods during divine service and profanation of the Sabbath. In May 1814 there were fourteen people charged with working on the Sabbath. In December fifteen people were charged with that offence.[201] From October 1816 the fines are listed alongside information on how this sum was disposed of. The fines for travelling or working on the Sabbath usually went in part to informants. For instance in 1818 on 26 September David Horton was fined five shillings for travelling on the Sabbath and that money went to an informer.[202] These offences, then, cannot be directly traced to constables; some part of the local population was involved.

The Windsor fines are unlike the activities of the benches in Sydney and Parramatta. An early offence is listed as 'harbouring a runaway', for which the fine was £5.[203] Trespass appears in these early years, though there were no proper fences or boundaries in the Windsor area even in the late 1820s.[204]

These records of fines suggest that the Windsor bench operated as a court where complaints could easily be made of neighbours. The role which the constables played in such disputes is unclear. They may have served summons for the defendant to appear before the bench or they may have made arrests themselves on information. In 1818 Elijah Lane was charged with employing a bushranger, for which he was fined £10. Immediately below this entry is another charge listed for Elijah Lane and that is 'abusing a constable'. For this he was to be fined the sum of five shillings.[205] This suggests the constable was directly involved in apprehending Lane and the bushranger.

In Windsor the records of the bench show offences relating to the number of carts, the killing of animals without a licence, and the distilling of spirits, so the court apparently policed the economic life of the town. The acceptance of such offences and the concentration on the Sabbath led to dissatisfaction with the legal structure, hence there was swearing in court which the magistrates saw as an offence also. However, the magistrates recognised poverty and were prepared to waive fines if the defendant was a poor person. Seven persons were allowed to leave the court without paying a fine, it being considered that their poverty warranted such compassion.[206]

Table 25   Reasons for appearances of constables before the Windsor Quarter Sessions, November 1824–January 1830

Reason	1824	1825	1826	1827	1828	1829	1830	Total
Search convict huts	1							1
Search warrant		6	14	2	9	2	2	35
Street arrest		2	4	1	4	1	1	13
Abuse of constable in public house		2						2
Drunk in street		1						1
Assault of constable		2	4	2		4	1	13
House searched on information to constables		2	2	11	6		2	23
Breach of peace			1					1
Galloping through street			1					1
Riot			2					2
Call for constable			1	2				3
Disorderly house				1				1
Cart search				1				1
Arrest in public house				1				1
Mounted Police arrest						1		1
Total	1	15	29	21	19	8	6	99

Windsor inhabitants were likely to appear before the bench on more than one occasion. Joseph Onus, for instance, appeared in August 1812 for assault, in November 1813 for assault, in June 1814 for swearing in court, in June 1815 for drunkenness and in October 1829 for assault.[207] To appear five times is somewhat excessive but most people appeared twice or three times before the bench. From such records we can see the stability of the population in the Windsor region. These small settlers did not move out of the area and became involved in similar offences.

It is apparent from information in the list of fines that the Windsor inhabitants were quite clearly involved in the process of law. The major involvement of informants listed as receiving part of the fines was in cases against travelling on Sunday or driving a cart without a board attached showing their name. These offences do not harm anyone but rewards were taken for them; they may well have been some kind of revenge against a neighbour. The Quarter Sessions certainly evince a familiarity with the bench that does not seem present in either Parramatta or Liverpool. This familiarity extended to the activity of constables. The number of cases that involved constables and the reasons for constables' appearance in the courts is shown in Table 25. Further discussion of individual cases follows.

There are thirty-five cases involving the use of a warrant in the Quarter Sessions records between 1824 and 1830. Very few of these searches were initiated by constables, but constables were called upon. The thefts involved were rural in nature and the property stolen was wheat, pigs or farm tools. The inhabitants attempted quite often to detect the thieves themselves. Mrs Kezia Roberts reported in 1825 how she attempted to detect stolen pigs belonging to her daughter: when she was informed by her daughter that pigs were missing,

> deponent immediately got up and discovered some of the paling in the stye had been pulled out and the gate of deponents yard pulled off the hinges. Deponent immediately made an alarm and sent her man Richard Butler to Thomas Welsh the district constable and others of her men endeavoured to track the pigs.[208]

In 1826 Henry Baldwin gave evidence concerning the loss of his pigs:

> knowing that Matthew Brown and the prisoner that resides with him sell more spirits than any other licensed house in the district and finding his men frequently drunk . . . he obtained a search warrant to search the place where the two prisoners live.[209]

Complainants would obtain a search warrant from the magistrate and take it to a constable who would then execute it.

The search warrant was very formal in the Windsor area and it was used despite the complainant having seen the stolen property him or herself. In January 1827 John Blackmore was arrested after a warrant had been obtained to search his house. Thomas Silk said he had seen a cask that had been stolen from him at the house of Blackmore. George James, constable, recommended that he procure a warrant; Silk did, returned with it and gave it to James.[210] The search could then begin.

Good use was made of the warrant in the Windsor region and there are consequently few cases of assault over freedom and the warrant in the Quarter Sessions records. In December 1827 when Edward Merrick, constable, tracked stolen wheat to the house of Thomas Douglass, he said he did so 'because he felt it was his duty'. Douglass asked him for a warrant and Merrick said he did not have one. Douglass 'said he would soon drive them off and fetched an axe', but Merrick added that Douglass used no violence. The person on whose behalf Merrick was acting, William Madgwick, went to obtain a warrant.[211]

Along with careful obtaining of warrants, tracking was much used in the Windsor area. In 1827 William Douglass, chief constable, was searching for pigs when he followed footprints, 'one of a very small another of a very large foot'.[212] The use of tracking meant that emphasis was placed on detection rather than suspicion, and in this case the complainants had no idea who was responsible. Most cases involving theft in the Windsor Quarter Sessions were between persons of equal status so suspicion did not settle on ticket-of-leave holders or small emancipist farmers because such persons constituted the population of the Windsor region.

There were only three cases in the Windsor Quarter Sessions records where constables apprehended thieves without a complainant accompanying them. In 1824 John Hunt, town constable, said that in consequence of an attempt being made to steal some of Mr Harpur's sheep that he, Hunt, 'had occasion to search the huts of the clearing party accompanied by two older constables'.[213] In May 1826 Thomas Hill, constable, received information that Joseph Crawford 'had found two shifts'.[214] He consequently searched the hut of Crawford, a free servant.[215] In May 1828 Benjamin Hughes had everyone in Smiths' public house searched for stolen property.[216]

The policing of bushranging moved beyond the great care taken by constables and complainants in establishing guilt. In bushranging cases constables were sent 'in search of robbers', and farms, huts of government servants and of small settlers were searched. In 1828 Edward White received directions from the chief constable to go in search of robbers with a man who said he had been stopped on the Richmond road. They 'searched several places in the neighbourhood' and went into the house of Carney on the Richmond road where two of the robbers were recognised.[217]

Except for these cases of search and indications that these searches were of numbers of households rather than one, there is no evidence of Windsor constables being opposed in the searches reported for bushranging cases.

Although harbouring had been a practice since 1810 in Windsor, as the records for the fines of free persons show, there are few cases of harbouring brought in the Quarter Sessions or the criminal courts. Those that are brought involve approvers and informants rather than constables initiating the arrest. In 1820 Patrick Keegan of the Richmond road party gave evidence against Patrick Hand, Catherine Hatch and Thomas Baker, all free, for being involved in harbouring him and receiving government property. In her defence Catherine Hatch said that she did now know he was a bushranger but thought he was a traveller.[218] She was convicted for harbouring.

In January 1828 a conviction against Richard Kelly, farmer, for harbouring, was quashed because of irregularity.[219] The case was originally brought in November 1827 when the constable Constantine Molloy had gone to the farm of Richard Kelly with three Mounted Police. They found Hugh Thompson, a runaway from No. 2 Iron Gang. Thompson gave evidence himself in the case and said he had met Kelly in gaol where Thompson was recovering from an illness and Kelly was serving a sentence. He asked Kelly if he had a 'thronged'[220] harvest and Kelly said he had. Thompson offered his services and Kelly said he would pay him the same wages as a free man.[221] Thompson's was the only evidence in this case and it was insufficient to convict Kelly which is why his appeal was successful. Kelly could quite easily prove that he thought Thompson was free, as he employed him on the farm.

The Mounted Police were involved in this case, and this was one of their few appearances before the bench to give evidence of their activities. In October 1828 the magistrate and Superintendent of Police, Archibald Bell, wrote to Alexander McLeay, Colonial Secretary, that he found the corporal of the Mounted Police difficult to work with. He described the activities of Moriaraty, the corporal:

> Moriaraty and the town constables on one occasion having prisoners in custody called at a private dwelling after dark, the man of the house accommodated the whole with refreshment and lodging, the thieves contrived to purloin from the possession of the keepers part of the stolen property which was to have been brought against them the next day. Owing to this fact Moriaraty threatened the inmates, presented a loaded pistol, was outrageous to the people, threatened to handcuff their government servants to the stump iron to drag him to Windsor gaol, the Parties complained to me at my residence. I admonished Moriaraty and the business terminated without confusion and without intimating [sic] the public mind.[222]

He reported that Moriaraty was involved with a female in a public house and was unseemly to the police officers who were called; he acted counter to Bell's instructions and treated Bell with disdain.[223]

Bell was cautious in his treatment of Moriaraty because of his concern for 'the public mind'; his interest in the stability of Windsor may well have prevented criminal cases being heard against Mounted Police or constables. The public reaction to constables in Windsor throughout the period, however, was not as quiet as the response to house searches. Where the Windsor constables were assaulted and opposed was in the streets of Windsor or the smaller towns around it.

In March 1825 James Freeman was charged with attempting to rescue a prisoner. The constable John Williams pursued a prisoner who escaped from him and James Freeman came out of his house calling the constable a rogue and throwing a brickbat at him.[224] In 1829 Robert Grundy attempted to take the staff of Samuel Blackman, constable; he said, 'he would take the staff from any bloody constable on the watch'.[225] In December 1826 Richard Watts assaulted George James, constable, saying, 'you old bugger you ought to have been hung years ago and may you be the first man that is hung and I'll stand Jack Ketch [hangman] for you'.[226] In December 1824 Thomas Donahue seized constable John Hunt in the street and called him a 'bloody hangman, a bloody Orangeman and a bloody constable'.[227] Outright hostility to constables was also expressed in criminal cases. In 1823 Henry Fleming threw a glass of rum in Thomas Welsh's face, saying 'there you bugger'; asked why he did it, Fleming told Welsh to go away, 'he was a bloody trap, he had nothing to do with him'.[228]

This abuse of constables and outright aggression towards them is apparent throughout the period and does not increase due to policing of bushranging or seem linked to the execution of new laws. The abuse and the obvious reliance on constables for search warrants and detection of stolen property seem contradictory, but may well have been part of a propensity for dispute apparent in the Windsor area. In 1829 and 1830 the use of search warrants by constables decreases but assault and hostility levels do not increase.

The nature of violence towards constables in Windsor does not stem from any particular conflict such as freedom or the warrant; rather it stems from constables initiating policing activity themselves instead of remaining the servants of the magistrates or the populace. But constables were called for in the most violent and aggressive activity in the period, the riot.

In 1822 a letter from the Windsor courthouse to the Attorney-General stated:

> The disorderly and outrageous conduct of some of the young men in the neighbourhood of Windsor, especially the Kables who have become a terror to the peaceable inhabitants have rendered it incumbent on the bench to make the present representation .. it would appear that under the erroneous notion of being born free, they are subject to no control or legal obligation and with these false and dangerous opinions they set at defiance all the constituted authorities—assaulting wantonly and maliciously peace officers and treating the magistracy with sovereign contempt both in public and private capacities.[229]

The magistrates added that the one case they sent to the October sessions 'fell far short of the many cases of an atrocious nature which have from time to time been exhibited'.[230]

There were five criminal cases involving the Kables and riot or assault of constables, and two cases before the Quarter Sessions. There were three other cases of riot in the Quarter Sessions records.

The Windsor magistrates were correct when they stated that the Kables had no respect for constable or magistrate. In 1821 George Kable was in a crowd of people in Windsor when the magistrate Mileham came and ordered the Kables home. George Kable refused, saying to Mileham, 'no he was as free as he was'; he later told Mileham to go home himself, 'for a good fuck would kill the old fellow'.[231] The crowd had formed for the purpose of watching Kable fight and fights were the reason for all crowd assemblages in Windsor. A boxing match at any time of the day or night gave the 'young natives' reason to assemble in such numbers.

By July 1822 the Kables opposed constables they met. Charles Kable told Thomas Wood, town constable, that he should go to Kable's house as he was 'a starve gutted bugger'; Kable said he (Kable) had supported most of the watch.[232] He added that the magistrates were as bad as Wood 'for making such a bugger a constable'.[233] In June Thomas Newton, constable, heard Kable say of him 'here comes a Windsor pig, a friend of yours'.[234] In September 1822 a huge crowd gathered behind John and Charles Kable who were waving their hats and challenging anyone to fight.[235] One of the inhabitants of the town requested Howe, chief constable, to call in the military. He did not think it serious enough.[236]

In 1824 John Kable assaulted constables in the streets of Windsor. He was speaking in infamous language when the constables attempted to calm him. He asked constable O'Neal if he wanted to fight, saying, 'I have an arm like a tree and in menacing language he wished there was a bloody good meeting he would fight till his head was off'.[237] In 1828 John Kable found the sport he wanted. William Salmon, a private in the 57th Regiment, said that on the night of 12 December at George Smith's public house, 'some of the company were jumping' and an observation was made that Sergeant Meloney, who was present, might jump further than any of the company.[238] John Kable said, 'I lay you a wager I can kick the hat off your head first kick.'[239] He challenged the military to fight and struck William Salmon. John Connor, town constable, was present but considered it prudent to let Kable remain in the public house as he would not be taken without a warrant.[240]

In 1826 the town constables of Windsor went to Pitt Town because it was rumoured a fight would take place. It was to be between Edward Hobbs and Joseph Smith the younger, who were later arrested for fighting a pitched battle.[241] William Douglass, district constable, said 'he never saw so many persons collected before at Pitt Town'.[242] Thomas Nixon and Joseph Hobbs began to fight and Griffith Parry, constable, attempted to stop them. Thomas Nixon told him, 'you go away and be buggered I will fight, I don't give a damn what you can do'.[243]

The willingness of young men to fight for entertainment is central to the examination of law in Windsor. The Windsor magistrates wrote to Frederick Garling, clerk of the peace, during the 1825 Kable case:

> under ordinary circumstances we certainly would have considered it only necessary to have commit-ted him [Kable] to the Quarter Sessions but reflecting on the possible consequences which might arise out of the feelings entertained by the generality of the young men in this neighbourhood, and who constitute the juries, to support one another in cases of this nature deeming unhappily these wanton acts of prowess rather in a meritorious than criminal light we thought therefore that the ends of justice and the public peace would be best served by sending him before the Supreme Court.[244]

Saxe Bannister wished the case to be heard before the Quarter Sessions.[245] The case was not heard because there was no prosecution, the witnesses being at places as diverse as Moreton Bay and Hunter River.[246]

These young natives with scant respect for magistrate or constable sat on the jury of the Windsor Quarter Sessions. What they represented in their attitudes and in their role as jurors was an important juncture in the relationship of the law to convict and free in the Windsor region. In Parramatta and in Sydney there were battles being fought over freedom and the rights of free or freed persons in the streets and in their houses. The rejection by the native youths of Windsor of constable interference in their form of enter-tainment, however violent, was couched in that same language of warrants and freedom. 'I am as free as you' says Kable to Mileham, at once a rejection and a statement, perhaps unwitting, of rights.

That support for Kable existed in the jury shows that Quarter Sessions juries were a threat to the old structure of magisterial authority. These magistrates reacted by playing an active role in transferring cases, hoping to move cases to the criminal courts and writing to fellow magistrates to explain the character of a defendant.

That such a challenge could occur in Windsor is undoubtedly because of the nature of the area. Small emancipist farmers who sought to detect stolen property themselves and then call in a constable provided the background for a very formal mechanical view of law. This was unlike Liverpool or Parramatta where constables pursued their own interests or sought to exercise their own authority.

The Cowpastures and Other Areas

In January 1817 Macquarie made the proclamation:

> that no persons whatsoever excepting the civil and military officers of the governor and the families of Mr. McArthur and Mr. Davidston holding sheep farms within the said cowpastures, themselves, or their shepherds or servants shall with dogs or otherwise under the pretext of hunting the kangaroo or looking for stray cattle or another other cause or business or pretence whatsoever shall cross the river Nepean or pass or travel within the lands and country westwards or southwards of the river Nepean unless on a pass or certificate under the hand of the governor or his secretary shall have been obtained.[247]

The reason for such a regulation was stated in a letter to Earl Bathurst, Secretary of State for the Colonies, from Macquarie in April 1817:

> I am sorry to be compelled to report to Your Lordship that the Wild cattle belonging to the Crown are very greatly reduced in Numbers, and I do not believe there is above one fourth now remaining of the Wild Herds I saw myself in that part of the colony in the year 1810; this great reduction has arisen from two causes, the first of which is the long and continued droughts with which the colony was visited for the four years preceding 1816 which proved most fatal to the Flockes and Herds throughout the colony and from which immense numbers of the wild Cattle perished; the second cause of their now reduced state is to be Ascribed to the Constant Depredations upon them by all the settlers and their servants, inhabiting the Banks of the Nepean for at least the distance of thirty miles along that River.[248]

He continued that repeated orders had been issued 'with a view of preventing those disgraceful practices, and Constables and Military Parties have been frequently sent to the Cowpastures'.[249] He said that despite these orders the depredations continued and in consultation with Judge Advocate Wylde he issued a proclamation declaring the stealing of wild cattle to be a felony.

In December 1817 he wrote that 'several persons have been apprehended in the very Act either of killing the old wild cattle or carrying off their calves. Some of the persons have been tried by the criminal Courts and some of them have been Capitally Punished'.[250] He planned to move the wild cattle across the Blue Mountains, 'which would free the Country of the Banditti of Bush Rangers (runaway convicts) and other idle persons who now subsist in the woods by these Depredations'.[251]

In the construction of this offence Macquarie sought both to protect the cattle and to limit the activity of the settlers and servants who crossed over the Nepean River to hunt. This was a further restriction on the movement of the population which had begun in the streets of Sydney.

To cross the Nepean, before or after the order by Macquarie, was to become suspected of hunting cattle. The policing of the Cowpastures included constables and informers. In September 1816 John Lowe, Joseph James, Charles Pickering and Patrick McGinty were charged with cattle theft. The informant was Joseph Broadbent, who said:

> I reside at the Punch Bowl ten miles from Sydney either on Friday 4 or Saturday 5 having been in Sydney I met the prisoner Charles Pickering in Hunter Street in conversation he informed me that he had provided lead, gunpowder, tea, sugar, tobacco, salt and asked me if I would be ready to go with him to the Cowpastures . . . on Monday 17 he called on me at my house . . . and asked me if I was

ready to go with him, being unwell I told him I could not. He afterwards I understand had some conversation with my man Joseph Aitkens, who thereupon came to me and asked permission to go with Pickering.[252]

Joseph Aitkens and his wife Ann were also informants. The story is continued in the evidence of John Reed, private of the 46th Regiment:

I am a member of the party which for some time past has been stationed at the Cowpastures and during my stay there have visited the government slaughter house, . . . Patrick Mitchell, who resides at the Slaughter House asked me to accompany him a mile distant he said he was going to kill kangaroos we met with Joseph Broadbent, Joseph Aitkens and Charles Pickering, spoke to them, rum was produced, a week later I saw the men at the slaughter house.[253]

In a search the meat had been found at Broadbent's house by two constables, John Russell and Thomas Dunn. Broadbent consequently informed, Aitkens informed and the soldier implicated both of them. As the punishment for cattle theft was death, the imperative to inform was intense.

By 1817, after Macquarie's order, the charge was no longer cattle theft but 'crossing the Cowpastures contrary to government orders'. Joseph Hodges was charged after being arrested by Joseph Scott, district constable. The case reads, that 'The prisoner accounts for being over the river in consequence to see a friend, he knew not it was contrary to general orders on that head he having been only 8 months in the colony.'[254] In 1818 the overseer of Macarthur, Andrew Murray, took a party of servants across the Cowpastures after receiving information from Aborigines that bushrangers had taken beef. They tracked the men and saw a fire where they demanded the men surrender; both were runaway convicts.[255] By 1817 the Cowpastures had their own constables and cases appeared before the Sydney, Liverpool, Bringelly and Parramatta benches. Groups of servants, however, also crossed the river in search of persons reported as stealing and killing cattle. Constables went from the Cowpastures to search houses for stolen beef.

The accounts in cases suggest that crossing to the Cowpastures to kill cattle was a common custom among servants and small settlers. This offence has a parallel with bushranging and in a sense prefigured the practices which were to develop in policing that offence. The search of the houses of small settlers, the pursuit and tracking of groups of men, runaways as well as small settlers, and the likelihood of the death sentence also appeared in bushranging cases. But this cattle theft involved habits which had developed among the population. By cutting off access to the Cowpastures, Macquarie cut off valuable food sources; he also made a strong encroachment on the free movement of persons about the colony.

The Cowpastures offence was established by Macquarie much as the activity surrounding bushranging was established as a criminal offence under the Bushranging Act. In this sense it heralded the suspicion that was to surround small settlers in the later charges of aiding bushrangers.

The policing grew up in the major towns of the Cumberland region, Sydney, Parramatta, Windsor and Liverpool, and it was not necessarily related to direct application of English law. This legislation concerning the Cowpastures and the Bushranging Act were specifically colonial developments by which the freed population became suspected, searched and questioned.

The outlying benches and the smaller country benches in essence policed convicts: constables were involved in the management of convict offences, being sent to collect recalcitrant convicts and to return them to their employers after punishment.

Two benches which diverged from this role of country constables were Newcastle and Bathurst. In the former penal settlement of Newcastle constables were intensely active in street policing and management of convicts involved in mining, brickmaking and town work.

James Calvert, the chief constable, was diligent in pursuit of his work. Alongside Isaac Elliot, superintendent of convicts, he reported arrests and searches of houses. Isaac Elliot in January 1824 appeared before the magistrate Henry Gillman, and said:

> I was ordered this morning to search some suspected houses for articles which had been stolen some time from Mrs. Evans. I found in a house inhabited by Ann Carr and James Styles the coat now before the court, it was placed on the floor and a box hid it completely.[256]

Carr was the defendant in this case but she was accompanied at the bar by Elizabeth Findley who was charged with 'being acquainted with a robbery without divulging the same'. John Taylor gave evidence:

> John Duncan told me last night that a little before he saw John Sage and Findley in Macquarie Street he heard Findley say she had the Carpenters things, upon which he replied, 'Don't talk too loud or you'll be overheard.'[257]

On this evidence Elizabeth Findley received the same sentence as Ann Carr: both were sent further north to Port Macquarie for the remainder of their original sentences.

Such policing practice represents an extreme of the street policing, searching and informing shown in the records of other benches. Newcastle as a former penal settlement in this case exhibits scant respect for the rules of evidence or guilt.

The Bathurst bench was concerned in particular with the role of convict servants, but the presence of military regiments, the 57th and the Buffs, meant that the role of constables was supplemented and modified by soldiers. The Mounted Police also appeared before the Bathurst bench to give evidence of their pursuits and activities. The diversity of the role of constables is reflected in the following evidence of William Carlisle in September 1825:

> On the 24 August 1825 I was at the head of a party of constables in pursuit of bushrangers in the neighbourhood of Bathurst we sent forward one of the said party disguised as a bushranger dressed in a factory frock and straw hat the disguised man went to the hut [of the servant of Captain Piper's] had some conversation and went inside the hut to conceal himself. We came to the hutkeeper and asked if he had seen a man pass he told a falsehood and said he had so we handcuffed him.[258]

The originality of this activity was a match for any of the activities of the Parramatta police with their disguises and raids of public houses. The hutkeeper was not taken into custody but taken a short way off and liberated and the party continued in pursuit of bushrangers.

The focus of the Bathurst constables and soldiers was the offence of bushranging and the related activity of absconding. In December 1825 John Walker, corporal of the Buffs, described how he broke up a mob of people watching a fight and chose to follow five of the persons thus dispersed. He overtook them, asked them for their papers and when they had none returned with them to Bathurst.[259] Soldiers were active in stopping and questioning persons they met. In June 1826 the Mounted Police arrested a man who claimed he was sent to Bathurst as a free man and that Mr Terry would swear to his character. He was sentenced to fifty lashes and returned to the government.[260]

The Bathurst bench exhibits close contact between overseers and the military: if a convict absconded the military were as likely to be informed as constables. The extent of policing and the close attention paid to servants is demonstrated by the charge against Thomas Moore in April 1826; he was accused of 'aiding and abetting a bushranger, endeavouring to entice away a Black woman who had formerly been in the bush with Johnston (a bushranger) and who was on the settlement in Mr. Evendon's charge'.[261] The offence was discovered by Mr Evendon, who described what he saw: 'the black women were seated around the fire near the stores, deponent saw the prisoner seated himself close to the woman who had been in the bush'.[262] When Moore left the farm, a soldier was sent out to follow him.

Bathurst police and soldiers attempted to place a tight web of policing over the settlement and what this created was a style of suspicion and questioning centring on the convict runaway. Evidence of harbouring or associating with bushrangers did not need to be exact or able to be proved. This policing with a logic of its own appeared throughout the colony. In areas inhabited by free persons it included them and shaped the nature of their freedom. The outer settlements exhibited extremes of colonial policing, rather than divergences from it. Newcastle and Bathurst showed the difficulty of extricating policing from a convict or penal system. The policing of the Cowpastures demonstrated the development of new modes of policing in the colony concerning freedom of movement and economy applicable to both freed and convict persons.

Sydney expressed new developments in urban policing; country areas were polarised between those like Parramatta, Bathurst and Newcastle, where policing methods were aggressive, and places such as Liverpool, where local financial interests influenced policing, or Windsor where authority existed almost with the permission of a local population which had its own definition of a constable's proper role. At the core of all of these different modes of policing was the issue of freedom. This was vigorously fought for throughout the colony.

As the focus of the Bushranging Act was the small settler, so the focus of vagrancy policing was the freed convict seeking to make a living for himself or herself in the town. In all areas the policing of the freed population was closely related to the convict system. This was largely because of the difficulties which magistrates and constables had with notions of freedom, guilt and the expiration of sentences. It is not difficult to see how magistrates who were used to managing convicts would find it hard to let go of ex-convicts and behave as if they were restored to their rights under English law.

The terminology relating to constables in New South Wales was, according to English standards, new. Rossi's introduction of the terms 'conductors' and 'wardsmen' was evidence of a deliberate reorganisation of the structures of policing. The establishment of the militaristic Mounted Police was a response to a perceived crisis, but their methods were simply an extension of those of ordinary constables pursuing runaways. Together these institutions express characteristics of 'police' rather than 'parish constables'.

Convict labour relations provided the basis of policing in the colony. This *extended* to the free population, rather than there being two systems of delineating offenders, suspecting or questioning them.

The free and freed population of colonial New South Wales expected a distinction to be made between policing of convicts and policing of themselves. Violence erupted when attempts were made to arrest free persons, and suggestions were made by the Windsor magistrates that free persons thought themselves out of the reach of law. But it was in Windsor, as we have seen, that popular use of the law played a large part in street policing and house searches. The colonial population, and most particularly persons from the lower orders, did not reject the law but brought disputes and their own versions of evidence, proof and suspicion to the courts. There is some recognition of law. A closer examination of use of law in disputes will uncover the nature of popular law in the colony.

Notes

1   R. S. Hill, *Policing the Colonial Frontier.*
2   See J. J. Beattie, *Crime and the Courts in England, 1660–1880,* pp. 66–7.
3   D. Philips, 'A Just Measure of Crime, Authority, Hunters and Blue Locusts: The "Revisionist" Social History of Crime and the Law in Britain 1780–1850', in S. Cohen and A. Scull, eds, *Social Control and the State,* p. 63; that 'rate payers and improvement commissioners' themselves introduced new methods of policing is suggested by D. V. J. Jones, 'The New Police Crime and People in England and Wales', *Transactions of the Royal Historical Society,* 5th Series, vol. 33, 1983, p. 154.
4   Macquarie to Bathurst, 3 November 1810, enclosure, *H.R.A.,* 1, VII, p. 479.
5   *ibid.*
6   *ibid.*
7   Stanley Allerding Thornton, 'Captain Francis Rossi, First Police Magistrate, Sydney and Principal Superintendent of Police, N.S.W. 1824–34', Paper presented to Stipendiary Magistrates' Convention, 3 June 1949, p. 12.
8   *ibid.*
9   Darcy Wentworth to Lachlan Macquarie, 25 July 1816, Wentworth Papers, A753.
10 Wylde to Macquarie, 20 April 1820, B.T. 21, p. 50592.
11 Thornton, 'Captain Francis Rossi', p. 12.
12 Redman, Evidence to Bigge Inquiry, B.T. 13.
13 List of Fines and Penalties, District of Sydney, 1813–16, B.T. 13.
14 Redman, evidence.
15 James Hargreave, P.M.B., 12 January 1812; John Baker, P.M.B., 16 May 1812; Thomas Dalton, P.M.B., 24 August 1812.
16 Joseph Brand alias William Branch, P.M.B., 8 October 1820; Richard Rochford, P.M.B., 2 February 1821.
17 George Brown, Sydney Q.S., February 1825, 3.
18 Thomas Connor, Sydney Q.S., February 1825, 5.
19 James Callaghan, Sydney Q.S., February 1826, 3.

20 J. H. Plunkett, *The Australian Magistrate, A Guide to the Duties of Justice of the Peace*, Sydney 1835, p. 42.
21 Morris Raine, Sydney Q.S., April 1828, 21.
22 Ann Ward, P.M.B., 2 March 1812.
23 Ann Doyle, P.M.B., 18 May 1812.
24 Ann Chapman, P.M.B., 22 May 1812.
25 William Quinn, P.M.B., 5 March 1820.
26 John Bucks, P.M.B., 29 March 1820.
27 Robert Williams, P.M.B., 28 March 1821.
28 Mary Banks, 5 January 1821; Sarah Dowsett, Elizabeth Hinsely, Hannah Chapell, 5 January 1821; Elizabeth Burne, 13 January 1821; Mary Leeson, 13 January 1821; Mary Doyle, Mary Troy, 13 January 1821; Ann Holloway, 3 February 1821; Hannah Cumberbreech, 16 March 1821; Mary Ann Wilson, 17 October 1820. All of these cases came before the P.M.B.
29 Mary Donelly, 8 March 1821; Mary Thomas, 28 March 1821; Elizabeth Haley, 7 March 1821; Ann Baker, 14 October 1820. All of these cases came before the P.M.B.
30 Jane Marcus, P.M.B., 16 September 1821.
31 Eliza King, P.M.B., 7 March 1821.
32 Mary Barber, P.M.B., 3 February 1821.
33 Darling to Bathurst, sub-enclosure, 15 November 1826, *H.R.A.*, 1, XII, p. 679.
34 Brisbane to Bathurst, 23 May 1825, *H.R.A.*, 1, XI, p. 612.
35 Grand Jury Report, Sydney Q.S., November 1824.
36 *ibid.*
37 *ibid.*, January 1827.
38 *ibid.*
39 *ibid.*, October 1827.
40 M. J. D. Roberts, 'Public and Private in Early 19th-century London: The Vagrant Act of 1822 and its Enforcement', unpublished paper, 1987.
41 *ibid.*, p. 36.
42 Mary Barker, P.M.B., 12 January 1812.
43 John Brown, P.M.B., 14 February 1816.
44 Jonathan Gorman, Patrick McGie, Owen McGie, William Harvey, P.M.B., 30 October 1820.
45 William Curtis, P.M.B., 9 October 1820.
46 William Cooley, Richard Jones, P.M.B., 8 January 1820.
47 Jeremiah Monday, P.M.B., 27 March 1820.
48 William Murphy, P.M.B., 27 November 1820.
49 Patrick Berry, P.M.B., 17 October 1820.
50 Thomas Sparkes, Q.S., November 1825, 42.
51 *ibid.*
52 Benjamin Smith, John Leather, Margaret Parsons, James Conning, Q.S., November 1826, 33.
53 Richard Nugent, Q.S., November 1826, 37.
54 Dennis D'Arcy, Q.S., November 1826, 36.
55 James Bryant, Q.S., October 1827, 45.
56 John Haughton, Q.S., January 1828, 28.
57 Barbara Sutherland, J.A.B., 4 August 1810.
58 R. vs Barbara Sutherland, C.C.J., 23 October 1810.
59 John McCabe, Mary McNally, John Dunn, J.A.B., 3 November 1810.
60 Evidence from Aaron Peckham, P.M.B., 25 May 1812.
61 *ibid.*
62 Charles Wright, George New, P.M.B., 31 January 1816.

63 Richard Hughes, William Murphy, Nany Coffey, P.M.B., 1 March 1821.

64 *ibid.*

65 James Gates, P.M.B., 21 February 1821.

66 Thomas Nickery, P.M.B., 31 January 1821.

67 *ibid.*

68 James Riley, P.M.B., 13 November 1820.

69 Fuller, P.M.B., 17 January 1812.

70 Elizabeth Burne, P.M.B., 13 January 1821.

71 *ibid.*

72 James Moon and others, P.M.B., 31 January 1821.

73 R. vs Edward Whitehouse, Archibald Wood, C.C.J., January 1818, 15.

74 Anne Murphy, Q.S., August 1825, 30.

75 J. Brewer and J. Styles, eds, *An Ungovernable People*, p. 13.

76 This point is stressed by C. H. Currey, 'Chapters on the Legal History of N.S.W.', Ph.D. thesis, University of Sydney, 1929, p. 261, and also by A. C. Castles, *An Australian Legal History*, pp. 70–5; see also D. Neal, 'The Rule of Law in a Penal Colony', LL.D. thesis, University of New South Wales, 1986.

77 Quoted in B. Fletcher, *Ralph Darling: A Governor Maligned*, p. 179.

78 H. King, 'Some Aspects of Police Administration in New South Wales 1825–1851', *Journal of the Royal Australian Historical Society*, vol. 42, pt 5, 1956, p. 217.

79 *ibid.*

80 J. K. McLaughlin, 'The Magistracy in N.S.W., 1788–1850', M.A. thesis, University of Sydney, 1973, p. 294.

81 Colonial Secretary: Circular to Magistrates, 20 April 1820, Bigge Inquiry, B.T., Box 24, p. 5270.

82 Currey, 'Chapters on the Legal History of N.S.W.', p. 261.

83 Brian Fletcher, *Landed Enterprise and Penal Society*, p. 57.

84 For example, A. G. L. Shaw, *Convicts and the Colonies*, p. 88; M. H. Ellis, *Lachlan Macquarie*.

85 C. H. Currey, *Francis Forbes*.

86 McLaughlin refers to both Stephen's and Forbes' attitudes to magisterial power, see *op. cit.*, p. 266–70. See also Currey, 'Chapters on the Legal History of N.S.W.', and D. Neal, 'Law and Authority: The Magistracy in New South Wales 1788–1840', *Law in Context*, no. 3, 1985.

• 87 Barron Field to Rev. S. Marsden, 16 December 1824, M.L., Af23/2.

88 Saxe Bannister to Sir Thomas Brisbane, 28 December 1825, Brisbane Letter Book, p. 56.

89 Enclosure 1, Brisbane to Bathurst, 28 September 1825, *H.R.A.*, 1, XI, p. 856.

90 *ibid.*

91 *ibid.*

92 J. Langbein, *Torture and the Law of Proof: Europe and England in the Ancien Regime*, p. 136.

93 *ibid.*, p. 139.

94 Referred to by Castles, 'Chapters on the Legal History of N.S.W.', p. 71 footnote 20.

95 Brisbane to Bathurst, 28 September 1825, Enclosure No. 1 Report of the Enquiry by Council on Alleged Illegal Punishments, 27 September 1825, *H.R.A.*, 1, XI, p. 856.

96 Currey, 'Chapters on the Legal History of N.S.W.', p. 148.

97 Government and General Orders, 26 May 1810, *H.R.A.*, 1, VII, p. 381.

98 *ibid.*, 3 November 1810, *H.R.A.*, 1, VII, p. 448.

99 Police Regulations Sydney N.S.W., *H.R.A.*, 1, VII, p. 479.

100 Ann Kelly, Parramatta Bench of Magistrates (P.B.M.), 10 August 1822.

101 Ann Birkin, P.B.M., 9 February 1822.

102 Mary Hutchinson, P.B.M., 2 January 1822.

103 Daniel Kelly, P.B.M., 17 June 1815.

104   John Sparrow, P.B.M., 23 October 1824, was asleep in his cart; Jonathan Suthors, P.B.M., 15 July 1815.

105   George Hibbard, P.B.M., 10 March 1826.

106   Samuel Hughes, Joseph Piggot, P.B.M., 21 August 1824.

107   Marsden, Evidence to Bigge Inquiry, B.T. 8, p. 3484.

108   Proclamation Court House Parramatta, 1 January 1820, B.T. Box 21.

109   Letter from Oakes to J. H. Grose, Wentworth papers, pp. 17–20, M.L. A754.

110   *ibid.*

111   R. vs John Clue, C.C.J., December 1818, 387.

112   *ibid.*

113   R. vs Benjamin Metcalfe, C.C.J., September 1817, 1.

114   R. vs James Callaghan, C.C.J., September 1823, 22.

115   R. vs Thomas Dutton and others, C.C.J., June 1821, 53.

116   *ibid.*

117   William Ashton, S.C.C.J., 1829 Miscellaneous.

118   George Booth, C.C.J., December 1822, 32.

119   R. vs John Burrell, C.C.J., May 1822, 5.

120   R. vs John Brown, C.C.J., May 1822, 13.

121   Grand Jury Report, Parramatta Q.S., October 1826.

122   R. vs William Harris, C.C.J., March 1822, 102.

123   James Bridges, John Bridges, Thomas Crossley, Elizabeth Buffy, Parramatta Q.S., February 1825, 1.

124   Richard Newham, Parramatta Q.S., February 1825, 23.

125   *ibid.*

126   R. vs Thomas Cooke, James Curry, S.C.C.J., 1826, 187.

127   *ibid.*

128   R. vs Joseph Kerr, S.C.C.J., October 1829, miscellaneous.

129   R. vs James Bailey, S.C.C.J., October 1825, miscellaneous.

130   Margaret Haslam, Parramatta Q.S., April 1826, 8.

131   George Yeates, Parramatta Q.S., April 1826, 20.

132   R. vs James Kirton, C.C.J., June 1821, 57.

133   R. vs Richard Edwards, C.C.J., March 1818, 8.

134   R. vs James Smith, John Cooke, Jemina Smith, C.C.J., June 1820, 17.

135   *ibid.*

136   Darcy Wentworth, Police Reports and Accounts, 1810–27.

137   *ibid.*

138   Macquarie to Liverpool, 18 October 1811, *H.R.A.*, 1, VII, p. 400.

139   *The New South Wales Calendar and General Post Office Directory*, 1832, repr. Dixson Foundation, 1966, p. 53.

140   *ibid.*

141   William Ikin, L.B.M., 19 February 1824.

142   Robert Lowe, L.B.M., 2 February 1824.

143   Lewis Solomon, L.B.M., 2 February 1824.

144   *ibid.*

145   John Quigley, L.B.M., 4 May 1824.

146   Lewis Solomon, L.B.M., 1 June 1824.

147   James McNamara, L.B.M., 28 June 1824.

148   *ibid.*

149   William Ikin, L.B.M., 11 February 1826.

150 Ann Marsden, L.B.M., 1 June 1824, and James Royal, L.B.M., 26 June 1824.
151 James Williams, L.B.M., 23 June 1824.
152 John Clements, L.B.M., 26 April 1824.
153 R. vs John Ferguson and others, C.C.J., January 1824, 34.
154 Charles Hensley, L.B.M., 22 March 1824.
155 Richard Barnes, L.B.M., 28 June 1824.
156 William Wollard, L.B.M., 30 June 1824.
157 William Davis, L.B.M., 28 June 1824.
158 James Noland, L.B.M., 30 June 1824.
159 R. vs Peter Geage, C.C.J., September 1822, 38.
160 e.g. R. vs William Cope, C.C.J., April 1817, 26.
161 William Mannix, L.B.M., 29 May 1824.
162 Thomas Bennet, L.B.M., 4 February 1826.
163 e.g. William Stephenson and others, L.B.M., 6 March 1826.
164 Charles Somerfield, L.B.M., 18 March 1826.
165 Reported, L.B.M., 3 March 1826.
166 Jeremiah Kennedy and others, L.B.M., 20 March 1826; John Sleett, Jonathon Davis, L.B.M., 20
     March 1826; Jonathon Madden, L.B.M., 25 March 1826; Peter Fitzimmons, L.B.M., 25 March
     1826; Thomas Herbert, L.B.M., 27 March 1826.
167 R. vs Patrick Kegney, S.C.C.J., September 1828, 144.
168 R. vs James Pretty and others, S.C.C.J., September 1831, 46.
169 R. vs Samuel Shaw, S.C.C.J., 1830, Miscellaneous.
170 Samuel Davis, L.B.M., 22 March 1824.
171 Howe to Parramatta Bench, Joshua Suttleby, Parramatta Q.S., April 1826, 24.
172 *ibid*.
173 *ibid*.
174 *ibid*.
175 R. vs Eliza Campbell and others, S.C.C.J., February 1825, 1.
176 *ibid*.
177 R. vs Andrew Ferguson and others, C.C.J., 1824, 34.
178 Letter enclosed, ibid.
179 R. vs John Lucas, S.C.C.J., Miscellaneous.
180 R. vs James Pretty, S.C.C.J., September 1831, 46.
181 R. vs Henry McAllister, C.C.J., September 1822, 39.
182 R. vs Archibald Campbell, S.C.C.J., April 1825, 135.
183 R. vs Daniel McLucas and others, C.C.J., September 1822, 39.
184 R. vs George Bedford, S.C.C.J., 1826, Miscellaneous.
185 James Butterworth, Liverpool Q.S., July 1826, No. 67.
186 Jonathon Madden, L.B.M., 28 March 1826.
187 Hugh Vaughan, John Murphy, Liverpool Q.S., December 1825, 17, 18.
188 William Winn, John Russ, Parramatta Q.S., February 1825, 22.
189 Richard Weavers, Liverpool Q.S., January 1828, 12.
190 Bishop Toft, Liverpool Q.S., January 1828, 24.
191 Weavers, Liverpool Q.S.; Toft, Liverpool Q.S.
192 List of fines of free persons. Windsor, January 1810 to May 1820, B.T. 12, pp. 190–216.
193 Windsor Police Magistrate letter book, 1828, M.L. A1397.
194 Evidence of John Howe to Bigge Inquiry, B.T. 13.
195 *ibid*.
196 Windsor Police Magistrate letter book, October 1830, M.L. A1397.

197 Evidence of Howe to Bigge Inquiry.
198 *ibid.*
199 Windsor Police Magistrate letter book.
200 Evidence of Richard Cartwright to Bigge Inquiry, B.T. 24, p. 5277.
201 John Lanahan, List of fines of free persons, Windsor, 1810–20.
202 *ibid.*
203 For example, Edward Kelly was fined £5 for harbouring on 10 October 1810, List of fines of free persons.
204 In 1828 fencing was becoming more common but the grand jury of the Quarter Sessions asked that information be given by the governor 'so as to enable the settler to place the fences on the proper sites and ascertain the lines by which communication between individual and neighbouring farms may take place which at present are sources of endless litigation', Windsor Q.S., January 1828.
205 Elijah Lane, 22 May 1818, List of fines of free persons, Windsor 1810–20.
206 Windsor seems to be the only region where poverty was formally recognised by the wealthy inhabitants. Cartwright in his evidence to Bigge said, 'a great many of the smaller settlers were reduced to wretchedness from one cause or another . . . From such a conviction the opulent part of the Parishioners . . . formed themselves into a society for relieving such distress', Cartwright, evidence to Bigge Inquiry.
207 List of fines of free persons, Windsor, 1810–20.
208 William Huggins, Windsor Q.S., February 1825, 9.
209 Matthew Brown, Windsor Q.S., October 1826, 17.
210 John Blackmore, Windsor Q.S., January 1827, 3.
211 Thomas Douglass, Windsor Q.S., January 1828, 3.
212 Edward Devine, John Faulkener, Windsor Q.S., July 1827, 6.
213 Patrick McNamara, Windsor Q.S., November 1824, 7.
214 Joseph Crawford, Windsor Q.S., May 1826, 31.
215 *ibid.*
216 Richard Noland, Patrick Byrne, Windsor Q.S., July 1828, 4.
217 R. vs George Kilray, S.C.C.J., January 1828, 4.
218 R. vs Patrick Hand, Catherine Hatch, Thomas Baker, C.C.J., November 1820, 483.
219 Richard Kelly, Windsor Q.S., July 1827, 30.
220 'Thronged' in this context probably means a good harvest ready for cutting.
221 Richard Kelly, Windsor Q.S., July 1827, 30.
222 Archibald Bell to Alexander McLeay, 17 October 1828, Windsor Police Magistrate letter book, 1828.
223 *ibid.*
224 James Freeman, Windsor Q.S., May 1825, 9.
225 Robert Grundy, Windsor Q.S., January 1829, 13.
226 Richard Watts, Windsor Q.S., January 1827, 13.
227 Thomas Donahue, Windsor Q.S., February 1825, 11.
228 R. vs Henry Fleming, C.C.J., March 1823, 30.
229 R. vs John Kable, Charles Kable, C.C.J., October 1822, 54.
230 *ibid.*
231 R. vs George Kable, Charles Kable, C.C.J., August 1821, 56.
232 R. vs Henry Kable, Charles Kable, C.C.J., October 1822, 28.
233 *ibid.*
234 R. vs Charles Kable, C.C.J., June 1822, 26.
235 R. vs John Kable, Charles Kable, C.C.J., October 1822, 54.

236 *ibid.*
237 John Kable, Windsor Q.S., February 1825, 10.
238 John Kable, Windsor Q.S., May 1825, 14.
239 *ibid.*
240 *ibid.*
241 Joseph Smith, Edward Hobbs, Windsor Q.S., July 1826, 8.
242 *ibid.*
243 Thomas Nixon, Joseph Hobbs, Windsor Q.S., July 1826, 9.
244 John Kable, Windsor Q.S., February 1825, 10.
245 Bell to Saxe Bannister, 17 February 1826, John Kable, Windsor Q.S., May 1825, 14.
246 *ibid.*
247 R. vs Joseph Hodges, C.C.J., April 1817, 8. The proclamation is included in the case.
248 Macquarie to Bathurst, 4 April 1817, *H.R.A.*, 1, IX, p. 348–9.
249 *ibid.*
250 Macquarie to Bathurst, 12 December 1817, *H.R.A.*, 1, IX, pp. 714–15.
251 *ibid.*, p. 715.
252 R. vs John Lowe and others, C.C.J., December 1816, 17.
253 *ibid.*
254 Joseph Hodges, C.C.J., April 1817, 8.
255 R. vs George Miller, George Blackridge, C.C.J., August 1818, 15.
256 Elizabeth Findley, Ann Carr, Newcastle Bench of Magistrates, 21 January 1824.
257 *ibid.*
258 Bathurst Bench, 28 September 1825.
259 Bathurst Bench, 6 December 1825.
260 Bathurst Bench, 27 June 1826.
261 Bathurst Bench, 11 April 1826.
262 *ibid.*

7

POPULAR USE OF LAW

The importance of exchange to the survival of bushrangers drew numbers of the population into an illegal economy. This economy was intricately tied to law due to the rituals of hiding and transferring property and the possibility of information being given. The practice of criminal law was thus bound up with popular understanding. The local population could take law out of the hands of legislators, administrators and magistrates and put it to community use. Between 1810 and 1830 the colonial population shaped and modified what it understood to be criminal law. It made use of some regulations and ignored others. It brought information to courts for various reasons associated with revenge or personal acquisitions, as well as what was felt to be a wrong. Like bushranging, these understandings of criminal law created a particular culture of hiding and transferring property, of accusation and defence.

'Community' has been a subject pursued with some difficulty by historians. As a term it has created problems because of its connotations of 'togetherness, the warmth and security of relations among people'.[1] When historians of early modern England looked for such warmth they found that it barely existed: social relations were intolerant in the pre-industrial village.[2] It is possible to reject the term but, as C. J. Calhoun has argued, 'community' is useful in exploring how people relate to each other, how they see themselves in society. Calhoun discusses community in terms of its 'weakness' and 'strength', thereby valuing good relations.[3] However, poor relations may also tie people closely together and may dominate social interaction. 'Community' may then incorporate both good relations and poor relations. While it is perhaps best to see community as an 'elusive quarry'[4] and thereby avoid valuing the term, historians are then confronted with the problem of methodology—where is one to look?

In considering community, historians have followed two approaches. The first is to examine kinship, social contact, mobility or the spatial outlines of settlement. Such an approach leads to the use of mathematics and the dominant image is that of the social web.[5] This changes over time but always remains a web, a static image. The second approach has been used recently by David Garrioch, who is critical of the first approach. As he points out, 'it is often possible to find out where people lived, with whom they socialized, where they worked and with whom and to whom they were related but none of this necessarily provides evidence of community life and nor does it tell anything about community structure.'[6] To overcome such limitations Garrioch provides another image—that of living tissue. Only with such an image can we understand the community, rather than stopping it and breaking it down into its different parts. Garrioch argues that the subjective element of human relations must be included in any analysis of community: historians must show the quality of human interaction and that interaction may not be friendly.[7] Garrioch moves the emphasis away from warmth or good relations to see how people manage disputes.

The historian of law finds that the law has only limited connection with social norms. Because law stands in a peculiar relationship to everyday life—it deals with the sudden event, the outraged or offended person—it is impossible to use law to build up a picture of social life. J. A. Sharpe has argued that litigants in early modern England 'were aware they were acting within a context of some sort of community social values and were concerned that their conduct should be, and should be seen to be broadly in accord with those values'.[8]

Implicit in such a statement is a perception by historians that law is an institution which solved disputes and validated social norms. But law may serve many purposes. In the colonial environment it was used by female servants to get out of service; it was used for the profit of the informer and the constable. Such use of law produces another kind of norm—that of use of law itself. How accessible the courts were, how easily magistrates or constables were convinced, how much evidence was needed: all played a part in producing this use of law. In colonial New South Wales the instability of currency and the economy and the importance of personal property meant that the use of criminal law was closely bound to economic competition.

Property

From the beginning of Macquarie's administration there were attempts made to curtail the effects of the competitiveness of the local economy. One of the earliest of these involved the market in bread. This market was felt to be orientated to those who could afford to pay high prices. The Colonial Secretary, Castlereagh, wrote in 1810 to Judge Advocate Bent:

> In consequence of the present scarcity of grain and numerous representations having been made to his excellency regarding the quality and weight of bread it is his wish that you take the earliest opportunity of a Bench of Magistrates being assembled to enter into such regulations with respect to this important subject as to restrain the bakers from devoting so much of the best quality of flour to the accommodation of the more wealthy inhabitants and by equalising the quality and prescribing the weight and price to relieve the poor from the injury sustained by them at the present time of scarcity.[9]

The bench, having taken the letter into consideration, introduced a number of regulations regarding the price, weight and constituents of bread. The penalty for disobeying these regulations was a fine of ten shillings.

The second Saturday following the announcement, the first charge appeared. William Lewis complained against Andrew Frazer, a baker, who sold him a loaf of bread 'differing in quality from the assize'. In all Frazer was fined forty shillings. That day it was decided by the bench that such fines arising from the charges relating to bread should be divided: one half would be paid to the informer and one half was to be used by the magistrate in carrying regulations into execution. Each loaf of bread, they decided, should be marked by its maker with his or her initials. The bench decided no biscuits should be made or sold unless they were composed of two-thirds wheaten and one-third maize flour.[10]

In Sydney this regulation produced its own structure of policing, relying heavily on the informant, who was able to obtain half the fine. In August 1811 several offences appeared related to the use of unstamped weights; the fines went to the Police Fund. The offence of selling lightweight bread or overcharging did not become major until 1815. This charge appeared less often than the charge of having light weights. Between 1813 and 1820 there were only ten fines for selling lightweight bread; there were seventy-three charges against persons who were found to have unjust scales or light weights.[11] The beneficiaries in these charges were the informers. They obtained payment through a constable and either part or whole of the fine was distributed by constables. From 1816 the major beneficiary of such charges was the clerk of the market. Fines varied from five to thirty-five shillings.

So while such regulations were introduced with the intent of curtailing the improprieties of the bread market they, in turn, produced another lucrative sideline, that of informing. It might be said that such informing could bring in more money than the making of bread itself.

Even more lucrative were the regulations introduced for curtailing the spirit trade. The fine for selling spirits without a licence was up to £30 and informers stood a chance of obtaining part of that sum as a reward. The structure of cases regarding distilling can be demonstrated by reference to Mary Turley and Robert Whitmore, charged in February 1811 with illegally distilling spirits.

The first person to give information in the case was the constable Daniel Cubbitt who said,

> he received instructions from Mr Lord to go on board a vessel called Chance just arrived from the Hawkesbury, of which Robert Whitmore was master, to search for spirits supposed to be on board of her ... the master then observed that Turley brought a quantity of wheat on board and if there was any liquor on board it would be hers.

Ann Chapman gave evidence that Mary Turley went to her house in George Street: 'I poured her out a glass of spirits thinking she wanted it, she smelled at it and asked me what I have a gallon for it ... I told her I gave £2.5 a gallon. She said she had some for sale and she could afford to sell it cheaper than that.' Ann Chapman went on:

I told her I would not have it and if she had any to be very careful for the governor had given very particular orders last week and that I would not have it in my house for £20, poor as I was. She then went away and came back in half an hour to ask if I had lodged any complaint against her about the spirits, as it was seized—I said no—I had some other employment.

The court decided that Robert Whitmore did not know that the bag in question contained spirits but they decided Mary Turley was guilty, fined her £20 and sentenced her to three years' hard labour at a place the governor would appoint.[12] Mary Turley assumed that an informer had been crucial to her arrest, and Ann Chapman was careful to distance herself from the whole transaction.

Such collusion between constables, informers and the courts meant that policing of the economy could be quite effective: informing produced another kind of economic pursuit. This did not occur with all regulations. In the 1820s there were attempts by the grand juries to influence the kinds of economic activity which could be engaged in on the streets of Sydney. Business concerns came under attack as 'public nuisances'.

These no doubt appeared because of the presence on the grand jury of wealthy merchants and shopkeepers. The most common complaint was the offal and blood from slaughter houses being allowed to run into the streets, but there was far less interest in this kind of offence than bread and spirit offences.

In 1827, for instance, William Small, constable, went to ascertain 'the cause of filth running into the tanks in Sydney'; he proceeded to the premises of Michael Burns in Pitt Street and saw that the 'common drain from the necessary ran into a stream of water'.[13] This charge was not preferred, but the policing of nuisances intensified. In 1828 eleven persons were charged together on one day in April with having concerns which were a nuisance. Constables ascertained the Christian names of persons who occupied houses which 'are presented as nuisances' and the names of the nearest neighbours who could prove the nuisance. Nothing was to come of these cases because, as was stated in Harpur's case, 'the witnesses that were subpoenaed to support this case ... declared they were near neighbours of Harpur did not find any inconvenience from his slaughter house and did not consider any nuisance.'[14] Though constables brought the initial complaint, it was necessary to obtain some agreement from neighbours; those neighbours did not perceive the nuisance of the slaughter house or gained some advantage from living next to it. Similarly, disorderly houses were reported primarily by constables and in 1830 constables appeared in the courts as respectable inhabitants of a parish to complain of bawdy houses.[15]

In these cases the effectiveness of policing depended upon the interest of the public in reporting the case or prosecuting it themselves. This interest certainly does not seem to come from a concern on the part of the public for the legitimacy of economic activity; rather, the rewards involved in informing were utilised to advantage, or perhaps cases were brought for other motives of economic competition.

Theft from the person in the streets or on the roads was invested with particular importance through its association with bushranging and the safety of the streets of Sydney. In January 1830 an article appeared in the *Sydney Gazette* concerning 'several spirited inhabitants' of Pitt Street who clubbed together and engaged 'a smart young man as guardian of the night, he is to be equipped after the London fashion with pistols, cutlass, stick, rattle and lantern and will sing "All's well" '.[16] This action was in response to fears for public safety and was related to complaints of inadequate street lighting.[17] In April 1830 the *Gazette* informed its readers that the Liverpool road 'is now well lined with Police, both civil and military . . . any individual who is apprehensive of travelling the road alone is at full liberty to call on the police to accompany them'.[18]

In the streets and roads of the colony the wealthy found themselves directly confronted by the menace of bushranging; concerns about street safety came from the merchants or wealthy shopkeepers of Sydney who were liable to be attacked at night. The offence of robbery thus provided an impetus for extensive street policing: arrests of persons considered suspicious, who were 'lurking about' or thought to be 'rogues and vagabonds'. The residents of Pitt Street, however, thought it necessary to create their own constable, thus exhibiting a dissatisfaction with Sydney constables, who were themselves, late in the period, subject to attack by street crowds. Fear of robbery, then, creates notions of 'public order' on the part of wealthier persons in the colony. Those persons deemed most suspicious by constables were convicts and recently freed men. The *Gazette* provides us with an example of the intersection between the suspicions of constables and magistrates and the wealthier segments of the population fearful for their own safety. In January 1830 its editor records:

> The sitting magistrate at the Police office yesterday sentenced a man free by servitude to three months in gaol as a rogue and vagabond. The Chief Constable deserves much credit for taking this description of gentry to task as we are certain every man who is honestly disposed may obtain a livelihood in this colony if he will work.[19]

The *Gazette* saw a rogue unwilling to work, and the magistrate sentenced a man found idle on the street. This, along with the complaints of employers, and their own disputes were the means by which free persons appeared before the courts. The offence from which such fears arose was robbery. It did not need to occur frequently to be regarded as endemic. This offence was described in the courts by its victims. The picture they painted provided the basis for the *Gazette's* information and for popular gossip and concern. This picture was provided by all levels of the population.

In 1816 Elizabeth Gallagher went before the Police Magistrates' Bench in Sydney to say she 'was walking along George Street when she was seized by two footpads who stole her pocket book'.[20] Elizabeth Pear two months later gave evidence that she was travelling in her horse and cart when 'she met two footpads who threatened to attack her servants, took spirits, one of them said that examinant should have her property again as she was a civil woman'.[21] The description of the defendants as 'footpads' derives from English terminology and these attacks occur at the beginning of the establishment of bushranging as an offence.

By 1820 Liverpool began to figure as a dangerous place for travellers and the Reverend Robert Cartwright expressed similar concerns to those voiced later in the *Gazette*:

> I think there is not in any part of the colony a worse police than at Liverpool. In so much as it is really dangerous to stay out at night. Several most daring highway robberies have been committed I may say within call of the Chief Constable's house . . .[22]

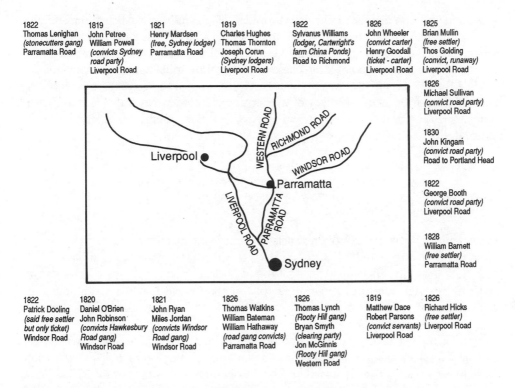

1822
Thomas Lenighan
(stonecutters gang)
Parramatta Road

1819
John Petree
William Powell
(convicts Sydney
road party)
Liverpool Road

1821
Henry Mardsen
(free, Sydney lodger)
Parramatta Road

1819
Charles Hughes
Thomas Thornton
Joseph Corun
(Sydney lodgers)
Liverpool Road

1822
Sylvanus Williams
(lodger, Cartwright's
farm China Ponds)
Road to Richmond

1826
John Wheeler
(convict carter)
Henry Goodall
(ticket - carter)
Liverpool Road

1825
Brian Mullin
(free settler)
Thos Golding
(convict, runaway)
Liverpool Road

1826
Michael Sullivan
(convict road party)
Liverpool Road

1830
John Kingam
(convict road party)
Road to Portland Head

1822
George Booth
(convict road party)
Liverpool Road

1828
William Barnett
(free settler)
Parramatta Road

1822
Patrick Dooling
(said free settler
but only ticket)
Windsor Road

1820
Daniel O'Brien
John Robinson
(convicts Hawkesbury
Road gang)
Windsor Road

1821
John Ryan
Miles Jordan
(convicts Windsor
Road gang)
Windsor Road

1826
Thomas Watkins
William Bateman
William Hathaway
(road gang convicts)
Parramatta Road

1826
Thomas Lynch
(Rooty Hill gang)
Bryan Smyth
(clearing party)
Jon McGinnis
(Rooty Hill gang)
Western Road

1819
Matthew Dace
Robert Parsons
(convict servants)
Liverpool Road

1826
Richard Hicks
(free settler)
Liverpool Road

Figure 9   Highway robbery on the roads to Sydney, 1819–30: cases appearing in the criminal courts.

Highway robbery in the 1820s occurred on the well-travelled roads of the colony. Figure 9 shows some of the perpetrators of highway robbery. These people were not bush-rangers and returned to their houses or huts after the attack. George Haley, a convict, described his experience on the Liverpool road in 1822:

> yesterday coming from Bunbury Curran coming through Liverpool toll bar I saw the prisoner in company with a woman, I asked the woman where she was going, she replied she had a pass to Parramatta. I desired her to go with me as I thought she had bad company with her. She came a mile or two and she said she would go to Parramatta but she would go home to Irish Town . . . as soon as she was gone the prisoner came up and said if I did not give him the price of a pint of rum he would cut my guts out, I was knocked down with sticks and my waistcoat cut.[23]

The defendants in this case were from the Liverpool road gang; they were met on the road by a constable, identified and taken in charge.[24] Members of road gangs, clearing parties and servants employed on private farms were often suspected and searched for property stolen from carts.

The 'spirited inhabitants' of Pitt Street reported in the *Sydney Gazette* were representative of wealth in the colony; they could employ a constable and could conceive of doing so. Rather than there being one public interest in the colony, there are distinctions to be made between wealthy persons who were represented on the grand jury and in the press, and the complaints of the lower orders. The kinds of participation and the purposes for which law was used varied in these two sectors of society. When the authorities modified the nature of policing in the colony, as in placing more constables on the Liverpool road, they did so at the request of the wealthy inhabitants of the colony.

While the interests of the wealthy can be clearly seen in cases concerning robbery, there is less clarity in the position of master and servant in cases of theft and work complaints. As Frank Crowley has written, the position of master and servant was uncertain:

> much of the traditional outlook on the relation of master and servant was imported together with English law, yet the reciprocal rights and duties involved in the idea of contract grew only slowly, this was due in part to the tendency of employers to measure out equal treatment to all labourers whether bond or free, and in part to the penal character of the settlement.[25]

It was originally to settle such discrepancies that the Masters and Servants Act was introduced to the colony in 1828. J. B. Hirst argues that this brought servants in New South Wales into line with English practice.[26] Hirst also writes that masters were given more credence by magistrates in their hearings of complaints and that the major source of disputes was the payment of luxuries rather than money. Masters claimed that luxuries were payment for work.[27]

A small number of free servants complained of their masters for non-payment for work and these included apprentices and Indian and Tahitian servants.[28] The difficulty of obtaining wages was emphasised in cases involving free servants. In May 1826 Mark Russell, free, said he had agreed to break up three acres of ground for which he was to be paid four shillings; he applied three different times for wages but did not receive them.[29]

Such cases involving such arbitration of wage disputes are very few before 1830 in the records of either magistrates' benches or Quarter Sessions. It was far more common that free servants were brought forward for theft from their employers.

Like cases involving female convict servants, these cases show confusion over ownership of property as well as the disputes over perquisites and work time. Also, as with female convict servants, there was room for exploration on both sides and the law could be used to benefit either. When we consider the cases they show the same instability as cases involving female convict servants, suggesting a fragility of relations with no clear pointers to proper behaviour for master and servant.

In the criminal court in 1830, John Jamison described how he came to blame his servant for theft:

> the prisoner calling himself George Stephenson came to deponent at Regentville on the 15–16 July and stated he had come from Bathurst under the recommendation of Mr. Blacket formerly deponent's superintendent, he produced a certificate . . . from this certificate and the distressed situation he represented himself to be in, deponent employed him to superintend the erection of several stockyards. The prisoner then presented to deponent that his bed and clothing were detained for a small sum in a house in Sydney and without the advance of £5 he would not be decent. Deponent refused several times to advance any money to him but at length consented to advance him £10 and sent him to get his things and purchase several articles for deponent . . . deponent understood the prisoner did not make any of the purchases, . . . the prisoner immediately absconded and has been absent since.[30]

The type of employment situation described by Jamison, where work was agreed upon and the employee became bound, is also a source of discontent in other cases. In a voluntary statement given to the Liverpool bench in 1824 by Andrew Ferguson, the conditions on William Howe's farm were described:

> [I said] he must have a good place of it at Mr. Howe's, he replied the place is not worth a damn, don't you see how he left me without breakfast. I said there must be perquisites in your situation besides your wages. [He said], No I can't get a half penny for I can't weed the corn or anything under my charge, everything is measured so particularly.[31]

In 1821 William Lahy was brought before the Windsor bench by his employer's son who stated, 'the prisoner has lived with his father six weeks he came to the house in rags and now has a quantity of good clothing and £1.2.6 was found on him'.[32] Free servants were likely to be suspected; their property was searched and careful note made of wages and dues.

While attitudes concerning work for wages were well established by the time of Macquarie's administration, the extraction of work from other aspects of life was a slow process in both Britain and Europe. Michael Sonenscher has written:

> there was no 'natural' market for labour in eighteenth-century Paris, no mechanism which ensured that it would be the wage rate which responded to fluctuations in the demand for labour. The assumption that there was has meant that all those concerns which can be placed under the general rubric of 'reproduction'—eating, drinking, housing, marrying, bequeathing or inheriting property or rights to property—have been separated off from work itself—this is an anachronistic procedure . . . all of these concerns were imbricated within the texture of work itself . . .[33]

There could well be a disjuncture between expectation and the market in labour in colonial New South Wales. While contract work is dominant for free servants, these cases show instances where servants expected more, or misunderstood what was owing to them. In 1821 Hugh McMullens was brought to the court by John Howe, chief constable of Windsor. Howe said that McMullens had been employed as a carpenter about the house and a coat went missing. In his defence the prisoner said the coat had been given to him by Howe's daughter, Eliza Kennedy. It had been

> put on him by Eliza Kennedy while asleep he was very thankful. The coat was on his bed fifteen weeks and was visible to everybody. Nothing being said about it he considered it as a gift. Being in need of a little money to purchase a plane and not having money, neither could obtain money in possession at the present time prosecutor owes me £8.9. I obtained 5/- supposing the coat a gift.[34]

The defendant explained that when his wages were not paid, the magistrates advised him to go to a full bench. McMullens said that his employer, Howe, became so enraged that he charged him with theft of the coat.[35]

When free servants came before the benches for theft throughout the period, their cases emerge from this situation of itinerant employment or short-term contract work, where wages are carefully set out and employer's property delineated from servant's property. Tables 26 and 27 show reasons given by employers for bringing servants to court. Such a situation was clearly open to exploitation on both sides, if it were not for the fact that the magistrates invariably supported the employer in cases of a serious nature.

Table 26   Reasons given by employers bringing free servants to court for theft, 1816–24

Received information	Suspected or watched servant	Checked servant's work	Servant absconded	Missed property at end of service
COURT OF CRIMINAL JURISDICTION, SYDNEY:				
Wealthy				
Will Hutchinson (Waterloo Mills)	Simeon Lord (Merchant)	Robert Cooper (Merchant)	D. D. Matthews (Farmer)	
Joseph Underwood (Merchant)	Solomon Levi (Shopkeeper, female servant)	Vickers Jacob (Merchant)	Robert Cooper (Merchant)	
John Dickman esq. (Steam Engine)				
John Jamison (Building of his)				
Mr Drennan				
Small Traders				
	James Wilshire (Tanner)	Joseph Wilmot (Publican, female servant)	Peter Quigley (Shopkeeper)	William Freeman (Small Farmer)
		Thomas Henry Hart (Publican, female servant)		
COUNTRY AREAS:				
Wealthy				
John Palmer (Parramatta)	William Howe (Liverpool)	William Campbell (Cooke)	Francis Settie (Liverpool)	
Mrs. King (Penrith)				
John McArthur (Liverpool)				
Small Farmers				
	Thomas Dargon (Windsor)		Mrs Pearce (Liverpool)	
	John Howe (Chief Constable Windsor)		William Ridgley (Sydney - farm Cooke)	
			John King (Liverpool tailor)	
			George Hall (Windsor)	

Table 27 Reasons given by employers bringing free servants before Sydney Quarter Sessions, 1826–28

Employer	Servant	Reasons
Barnet Levy (trader)	Maria Hunt	Master communicated intentions of dismissing her while she laid cloth for dinner inconsistently with directions. Absconded, property missing.
Mary Dillon (shopkeeper)	Phillip Kellow	Employed as cook, missed property, obtained search warrant.
William Wilmot (publican)	Ann Widgett	Lost articles during employ, suspected her.
Susan Adams (shopkeeper)	Thomas Youdall	Missed salt pork, suspected prisoner, met him with pork.
Robert Cooper (merchant)	Hugh Carline	Received information that prisoner had let nails off cart.
Eliz Fowler (settler)	Robert Grant	Employed to drive dray, seen taking property.
William Riley esq.	William North (personal servant)	Employed assisting in cooking, left house, property missing.
George Burn esq.	John Williams	Employed in store, suspected, searched jacket for pork.
Waterloo Stores	Samuel Kendrick	Employed as cooper, seen by constable carrying property.
Charles Pickering (market stallholder)	Thomas Fletcher	Employed casually at stall, property stolen.
Mary Reynolds (householder)	Jane Catty	Informed that the stockings prisoner was wearing were her own.
Joshua Raphael (tradesman)	Bartholomew Flinn	Suspected of robbery, constable called to search.
Benjamin Kirkby (householder)	Thomas Strutland	Missed money, suspected servant.
Nicholas Aspinall (soap manufacturer Clarence St)	Thomas Turner Thomas Gribberne	Watched by superintendent, soap concealed.

As with cases involving lightweight bread or selling of spirits, the courts could be used in cases involving master and servant to ensure that wages would not have to be paid or work would not have to be done. Uncertainties about what constituted payment and uncertainties about the proper relationship between master and servant were at the base of such cases. It would be wrong to see the courts as arbiter in such disputes. Rather the law was a battleground between master and servant when there were no clear reference points for either. Since employers were more likely to be listened to, and were more likely to use the courts, the law worked in their favour.

It was not only payment of servants and their rights and dues which led to dispute: the whole currency system of the colony opened the way for argument and exploitation. Sid Butlin described the different kinds of currency available in the colony between 1810 and 1830.[36] The promissory note and the store receipt were articles of exchange, along with wheat and rum. We may add clothes to Butlin's list. The records of the courts show how such a system could be exploited.

The promissory note and the store receipt were articles of exchange, along with wheat, clothes and rum. Forgery of notes and receipts was reported by shopkeepers who presented the bills for payment and discovered they were not authentic. In 1810 Francis Lawless and John Dalton were charged with forging a paymaster's note for the sum of £2. Elizabeth Shannon described her dealings with them:

> I live in Cambridge Street and keep a shop for selling little trifling things. I received the bill now produced from a man of the name of Ingram about three weeks ago. I received the £2 Paymaster's note and gave him one calico shirt 10/- and 30/- in colonial bills and I sent out and got him a pint of rum for £2 8/-.[37]

The case was further complicated when Elizabeth Shannon stated the following:

> When Ingram came to me with the fake bill he said he was a Hawkesbury settler by the name of Joy, that he had just came from the country and had frequent dealings with me there . . . I often go there on business. I never engaged Lawless to build a partition for me or anything else I never employed him.[38]

The complication of commercial dealings in the early colony meant that labour could also become an article of exchange. Perhaps some false swearing is suggested in the claim that Lawless had been employed; perhaps it was indebtedness which compelled Elizabeth Shannon to bring the complaint because of the nature of an economy based on contract. The colonial economy was open to such dealings.

Elizabeth Shannon brought another case the same day when Thomas Parnell was charged with uttering a forged paymaster's bill. Elizabeth Shannon said she took the £2 paymaster's bill from a woman by the name of Ann Hendon, and she gave for it a £2 bill on Frances Williams, a quarter of a pound of tea, and a pound of sugar, the whole totalling £2 6s. She passed the paymaster's bill to a man by the name of Browning and he returned it as a bad bill. Ann Hendon gave evidence that she had received the paymaster's bill from Parnell for whom she had washed for nine or ten months. She could not read and so she showed the bill to Ann Chapman who identified it in court. Thomas Parnell denied that the bill he gave Ann Hendon was the one presented in court. The Judge Advocate's Bench, thinking the evidence insufficient, discharged Parnell.[39]

Though notes may have been in circulation for some time, the reckoning came when they were presented for payment. In 1811, however, Mary Reiby used another means of detection. She received a note and took it to the person named, Mr Blaxland, to ascertain the authenticity of the handwriting.[40] The defence of Hannah Bent in this case was that she could not read so could not tell if the bill was forged.[41] She received a sentence of six months in the Female Factory.

Before the establishment of the Bank of New South Wales in 1816, forgery cases concentrated on promissory notes, orders and obtaining credit with fake notes. The detection was through shopkeepers like Mary Reiby and Elizabeth Shannon who remembered where they obtained the notes or orders from and reported the circumstances to the constables. A forged bill may have been in circulation some time before it was detected and orders for property circulated in the same manner. This left the cases quite open to false accusations.

Such offences continued when the Bank of New South Wales was established and they included the forgery of bank notes themselves. William Mahoney appeared in 1817 before the criminal court charged with forgery, an attempt to defraud Andrew Nash and the directors of the Bank of New South Wales. Johanna Rotton, housekeeper to Joseph Morley, a shopkeeper of Gloucester Street, Sydney, reported that a woman named Ann Hayes or Ann Mahoney obtained credit in the shop for £1 and 'yesterday called and gave a £1 note of Riley and Jones for it'.[42] Johanna Rotton handed the note to Morley half an hour later and he immediately pronounced it a forgery. The publican Francis de Silva also appeared and said he had sold rum to Ann Hayes and received a note in part payment. De Sylva went to Moss, a publican in George Street, who said it was a forgery. He went to Ann Hayes' house with the note and she said of the note 'never mind if it's a bad one, I'll find you a good one'[43] and gave him another note which also proved to be bad.

Six months later in the town of Parramatta Andrew Nash, publican, received a forged note which was verified as fake by the magistrate Marsden. He had received it from Mary Ann Wright, daughter of Gorman. She said she obtained it from William Mahoney. On 25 August 1817 three constables were to search the house of Mahoney where they found the plates for the production of notes and bank notes made out in the handwriting of Riley and Jones, merchants.[44]

The possibility for such forgery and the length of time it took for Mahoney to be searched and the forging equipment found was due to the structure of the economy, where bills were commonplace. The Bank of New South Wales notes were forged with the same distribution techniques as the promissory note. In 1822 a direct attempt of obtaining money from the bank was made by a fifteen-year-old, Mary Leighton. She presented the accountant of the Bank of New South Wales with a draft with the forged signature of William Wemyss. Despite her defence that she was led astray by 'a young man in the service of government house', she was transported for life.[45]

Very few persons were apprehended for such direct attempts on the bank: forged notes passed through the channels of shopkeepers and publicans until a case could be made. The victims of forgery in cases before the court were primarily wealthy merchants or landowners whose bills would possibly be more assured of identification, as well as the Bank of New South Wales. Table 28 sets out forgery cases and the means by which they were brought to the Court of Criminal Jurisdiction. Those that involve production of large quantities of notes include the involvement of informers and approvers. Forgery cases automatically drew in numbers of accused persons who, in order to defend themselves, gave evidence.

Defences such as Mary Leighton's depended on intent, and earlier cases where illiteracy was claimed followed the same pattern. If a search was made and plates found, or the prisoner pleaded guilty, such a debate of course did not apply.

Table 28   Means of discovery of forgery cases appearing before the Court of Criminal Jurisdiction, 1816–24

Year	Defendant	Victim	Article	Presented to	Means discovered
1816	Henry Pearce	Joseph Morley, shopkeeper	Promissory note	Samuel Terry, store	Terry requested payment three weeks later from Morley.
1817	Ann Eliza Prosser	Robert Campbell, merchant	Promissory note	Robert Cooper, dealer	Cooper met Campbell and informed him; Campbell denied note.
1817	Patrick Hannon, Windsor convict	Windsor Commissariat	Bill of exchange	Charles Thompson, shopkeeper, Hunter Street; Eliza Cassidy, public house, Gloucester Street; Joseph McKinley, shopkeeper	All three shopkeepers suspected prisoner for having so much money and constable informed.
1817	William Mahoney	Bank of New South Wales	Bank note	Johanna Rotton, housekeeper to Joseph Morley, Gloucester Street; Francis de Silva, publican	Ann Mahoney/Hayes gave note; Morley recognised forgery; Morley and de Silva went to house of Mahoney
1817	Thomas Brown	Bank of New South Wales	Bank note	Mr Brown, warehouse	Woman from Brown's went to bank. Prisoner came to bank.
1818	Joseph Salter Susannah Knock	Bank of New South Wales	Bank notes	Mary Gotham for bread and cheese. Celia Wright with defendant.	Gotham and Wright informed. Constables searched.
1820	James Garland Elizabeth Hannell James Stubbs	Commissariat	Store receipts	Clerk commissariat was told by prisoner that he had been passing forged receipts for several years.	Informers, constables picked up defendant on race course.
1821	William Williams Gilbert Brown William Lansdown John McGuire William Turncliffe Edward McAvoy Convicts	Bank of New South Wales	Bank notes	Mrs. Wilmot, Talbot's public house, Geo. Street; Mr Klensendorrfe, Liverpool publican	Shopkeepers recognised '£1' altered to '£10'.

Table 28   *(continued)*

Year	Defendant	Victim	Article	Presented to	Means discovered
1822	Charles Merrit, watchmaker	Bank of England	Plates to forge notes	Anonymous informer	Constables searched.
1823	John Glasside, free	Order of Edward Bates	Order for stores	Thos Catterwell, clerk to Mr. Hart, Pitt Street.	'It was not till Mr. Bates came to look at order it was discovered false.'
1823	Charles Eaton	Order of C. Walker	Order for stores	John Hobcroft, servant to Mr Wilshire by Thomas Smith	Smith claimed Eaton gave order in exchange for money.

A total of 53 cases of forgery were brought before the courts, as follows: Judge Advocate's Bench, 8; Police Magistrates' Bench, 3; Court of Criminal Jurisdiction, 1810–21, 12; Supreme Court of Criminal Jurisdiction, 30.

Obviously, if the defendant was found with forging equipment by constables a much more successful case could be made out. Mary Leighton was apprehended for forging one bill, but other cases like William Mahoney's involve forgery of large numbers of notes where constables discover production lines for them. These cases involve informants and approvers.

In 1821 Gilbert Brown, an approver, gave evidence in a case against six men for forging:

> Williams came up to Parramatta and said if I would pass a few £10 notes he, Williams would get my liberty. I went with Williams to Cook's River to a hut put up for the reception of bushrangers. He gave me a £10 note which I came to Sydney with and passed to Mr. Wilmot . . . Williams and I divided the change . . . I have passed one other note to a person who keeps a public house at Liverpool whose name I do not know.[46]

All of the prisoners were apprehended after the constable John Lucas went in search of them after reports from Wilmot and the publican. Williams attempted to swallow some notes when apprehended.[47] Williams described himself as part of a large operation and the initial note discovered had been altered from £1 to £10 rather than being completely forged. Williams gave evidence to avoid being charged himself. His evidence shows the centrality of shopkeepers and publicans to the discovery of forgery cases. At the same time, because of the need to prove intent, forgery cases were very hazy in establishing guilt and were obviously open to false swearing or manipulation.

These cases arose out of the structure of the economy where promissory notes or orders of some kind were the main currency. The forgery case in the colony did not simply involve the defendant and his tampering with notes: it also involved a complex system of informing, searching and signs of guilt. The connection between the economy and the use of law is further illustrated in examination of other cases involving payment in the colony.

Shops and public houses were important centres for the exchange of debts, which notes represented. As we have seen, they were also the centre of constables' attention for the illegal sale of spirits and the presence of government servants in the house. James Kirton at Parramatta, William Widgett at Windsor and all of the Liverpool publicans were subject to searches and raids by constables.

Though quarrels over debts could be solved in the civil courts, certain publicans appeared before the benches on complaints made about their activities as creditors or debtors. The Liverpool publicans were particularly responsible for such complaints. Henry Turbett claimed in September 1824 that he presented a bill to William Klensendorrfe, Liverpool publican, to have it settled. Klensendorrfe at the same time billed Turbett for articles in part payment and gave him a bill on Jonathon Pearce in Liverpool for the remainder. Klensendorrfe asked Turbett if he would sign an agreement to furnish certain work at Klensendorrfe's residence but Turbett would not agree to terms. Klensendorrfe assaulted him, ordered his wife to assault him and they both tried to take Turbett's tools.[48] It is clearly demonstrated in the case that both men were involved in a complex state of indebtedness. Klensendorrfe wished it to continue.

In 1824 John Quigley was brought before the Liverpool bench by the chief constable Ikin. Quigley, it was claimed, was drinking in the Ship Inn; he called for spirits he could not pay for and got so drunk he was unable to talk. The prisoner, though, gave a defence. He said he had left a note in the hands of Mr Browne, publican of the Ship Inn, and on account of that had occasionally drawn property there. He knew that a balance was still due to him, which was why he called for spirits. He was never able to get a statement of any kind from Mr Browne.[49] In this case the court was used as part of a financial transaction, in order to enforce payment of a debt that was claimed. The blur between legality and illegality in the presentation of this case is certainly reflected in other cases involving disputes in country regions. Law is used or incorporated into a dispute rather than being used to solve a dispute.

The area of disputes in all country regions concerned the lack of fencing: there were arguments over boundaries, the destruction of crops and the impounding of animals. In 1818 Andrew Johnstone, constable, appeared before the Windsor bench for assault. He said he had sent two of his men and his sons to clear some ground for wheat. He was called to the field and found William Johnstone wrestling with Ralph Turnbull. Johnstone asked what right Turnbull had to be there: 'Turnbull replied he had a right to be there from the Governor's permission to occupy the same. He had refrained from cropping the ground in consequence of it not being measured.' Turnbull gave a defence in this case:

> the ground is supposed to belong to a farm he rents from Mr. Hall, he met young Johnstone who drove the pigs away, the defendant's wife [Turnbull's] and Elizabeth Stubbs came over attempting to persuade him to go home . . . Andrew Johnstone knocked him down with his staff saying if he did not submit he would knock him down again and that it was in his power to take his life.

The Windsor bench decided that Johnstone had abused his authority in 'making the same instrumental to private pique'. They dismissed the complaint and also Johnstone from his duty as constable. Andrew Johnstone became the defendant himself and was sent before the criminal court for assault, of which he was found guilty. He wrote a petition addressed to the Judge Advocate:

Your petitioner submits for the humane consideration of this honourable court the very severe and heavy losses he has sustained by the late floods, having nearly all his grain, growing crops, poultry and other stock destroyed by these floods to nearly his ruin in point of circumstance.[50]

Floods invariably intensified disputes over boundaries in Windsor. In 1828 the grand jury reported that fences and boundaries were sources of endless litigation,

to which these districts are more liable than any part of the country by reason of flood having induced many of the settlers to remove their dwellings to the highlands for safety a circumstance itself prejudicial to the necessary intercourse of the farm with the farmyard independent of the obstacles of sufficient access and circumstance needs.[51]

Trespass and consequent assault cases appeared in the records of the Windsor bench and the Quarter Sessions. It was necessary to establish the boundaries of one's own property for economic survival.

In Liverpool the same kinds of disputes occurred, but these involved wealthy landowners. Thomas Campbell was tried for the assault of Elizabeth Neale when he attempted to stop her ploughing in 1818.[52] The Parramatta bench also heard such complaints: in 1822 Margaret Downey went before it to give evidence that Thomas Saunders Junior and Mrs Saunders had gone down to her fence with a horse and cart to go through. Margaret Downey opposed them going through and Mrs Saunders replied she would tear down palings. They pulled down the fence and struck Margaret Downey, calling her an Irish bitch.[53] Saunders was fined £2 by the criminal court.[54]

The poor fencing and inadequate roads were not simply a result of relocation because of floods. Governor Brisbane complained in 1823 of the impossibility of establishing true ownership of land because it changed hands so many times and no records were kept.[55] Similar competitiveness between neighbouring farmers has been explored in studies of early nineteenth-century America. Access to land meant great opportunity, but the uncertainties of land claims meant constant skirmishes between neighbours. Alan Taylor has written of the Sheepscot back country in Maine 1801: 'conditions encouraged many (but not all) to conclude that outstripping their neighbours in a competitive race for wealth and its power provided the only sure independence.'[56] Such studies have been directly related to the emergence of a capitalist mentality among farmers, attitudes well recognised by Australian historians Brian Fletcher and George Parsons.[57] In New South Wales we can see the law as a powerful means of extending competition between farmers. The competitiveness of the market was expressed in the use of the courts. The inadequacy of boundaries, combined with an economic system dependent on many differing kinds of currency, resulted in highly competitive neighbours who were jealous of their own harvests and animals. Such a situation was not helped by the habit of animals of wandering in search of food and their tendency to feed on wheat crops and corn.

In 1822 William Hovell interrupted the proceedings of the bench of magistrates at Minto, shouting at Howe the magistrate, 'I do not know whether to complain of you or your stockman, your cattle destroyed my wheat.'[58] Two years later William Hovell's cattle went into the wheat of Robert Brierson, ticket-of-leave. When Hovell stopped Brierson and offered him the 'poundage' (i.e., the sum of the fine), Brierson replied, 'I am no poundkeeper.'[59]

These two cases demonstrate the means by which wandering animals were dealt with all over the colony. No recompense could be obtained for destruction of a crop, but revenge could be obtained by impounding the animals of the neighbour. Assault cases resulted from the anger of the person whose crop was destroyed or the anger of the person who saw his animals being taken to the pound. All social classes participated in this violence, Sir John Jamison being one defendant.[60] Such quarrels could well break down the distinction between wealthy persons and poorer defendants.

Those who suffered quite clearly, though, were persons who could not afford the poundage or destruction of the crop. John Guildford gave information concerning the circumstances of the harbouring of the bushranger John Price by the settler John Phena-more. Guildford noted that they saw Mr Johnstone's horses go into the wheat of Ikin the constable. Ikin sent the dogs and children after them and said the only way to keep horses out was to set up a single rail fence, leave a cart open, drive the horses in and tell Mr Johnstone. Price said, 'that is not the way to receive satisfaction, they are gentlemen, a poor man has no chance with them. There is only one way to receive satisfaction and that is to blow the brains out of some of the horses.' Ikin replied he was only newly out of trouble (this probably concerned his liquor dealings) and would never do anything again which would affect his life.[61]

The uncertainty of economic relations is reflected in the numbers of cases brought for theft of pigs, turkeys and cattle between small landowners. The animal most commonly stolen in the Windsor area was a pig. The descriptions which complainants give of their behaviour and suspicions show the incorporation of law into dispute.

In 1822 Charles Wilkins, free, of Wilberforce, was charged with theft of a pig. Thomas Graham, of Wilberforce, had said he had lost two sows from amongst his running pigs. He recounted how he discovered the theft. He had 'made every search in the neighbour-hood particularly about the prisoner's premises'. The pig was in a log sty and seemed to have been driven in there. Wilkins reportedly told the constable James Tester that if the constable had not been there when Graham came he would have shot Graham. Wilkins was transported for fourteen years.[62] In March 1822 Thomas Graham brought a case against another settler, Richard Rustin, for possessing a sow stolen from his property. He had been informed by John Cobcroft Junior that the sow was in the possession of John Bailey, who said he purchased it from Rustin.[63] Rustin was acquitted on this charge.[64]

Michael Ford was charged in 1826 with stealing a pig from John Lyons. Lyons too had immediate suspicion of who was responsible for the theft. He said his pigs were in the habit of going to a lagoon near Ford's house, and 'the prisoner generally was a suspected person of having other pigs in his possession and in consequence his wife [Lyons'] obtained a warrant'.[65]

Suspicion could result from bad relations; if there was no suspicion of a particular person, tracking was often resorted to. Kezia Robert's servants began to track pigs stolen from her daughter,[66] and as a result William Nash, Edward Higgins and Jeremiah Buffy were apprehended after they were tracked to their house.[67] In 1821 Joseph Onus lost his barrow pig and he said, 'a native tracked the steps of some persons and blood to the

Table 29 Theft accusations between small landowners, traders and itinerant labourers appearing before Windsor Quarter Sessions, 1824–27

Defendant	Accuser
1824–May 1826	
Luke Stamforth	Thomas Hodges, itinerant labourer
Ann Wright	Sarah West
Thomas Dargon, trader	James Cox, itinerant labourer
James Dargon } Joseph Windred }	Cyrus Doyle
Patrick McNamara	John McDonald
James McKenzie } Henry Richardson }	Thomas Howard
Matthew Wood	Catherine Lunch
Richard Holloway	Daniel Smallwood
Mary Russell } Mark Russell } William Dixon, itinerant labourer }	Thomas McKeever
Michael Leydon	Thomas Rainbow
Thomas Jones	William Baker the younger
Samuel Freeman } Thomas Baker } Elizabeth Freeman }	Morris Breaknook Jeremiah Hill
Daniel Bigley	Ann Birken
James Hill, prisoner to Elizabeth Hill	James Timms
Charles Beales, itinerant labourer	Henry Fleming
Richard Whittington } James Irvine }	Richard Kelly
James Mahoney	Elizabeth Quinn
Thomas Kelly } Thomas Sparse }	James Roberts
Mary Huggins } George Clarke }	Mary White
John Drake	Thomas Cooper
John McCabe	Patrick McCabe
James Tomlinson	James Rose
July 1826–April 1827	
George Davis	Revd Mathew Meares
Patrick Joice	Michael Brookes
William Williams } William Lahy, itinerant labourer }	William Clemson
John Blackmore	Richard Nowland
William Brown	Mr W. Hayes
William Brennan	John Fox
William Binge, tenant	Isaac Gorrick

Table 29   *(continued)*

Defendant	Accuser
Patrick Keenagh	Patrick Lahy
John Hughes	George Bowman, trader
Catherine Fox	James Chapman, shoemaker
Ann Rustin	Michael Lamb
William Higgins }	Thomas Wright
William Thompson }	
John Robinson	Patrick Byrne
Isaac Salter	Joseph McCaulding
Joseph Keen	Thomas Parnell
John Hobbs	Henry Flemming
John Pearce	James Kelly the elder
John Howe	Mr Smith
Matthew Brown }	
Joseph Copson, convict }	Henry Baldwin
Thos Church, convict }	
Thomas Green }	
Patrick Carroll, itinerant labourer	Richard Kelly
Michael Ford	John Lyons
Thomas Freeman, convict }	George Smith
John Burton, itinerant labourer }	
James Calloughy	Edward Baldwin
Edward Devine	Mathew Lock
Thomas Chasling	James McDonald

lagoon, and reaching a spot Job Moore found a quantity of meat concealed'.[68] In 1820 James Steel reportedly sold a pig to John Teale for 20/- (paid in one shirt and jacket). The pig came back and Steel did not inform its new owner but supposedly knocked it down and killed it. John Teale said that Steel denied twice that the pig had returned.[69] Cases between persons of equal status formed the bulk of theft cases in the Windsor region (see Table 29).

Accusations of pig theft in the Windsor region resulted from the economic structure of the area where small farmers lived in close proximity and disputes were common. That the defendant might be transported for fourteen years did not seem to concern complainants. Relations of indebtedness possibly encouraged such litigation whereby a fine could financially ruin a defendant or the property be left barren or sold while a sentence was served.

While Windsor exhibits a particular propensity for persons of equal status to challenge each other with theft, there is evidence of similar cases in other areas. In 1817 at Parramatta Moses Watson and Hannah Spencer were charged with pig theft through the activities of an informant, Ann Waddie, a woman in the Female Factory. She had seen Moses Watson go to the house of Hannah Spencer with a bag on his back in which she thought he had a pig. He came out of the house with four loaves of bread and without

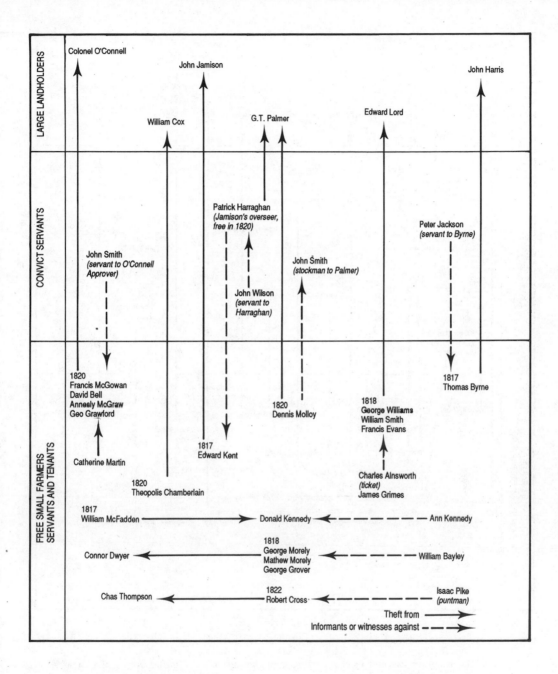

Figure 10   Status and relationships of persons appearing in cases of horse, sheep and cattle theft, Windsor region, 1817–22.

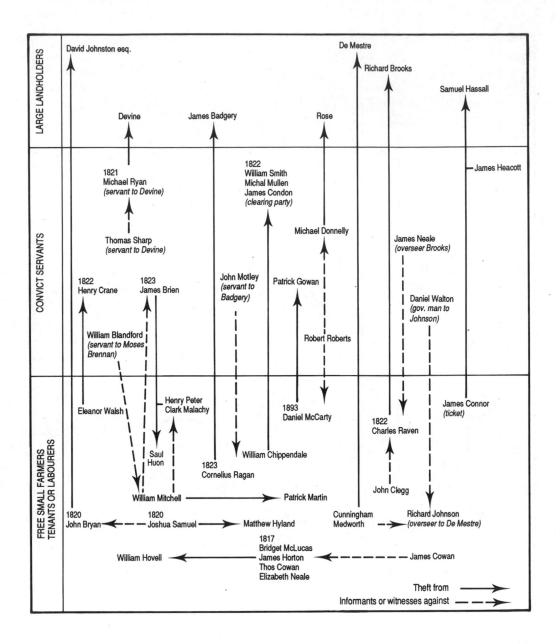

Figure 11 Status and relationships of persons appearing in cases of cattle theft, Liverpool and Campbelltown region, 1817–23.

the bag.[70] The owner of the pig, Thomas Weyman, obtained a search warrant on this information.[71] In 1820 in Liverpool, Joshua Cunningham and Samuel Medworth were charged with theft of a cow from Matthew Hyland. Hyland had found all of his cattle missing one morning and the rails taken down from their yard. He had sent two boys to Liverpool where they saw cattle in the slaughter yard. Two constables informed the court that they had seen Cunningham driving the cattle.[72]

Theft between small farmers of the same status occurs throughout the colony and through tracking, through obtaining search warrants, through receiving information the farmers did much of the work of cases themselves. Theft from larger landholders followed the same pattern, except that it included overseers and government servants as informers as well as small landholders (see Figures 10–13). In 1827 in Windsor at Colonel O'Connell's farm, Riverston, a calf was taken from the calf pen. The overseer Thomas Munday said he suspected the farm's nearest neighbour, John Connor. Munday and his wife gave the reason that Thomas Welsh, servant to Connor, came to O'Connell's farm and said that the calf 'may have been cleverer than they thought'.[73] Informants were mainly government servants who gave evidence of seeing a calf or sheep slaughtered or being carried to the house of a settler or the hut of other government servants. Small settlers acted as receivers. Theft of sheep or cattle occasionally involved groups of servants and sometimes one turned approver.

In 1822 Robert Harmer gave evidence concerning the theft of a cow belonging to Captain Richard Brookes: 'Charles Raven said to this deponent your master has some fine cattle can't you get some for me. Deponent replied, I do not know, but I'll see. Shortly after deponent drove a cow and calf there.'[74]

In 1823 Thomas Perry, a small settler in Penrith, was charged with soliciting Jonathon Doyle to steal the magistrate McHenry's calf. He said:

> sometime back the prisoner Thomas Perry was at deponent's house—asked him how he was for meat. Deponent replied he had a cask. Perry said he was very ill for meat, deponent replied, 'but you have plenty of pigs?' 'So' 'none to kill' he said it would be easy to get some meat if he had someone to assist.[75]

Perry's case was referred back to the magistrate and he was given a bond for good behaviour.[76] Perry wanted someone to help him and it was difficult to steal cattle alone. Consequently cattle theft was very risky as convict servants or small settlers could easily become approvers and avoid punishment themselves.

Disputes over property escalated into informing or accusation. The suspicion and attentiveness evident in animal theft cases meant that the use of law in disputes in such a manner also gave the courts enormous power over illegal behaviour. Just as the dramatics of bushrangers referred to the rituals of law, so too the care people took in hiding stolen property or guarding against informers bore relation to the likelihood of being caught. Hiding became almost ritualistic in the colony.

In 1822 Charles Fell, a shopkeeper, found a hide in a hole in the ground covered with loose soil;[77] the legs and tail of a calf were found hidden under a stump near the hut of Richard Crisp.[78] In 1822 also Joseph Morley, settler of Prospect, found the skin of a lamb in a post hole.[79]

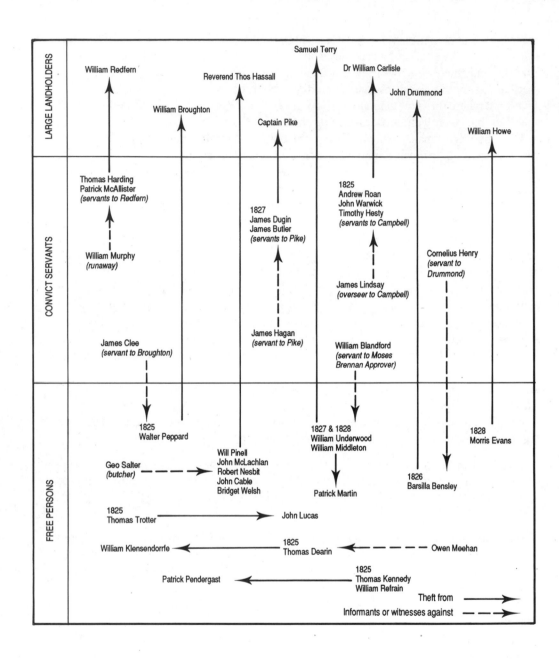

Figure 12 Status and relationships of persons appearing in cases of horse, sheep and cattle theft, Liverpool and Campbelltown region, 1825–28.

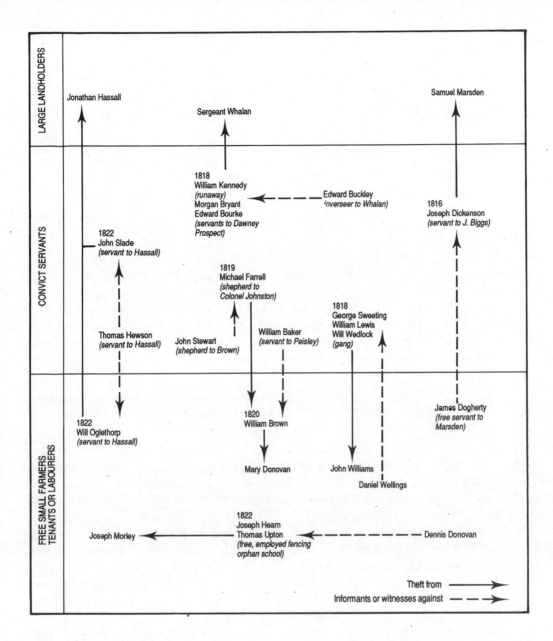

Figure 13 Status and relationships of persons appearing in cases of sheep and cattle theft, Parramatta region, 1818–22.

Susannah Newman of Cockle Bay demonstrated in 1818 quite clearly how important it was to have an explanation for meat found in the house:

> Sunday I went to church and left my pigs feeding close to the house of John Baker I returned, some pigs were missing . . . I went to Baker's where I found a pig's head in an iron pot. I charged Baker with having stolen my pig, examined his harness cask found the meat . . . soon after I went out for a search warrant.[80]

The harness cask was where meat was meant to be kept and Susan Foley, who stayed to watch Baker, told Susannah Newman on her return that Baker had removed some meat from under his bed into the harness cask. This was suspicious behaviour in itself and meat under beds, found in bags in holes and strung in a creek was evidence as much as the skin or feet.

The only way to keep meat was by salting it so if someone was seen to be buying or obtaining salt after a cattle theft this was grounds for suspicion. When Thomas Fletcher, overseer to Samuel Hassall, lost two heifers, he strongly suspected a ticket-of-leave farmer, James Connor, because he heard that Connor had obtained a quantity of salt up to sixty pounds.[81]

From the numbers of accounts of rotting meat it can be gathered that the market for stolen beef was not a profitable one. It was a market in which requests for beef were made to government servants rather than open selling of stolen meat. Edward Farrell confessed in a case of sheep theft:

> the first conversation I had with Sheehan he said could we do anything with sheep. I have a fence [person to buy] he said he had not 3lbs of meat since he'd been with his master, 'I am half starved'. Sheehan replied you need not be afraid I have a person who will buy anything I bring her. I slept at Styles all night repented in the morning and went to Mr. Blaxland to lodge information.[82]

Farrell's references to hunger and to the need for someone to buy the remaining meat were similar to other cases, and the difficulty of obtaining a 'fence' to sell the meat to was also common. It was much better to keep the animals alive and sell them to small farmers or slaughter yards. The secretiveness about hiding the remains of the animal well illustrates the extent to which cattle, sheep and pig theft was policed.

Yet if the animal was kept alive it had to be driven down the roads or to the markets in order to be sold, and careful note was made by locals of passers-by and the animals they possessed. Horses were noticed very quickly and it was unusual for a poor man to own a horse. They were also highly valued by persons who did own them. Patrick Pendergast gave evidence in 1825 that he had lost a mare and 'never heard anything of her until he saw her in the possession of Thomas Kennedy in Irish town'.[83]

Although boundary fences were either very poor or non-existent in country areas, inhabitants had clear ideas of which property was theirs and what was trespass. This resulted in quarrels over land and crops. Wandering pigs and other animals were also a source of discontent in country areas, and resulted in many cases of assault and rescue. The monetary system, dependent on indebtedness, also resulted in criminal cases. The theft of animals could be used as a kind of revenge or collection of debts. Policing of stolen animals was quite intensive by both small landowners and government servants and it was partly assisted by the activities of informants and approvers. The second economy in meat and stolen animals does not seem profitable and intense policing created its own activity of hiding, planting and 'fences' or receivers.

In 1828 a series of offences were heard at Windsor which were listed in 'Records of Conviction under Mr. Peel's Act'. John Garrick was charged with trespassing on the growing crops of Robert Farlow of Wilberforce and destroying the crop by feeding it to horses.[84] He was fined thirty shillings. Robert Reeves was charged with shooting and injuring a dog, the property of Edward Standing of Richmond; he was fined the sum of thirteen shillings and imprisoned till it was paid.[85] James Bryant was charged with stealing turnips from Joseph Jones, and Thomas Thomas and John Birtles were charged with cutting and carrying away timber, the property of Henry Robinson.[86]

All of these people, defendants and prosecutors, were small settlers. Such struggles, as we have seen, occurred throughout the period, in Windsor and in other areas, These new charges under Mr Peel's Act concerning trespass and theft dealt with struggles that underlay many charges of assault and theft in country areas. Rather than boundaries of land becoming less important in the courts, the defence of them became more important as they were established.

The offences so far discussed resulted from the ease of transgressing 'proper' economic relations. The struggles that marked the countryside resulted from the newness of the economic system. Indebtedness, boundaries, the loss of animals, the damage done to crops, all resulted from the inadequacies of the system of land grants. The difficulties of indebtedness and the management of accounts resulted from the nature of a currency system in which several different methods of exchange were used. Theft, though, was beset with similar problems. The impossibilities of obtaining trustworthy 'fences' or receivers of meat or cattle meant that cattle theft was risky. The illegal economy of stolen animals or meat relied on careful hiding of stolen property and transferring of animals. Even if meat was hidden under soil or forty yards from a house, it was likely to be found. The economy of the towns was also dependent on buying and selling through various means of exchange. It was subject to embezzlement, forgery and shoplifting. The channels through which stolen goods passed and the means by which they were discovered show the patterns of theft and the quarrels which surrounded them.

In 1819 Robert Hobbs, the district constable of Pitt Town, overheard a conversation of Joseph Smith, servant of Mr Grimes, in which he stated:

> that some months since being in search of a young bullock . . . he found the hopper of a mill near to the stockyard of Mr. Gilderthorpe, he kept the same for two months and sold it to James Palet upon condition if the same was owned he should deliver it up . . . witness [the constable] found the said hopper in the possession of James Palet.[87]

The hopper of the mill had been stolen seven months before from the farm of Colonel O'Connell. Joseph Butler, stockman to Gilderthorpe, said he had purchased the mill from Thomas Myles of Pitt Town for £3 providing Myles had liberty to grind wheat with it. The mill was identified by O'Connell's servants. Thomas Myles received twelve months at Newcastle. The mill was extremely important to the financial status of the small or large farmer alike. It was one of the most commonly stolen articles in the countryside.

It is possible to discover a long link of stolen property through accounts of overheard conversations or through the work of informers in both country areas and Sydney. Neighbours were one group of informers. When Thomas Moore's house in Sydney was broken into, Ann Eastern gave evidence that she resided 'opposite, that she saw Catherine Leeson go to the door, finding it locked, go to the window put in her shawl and bonnet and finally managed to open the door. Moore's housekeeper Mary Shea returned and both women left later after Catherine Leeson had put a bundle through the stable window.'[88] This evidence was not sufficient; Judge Advocate Wylde wrote of the case: 'there is evidence of an entry and removal from the house but not from the premises, of such articles taken and enumerated none are found upon her or in her possession—the evidence of Eastern is questionable on the whole conduct.'[89] The evidence was questionable to Wylde, but not the the magistrates who passed on the case. The words of informants or approvers often sealed a case for the magistrate when it may well have been unfit for the criminal court. The informer did not necessarily hold a grudge against the defendant: Ann Eastern could well have been describing what she saw as suspicious behaviour. In 1818 in Parramatta Elizabeth O'Hara gave evidence against Henry Hitchcock. She had seen him with a new pair of shoes and before that had gone to his house and observed a quantity of flour. She suspected it belonged to a household recently robbed.[90]

The complexity which sometimes lay behind the actions of an informer is suggested by the case against Felix McClinton in 1827 in Bathurst. Maurice Maroney, free, gave evidence that Peter Cooney came to him and said, 'Maroney here is this villain, McClinton, that cursed Orangeman who has been trying to do me a injury, if you will take these spoons put them into the house where they might be found I'll give you £5.'[91] Maroney said that he asked Cooney who would go and find it: 'Cooney said it would be neither the constable at Bong Bong or Macyntyre Creek but the chief constable at Cawdor who was a friend of his.'[92] This case had begun with a different set of evidence, that of Edward Farley, chief constable of Cawdor, stating that he had proceeded with a search warrant to McClinton's.[93] This constable claimed he proceeded because of 'information given', and the informer was initially unnamed. The second informer, Maroney, claimed he gave evidence because he considered wrong had been done.

Exactly what motivated informers is difficult to ascertain. Maroney may not have been as concerned as he suggested. Those informers who were named in cases before the magistrate's bench in 1820–21 were of the three kinds: servants who saw their interest as compatible with their employer's or who wished to protect themselves from accusation; those who had bought stolen property or were offered property to buy; and persons who reported suspicious behaviour. Informers, therefore, went with various intentions to the courts. There were also pecuniary advantages, as it is clear that police in Sydney paid informers.

Cases before the criminal court provide more detail. Among persons who noted suspicious behaviour were gentlemen. Captain Piper, in 1821, wrote 'a memorandum to Captain Rossi respecting my robbery'. He wrote that a man named Patrick Byrne overheard a conversation. This involved:

> two persons answering [i.e. speaking] about the robbery committed and one of them said he might as
> well be in it as he had been asked by John, conversation appeared to suspect a man by the name of

Carey between twelve and 1 a.m. in the ward where the tradespeople are kept, the man is large, Irish by birth.[94]

Those in possession of stolen property were under threat from persons living in the same house. Constables searched the house of William McDonald because of information given, and later one constable reported what had occurred: 'I told McDonald he might give us a great deal of trouble he knew what we were looking for . . . he said he dared say he did know and pointed to the other prisoners saying they brought it and it was up the chimney.'[95]

Cases from the 1826 Supreme Court and Quarter Sessions were similar to those of 1820–21. Shopkeepers were prominent. There were cases in the Supreme Court where constables worked according to information they received. John Purcell, chief constable of Penrith, appeared before the Sydney bench to give evidence against eight persons for receiving after he had been given information.[96] Cases from 1826 show an absence of concern for the welfare of neighbours; there is increasing complication in the bringing of cases, with the accusation passing through several receivers until settling on one person.

Esther Hands reported in February 1826 that five months before, her husband's house had been broken into and forty-two of forty-three veils had been stolen. The informant in this case was Elizabeth Thompson, who gave information that four months before she had purchased five veils from Mary Trainer and had sold one to another woman. One veil had been taken out of a drawer by Mary Trainer's daughter who said she had 'planted' it.[97] It was through this evidence and the evidence of other persons involved in the sale of the veils that Mary Trainer was arrested. In such a situation Elizabeth Thompson may well have been charged with receiving stolen property.

Country benches were more open to false information, and to information given for particular reasons other than concern for justice or self-protection. In 1820 Michael Smith was accused by John Mackenzie of entering his house and taking away pork and spirits. In his defence Smith said:

some time in November John Mackenzie accompanied by two constables came to the prisoner's house by virtue of a search warrant. Mackenzie alleged he had been robbed. Prisoner having some pork and rum his own property the said Mackenzie . . . said he lost pork and rum and claimed the prisoner's rum and pork . . . the following day the investigation of the business took place at Windsor when he stated he could not swear to any part of the pork or rum. Eight days after Mary Mackenzie came to said court and swore to some of the pork very probably from the description she had received of it from said John her husband. The prisoner had on this occasion informed the magistrate of a stolen pig being in the Mackenzie's possession which he is apprehensive is the cause of the present unfounded and malicious charge.[98]

Despite this evidence, Smith was found guilty and was sentenced to seven years' transportation. This case is typical of reciprocal charges where small farmers accused each other of theft or participated in cases against each other. Smith did not have enough evidence for a false swearing case and so in the eyes of the court a theft had occurred.

Country theft cases present a pattern of interference in the economy different to Sydney cases. Cases brought up against people who participated in other cases form a substantial part of country Quarter Sessions records. While there are thefts in Sydney from households which result in this kind of cross-accusation of neighbours, this pattern does not extend outside immediate neighbours and household theft. In the countryside the workings of the economy closely resemble relations of the illegal economy, i.e. property is stolen from someone who was of the same status as the thief and who no doubt had commercial relations with him or her. In Sydney those who informed were mainly shopkeepers or persons observing suspicious behaviour. In the country those who informed may well have been closely related to the thief.

The sensitivity apparent in cases involving informers suggests that theft was very risky in the colony. The accused may well have been innocent: he or she might have been caught at a particular point in the transferring of property as money or the charge might have been brought by someone who wished to protect themselves or construct a case as revenge. The variety of motivations for informing made the policing of theft in the colony quite ruthless.

Informers and approvers also give us information concerning the receivers of stolen property. Through them we can ascertain the channel of goods through the illegal economy.

In 1817 Ann Podmore went to her master's house, inquired if he was home and went up the stairs where 'she committed several acts of violence'. After she left, a watch, three yards of calico and a bonnet were found missing. Two constables interviewed Ann Podmore in the watchhouse and Podmore said if she could go home she would find it. They went to her lodgings and asked her room mate Susannah Knock for the watch. She said they could not have it till morning. Rachael Field was brought from the watchhouse in Pitt Street in consequence of Ann Podmore saying that Knock was receiver to Rachael Field. Field asked for the watch back, and Susannah Knock said, 'I can't, I can't.' Samuel Chapman, in company with two other constables, searched the house; upon digging up the garden they saw something shine and found the watch.[99] Susannah Knock was charged with receiving. The property in this case did not move outside the house of the prisoner because another household member was a receiver.

In 1822 Henrietta Bray was given two shirts to plant (i.e., hide) for Ann Crane. They belonged to Mr Harpur. Harpur sent Ann Crane word that he saw his shirts being sold around the town. Sarah Wise gave evidence that the prisoner had come to her with the shirts and sold them for half a crown.[100] In 1821 James McGreevy and Margaret McGreevy were charged with receiving property from Ann Kennedy. The constable involved in the search, Thomas Dunn, said that Kennedy had told him, 'Margaret McGreevy invited her to rob her master's house. Cash had been given to Margaret McGreevy who returned some of it and said to give it to James McGreevy and get for him the makings of a pair of Dane Trousers to keep him in temper against Christmas.'[101]

These receivers charged were not people who made profits on stolen property, nor were they shopkeepers. The property passed from the original defendant to persons to whom something was owed or something was given. Shopkeepers, like Sarah Wise, could give evidence that they knew nothing of stolen property and bought in ignorance. It is rare to find a shopkeeper in a receiving case, though they give evidence enough in theft cases.

Receivers were often small householders who were involved in buying and selling for themselves. In 1824 Martha Dunn said she would tell constables where she had sold stolen property. She took them to the house of Warren Lindsay; 'she said she had made a present of a shirt to Lindsay and the others she got £2 upon'.[102] That some persons were wary of buying stolen property is demonstrated by the kind of evidence Thomas Siddenmam gave against Thomas Clarke: 'Ten days since the prisoner Clarke sold to him five table cloths, paid 20/- he said he had won them in a raffle and they were "all right".'[103] Property that was not 'all right' was often traced through several buyers to the original thief, or the last person, perhaps, who could not give a reason for selling it. In the case against Thomas Slater, free, of Sydney, three jewellers gave evidence against him. Richard Pante said Slater had purchased a silver watch for which he paid four Spanish dollars and James Oately said he had worked on the watch for Slater. Edward Thurston described how he had purchased the gold watch key from Slater. The inform-ant John Hugo, resident of Sydney, explained how Slater had come to own the property:

> Three months ago I was at a house kept by Thurston on the rocks . . . between 8–9 a man named Marten came in, went into the yard with Thurston, Thurston shortly after called Slater thrust a gold key in his hand appeared to be bargaining. Slater was called to give his opinion. Thurston said don't let it be a dry bargain lets have some rum—the gold key is very much like Thurston's. As going out Thurston told Slater to ask Marten if there was anything else to sell.[104]

The house of a publican was not a particularly safe place in which to sell stolen prop-erty, but some publicans are named as receivers. Patrick Conner, publican, was impli-cated in a case in 1824 when he bought a shawl for eight shillings,[105] and in 1825 he appeared on a charge of receiving material. Catherine Doyle gave evidence that she purchased for Patrick Conner eighteen yards of dimity. She was attempting to resell it in the market when it was claimed by Mr Robert Cooper, merchant. Jane Hughes of Cambridge Street said Conner had left a box at her house which the constables later came for.[106]

The Conner case is one where a person appears twice as a buyer of stolen property. Receiving cannot be located in one public house or shop nor in particular households in Sydney. Cases of receiving involve often some kind of personal relationship alongside that of buyer and seller, or possibly buying forms part of that relationship.

If we were to look for a structured illegal economy where certain channels were consistently used, we would not find it before the courts. The receiving that occurs in Sydney is between persons who know each other and can be informed on. Alternatively it may be that successful receivership was in the hands of shopkeepers who could easily disclaim any knowledge that the property was stolen. It is clear that property often passed through several hands before it successfully reached a shopkeeper, without that shopkeeper or stallholder informing.

Also, from the number of cases which appear after months it seems as if articles were 'planted' or hidden before they became 'all right'. The sellers did not anticipate the sharp eye of a woman whose dress had been stolen months before or the eye of the merchant who saw before him material which was 'one of a kind' in the colony.

In Sydney receiving was part of petty theft and in the courts it had the same pattern as petty theft. Small sales were made from house to house by acquaintances: one had to be certain they would buy and not inform. It was perhaps only close acquaintances who were trusted with such property and information. Suspicion and uncertainty of trust are suggested by receiving cases as well as cases involving informers.

Country cases of receiving involved more planning and foresight. In 1825 William Ikin, constable, said he 'heard' that two highway robbers were connected with William Kendle so he searched the house of Mrs Moore which Kendle frequented.[107] Jane Barber gave evidence that she was stopped in the street by Kendle and asked would she buy a blanket.[108] William Kendle was questioned by the Liverpool bench and said that he 'met the prisoners, at Michael's Road Party and they asked me to buy linen. He bought shirts and trousers, Campbell was the salesman. I told Moore I'd bought it off the prisoners.'[109]

This was typical of receiving in the countryside: a small farmer bought from government servants who had robbed a cart stolen from their employers. The property was not meant for resale but for consumption by the household. In bushranging cases also, receivers fitted this pattern: they were not large-scale entrepreneurs in stolen property, but accepted goods as tokens of friendship or as exchange for harbouring, and then perhaps used these goods as currency. Unless there was an attempt to sell stolen articles, as much care went into hiding them as into hiding stolen meat and the skins of animals. Property was found locked in boxes, under beds, hidden in wells and in lofts. It is clear from evidence about where articles were found that people expected their houses to be searched or information to be given to constables. During searches property was often hidden on the person of the suspect, in a hat, or in the bosom of a dress.

Cases eventuated only when stolen property was found and therefore there was good reason for a search; it is difficult to ascertain how many houses were searched where property was not found. Geographical relations of suspicion, however, can be established. In 1815 Mary Miller of Cambridge Street missed her pigs. She heard a noise from William Ryder's house. A crowd assembled outside his house and Ryder attempted to climb out the back window. For pig theft he received twenty-five lashes by the order of the magistrates' bench and was sentenced to the gaol gang for six months.[110] Neighbours were the first group of persons to be suspected in Sydney. These were immediate neighbours or persons living in a skillion at the back of the house. Other persons suspected were stallholders involved in a similar business to the victim. Thomas Shaughnessy of Hunter Street, a shopkeeper, was robbed of a large quantity of black crepe; he suspected Richard Gilbert, a tailor, and had his house searched.[111] In country areas suspicion followed the same pattern as in animal theft: neighbours or government servants were suspected. Bushranging did not alter this kind of accusation and consequent searching.

In early colonial New South Wales law formed part of disputes, particularly in country areas: it could be used as protection or revenge and it carried with it numbers of effects that could net the uninvolved into court. Law was very closely related to the economy, where exchange of property as money from person to person created a long chain of receivers, buyers and sellers. The difficulties of existing in the colonial economy made use of law more likely and the nature of that economy made for suspicion, secrecy and a certain type of illegal behaviour. In many ways such results created a highly effective policing system.

As with bushranging, the nature of the policing system, with its informers and its receivers, created a culture of illegal behaviour. At night a watch would be carefully buried in the garden, meat wrapped in shirts and hidden in a bed; to 'plant' in colonial New South Wales was very difficult. A knock at the door could mean the constables and the honest or dishonest victim. The hiding place, which had seemed foolproof, would be swooped upon and the property found. Justice would begin to be done.

The courts were used not only in cases of theft but also in assault cases. To examine such cases will show further when law was called into people's lives.

Violence

In 1816 William Best went before the Sydney magistrates' bench to explain a dispute between himself and his neighbour, Robert Williams. The quarrel began when Best found his chickens dead and blamed his neighbour's cat, which he then killed. Robert Williams went to the door of Best's house with a constable and struck Best. The explanation continued: 'I said if he struck me again I would take him before Dr Wentworth, he replied with a threat.'[112] Both sides in this quarrel sought to use the law: Williams brought a constable and Best threatened to take Williams to court. Neither was going to the court to solve the dispute; they used law as a threat. As this case suggests, the law could fulfill a number of roles in community violence. In using the law the colonial population was shaping it to their own interests and these interests may have had little in common with preserving good relations or with the intentions of the law.

Assault cases can be divided into those where some cause of the dispute was given, as in William Best's case, and those where no reason was given. In country areas assaults occurred over boundaries of land and wandering animals. In Sydney, indebtedness and financial relations were given as causes of dispute.

In February 1821 Ann Williams of Castlereagh Street asked for repayment of a debt of £2 16s. from Catherine Caine, also of Castlereagh Street. Ann Williams claimed in court that Caine had said she would borrow a pistol and fire it at Williams' head.[113] Catherine Caine was bound to keep the peace. The following month Catherine Caine appeared before the magistrates' bench and claimed that for a month previous she had had stones thrown at her doors and windows, one of which cut her head; Samuel Rowley of Castlereagh Street gave evidence that he saw stones thrown from Ann Williams' skillion.[114] Such reciprocal charges by neighbours were quite common: this incident resulted from indebtedness to a neighbour which was followed by a quarrel lasting at least a month. In 1821 Elizabeth Gray reported how she bought three tumblers from one Jennings when she did not have the money for them: 'I went in company with Mrs. Powell to the house of Jennings and while I was there I agreed to take three tumblers at 1/3 each but as I had not any money in my pockets I begged of Mrs. Powell to account with Jennings for the tumblers.'

That such a claim was not expected by Jennings is apparent in the incident that followed: Jennings and his wife tore Elizabeth Gray's clothes and charged her with stealing the tumblers.[115] Throughout the period, though in a small number of cases in comparison to country assault, shopkeepers, landlords and bailiffs were assaulted when disputes over money developed. Women were extremely active in these assaults.

In assault cases involving debt, women and men acted in the same manner. For instance, Dennis McAnany assaulted Mary Wright of Phillip Street when she was discussing rent with another person.[116] William Burke intervened in 1826 in a discussion over money between William Moore and John Dunn who shared part of the house with Burke.[117] As in country areas, the system of exchange resulted in tensions which produced violence. These appeared in court alongside property cases, and all levels of society were involved. Figure 14 gives an indication of the use of the courts in serious cases between 1816 and 1820.

However, most assault cases required the statement that no provocation was given to the defendant, and women were more likely to bring neighbours to court for reasons that remain unexplained. This is also illustrated by the records of the benches of magistrates in 1820–21 set out in Figure 15. In further analysis of such cases we can ascertain what kind of assaults were reported and what was said in other cases where reason was given.

Catherine Caine of Castlereagh Street was apparently not very popular, for John Tucker and John Smith were charged in 1821 also with throwing stones or brickbats at her house. Thomas Dunn, chief constable, was certain that the brickbats came from the house of the prisoners.[118] To throw stones or brickbats was one method of abusing a neighbour and there was usually several days or perhaps weeks of such activity before it was reported. Sarah Edwards combined such throwing of stones in 1812 with killing the cat of Mary Jenkinson.[119] Stone throwing appeared in courts throughout the period: in 1827 Margaret Parsons was charged with throwing stones at the house of Ann Barnett.[120]

Stones were generally thrown by women. Women would be defendants one week and prosecute the next. In 1828 Sarah Crane called Mrs Susannah Perry 'many approbious names without any cause' and struck Mrs Perry and her husband.[121] Three days later Sarah Crane appeared before the bench to give evidence that Mr Perry had met her and 'without any cause or provocation gave her a violent kick in the thigh, deponent had words with his wife when he came up'.[122] Both of these cases were 'not found' to be cases for the Quarter Sessions. It appears as if the person who could get to the magistrates first complained of being assaulted 'without provocation'.

When any reason was given, it was related to the court process itself. Catherine Martin gave evidence in 1819 that her father's house had been broken open and a quantity of her household utensils broken to pieces. She went into her house and was followed by Margaret Lawrence and Elizabeth Biggers who asked her 'if I liked it' and proceeded to break more property.[123] They implied that their activity was in revenge. Elizabeth Tully in 1812 made use of gross language to Jane Styles and said that Styles had 'hanged two men innocently'.[124] These cases do not concern violent women attacking well-dressed or wealthy women in the streets; rather, in a manner similar to women's involvement in household theft cases, they resulted from conflicts between persons of equal status who lived near each other and who developed animosities which were played out in the courts. Both the magistrates' benches and the Quarter Sessions were open to such cases.

This kind of assault between male neighbours is presented in the courts quite clearly and reasons for it were plain. Edward Williams had unwisely decided to watch a fight

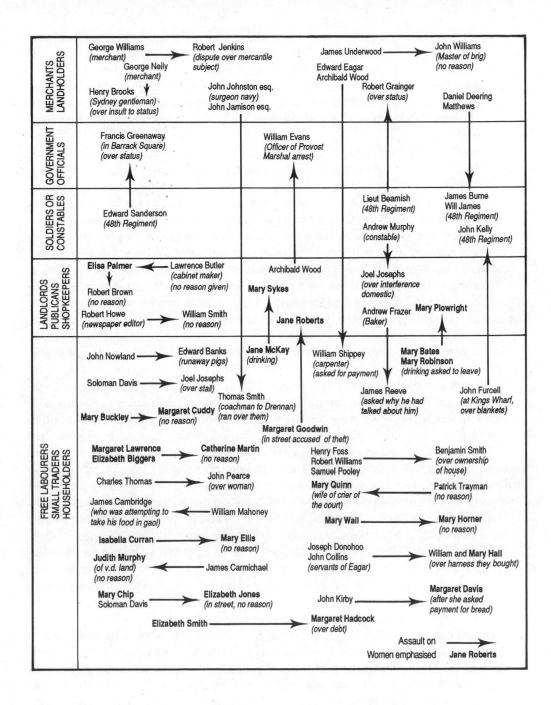

Figure 14 Status and relationships of defendants and complainants in assault cases before the criminal courts, 1816–20.

between William Wall and Wall's wife and he was assaulted.[125] William Wall was reported in 1816 by John Jamison who said that Wall, the storekeeper, abused him in the street constantly.[126] John Mitchell returned home with the wife of Nathaniel Lawrence and assaulted Lawrence, saying the house was his.[127] In 1827 Mr James Robertson received a letter from Francis Girard: 'you must be a damn coward to have insulted Mrs. Girard as yours did in your shop—and if you are instilled to this wound you may come and see me.'[128]

Though the violence described—jumping on stomachs, kicking in the face, hitting with brickbats—was the same whether the assailant was male or female, we find differences in the use of the courts between men and women. Women, as in theft cases, brought personal vendettas to court, sometimes coming week after week as defendant or assailant. This accounts for the absence of a reason for assault in many cases involving disputes between women, while men were careful to explain the source of their dispute. For both men and women in Sydney and the country, financial relations were given as a cause of assault cases; both were equally involved in financial transactions.

Assaults in the streets that did not result from disputes with neighbours were closely related to robbery, fighting, drunkenness and free passage down the streets. If people used any kind of abuse it was in terms of convict origins. In 1816 Ann Smith was sent to Newcastle during the governor's pleasure for abusing George Smith in George Street. She said, 'Smith you bloody wretch you are not now at the coal river you bloody convicted wretch.'[129]

The ritual of fighting drew large crowds, and such events resulted in assaults themselves. In 1827 Henry Taylor claimed that Charles Bayley had assaulted him in George Street although he gave no provocation. Bayley's defence was that Taylor had told him he would find a man to fight him for £20 and Bayley, feeling aggrieved, knocked him down.[130] In 1826 William Wemyss interfered in a fight because he saw John Edwards strike a man he was fighting when the man was on the ground.[131] Assaults in the streets by men related to robbery were invariably of persons who were wealthier than the defendant and possessed some money which the defendant had failed to steal. James Davison, a seaman, was attacked by two men in 1821; his cries of robbery and murder brought the publican John Neale who took the attackers into custody.[132] Passers-by gave evidence in assault cases and some attempted to intervene. What brought all witnesses and constables was the cry 'murder', and this was invariably used by women and persons being robbed. In 1818 a deponent in a murder case claimed he did not go to the assistance of the victim because if he got out of bed every time the cry of 'murder' he would get up twenty times a night.[133]

Cases of assault in the streets do not centre on one particular group, with the exception of the military. Soldiers were both complainants and defendants in cases of street violence. In 1812 John Stewart, private of the 48th Regiment, said he was going to the tanks for water when he was violently assaulted by a number of boys. One of them, William Bigg, was very active and called out 'pin the bloody bugger'.[134] Soldiers were often subject to physical attack in the streets of Sydney. In March 1827 Michael Leary, private of the 39th Regiment, was attacked when he attempted to go into a public house.[135] Soldiers were also responsible for attacks themselves. In July 1827 John Owen and

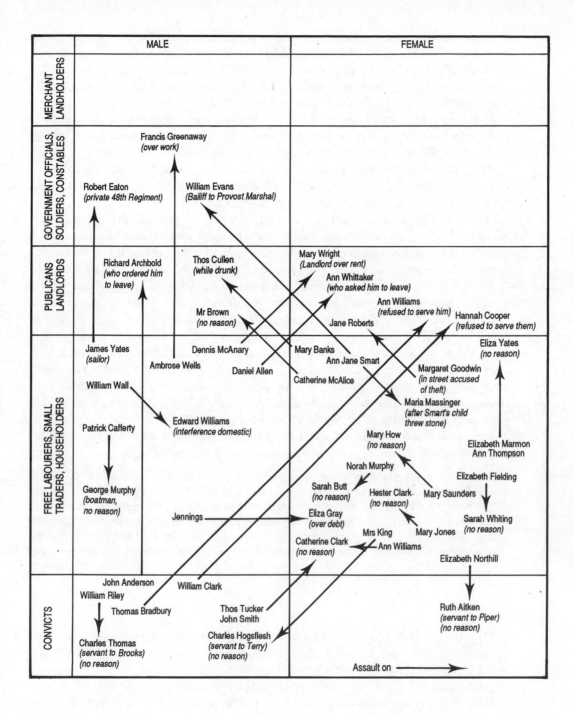

Figure 15 Status and relationships of defendants and complainants in assault cases before the Police Magistrates' Bench, 1820–21.

Patrick Sullivan, soldiers, attacked Mary Ellam in Pitt Street, saying 'they would rip up the first convict they met'.[136] Mary Ellam and her husband, 'as there was no assistance to be had where [they] lived', took the soldiers to the watchhouse but the constable, Fitzpatrick, refused to take them in charge and told Mary Ellam, 'she might kiss his boot and if she did not go away he would throw a bucket of water over her'.[137]

In the late 1820s attacks on constables by soldiers were increasing in the streets of Sydney and so Bernard Fitzpatrick may have been unwilling to provoke a possible riot by imprisoning the two soldiers. During the same sessions Thomas Amsden, constable, reported how a mob of persons attacked soldiers with palings in an attempt to rescue their prisoner John Bates. He described how the military 'drew their bayonets and would have attacked the mob but for deponent's persuasions'.[138]

The behaviour of soldiers in drunken groups possibly exacerbated already tense situations. In 1814 a group of drunken soldiers were charged with the rape of Ann Fagan. It was claimed that they had burst open the door of her house and raped her; there were twenty soldiers involved but only two were recognised. Those two were found not guilty by the Court of Criminal Jurisdiction on the grounds that she could not positively identify them as the soldiers who had raped her.[139]

In 1813 two soldiers, Conner and McNaughten, were charged with the murder of William Holmes. They had, it was claimed, attacked a young man and woman walking along the street. The woman, Elizabeth Winch, ran to the house of her employer, Holness. Shortly after, Ann Holness arrived home with her husband William, and asked what were two soldiers standing near her door with sticks doing. The soldiers hit the doors and windows saying they wanted the woman there. William Holness attempted to stop them and they hit him with the sticks, killing him.[140]

The soldiers were charged with manslaughter and received a sentence of six months' imprisonment with a fine of one shilling each. Macquarie wrote of this:

> But whilst the clemency of the court supported by the general tendency of the laws to the side of mercy has pronounced the lenient sentence of manslaughter . . . it rests with the Governor and the Commander in Chief to mark in the strongest terms his indignation of an occurrance so disgraceful to the Military Character and he trusts with confidence that the high sense of honour which characterizes British Army in every quarter of the world and which the 73rd Regiment in particular has possessed a most flattering Portion of will induce them to look to this lamentable event as a Beacon set up to guard them against the fatal Consequences attendant on the life of drunkenness, debauchery and riot which inevitably tends to the debasement and degradation of the upright and manly Character of a British soldier and necessarily induces the Contempt and Indignation of all brave and honourable men.[141]

The offences in which soldiers were involved throughout the period resulted from drunkenness and debauchery, but the assaults on them also occurred when they were either officially acting or walking about the streets.

While soldiers were a focus of violent attitudes, so was the public house a site of violence. Marion Aveling has pointed out that the public houses of the colony tended to cater for various social groups.[142] Her work, which centres on the late 1830s, also suggests that women were less likely than men to frequent public houses. By contrast, disputes in public houses during the period 1810 to 1830 included women as well as men, and both sexes were equally involved in murder in public houses. The contrast between the two periods suggests perhaps that as the Sydney economy changed, the nature of public houses changed.

In this period publicans were assaulted when they requested money for drink or when they refused to serve particular persons. The reasons for refusal to serve drink are not given but Robert Haskett, assigned servant to Daniel Cooper, implied in 1820 that certain types of people were not welcome in Cooper's hotel: 'Last night William Clark and his reputed wife came with several others, [they] came rushing into my master's house and after asking for a drink and being refused he knocked me down.'[143] Mrs Ann Williams reported a similar refusal in 1820 involving Thomas Bradbury.[144] Assaults also resulted from requests being made for the prisoner to leave the house due to obnoxious behaviour. In 1816 Jane McKay went to the house of Mary Sykes 'and spat and vomited about the place'; she was asked to leave and did so, but returned and assaulted Mary Sykes.[145]

More violent were disputes between customers in public houses, and often soldiers were involved. A group of sailors entered the Chelsea Pensioner and saw the soldier Robert Eaton, private of the 46th Regiment. They said, 'damn them, how many of them is there, we will give them a good thrashing'.[146] In 1816 Thomas Whittaker, publican of Harrington Street, saw Timothy Griffen in argument with a private of the 46th Regiment. Griffen with several others pushed the private into a corner and beat him with bludgeons.[147] Assaults against soldiers do not appear as often in Quarter Sessions records, but in these early cases it is clear that the soldiers were seen to be out of place in the public house in which they chose to drink.

Riotous and turbulent conduct also occurred in public houses and was reported by constables. In 1827 Mr W. G. Whitfield reported how Thomas Howell, free, came into his public house and caused great disturbance, assaulting Whitfield.[148] William Thompson in 1828 was charged with stabbing Thomas Crossman. Thompson called Crossman into the Bristol House public house, and gave him spirits. Crossman reminded him about 'cutting his throat twenty years ago and a young woman', Thompson became violent after begging Crossman to say nothing and stabbed him.[149] In 1819 Mary Plowright's public house had its doors broken down after Mary Bates and Mary Robinson were thrown out for fighting.[150] In 1827 the publican Mr Hodges of the Blue Lion managed to tie the hands of John Lynch who became riotous in his public house.[151]

Those publicans who appear as complainants reported that they did so to assure some kind of stability in their houses. Murder in the colony most commonly occurred in houses, or on roads and isolated farms, but a number of murders occurred in public houses in Sydney. The statements of witnesses and the kinds of information they give provide further explanations of violence in public houses.

In 1812 John Hunt, soldier, was charged with the wilful murder of Mary Connor at Sydney on 17 March 1812. She had been drinking in William Wright's public house. William Wright gave evidence:

> It might be an hour and a half after she first came in that the prisoner [Hunt] came into my house nobody was with him. He went into a back room and shook hands with a man by the name of

> Michael Cassidy. He [Hunt] was very drunk. He came out from the back room into the front room immediately and said 'Is there any soldiers here.' My wife answered 'No—nor has been today.' The deceased was standing at the corner of the table. She was tipsy. She said to the prisoner 'what do you think we want with soldiers'. It looked very disrespectful. He was standing almost close to her and he lifted up his hand and struck her in the breast . . . she fell and struck her head against a cupboard.[152]

Wright continued that they did not call for any medical assistance. The injured woman was taken away in a wheelbarrow by two men. Wright believed it was an accidental blow. 'The deceased was a woman between 50 and 60, the deceased was very much addicted to drinking.'

John Boxley, who worked with Mary Connor selling fish, took her home in a wheelbarrow 'because she was too ill to walk'. Joseph Edwards, who lived in the same house as Hunt, helped to take her home; she claimed constantly she would die from the blow. Darcy Wentworth, principal surgeon, examined the body of the deceased and could find 'no appearance on the body either internally or externally that could indicate the cause of her death . . . I should have supposed the deceased had come to her death naturally.'[153] The defence brought forward a witness, Benjamin Haywood of the 73rd Regiment, who said the prisoner was not out of his sight the entire night of the incident. John Hunt was found not guilty.

In 1814 Ormsby Irwin and his wife Eleanor were charged with the murder of a sergeant, Robert Morrow. The incident occurred in the licensed public house of Elizabeth Watson, the housekeeper of Michael Casey, who also kept a shop on the premises. In the house were Sergeant Connell of the 73rd Regiment and Corporal Connell of the 46th Regiment, the Irwins, and Morrow with his woman, Honar Fahey. Fahey gave her version of the evening:

> Corporal Connell . . . began to sing a song the deceased [Morrow] objected to the song. I do not know the reason he objected to it. It was what they called a croppies song. The prisoner Eleanor Irwin made answer that he insisted the song be sung over again, Mrs. Irwin and Sergeant Connell then both joined in the same song. The deceased objected to it again. She (Eleanor Irwin) said she was a free woman, and not lately came from being transported at the coal river; although she was not a croppies wife she was a croppies sister. The deceased then said you are no society for me, take yourself away and walk.[154]

Eleanor Irwin then assaulted Morrow with a bayonet. Honar Fahey claimed that the Irwins began beating the prisoner. She ran for the guard who arrived and were told to take no notice as the man was in liquor; she ran to the barrack and returned to find Morrow lying on the sofa, hurt in the stomach. Corporal John Connell, also for the prosecution, gave evidence of a slightly different nature; he described a scuffle between Honar Fahey and Eleanor Irwin. He saw Eleanor Irwin jump on the deceased. Sergeant Connell came in and said, 'Irwin you've killed the man, Irwin (the prisoner) said it makes no consequence the fellow was sent to the coal river for his misdemeanors and you know that Connell.'

Sergeant Connell claimed he did not think the song was a croppie song and that the real dispute began with a quarrel between Eleanor Irwin and Honar Fahey. Benjamin Butcher, private of the 73rd Regiment, gave evidence that Morrow had told him that

Ormsby Irwin had hit him and murdered him. He also said that the deceased and the accused were great friends. Thomas Fisher, surgeon with the 46th Regiment, gave evidence that the deceased had died from injuries received. The defence argued that Irwin had fallen among some chairs. Lieutenant Skullhouse gave evidence that Morrow had been an excessively violent and intemperate man during his sentence at Newcastle. The Irwins were found not guilty of murder but guilty of killing and slaying. They were sent to Newcastle for two years.[155]

In 1811 John Gould was charged with the murder of Margaret Finney after they had been drinking in the house of Swinburne. Swinburne described part of the evening:

> She began to play with the prisoner and pull him about. She sat upon his knee. My wife made answer 'Mrs. Finney do not make so free with that man for he will not stand it.' She got up from his knee but did not say anything . . . After this Catherine Deveraux sung a song, after that my wife sung one. After that the deceased said she never saw two old women so comfortable in her life 'Now old Betty, I'll give you a jig first to please'. The deceased was quite sober. This is her usual mode of behaviour.[156]

When Margaret Finney and John Gould left the house, Swinburne thought he heard Finney cry out; he did not hear the cry of murder: 'I thought her husband had come home and caught the prisoner with his wife and that he was ill using her.'

Isabella Mansfield who lived across the road reported that she had heard the cry of murder three times. She opened the door and looked out. It was moonlight. 'I saw a man standing at the outside of the gate and the deceased standing on the inside . . . the deceased said "Oh dear you have almost murdered me" the man made answer "you whore see how you have scratched me face".' Isabella Mansfield turned and said to Nicholls who lodged with her, 'Oh my God what a heavy beating Gould is giving Mother Finney.' Isabella Mansfield had not spoken to Margaret Finney for a month and in court was uncertain if the man she saw was indeed Gould.

Margaret Finney's husband gave evidence that his wife was in good health when he left and that she was worried about staying in the house by herself as she might be attacked. The surgeon who examined the body found the face very much injured and the death, he thought, resulted from injury. Gould's defence was that he went home and fell over, thereby accounting for blood on his clothes. Several persons testified to his good character. Gould was found guilty, hanged and anatomised.[157]

These three cases involved soldiers socialising with the ordinary populace. The persons killed were initially on good terms with those who were accused. In two cases violence results, not from a long-standing quarrel, but from something that was said, deemed to be offensive and acted upon. What was said produced violence which resulted in a death. Public houses in these cases are presented as extremely volatile places where a song sung or a phrase uttered was enough to result in attack. Assault cases following these early murders result from similar circumstances: an argument began and violence followed. It was uncertain if it was 'the croppies' song which resulted in the quarrel between Irwin and Morrow. In both of these cases the insults traded were related to status—a Coal River transportee, an offensive song. Insults against ex-convicts and aspersions on soldiers resulted in violence.

If we hear any abuse in the streets it is along these lines of status that it occurs. The two public houses mentioned seem to be only partly full of people and in Swinburne's only four persons were dancing. The silence of Isabella Mansfield and her lodger suggests a similarity with assault cases between women: when enmity existed between neighbours, stones were thrown and court cases were entered into.

In 1823 a murder case where women were defendants occurred when Happy Fuller died in her bed. All of the witnesses in the case gave evidence that she had been drinking and smelt strongly of liquor; she went upstairs to bed and had a fit which caused her death. These witnesses gave evidence in January. In April at the Parramatta courthouse Francis Henry, convict servant to Mrs Slade and a former patient of the Parramatta Hospital, said he had asked Sarah Quinn, a witness to the killing, if there were any marks of violence on the body of Happy Fuller at the time of her death. Sarah Quinn had replied that there were and that was because, she said, Mary Redman and another woman who were in the house beat her and were in the act of dragging her downstairs. Francis Henry asked why, and was told it was for £6, and when Mary Redman was going out of the house she took the shoes off the feet of the dead woman and put them on her feet.[158] This evidence was hearsay, yet was enough for the magistrates to present a case.

The ease with which women used the court gave rise to accusations of false swearing and false information. In 1811 Mary McDonough interrupted the funeral of William Howarth, shouting:

> she hoped the bloody devil would fly away with his bloody soul before he got to the bloody church. That her bloody husband had not half the attendance of that bloody informer. She said she would give a bottle of rum to the man that would nail him up and she would attend the bloody funeral with the bottle.

Mary McDonough was ordered to pay £10 to the Police Fund and was imprisoned for three months.[159] In 1812 Elizabeth Tully assaulted Jane Styles, saying she had hanged two innocent men.[160]

False information was related to theft cases and this was where violent offences linked up with property offences. In Sydney patterns of theft were much more anonymous than in country areas, where neighbours were likely to accuse each other and search each other's houses for stolen property. Though this did occur in Sydney, it was in country areas where disputes over property had strong ulterior motives of economic competition.

Assaults in the country were closely related to economic disputes or the threat that information would be given of criminal activity. The public houses were important meeting places for servants and small landowners, and the disputes surrounding them were closely related to the kinds of economic activity that took place in them. Murder cases were also related to economic activity, as well as to theft and receiving.

In 1828 Patrick Tighe, a government servant, was found dead on his master's farm. It was claimed in the case that Thomas Ryan had threatened to kill him because he told of a pig they stole together.[161] When there was a death, deponents were sometimes quick to find a reason they thought could account for it. In a case concerning the death of Mary Hogan, Sarah Clements gave evidence that though Mary Hogan seemed sprightly, being about to give birth, she was suddenly seized by a violent fit of coughing and 'blood spurted like a fountain from her nostrils and mouth'. She died within ten minutes. Sarah Clements remembered that four months before Mary Hogan had said she had a stone thrown at her and was injured which made it difficult for her to lie on her side. She said the name 'Eaton'. Mary Hogan's husband 'was not aware of any ill will but on the account of the conduct of Mrs. Fowler's servants of whom Eaton was one, Hogan was ordered by Mr. Fowler to make away with the game fowls belonging to Eaton and others'.[162] Neither of these cases provided enough evidence for a criminal trial.

The amount of bargaining evident in criminal cases from country areas is apparent in the case against Rosannah Smith alias Mary Banks. William Scott, a free settler of Minto, claimed he went to her house to get washing from her. She called out 'Murphy' and cut Scott across the throat with a knife. The next day the man who lived with Rosannah Smith, Robert Maxwell, went to see Scott. Scott reported:

> he asked me why I came to abuse his wife I said I had not he told me she said so and that she intended to swear against me he said that he would advise her from that as much as possible but if she did not do it he would assist her in all his power which was his duty but if it could be made up otherwise he did not wish to carry it further.[163]

'Otherwise' in this case could be money, the cancelling of a debt, or payment in property.

Assaults occurred in country areas along these economic lines and Table 30 sets out differences and similarities in reasons for assault before three country benches and Sydney. Table 31 shows a series of assaults in Windsor over crops and animals and Figure 16 shows interaction of accusations of theft and assault in Windsor.

A further area of murder in country regions was the sporting event, such as the boxing match in which a contestant was killed. Witnesses in these cases would stress the fairness of the fight: 'He saw no unfair means towards either party but observed the deceased fall and immediately after arise and put himself in the attitude of fighting.'[164] So claimed a bystander at a fight in which Henry Henessy was killed in Newcastle in 1818. In 1823 Bob Wilson was killed trying to get fair play when people were fighting.[165] In 1820 James Neal was killed when he was involved in a fight in which he had asked his master to observe fair play.[166]

'Fair play' in fights bears comparison with behaviour in public houses: both forms of entertainment had their difficulties. A blow in play could kill, and a word out of place in a public house could result in violence. Where poor relations are most obvious, however, is in the realm of debt, exchange of property and demands for payment. These are the reasons presented to court; they are hardly elaborate. The point at which dispute broke into violence was represented as extremely delicate, liable to explode quite easily.

Theft and assault cases are very different from murder. In theft and assault, the courts are sought out and the terms of reference are shaped by the complainant. By contrast, murder inquiries were often unwelcome. When Mary Connor, fishmonger, was killed by a blow, some witnesses were willing to speak, others more reticent. Happy Fuller's death was effectively covered up until Francis Henry decided to inform. In theft and assault cases we meet aspects of the community we are meant to hear, whereas in murder we have access to areas that the community is reluctant to speak about. If we see the law as

Table 30 Reasons given for assaults appearing before Quarter Sessions

Sydney	Parramatta	Liverpool	Windsor
Male accused			
Work agreement	Debt	Debt	Debt
Trespass	Harvest	Sale of Property	Work agreement
Debt	Passage through land	Passage through land	Fencing
Business agreement	Trespass	Rescue of animals	Harvest
Woman	Ownership of cart		Accusation of theft
Rent	Rescue of animals		Boundaries
Sex with woman			Rescue of animals
Neighbour's activities			Drunken argument
Free passage through			public house
the street			In street; no reason
Status of person			given
in street			Acting improperly
Begging			Interference
Drunken argument			domestic violence
public house			False swearing
Female accused			
Debt	Rescue of animals	Friend: in street;	Religion
False information	Passage through land	no reason given	Giving evidence in
in court			court
Friend in house			Relationship with
Drinking: on			husband
publican			Work agreement
			Borrowing
			Ownership of crop
			Fencing

inhabiting a particular juncture in silence and speech in the community—as having uses, and as sometimes invading where it is not wanted—we are closer to the practice of law than if we merely assume that it solves disputes. That silence in comparison to that speech plays a different role for women than men. Sexuality is not only a focus of the authorities but also a focus for the community: women as murderers were more likely to be handed over to the constable or the magistrate with a set of evidence that perhaps would mean nothing in court.

Isolating Women: Infanticide and Suspicion

Cases involving murder by women seem more divisive and upsetting to community relations within local populations. The scramble for economic subsistence through trade or theft was momentarily shattered by scandal. Such is also the situation with infanticide: the offending woman's body and history were open for discussion and it was the

Table 31 Assaults over boundaries, crops and animals appearing before Windsor Quarter Sessions, 1824–27

Defendant	Complainant	Complaint
John Woodbury and John Hunter, Small landholders	Geo. Smith, baliff to provost Marshall	
John Amos/Parchment, small landholder	William Holmes, small landholder	Boundary
Hugh Hockey, small landholder	Geo. Davis, small landholder	Accusation of theft
Thomas Bond, small landholder	Daniel Kelly, small landholder	Rescue pigs
John Evans, small landholder	Joseph Bannister, servant	Rescue pigs
Charles Williams, servant to Harper	Festus Tang	Dogs set on him
Thomas and Ann Cribb, small landholders	Edward Conlon	Fencing
Thomas Martin, small landholder	Michael Leydon, small landholder	Accusation of theft
William Kiss, small landholder	William Ashton	Debt
Henry Flemming, small landholder	John Waters, small landholder	False swearing
George Howell, small landholder	James Timms	Boundary
Thomas Jones, small landholder	John Riley, small landholder	For searching farm
Michael Ford, small landholder	John Lyons	Accusation of theft
Peter Daley, small landholder	Robert Nunn, small landholder	Debt
James Kelly, small landholder	James McKane, government servant to John Brown	Rescue pigs
Thomas Hodges	Thomas Lewer	Over work agreement
James Stepheton, small landholder	Joseph Hibbert	Trespassing pigs

woman's body, her sexuality, her person which was subjected to scrutiny by men and other women. This left the woman alone under scrutiny, even if others were involved. As we have seen all through this study, finally, despite all their involvement in the economy, legal or illegal, despite all of their participation in violent attacks, it was women's sex which isolated them.

There are six cases of infanticide in the entire period. One of these was concerned with the practice of midwifery, when a woman attending the birth of a child held the newborn child up by its feet and shook it while saying prayers; the child subsequently died and the midwife was charged with murder.[167] All of the other cases were concerned with the concealing of a birth by the mother and the subsequent discovery of the body or other evidence of a child. These women were charged with infanticide or 'murder of a bastard child' which since 1803 had had the proviso that if a women concealed the birth of her child she could be imprisoned for two years.[168] One of the remaining five cases comes

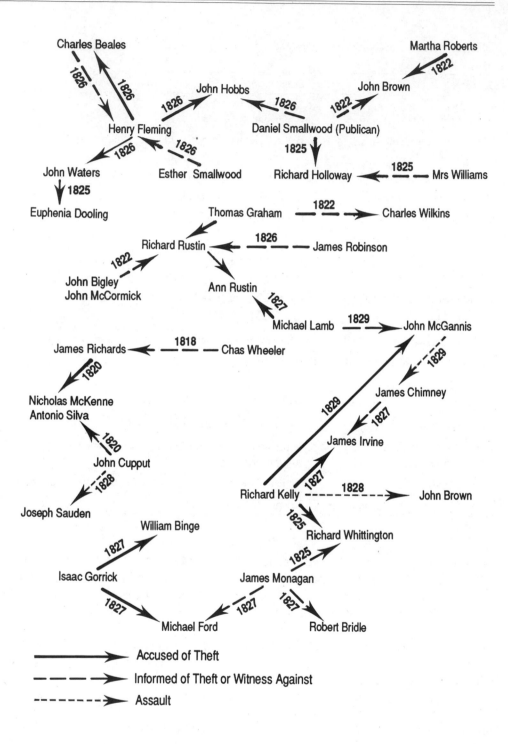

Figure 16   Examples of interactions between small landholders in theft and assault cases before the criminal courts and Quarter Sessions, Windsor, 1818–29.

from Hobart in 1817, and others come from Sydney in 1817, Parramatta in 1818, Newcastle in 1824 and Windsor in 1829. The cases, then, arose out of different situations and geographical areas in the colony. Infanticide, or concealment of a birth, appears rarely as an offence at all and so these cases are of interest in themselves. They arose out of peculiar situations. We will examine the interlocking circumstances which resulted in these cases coming to court, and also consider the way in which infanticide was described, what hallmarks of guilt there were and what behaviour was considered unusual.

Initially, it must be understood, all witnesses close to the woman were careful to state that they were not involved in the concealment of the birth; to us the woman appears isolated and alone when she may not have been. The birth is a lone one and discovered after: it is never described to us by anyone but the woman. The woman did not tell people in the house that she was pregnant, or she strenuously denied it when it was suggested. Women were singly charged with concealment, even though all of these women lived in a household with a number of people. It is an isolate crime which centres on the mother and her attitudes: no others were accused. In one case, Lily Mackellar's, her brother-in-law and sister were accused of concealing the burial of the child.

The women who were accused were not of the same status. Ann Williams in 1817 in Sydney was a free servant. Lily Mackellar was a spinster residing in Hobart with the family of her wealthy sister. Harriot Marks worked in the Female Factory and lodged in Parramatta in 1818. Sophia Ward was living with her mother after returning from service in 1829. Eliza Evans was living with her sister in Newcastle in 1824. All of them appeared to have reasonable relations with the households they lived in; none seemed to be brought to the courts out of household spite. Though all these women except Lily Mackellar were from poor backgrounds, their situations were not unusual for the colony. They had different positions in the household: a daughter returned from service was not similar to a sister or servant, though the work they performed in the house might have been the same. All, however, were single women.

In 1829 John Cobcroft of Wilberforce, constable, went before the magistrates at Windsor and gave evidence that 'a young woman of the same place aged twenty years has been considered by the neighbours in a state far advanced in pregnancy . . . these few days the said Sophia Ward appeared much reduced in size'.[169] Cobcroft felt it necessary to report this to the magistrates but he did so with reference to the 'neighbours'. It is generally the neighbours who initiate these cases. When Mary Sutherland saw the body of a child in a ditch at Parramatta in 1818, she called, 'for God's sake! go down into the ditch and pick up that dear infant that some unfortunate mother has flung there'. Francis Oakes immediately went to Harriot Marks' house when he heard the body of a child was found, because he suspected her.[170] In Eliza Evans' case Peter Ryan, a prisoner, saw three soldiers in the street quarrelling with each other: 'one of them expressed determination to report to Mr. King that the accused had been delivered of a child'.[171] In all of the cases neighbours or members of the community noted the pregnancy and appeared in the courtroom to say the woman was obviously with child and then suddenly was not. The pregnancy was a community concern, even if it was never spoken of to the woman herself. Elizabeth Kemp, in Lily Mackellar's case, said, 'I was certain from her appearance she was in the family way.'[172]

The state of pregnancy was obvious and suspected by the neighbourhood but it was denied and claimed to be denied often inside the household. Ann Williams claimed she was swollen because of the dropsy when asked by Daniel Pegg, a fellow servant, if she was pregnant. Harriot Marks told her landlord, who had threatened to throw her out if she was pregnant, that she was not and that it was an infirmity.[173] Sophia Ward's neighbour said he had taxed her with being pregnant but she had always denied it was so. In Ann Williams' case the denial was carried on so long that in the case before the magistrates the surgeon was asked, 'Do you think a female can carry a child nine months within her womb and not know herself to be pregnant?'

The case was begun by community knowledge and suspicion as well as denial. It was to be established by medical or material evidence, much as theft cases were proved by the presentation of stolen goods and murder cases by the presentation of the body. Evidence of infanticide, or concealment of a birth, rested on the issue from the mother's body, and this formed most of the evidence. It was not enough that the mother appeared pregnant and suddenly was not: stained clothing, congealed blood had to be spoken of before a case could be established. When Francis Oakes went to the house occupied by Harriot Marks, he was accompanied by Sergeant West and others. He examined a tub and found congealed blood, and more congealed blood under the bed; he found blood in the bed and clothes stained 'in a most dreadful manner'. Ann Williams' employer forcibly pulled the bed clothes from under her and discovered evidence of birth. Bridget Cline, a midwife, was called by Mrs Smith, sister of Eliza Evans, to examine her and discover evidence of the afterbirth. Susannah Douglas, who worked for Lily Mackellar, saw the clothes she was to wash and found their appearance very extraordinary as if there had been a lying in.

Despite the blood, Harriot Marks continued to deny the existence of a child. Ann Williams admitted the birth and said she was very sorry not to have discovered it to her mistress and said the child was in a trunk under the bed. It was found dead, wrapped in an apron. Lily Mackellar's 'almost perfect child' was found where it had been buried with its umbilical cord torn out; it had bled to death. The case against Eliza Evans rested on the evidence of 'afterbirth' and the child was described as being 'not full grown'. There was also no body of a child in Sophia Ward's case: the evidence rested largely on the shape of her breasts, suspicion, and some congealed blood found in the garden.

The examining of the mother and the afterbirth was the task of surgeons and midwives, and they played a major part in the cases. Bridget Cline in Eliza Evans' case stated, 'What I saw appeared to be afterbirth . . . I am a mother of children and have frequently assisted in deliveries.' William Redfern, surgeon, was consulted with on the pregnancy of Ann Williams: 'I advised Mrs. Marr to send Ann Williams to hospital whereby I might determine the actual character of the disease where her condition and other circumstances would not prevent the [surgeon] from a delicate examination.' Mary Buchan, a midwife, was called to the room of Harriot Marks by Dr West to examine Harriot Marks' breasts to see if there was milk in them. William Richardson, surgeon, examined the breasts of Sophia Ward and found 'her breasts were large, though they were not larger than a stout woman's might have been, there were hard lumps in part of them and other parts were flaccid, her breasts were also streaked as is usual the case where they have been much distended with milk'. It was mentioned in all of the cases that an attempt at abortion had previously failed or that the birth was an abortion. Ann Williams had been to a Mrs Beggs for 'medicine'. Lily Mackellar asked the surgeon for calomel which he refused because he knew it to be an abortifacient. Sophia Ward asked Mary Lewis' mother to 'procure some stuff to cause a miscarriage'. This kind of procurement appears in criminal cases when husbands were accused of attempting to murder their wives with such medicine.[174] It also appears occasionally in the records of the magistrates' benches, the procuring of such medicine being a common law offence.[175] The sudden onset of menses after months of waiting was met with relief in the household of Harriot Marks: Mrs Oldsworth, the landlord's wife, proceeded to tell the neighbourhood and gave this evidence in court.

Both the medical excuses given by the women and the presence of midwives and surgeons in the courtroom support the assumption that medicine and its analysis of the body were central to the establishment of guilt. The case rested on a close analysis of the woman's body: if she was considerably reduced in size, it was a sign that a child had been murdered or a birth concealed. What is notable is the collusion of local midwives and surgeons and their cross-referencing and consulting of each other in these cases. It was not the surgeons' task to deal with childbirth and they often exhibit 'delicacy' or uncertainty about the condition, but they were consulted and called for.

Community suspicion or 'common sense' was not enough. However, the surgeon's or midwife's evidence alone was not enough either. For a case of infanticide to be proved, the child had to be born alive. The distinction was explained in 1824 by the Judge Advocate in his letter to the magistrate Gillman, on returning the Eliza Evans case to him:

> 43 Geo 3 c.58 s.54 makes it lawful for the jury by whose verdict any person charged with the murder of a bastard child shall be acquitted to find a case if it shall appear in evidence that the prisoner was delivered of issue of her body, male or female which if born alive shall have been born a bastard.[176]

Eliza Evans was consequently found guilty of concealment and not of infanticide. Surgeon Redfern examined the lungs of a child found in a ditch near Harriot Marks' house and discovered they swam in water, suggesting the child had been born alive. Edward Suttrell, principal surgeon, examined the body of the child claimed to be that of Lily Mackellar and thought it had been born alive; he had never seen a better or more perfect child; he decided it had bled to death. In Ann Williams' case, surgeon Redfern said he felt the child had been born alive. In their confessions Harriot Marks and Lily Mackellar both claimed their children had been born alive. Harriot Marks said:

> between the hours of 10 and 12 she was delivered of the male infant child, now produced, between the tub and the harness cask before mentioned—the child lay on the ground on the stores, she looked at it and saw it open its eyes and shut them but it never cried, she contemplated for some time what to do with it she took it up off the ground and laid it on the lid on a napkin when something broke in her and blood flowed down the skilling she did not know what to do, she took a tub and a silk handkerchief and washed herself with it for some time to try and stop the blood she took a lamp down and looked at the child and found it quite cold.

Harriot Marks had given birth in June and complained of how cold she was. Lily Mackellar in her confession said:

at 5.30 the child was born I took the child up and laid it on my arm it was a male child, it was alive, I fainted and when I came to myself it was dead. I do not remember how the navel string was broken except it was when I first took it up, it was broken off close to the child's body.

The lack of medical knowledge of cause and effect exhibited by these women was not restricted to their defences alone. The whole medical case rested on such uncertainties. When the surgeon Flood was questioned as to the death of Lily Mackellar's child, he was asked, 'would not the entrails protrude before the cord would break?' He answered, 'it is possible the bowels might, the cord seems torn away how that would occur in a healthy child I cannot say'. Flood disagreed with the principal surgeon, Suttrell, but said the mother had gone full term, he said he could not tell if the child was born alive or dead and there was a possibility 'it might have died at birth'. Mrs Oldsworth, wife of the land-lord of Harriot Marks, had told the overseer of the hospital that 'nature had been stopped on Harriot Marks for eighteen months past and that it had now returned so powerfully that it had run through the bed and everything she had'; the overseer had replied that if that was the case it was very probable she would soon get better. These cases of infanticide were not definite then: so much had to be proved medically which was virtually impossible to prove. The state of medical practice regarding birth can be illustrated by reference to Darcy Wentworth's medical notebooks. As well as being a magistrate he was a popular surgeon and was frequently called to attend births. In a case such as Harriot Marks' haemorrhage, his notebooks say the best thing to do was to pour as much water as possible into the woman's vagina and 'women exhausted by loss of blood at their labour would take with impunity as much brandy as would intoxicate them several times over'.[177]

Medical evidence alone was not enough: there were questions to be asked concerning intent. 'Did you observe any child bed linen?' asked the inquest of Ann Williams' fellow servant. The servant answered, 'nothing of the kind, nor anything for a woman in her state'. 'I never saw Miss Mackellar making baby linen', said Mary Evers to the inquest in Hobart. Mary Lewis gave evidence to the magistrates in 1829 that she had asked Sophia Ward if 'she had anything (meaning clothes) ready for the child'; Sophia Ward replied, 'Oh I am not with child.' In England 'pleading linen' formed part of the defences of women accused of concealing a birth—the defendant would argue that she had sewn baby linen.[178] In New South Wales witnesses were questioned on this. Despite all denials of pregnancy, it was expected that the woman would be sewing baby clothes, even secretly. Rather than allowing this opportunity to plead linen, the courts in colonial New South Wales made the absence of linen part of the prosecution.

The charge of infanticide came after three or four months of expectation and waiting on the part of neighbours who brought the case. Sarah Longford was asked why she had suspected that Harriot Marks would make away with the child. She said 'because they kept it so secret—Mrs. Oldsworth and Harriot Marks'. The other cases resulted from such situations of suspected unacknowledged pregnancy, suspicious behaviour, the report to magistrates and medical intervention. Major West, surgeon, examined Harriot Marks to see if she was pregnant, disagreeing with the midwives who said she was not. West told Harriot Marks, 'he was so convinced of her being in a state of pregnancy that if she persisted in concealing it he should be under the necessity of reporting it to the Magistrate or Chief Constable'. Harriot Marks admitted to him that she was pregnant to the chief constable of the ship which had brought her from Ohtahiti and so Major West did not report the pregnancy and heard nothing of her until the body of the child was found.

Infanticide was not a sudden unexpected event. In this sense it was markedly different from any other offence which came before the criminal court. All of the evidence given suggests that people were familiar with the idea of women killing newborn children and had apprehensions that these women would do so. In effect the community suggested infanticide and the courts took it up; the community waited out a pregnancy and noted what would happen. These cases involved young single women and it is possible that other women did commit infanticide but were not regarded with such close attention. The women who were charged were not cohabiting with men and it was their secrecy which singled them out. Harriot Marks explained in her confession that she had become involved with the chief officer and when they arrived in Sydney he told her he was already married and could not marry her. James Taylor had 'paid his addresses' to Sophia Ward, intending to marry her. He

> suspected she was with child and mentioned his suspicions to her in her father and mother's presence. These suspicions were the cause of his not fulfilling his engagement to her. The prisoner as well as her mother denied that she was in that state. He therefore determined to wait until he saw the result.

The actual father of the child was referred to by name, James Henry Gardiner, only once. The 'cause' of an infanticide case was not immorality, but secrecy. Harriot Marks was to be thrown out of her house because she already had three children and her landlord 'did not want a nursery'. It was not simply because she was pregnant.

The infanticide case was produced by a set of relations between community, medicine and law which centred on and isolated the woman involved. The case was first held by the local coroner and jury and then passed on to the criminal court. None of these women were found guilty of infanticide by the criminal court because of the strictures of evidence necessary to determine a live birth. They were consequently found guilty of concealment and were sentenced to two years in prison.

Infanticide cases were produced by a coalescence of interests. In these cases the local populations were willing to speak, to explain what had been hidden from them and what were the signs of guilt. Such a coalescence was rare in the colony. In these cases the people and the court do not speak at cross-purposes, and hidden motives do not appear to be relevant. In a sense the infanticide cases are a kind of perfection in the performance of a legal system: they saw the way law should work, the way law is imagined to work, with clear understandings and agreement on the legal process.

Reasons for popular use of law have been suggested by J. A. Sharpe. He argues that settlement out of court was quite common in early modern England, thereby allowing law to serve local purposes.[179]

In disputes in early colonial New South Wales settlement out of court was also common, particularly before the Quarter Sessions hearings in Windsor and Sydney. The nature of the Quarter Sessions and the higher courts gave complainants and defendants time to enter negotiations: as Robert Maxwell stated with reference to the higher courts, it was time 'to make it up otherwise'.[180]

Where there was greatest access to the courts, in Sydney through Dr Wentworth, and in Windsor through magistrate Bell, they were used extensively in dispute. Thus some courts were more 'closed' than others. The arena for the whole colony seems widest in the period of Quarter Sessions when juries judged cases between 1824 and 1828. These sessions could be aimed at by complainants, they could use both the opportunity of the case and the opportunity of forgoing prosecution. The most important aspect of this use of courts was the role of the courts in economic disputes. Exchange of property as money, boundaries of land ownership, runaway animals, debt and the uncertainties surrounding what constituted a debt: these figure again and again in criminal cases. In these cases we see law as a weapon as well as an attempt to resolve conflict by effectively silencing a defendant. In such an environment there is much room for false information and false accusation and this is where the use of law by the population combines so effectively with the developing policing methods in the colony. House searching, the use of the warrant and the powers of constables were endorsed in the colonial environment. There was a willingness to utilise law in the colony, to take law and make it useful.

Notes

1 C. J. Calhoun, 'History, anthropology and the study of communities: Some problems in Macfarlane's proposal', *Social History*, vol. 3, no. 3, October 1978, p. 369.

2 J. A. Sharpe, ' "Such Disagreement betwyx Neighbours": Litigation and Human Relations in Early Modern England', in J. Bossy, ed., *Disputes and Settlements*. See also L. Stone, *The Family, Sex and Marriage, England 1500–1800*, London, 1977; A. Macfarlane, *Reconstructing Historical Communities*, Cambridge, 1977.

3 Calhoun, *op.cit.*, p. 372. While this article is devoted to a critique of the methodology of A. Macfarlane, Calhoun returns to this definition in closing.

4 David Hall used these terms to discuss popular culture. D. Hall, Introduction, in S. Kaplan, ed., *Understanding Popular Culture*, p. 5.

5 See, D. Rutman, 'The Social Web: A Prospectus for the Study of the Early American Community', in W. O'Neil, ed., *Insights and Parallels Problems and Issues in American History*, Minneapolis, 1973, p. 58.

6 D. Garrioch, *Neighbourhood and Community in Paris, 1740–1790*, pp. 3–4.

7 *ibid.*, pp. 2–13.

8 Sharpe, ' "Such Disagreement betwyx Neighbours" ', pp. 167–8.

9 Colonial Secretary to Judge Advocate Bent, J.A.B., 28 May 1810.

10 Andrew Frazer, J.A.B., 9 June 1810.

11 From Fines, Penalties, District of Sydney, Evidence to Bigge, B.T. 13.

12 Robert Whitmore, Mary Turley, J.A.B., 2 February 1811.

13 Michael Burns/Byrne, Sydney Q.S., April 1827, 26.

14 John Harpur, Sydney Q.S., April 1828, 29.

15 In July 1830 five constables continually brought cases against bawdy houses in the parish of St Phillip: see Sydney Q.S., July 1830, 24–31.

16 *Sydney Gazette*, 29 January 1830.

17 *ibid.*, 5 January 1830.

18 *ibid.*, 3 April 1830.
19 *ibid.*, 7 January 1830.
20 William Pugh, P.M.B., 27 January 1816.
21 Nicholas Knight, P.M.B., 12 March 1816.
22 Richard Cartwright to Bigge, B.T. 23, p. 4399.
23 R. vs George Booth, C.C.J., September 1822, 32.
24 *ibid.*
25 F. K. Crowley, 'Working Class Conditions in Australia 1788–1851', Ph.D. thesis, University of Melbourne, 1949, p. 261.
26 Hirst, *Convict Society and Its Enemies*, p. 101.
27 *ibid.*
28 In 1812 three 'natives of Otahiete' made complaint against Simeon Lord, Sydney merchant, for not providing them with proper food and clothing: see J.A.B., 23 July 1812. For other cases involving proper treatment see J.A.B., 15 June 1819 and 11 October 1813.
29 Argyle Bench of Magistrates, 29 May 1826.
30 R. vs George Stephenson, S.C.C.J., December 1830, 2.
31 R. vs John Ferguson and others, C.C.J., January 1824, 34.
32 R. vs William Lahy, C.C.J., August 1821, 61.
33 M. Sonenscher, 'Work and Wages in Paris' in M. Berg, P. Hudson, M. Sonenscher, *Manufacture in Town and Country before the Factory*, p. 171.
34 R. vs Hugh McMullens, C.C.J., August 1821, 59.
35 *ibid.*
36 S. J. Butlin, *Foundations of the Australian Monetary System, 1788–1851*.
37 Francis Lawless, John Dalton, J.A.B., 29 December 1810.
38 *ibid.*
39 Thomas Parnell, J.A.B., 29 December 1810.
40 George Graves and Hannah Bent, J.A.B., 9 February 1811.
41 *ibid.*
42 R. vs William Mahoney, C.C.J., September 1817, 27.
43 *ibid.*
44 *ibid.*
45 R. vs Mary Leighton, C.C.J., March 1822, 60.
46 R. vs William Williams and others, C.C.J., April 1821, 16–17.
47 *ibid.*
48 R. vs William Klensendorrfe, S.C.C.J., 1824, 32.
49 John Quigley, L.B.M., 4 May 1824.
50 R. vs Andrew Johnstone, C.C.J., May 1818, 21.
51 Report of the Grand Jury, Windsor Q.S., January 1828.
52 R. vs Thomas Campbell, C.C.J., January 1819, 180.
53 R. vs Thomas Saunders Junior, C.C.J., March 1822, 74.
54 *ibid.*
55 Brisbane to Bathurst, 3 September 1823, H.R.A., 1, XI, p. 121.
56 A. Taylor, 'The Seed Plot of Seduction: The Struggle for the Waldo Patent Backlands 1880–1801', in G. Eley and W. Hunt, eds, *Reviving the English Revolution*.
57 B. Fletcher, *Landed Enterprise and Penal Society*; T. G. Parsons, 'The Development of Colonial Capitalism', *Journal of the Royal Australian Historical Society*, vol. 68, no. 2, pp. 155–9.
58 R. vs William Hovell, C.C.J., June 1822, 24.
59 R. vs William Hovell, S.C.C.J., 1824, 38.
60 R. vs John Jamison Senior, C.C.J., December 1820, 47.

61   John Price, L.B.M., 6 March 1824.
62   R. vs Charles Wilkins, C.C.J., October 1822, 59.
63   R. vs Richard Rustin, C.C.J., March 1822, 78.
64   *ibid.*
65   Michael Ford, Windsor Q.S., October 1826, 19.
66   R. vs Moses Watson, S.C.C.J., 1827.
67   R. vs William Nash, Edward Higgins, Jeremiah Buffy, C.C.J., September 1816, 10.
68   R. vs William Clarke, Andrew Muntagh, C.C.J., August 1821, 62.
69   R. vs James Steel, Michael Cassidy, C.C.J., 1820, 421.
70   R. vs Moses Watson, Hannah Spencer, C.C.J., January 1817, 12.
71   *ibid.*
72   R. vs Joshua Cunningham, Samuel Medworth, C.C.J., March 1820, 3.
73   R. vs John Connor, Thomas Welsh, S.C.C.J., 1827, Miscellaneous, 3.
74   R. vs Charles Raven, C.C.J., December 1822, 4.
75   R. vs Thomas Perry, C.C.J., August 1823, 65.
76   *ibid.*
77   R. vs William Smith, Michael Mullen, James Cardon, C.C.J., September 1822, 23.
78   R. vs Richard Crisp, John Dent, John Pierce, James Hall, C.C.J., March 1822, 72.
79   R. vs Joseph Hearn, C.C.J., June 1822, 22.
80   R. vs John Baker, C.C.J., June 1818, 3.
81   R. ys James Connor, James Heacott, C.C.J., March 1823, 35.
82   R. vs Edward Farrell.
83   R. vs Thomas Kennedy, William Refrain, S.C.C.J., April 1825, 45.
84   John Garrick, Windsor Q.S., October 1828, not numbered.
85   Robert Reeves, Windsor Q.S., *ibid.*
86   James Bryant, Windsor Q.S., *ibid.*, Thomas Thomas and John Birtles, Windsor Q.S., *ibid.*
87   R. vs Thomas Myles, C.C.J., September 1819, 256.
88   R. vs Catherine Leeson, C.C.J., September 1817, 1.
89   *ibid.*
90   R. vs Henry Hitchcock, C.C.J., December 1818, 4.
91   R. vs Felix McClinton, S.C.C.J., July 1827, 44.
92   *ibid.*
93   *ibid.*
94   Piper, 'Memorandum to Captain Rossi respecting my robbery', C.C.J., 1821, 103.
95   R. vs William McDonald, Joe Bird, Henry Singer, C.C.J., 1821, 95.
96   R. vs Hannah Pendergast and others, S.C.C.J., 1826, 33.
97   Mary Trainer, Sydney Q.S., May 1826, 18.
98   R. vs Michael Smith, C.C.J., December 1820, 36.
99   R. vs Ann Podmore, Rachael Field, Susannah Knock, C.C.J., September 1817, 13.
100 R. vs Henrietta Bray, C.C.J., 1822, 19.
101 R. vs Ann Kennedy, James McGreevy, Margaret McGreevy, C.C.J., 1821, 2.
102 R. vs Martha Dunn, S.C.C.J., July 1824, 13.
103 R. vs Thomas Clarke, S.C.C.J., July 1824, 58.
104 R. vs Thomas Slater, S.C.C.J., September 1824, 44.
105 R. vs Theo Willougby/Johnson, S.C.C.J., 1824.
106 R. vs Patrick Conner, S.C.C.J., 1825, 121.
107 R. vs Archibald Campbell and others, S.C.C.J., 1825, 135.
108 *ibid.*
109 *ibid.*

110 William Ryder, P.M.B., 11 December 1815.
111 R. vs Richard Gilbert, C.C.J., June 1821, 18.
112 Robert Williams, P.M.B., 20 April 1816.
113 R. vs Ann Williams, C.C.J., June 1821, 15.
114 *ibid*.
115 Jennings and his wife, P.M.B., 15 March 1821.
116 Dennis McAnany, P.M.B., 12 December 1820.
117 William Burke, Sydney Q.S., June 1826, 33.
118 John Tucker, John Smith, P.M.B., 7 March 1821.
119 Sarah Edwards, P.M.B., 3 January 1812.
120 Margaret Parsons, Sydney Q.S., July 1827, 38.
121 Sarah Crane, Sydney Q.S., February 1828, 50.
122 John Perry, Sydney Q.S., February 1828, 51.
123 R. vs Margaret Lawrence, Elizabeth Biggers, C.C.J., January 1819, 48.
124 Elizabeth Tully, P.M.B., 19 December 1812.
125 William Wall, P.M.B., 24 October 1820.
126 William Wall, P.M.B., 8 March 1816.
127 John Mitchell, P.M.B., 19 October 1816.
128 Francis Girard, Sydney Q.S., December 1827, 22.
129 Ann Smith, P.M.B., 9 April 1816.
130 Charles Bayley, Sydney Q.S., March 1827, 47.
131 John Edwards, Sydney Q.S., May 1826, 35.
132 John Hughes, P.M.B., 16 March 1821.
133 R. vs John Gould, C.C.J., 9 March 1811.
134 William Bigg, P.M.B., 15 February 1821.
135 Charles Bogg, John Norman, Sydney Q.S., April 1827, 40.
136 John Owen, Patrick Sullivan, Sydney Q.S., July 1827, 41.
137 *ibid*.
138 John Bates, Sydney Q.S., July 1827, 42.
139 R. vs James Blackstock, James McDonald, Neil McClaud, C.C.J., 17 March 1814.
140 Macquarie to Bathurst, Enclosure No. 2, 31 July 1813, *H.R.A.*, 1, VIII, pp. 7–27.
141 *ibid.*, p. 6.
142 M. Aveling and A. Atkinson, eds, *Australians 1838*, p. 247.
143 William Clark, P.M.B., 16 September 1820.
144 Thomas Bradbury, P.M.B., 20 November 1820.
145 R. vs Jane McKay, C.C.J., January 1816, 4.
146 James Yates, P.M.B., 4 November 1820.
147 Timothy Griffen, P.M.B., 3 August 1816.
148 Thomas Howell, Sydney Q.S., May 1827, 48.
149 William Thompson, Sydney Q.S., December 1828, 17.
150 R. vs Mary Bates, Mary Robinson, C.C.J., August 1819, 229.
151 John Lynch, Sydney Q.S., March 1827, 51.
152 R. vs John Hunt, C.C.J., 7 May 1812.
153 *ibid*.
154 R. vs Eleanor Irwin and Ormsby Irwin, C.C.J., 23 June 1814.
155 *ibid*.
156 R. vs John Gould, C.C.J., 9 March 1811.
157 *ibid*.
158 R. vs Mary Redman, Bridget Lever, Thomas Frances, William Fenning, C.C.J., June 1823, 1.

159 R. vs Mary McDonough, C.C.J., 10 November 1811.
160 Elizabeth Tully, P.M.B., 19 December 1812.
161 R. vs Thomas Ryan, S.C.C.J., 1828, Miscellaneous.
162 Decease of Mary Hogan, S.C.C.J., 1828, Miscellaneous.
163 R. vs Rosannah Smith, C.C.J., April 1823, 17.
164 R. vs Michael Collet, C.C.J., March 1818, 9.
165 Bob Wilson, inquest, C.C.J., March 1823, 2.
166 R. vs Charles Leavy, C.C.J., December 1820, 91.
167 R. vs Sarah Mellion, S.C.C.J., January 1830, 29.
168 P. C. Hoffer and N. E. H. Hull, *Murdering Mothers: Infanticide in England and New England 1558–1803*, p. 87.
169 R. vs Sophia Ward, S.C.C.J., 1829, Miscellaneous.
170 R. vs Harriot Marks, C.C.J., December 1818, 297.
171 R. vs Eliza Evans, C.C.J., January 1824, 12.
172 R. vs Lily Mackellar, C.C.J., September 1817, 57.
173 R. vs Harriot Marks, C.C.J., December 1818, 297.
174 For example: R. vs Edward Hoar, C.C.J., December 1823, 55.
175 For example: Thomas Beardman, Parramatta Bench of Magistrates, 5 August 1815.
176 Letter enclosed in case of Eliza Evans.
177 D. Wentworth, Medical Notebooks, M.L., B196.
178 Hoffer and Hull, *Murdering Mothers*, p. 69.
179 J. A. Sharpe, ' "Such Disagreement betwyx Neighbours", Litigation and Human relations in Early Modern England' in J.Bossy, ed., *Disputes and Settlements*, Cambridge, 1983, pp. 167–8.
180 R. vs Rosannah Smith, C.C.J.

PART 4

The Courtroom

'How will you be tried?'
'O, the easiest way to yourselves, anyway you think proper!'
AN EXCHANGE BETWEEN CLERK OF THE SUPREME COURT
AND PRISONER, MAY 1827

8

Deciding What Was Good and Bad

Trial

For the defendant and the prosecutor, the process of arrest and hearing or committal was to lead to the trial. In minor cases heard before magistrates the depositions were quickly followed by judgment; for serious cases there were some weeks or months spent waiting for trial. Both magisterial decision and trial were governed by the ritual of English legal procedure. In discussion of the higher courts, Hay writes that 'a considered use of imagery, eloquent speech and the power of death . . . had considerable psychic force'.[1] When we consider the terrain this book has covered, the clamour to give evidence, the understandings of what was material evidence, the revenge, the suspicions—all of these were silenced. Pre-trial events and trial inhabited two different realms of understanding and the trial was an epilogue to all that preceded it. As the Chief Justice announced in the criminal court in 1826, 'in a criminal proceeding, the awarding of punishment was in the province of the Court alone, which could throw out what was bad and pronounce on what was good.'[2]

At every point in the making of a criminal case, decisions were made: as to what was suspicious behaviour, when property was interfered with, what was trespass, what was an assault, a murder, a horrific act. But the court made the final decision.

Case papers, as we have seen, often exhibited a clash between the perceptions of the magistrates and the perceptions of the ordinary population. When a husband should search for his missing wife, when a child was ruined, when a theft was proved were all points at which witnesses and defendants and magistrates unwittingly clashed. The decision on cases, though, rested with those magistrates and judges of the criminal courts.

At this time all material evidence was presented in court: the stolen pig, the bruises of a beaten women, the horse, the cow or sheep skin, all are recorded as being physically brought to court. Misunderstandings concerning what was considered suitable evidence for the court to see have been clearly shown in depositions discussed. Henry Crane's shoes, useless as they were in proving theft of a heifer, were dutifully exhibited.[3] Crucial to some cases was the presentation of the stolen property: for instance, cattle theft, because of the distinctive markings on each cow, was easier to prove than sheep theft. The need for material evidence was most apparent in cases where magistrates attempted to obtain information about stolen property by subjecting the prisoner to punishment until the place of concealment was divulged.

Central to cases of torture dealt with in the inquiry into the Parramatta magistrates in 1826 was the assumption that material evidence was concealed somewhere and would be found if the prisoner could be persuaded. Henry Grattan Douglass, magistrate, ordered, 'Henry Bayne, attached to the Domain party, sentenced to receive twenty-five lashes every morning, until he tells where the money and property is stolen from the house of William Jaynes, at Parramatta, by him.'[4] The need for evidence to make a case was no doubt one reason for the elaborate attempts to hide stolen property. For magistrates, lack of evidence did not have any relation to assumption of guilt. In bushranging cases and in theft cases we have found them writing to the Attorney-General hoping that the defendants would receive punishment although the evidence was poor. Before their own benches they were sometimes willing to punish prisoners brought on 'suspicion' of theft.

Depositions were sent to the criminal court where evidence was considered by the Judge Advocate, later the Attorney-General, and was accepted or rejected according to its validity according to law. In theft cases this process was quite straightforward. In cases of violence, the process was more complex: for instance, in a rape case it might be alleged that the victim was intoxicated.

It was here that tracking, suspicion, hearsay, superstition were weeded out and the ordinary population's understanding of the law, and often the magistrates' understanding of law, clashed with the legal mind of the Judge Advocate or Attorney-General. Nowhere is this process more evident than in murder cases. Eliza Campbell was suspected because she would not touch a shroud, Charlotte Dunn because she bought mourning before her husband died.

The defendants waited in prison or where granted bail until it was decided that the case was to proceed to trial. *Habeas corpus*, the right to inquire into imprisonment before trial, did not apply in the colony until after 1824.[5] Letters from the families of defendants and notes to witnesses found their way into court papers. It was in gaol that Edward Hoar was overheard by the turnkey to suggest his guilt in poisoning his wife and diligent search was made for the lock of hair belonging to a woman he loved.[6]

Letters were also produced in court after they had been desperately written by someone awaiting trial. The following letters are reproduced verbatim and the spelling shows pronunciation of words. In 1820 William Ring wrote to the prosecutor in his case:

> I have found the person that I had them things of that I was committed for and should be glad if you would come down to Sydney to me to see if it is the same man that you brought yours of no doubt by description. Five foot three inches, smallpox. So if you will come to Sydney Gaol you will find this man you bought the things of—as soon as possible.[7]

To subpoena witnesses and to pay for one's keep in gaol (food was not supplied) was expensive and some defendants resorted to writing their defence directly to the Judge Advocate or Attorney-General. Peter McCue wrote in 1820:

> Pardon the liberty that stake in laying these papers before you but hope that my present situation be my excuse . . . I take the liberty of explaining to your honour that carickter of the witness Mary Jacob and the reason that indulge to sade witness to give this melisious evidence against me . . . the witness a fellow servent in the house with me in the imploy of Mr. Faithful and during that time I formed a criminal connection with her with which connection caused me to draw the principle part of my wages of my master to give to her wich my master Mr. Faithful can prove if your honore will be pleased to aske him wich things I gave her I will mention in this to your honor but sometime oftene this i was informed that she had got somothear connection beasides that of mine wich so enraged me that I was determined to take those clouthes from her that I had given to her the first opertunity.[8]

McCue thought the situation could be righted through this letter and that the judge would ask questions on his behalf. For a person waiting in gaol for trial there were few options if money could not be obtained for witnesses, messages or solicitors.

Even after 1824 once the case did reach the court, trial hearings were very rapid. The magistrates' bench heard up to twenty cases a day, while the Quarter Sessions were thought to be working slowly if twenty cases were not heard in two days. The criminal courts were almost as rapid, the normal sitting for one session being two weeks. Executions occurred during sessions and those executed had been tried the previous day. To the *Gazette* it was the right of all to observe court proceedings as well as executions. This statement was made after the doorman at the Windsor Quarter Sessions refused access to a group of people[9] and it seems that court procedures were quite popular with audiences.

To Ellis Bent the pomp and ceremony of the criminal court was injured by the absence of a courthouse.[10] The early criminal court was crowded and inadequate.[11] The first session of the Parramatta Quarter Sessions stated the inadequacies of holding the sessions in an inn as it distracted from the duties of the court.[12] In late 1829 the Supreme Court began sitting on circuit and this is the first reference we have to ceremony at the beginning of sessions. The *Gazette* described:

> a cavalcade consisting of a number of the resident magistrates and gentry who accompanies the learned Judge and law officers into the town with similar demonstrations of respect to those which marked his Honour's entrance on the former circuit. The trials commenced on Tuesday last having been occupied in the usual ceremonies of opening the Court, reading the Commission and attending Church where the assize sermon was preached by the Venerable Archdeacon Broughton.[13]

Throughout the period the structure of criminal trials essentially resembles the depositions. Witnesses are called and give evidence; the defendant is asked if he or she will speak for himself which he or she may or may not; the military jury retires for decision and returns; if the finding is that the prisoner is guilty, sentence is passed or the prisoner is remanded and sentence passed later in session. The information given in these trial proceedings, therefore, does not differ from the information given in depositions. In fact, if divergences from depositions occur the trial is stopped, the witness questioned and a possible charge of perjury suggested. Thus this kind of criminal trial bears much relation to the magistrates' bench or Quarter Sessions where the depositions provide evidence of court hearings. This only differs in the criminal courts if a defending counsel appeared in the case.

We have access to the words of the defending counsel and the addresses of the judge and the Attorney-General which reported criminal trials faithfully. It is apparent that there was much to be gained by hiring a solicitor, for cases with written defences had a far lower rate of success. The texts of the written defences are available to us in court records, where they appear alongside the information which relates to the charge. These were read out in court and the judge, or earlier, the Judge Advocate, asked if the prisoner had anything to say in his or her defence. That these defences were not written by the defendant is quite clear: handwriting on many of them is uniform, and a great proportion of defendants could not write except for signing their names.

In 1822 Edward Melville, a government servant to Campbell, was charged with burglary in the house of another farm worker. His defence read:

> the kitchen is under the same roof as Peter Stuckey it is my place of abode . . . a child of about seven years perceived some remarkable communication between the said Mrs Stuckey and your petitioner—which Ann Stuckey was very afraid would reach Peter Stuckey bearing on her character, she thought she might impute this to clear herself.[14]

This defence was ineffective and Melville was sentenced to death. In 1820 Dominick McIntyre was charged with stealing mutton from George Thomas Palmer by Palmer's overseer, John Smith. His defence reads:

> Having no means to employ a solicitor I throw myself on the mercy of the court . . . begs leave to state he has given notice to the gaoler to subpoena three witnesses who had heard the prosecutor and his wife consulting together several times, the prosecutor's wife proposed to her husband that he should swear that the prisoner and a man named Turney, son-in-law to the prosecutor were the Persons that stole the sheep [in order] to extricate himself and that she would hang twenty [rather] than he should be hurt—further begs leave, although he lived in the same house with the prosecutor and son-in-law, he had no concerns with them as he rented part of the farm to himself and all his affairs were distinct, the property was found on the prosecutor's part of the farm.[15]

Dominick McIntyre and Daniel Turney were found guilty despite this defence.

When Francis Williams, employed by the Bank of New South Wales, was charged with embezzlement, his written address to the court read: 'In pleading guilty . . . I have been actuated by a sense of respect to this honourable tribunal in order to spare them the trouble of a tedious enquiry into circumstances and events connected with this case.'[16]

Hugh Taylor in his defence in 1822 said, 'No man can be secure in the colony if such evidence as has been produced on this day is to be credited.'[17] William Brown in 1820 said, 'The learned Blackstone says "if there is a doubt of a prisoner he must be acquit for better ten guilty men escape than one innocent man suffer" my paying the notes is no proof of my knowing it to be stolen.'[18]

Written defences appear on scraps of paper included in records; it is probable that they were easily lost, so we cannot be certain how many cases included them. Spoken defences are described by the newspapers and do not regularly appear, it being often noted, 'the prisoner had nothing to say in his defence'. However, in July 1827, Richard

Kelly before the Windsor Quarter Sessions informed the court that the sentence passed on him 'was illegal'.[19] He was continuing the tradition of a number of solicitors in the colony in this statement, for it is apparent in examination of the statements of solicitors that legal technicalities were the prime mode of defending cases.

Solicitors appeared in cases more often after 1824: with the likelihood of bail being granted defendants had possibly time to raise money or enter into agreement. They were not hired only by persons possessed of wealth. Before 1824 we see, in the few appearances of solicitors, the beginnings of arguments of legal technicalities. Solicitors read a written defence or made a statement of defence for their client. In 1819 during the September Sessions the *Sydney Gazette* noted of the case involving John Gilchrist for forgery:

> The evidence for the prosecution here closed and the prisoner went upon his defence. He was permitted to read a written statement; which bore chiefly on the non-intention to commit a fraud; which argument he endeavoured to sustain by a declaration of his design to have taken up the bill before it became due; and his Advocate, by whom he had been ably assisted on the examination, argued a point of law on behalf of the prisoner with much ability and perspicuity; but failed in his object.[20]

The point of law was not explained. It does, however, appear in the deposition. The solicitor was Frederick Garling. He referred to Geo. II, c. 28, the law regarding forgery:

> It is obvious from the wording of this act that the legislature contemplated only the great evils resulting from forgeries to a nation which had become extensive in Trade and Credit and did not intend to include the distant colonies . . . the prisoner is not answerable to these acts, [by the] 13th of his present majesty 139, the offence of forgery on a foreign Bill of Exchange constitutes only a simple larceny. Can it be for an instant contended that the forged bills upon which the unhappy prisoner is convicted are other than foreign bills as contemplated by acts of parliament made in England.[21]

As the *Sydney Gazette* reported, this argument was not successful as Gilchrist was sentenced to be transported for life.[22]

While such defences were sparse before 1824, after 1824 they became reasonably common, one at least appearing each session. In September 1824, two months after the institution of the Supreme Court of Criminal Jurisdiction, the *Sydney Gazette* reported the trial of the King against Sharland:

> The information contained a second count against the prisoner for assault with intent to murder but the statute being omitted the second charge resolved itself into a mere misdemeanour at common law. The Jury entered a verdict of 'Guilty'. Afterwards the Attorney General entered a nolle prosequi [decision not to proceed] but it was contended by the counsel for the prisoner, in arrest of judgement, that the information was irregular, because it did not lay the offence in any *county*, although facts were proved to have been done in the county of *Cumberland*; that the offence charged amounted in fact to a felony and could not receive judgement as far as a misdemeanour.[23]

The Chief Justice answered the next day:

> . . . the rule of law which requires the specific county to be named in the indictment or information, does not, in my opinion, apply here. In England, the institution is coeval at least with trial by jury. It is part of the law of trial by jury that the jury should be returned from the county where the offence was alleged to be committed. Hence for convenience of trial circuits were instituted throughout the different counties in England . . . I am of the opinion that it is not necessary on any criminal

proceeding in the Colony to state the offences to have been committed in any particular county, provided there be a word sufficiently descriptive of the place to bring it within the jurisdiction of the Court and to give the party accused every benefit of his defence . . . Upon the second ground I am of the opinion that as the offence charged is a misdemeanour does in fact amount for a felony, that judgement must be arrested upon it.[24]

The solicitor, unnamed in both accounts, argued the language of the indictment and the relevance of the terms used in the form of indictment to the colony. These arguments concerning the relevance of English law to the colony and its inapplicability to conditions in the colony were to appear frequently. In April 1825, the solicitor Rowe successfully argued that pardons were prerogative of the king and not transferable, thereby challenging another indictment.[25]

In July 1826 Rowe argued that a prosecutor in a theft case was a convict, therefore, legally, was not able to hold property, so no theft had taken place.[26] In November he argued that government property belonged to convicts and so a theft could not have taken place.[27] In May 1827 he argued that the laws relating to forgery were not applicable in the colony.[28] In August 1827 when he argued a convict could not give evidence as a witness, he was told by the Chief Justice to produce a record of the offence, and, as there was no sufficient means of doing so, his objection was overruled.[29] In February 1828 he argued the absence of records so that a witness, who, it was suggested, was formerly convicted of perjury, would be given credibility as a witness.[30] In May 1828 Rowe argued for an arrest of judgment in a conviction of forging a promissory note: 'the instrument alleged to have been forged was described as a promissory note whereas being for payment of a Spanish dollar and not the current coin of the realm—it could not in law be considered a promissory note . . . for which the defendant was indicted'.[31] In February 1830 the solicitor Therry argued that theft of emus was not relevant to Mr Peel's Act, which clarified theft offences concerning animals as food, as they were not considered food by the prosecutor.[32]

But solicitors, for all their skill in drawing out the inadequacies of witnesses and indictments or law itself, appeared in a minority of cases. For most defendants the hope that pertinent questions would be asked, or an attempt to ask them themselves, was their experience of the courtroom.

The first decision to be made by the defendant in court was the plea. The charge was read out and the defendant was asked how he or she would plead. Newspapers report some exchanges over this. In May 1828 the bushrangers Tennant, Ricks and Carne were indicted for stealing in a dwelling house:

the prisoner Tennant when called to plead said 'Guilty', Mr. Justice Dowling: Are you aware of the consequences of that plea. Prisoner: I don't care my Lord I am tired of my life and as they seem determined I am ready for it. We were tried and sentenced to death last Session and have been kept in chains ever since and now we are brought up to be tried again.[33]

The Attorney-General explained to the judge that the prisoners had been tried on a repealed statute and that the new charge was entirely different.

Justice Dowling: I advise you to withdraw your plea altogether and take your trial as you are charged with a capital offence. . . . Tennant replied: 'very well not guilty if you like' . . . the other prisoners replied in the same way 'Oh, anything you like, not guilty, you may try us the easiest way to yourselves'.[34]

Those persons who pleaded guilty were questioned by the judge or Judge Advocate in this manner throughout the period. Tennant's lack of knowledge concerning pleas is reflected in other cases. In January 1828 before the Windsor Quarter Sessions, James Butterworth, appearing for theft of shirts, pleaded guilty, whereupon 'the Chairman mercifully reminded him that if he persisted in the plea of guilty, nothing could appear in court in extenuation of punishment, whereupon the prisoner withdrew his plea and pleaded—Not Guilty'.[35]

Allesandro Portelli has discussed what he called the 'oral shape of the law', that is, what is said in the courtroom and what limitations there are on that speech.[36] In court transcripts, we are presented with two differing images of the progress of trials, one for the Court of Criminal Jurisdiction and one for the Supreme Court. In the Court of Criminal Jurisdiction the case proceeded according to the decision of the Judge Advocate who was both prosecuting counsel and judge. In these cases the defendant could ask questions of the witnesses but the court was dominated by the opinions of the Judge Advocate. In 1821 the following report appeared in the *Sydney Gazette* concerning the trial of Ann Kennedy James and Mary McGreevy.

> His honour the Judge Advocate declared his reluctance at unnecessarily occupying the valuable time of the court by bringing forward further evidence to support its charges that the prisoners seemed wholly unable to rebut and therefore they were called for their defence.[37]

The *Sydney Gazette* reports these trials from the perspective of the Judge Advocate; it devotes much space to his speech sentencing and often adds its own comments. In 1819 the *Gazette* commented on the trial of Buckley, Brown and Ford, 'the evidence being too clear to admit of a defence the prisoners where called upon acknowledged being together in the unhappy occasion'.[38]

The *Gazette* does not appear to disagree with the decisions of the court in these cases before 1824 and the image it presents of the court represents the structure of power relations in the courtroom. As Judge Advocate Bent was to complain, the Judge Advocate was both prosecuting counsel, judge, advisor to the six military officers, and advisor to the defendant.[39] To counteract this power there were the questions by the defendant which, as I have stated, seem rare; there were also the questions by defending counsel if there was one, the statements of the defendant's witnesses and cross-examinations.

When questions do appear, they concern points of fact or attack the credibility of the witnesses. In March 1814 in the trial of Caleb Wilson for unnatural assault, one of the witnesses, Edward Wright, was questioned by the defendant as to how he had always referred to the prosecutor: 'The prosecutor has always gone ever since I have known him by the name of Whangyjemmy—it means lying James. It is a native name, when a Black man thinks you are telling him a lie he says "Whanga".'[40] Another witness, this time for the defendant, gave evidence that the prosecutor was a notorious liar and was known by the name of Whanga Cunningham—'the children call him by no other name'.[41] This evidence, initiated by the prisoner, was successful, and he was found not guilty.

Once the defence had been heard, the court prepared to make its decision. In some cases the *Gazette* notes an address to the court on the part of the Judge Advocate and in other reports the members of the court retiring without address.[42] In 1813 the Judge Advocate delivered a lengthy address in the case of the murder of William Holness. This was a highly political case and its implications, involving the regiment of the governor, no doubt resulted in the length of the address. The Judge Advocate, Bent, commented extensively on the evidence presented:

> in this case even though struck by the deceased the prisoners in the eye [in the view] of the law would be guilty of murder, but if the death of the deceased cannot be clearly and distinctly traced . . . to the conduct of the prisoners charged in the information it would be the duty of the court to acquit them altogether of this charge.[43]

If the Judge Advocate did address the court, the content of his address followed from his own estimation of the legal certainties of the case. The court would adjourn for up to two hours and when the Judge Advocate and officers returned another address would be made to the court.

The *Gazette* made much of this second address by the Judge Advocate, particularly if the offence was a capital one. In 1820 in the cases concerning Cunningham, Medworth and others brought on separate charges of cattle and horse stealing, the *Gazette* noted:

> Upon this awful occasion nine unhappy men standing at the Bar of the Court in expectation of their horrifying doom presented to the pitying eye of the spectator or melancholy picture of calamity the dye was cast, and the token to be paid! What forfeit? Nothing but life itself extending to a new creation; in which the doom of mortals was to be irrevocably fixed.[44]

In his judgment address Wylde amplified the role of the criminal courts in regulating the morality of the colony. 'Crime' was more important to him than 'law'; his rhetoric was reflected in the 'awfulness' expressed by the *Gazette*. Wylde placed the court in this particular relationship to society. Yet both Bent and Wylde were critical of the institution they were operating in. Currey quotes Wylde:

> it may seem to be doubtful whether the same system of summary and simple procedure in the administration of civil and criminal justice, the conduct of which was committed in the few civil and military officers in 1789, who in conjunction with a population of 900 souls, were to witness and become interested alone in its operation, can be fitted to or supply the means of full and effective justice in a population increased to the number of 35,000 souls in 35 years.[45]

On 10 June 1824 the Supreme Court of Criminal Jurisdiction met for the first time and later in the year the first Quarter Sessions were held in the colony. Trial by jury, albeit military jury in the former case, had reached the colony of New South Wales. Frederick Goulburn, the Colonial Secretary, placed a notice in the *Gazette* in October 1824, declaring that, despite the Supreme Court, 'the solitary existing barrier that divides the mother country and Australia (as regards the liberty of the subject) will very shortly be removed and then we shall become altogether English.'[46]

The excitement that existed in the colony over the extension of such liberty to it is well conveyed in that quote. John Northall from his place of imprisonment in Port Macquarie wrote to the Attorney-General:

I most humbly and submissively beg leave to intrude myself upon your attention, fully sensible from your general conduct so eminently characteristic in the late trials at Sydney to lean on the side of Mercy and where a shadow of innocence betray itself to be the first to perceive it and appear gratified by the pleasing satisfaction of saving a victim from destruction . . . would to God my case had been tried when you held the high situation you do now at the Judgement Bench at Sydney . . .[47]

The year 1824 was one of change in the nature of criminal justice in the colony. The workings of the Supreme Court of Criminal Jurisdiction were described by the *Gazette*:

In our new Criminal Court the Attorney General exhibits the information and conducts the prosecution: Heretofore the Judge Advocate was Public Prosecutor as well as Juror. The Chief Justice has no voice in the verdict, having all, but nothing more than the powers of one of the English Judges vested in him; in consequence of which they Jury retire without the Chief Justice. Before the verdict was carried out by a majority; but now we are particularly happy to announce the Members (seven in number) must be unanimous in their verdict.[48]

Power relations in the court were now split three ways, whereas before they had been centred on one person. The Attorney-General, the jury and the judge replaced the Judge Advocate and six military officers.

The new role of the military officers as jury is well reflected in the following exchange, occurring in August 1824, in the case against Hugh McLusky for theft.

Upon this case the jury retired for upwards of an hour when the foreman returned and informed his honour the Chief Justice that the members could come to no decision and that it was not likely they would. His honour was pleased to observe that in similar cases, it was usual in England to retire to some coffee house till they decided upon the verdict, but no such convenience existed here the Gentlemen could retire to their quarters and that, most probably, by the following morning the verdict would be returned.

FRIDAY: Hugh McLusky was again placed at the bar, the Jury called over by the Prenthonorary, the Foreman stated, that the Jury could not agree, and were not likely to agree.[49]

In the earlier Court of Criminal Jurisdiction we find no such discussion of non-agreement. The Supreme Court of Criminal Jurisdiction worked according to the mechanism of trial operating in England. In the colony, if there was a counsel the debate would be between counsel and Attorney-General, and, as stated, the bulk of counsel's arguments centred on points of law. The court hearing after 1824 entailed *dialogue* between at least the judge, the prosecution, the witnesses and the defendant, if not the defendant's solicitor. For example, in the case against Alfred Bryer for forgery in 1826, the record reads:

Mrs. Julie O'Holland: States that she resides in Sydney and knows the prisoner about six weeks ago she received from him a written paper . . .

Cross examination by the prisoner; will swear that is the identical check she received.

By the Court; witness had it in her possession from half past ten at night until the following morning.[50]

This dialogue was usually continued in the address of the judge, either Judge Dowling or Chief Justice Forbes or Justice Stephen. The address played a crucial role in these cases for in it the judge repeated the evidence, brought up various points of law, and gave his opinion. In 1827 when Timothy Shea was tried for the murder of Patrick Henly, the

Chief Justice summed up: 'in all cases of this kind the great point of enquiry was the *animus* with which the act had been committed for death might be caused and still the crime not amount to murder, malice being the main ingredient.'[51] In the majority of cases, where the defendant did not have a counsel, this address to the jury on the part of the judge was crucial. Forbes, Stephen and Dowling set out the case for the jury's decision. In 1830 we find Dowling stating in a case of robbery:

> His Honour was of the opinion from the evidence before the court that a robbery had been committed on the prosecutor by someone, but the issue for the consideration of the Jury was, whether looking at the condition in which the prosecutor appeared, from the whole of the testimony to have been in on the night in question, they could safely act upon his evidence with regard to the identity of the prisoners at the bar.[52]

The point of the drunkenness of a prosecutor was revealed after extensive cross-examination by the defending solicitor, Therry. As in the earlier criminal court the judge summed up according to the evidence presented to him. Witnesses in these cases appeared to give evidence on alibis or points of fact rather than the character of the defendant. The summing up was closer to points of law. This was all part of the new Supreme Court but witnesses were still expensive to obtain, solicitors even more so.

In 1826 John Trotter, appearing on a charge of cattle stealing, handed a memorial to the court to obtain an arrest of judgment. It stated that he had approached the Attorney-General and told him he had witnesses to prove his innocence but had not the financial means to compel their attendance through subpoena, and, though given time, he still had not the means. The Chief Justice answered:

> the prisoner was tried in January last and from the statements he had made the Attorney General had put off praying judgement against him in order to give him an opportunity of bringing foward any evidence which would prove his innocence but it appeared that so much time had only been lost, as nothing had been brought before the Court in extenuation or in any way available, the Court could not try the charge over again and any proofs of innocence which the prisoner might be able to bring forward should be laid before the Governor.[53]

In this sense, prisoners without financial means were still greatly disadvantaged despite a court which worked according to law, with some dialogue, and with chances to request time for witnesses.

The announcement of a sentence was followed, as in the criminal court, with an address to the prisoners. Though none reach the lyricism of Wylde, Dowling was the judge most likely to bring in discussion of morality or the level of crime in the colony. Forbes and Stephen discussed law. In 1830 Dowling informed two defendants that he hoped the sentence passed would 'have a salutary influence on your future conduct and particularly on you, Howe—who have been born in the colony—instead of assisting in perpetrating a stain upon your native land'.[54]

When the Assizes were established in 1829 and the Supreme Court sat on circuit, Dowling was particularly inspired. The *Gazette* wrote:

> we are aware that the practice of Mr. Dowling in thus winding up the business of the local courts has not escaped the cavils of the censories as though it were a pompous and needless display of rhetoric; but they are only *cavils* and proceed from an imperfect estimate of the influence of judicial addresses

upon the feelings of society. That influence is strong and general. The people are reminded of their duties and privileges as English subjects.[55]

Dowling reported on the nature of the offences, the extent of crime. At the Maitland Assizes in 1830 he congratulated the district on the absence of highway robbery, applauded the existence of circuit courts and stressed the necessity for better roads.[56]

The *Gazette* also thought circuit courts were crucial. The jurors for the Assizes were not military but local residents. The *Gazette* wrote:

> The knowledge of character which is acquitted by gentlemen residing on the spot, who are called to serve the office of Jurors is obviously of the greatest benefit in the administration of Justice; more particularly as it affects the witnesses who are brought forward either on the part of the crown or the accused. In this Colony, where unfortunately for the character of the lower orders of society, witnesses can be obtained to swear anything that may be required of them this local knowledge is of utmost importance.[57]

Such criticism of local people had been made by the *Gazette* before in its criticism of the juries selected in country areas for Quarter Sessions. Between 1824 and February 1829 when the juries became military, the Quarter Sessions were able to set the limits of what they heard through the grand jury. As we have seen, in 1828 the Sydney Quarter Sessions limited the number of 'trivial' offences they heard.[58] The sessions were intensely local in character and as such exhibit some familiarity between defendant, prosecutor and jury. As in a coroner's inquest however, the importance lay in the verdict. Quarter Sessions juries were far more likely to give a 'not guilty' verdict than the higher courts.

This was the *Gazette's* objection, or suggested objection. In 1827 it reported on the Windsor Quarter Sessions, regarding the case of one Browning:

> Browning is a native of the colony and most of the gentlemen of the Petit Jury were natives of the Colony also, and although intended to show he was a hardened offender we must insert in our report the comment he thought proper, to pay his fellow Australian. The learned Chairman addressed the prisoner and concluded by passing sentence—7 years transportation. The prisoner immediately remarked 'Well there's a pretty set of fellows to be jury men they know more about a dish of ominey a good deal—what should they know about a jury.'[59]

In May 1827 the *Gazette* reported a rumour that in the July Sydney sessions the chairman was going to incorporate colonists from the emigrant order 'which would at least render them more intelligent if not respectable'.[60]

Whether any of the complexity of courtroom procedure was understood by the population is uncertain. Crowds might follow the solicitor Rowe and the Attorney-General might receive letters from prisoners commending him on his fairness, but there was also evidence of a rejection of the processes involved or some unawareness as to the result of a trial. 'I like 'em all well enough', said a defendant at Windsor Quarter Sessions when asked if he had any objections to the jury.[61]

The Supreme Court addressed a similar question to William Ward and William Power, charged with robbery in a dwelling house:

> The Clerk of the Court having read the information to which the prisoners pleaded not guilty put the usual interrogatory 'How will you be tried?' Prisoners 'O' the easiest way to yourselves, anyway you

think proper!' Being asked in the usual way whether they would challenge any of the Jury 'O it's all the same to us who you have, a parcel of blackfellows, would do just as well!'[62]

For most people who went through the court as defendants, their only speech was the plea they made. They had no choice of stating a defence, the choice of calling witnesses, the choice of having a counsel; but without means they could not utilise these choices. Their contact with the courts centred on their sentence. When William Webb and Sarah Webb appeared for house robbery they received the death sentence: 'at hearing which the unfortunate woman, who did not seem to anticipate such a result dropped on the floor and was carried shrieking out of court, her cries resounded throughout the building.'[63]

Punishment

The final stage in the making and processing of a criminal trial or a hearing by the lower courts was punishment. The courtroom hearing enabled only those with solicitors or bravery to speak; ordinary people were utterly powerless when they became subject to the machine of punishment. In New South Wales this was a curious machine. Transportation to New South Wales was, as punishment, subject to intense debate in England. Its opponents were Jeremy Bentham and evangelicals who sought to argue new concepts of the prison as effective punishment.[64] At the heart of such debate was the notion of reform: prisoners were to be reformed by effective means and for the opponents of New South Wales the colony fell far short of these requirements. De Tocqueville captured the essence of criticism in 1833: 'The criminal, a prisoner though he be, becomes, transported to Australia, in fact a servant at wages.'[65] This system, he said, was meant to be economical and it was not, but, he said, 'the question of economy is but a secondary one'.[66]

De Tocqueville had stated an old conflict in debates over punishment. The history of the colony from 1810 to 1830 was marked by continual tension in English parliamentary debate between 'reform' and 'economy'. Bentham had tried to combine reform and economy in his argument in *Panopticon vs New South Wales*.[67] His arguments were unsuccessful and in transportation the British government sought to combine effectiveness in reform and terror to potential offenders with economy in the transportation and assignment system. The government labourer was undesirable, according to Bigge, and we have seen how Brisbane was pleased with the solution of clearing gangs as both government labour and service for private employers. Darling was also impressed with his system of 'political economy' whereby employers would bear some administrative costs. Darling, however, was also concerned with the laxity of the system and wished all convicts to be worked in irons. This fear of laxity was to appear throughout the period: transportation was economical but was it also for the convict at worst 'a form of emigration'?[68]

A. G. L. Shaw has set out the history of the increasing severity of the convict system. It was strongly influenced by the arguments of reformers, Bentham, Peel, Romilly, Brougham and the evangelical prison reformers Fry and Howard. The dilemma existing in England is described by Shaw:

For half a century, bitter protagonists had been hurling figures at one another, giving conflicting estimates of costs; but gradually it began to appear that transportation would never be as cheap as some hoped. Colonial Governors were as repeatedly ordered to economize as they were told to be rigorous . . .[69]

Randall McGowen has analysed the tension between the old system of eighteenth-century terror and mercy as described by Hay, and its new opponents, the advocates of a mechanical law and scientific mode of punishment: 'Advocates of reform enjoyed striking success in setting the terms of the debate. What had once been accepted as the course of the law—severity combined with mercy—was now reinterpreted as a symptom of the breakdown of the judicial system.'[70] New South Wales figured large in debate about prison reform. This made the colonial governors the centre of powerful debates in the House of Commons. New South Wales was indeed born out of a legal system undergoing profound change and dilemma.

It is not surprising then, that the system of punishment operating inside the colony should be subject to scrutiny and political sensitivity both locally and in England. Evidence of torture was sent to William Wilberforce, the evangelist member of the British Parliament, by the enemies of magistrate Douglass (see Chapter 6); it could be well utilised.

On examination it appears that the system of punishment operating in the colony, though it originated in a system of transportation, did not lag behind developments in imprisonment in England.

The lash was the primary punishment meted out to male convicts. Bent complained that it was difficult for him not to resort to this kind of punishment in the Court of Criminal Jurisdiction:

the number of cases committed is owing to the want of punishment and I have been extremely embarrassed as to the mode or degree of punishment inflicted on offenders it frequently happens that prisoners are brought forward, charged and eventually convicted of a felony and when the bench is about to convict the offender it is perhaps objected that the prisoner is in the employ of the government and by imprisoning his labour is lost . . . the objection when admitted leaves no other alternative than corporal punishment.[71]

The logic of corporal punishment is well received in that settlement: a convict lashed could be returned to an employer and no labour would be lost in his punishment. The number of lashes ordered varied extensively between magistrates. It was the Sydney bench in 1812, 1815–16 and 1821 which revealed the most erratic use of the lash. Parramatta, despite its reputation, clearly had set punishments and awarded them accordingly. It was not until 1829 that suitable punishments were set out for the benefit of the magistrates.[72] 'Moderate punishment', as we saw in Chapter 2, was defined for them in an Act in 1825: ten days' work on the treadmill, flogging up to fifty lashes, solitary confinement on bread and water for a period not exceeding seven days, imprisonment with hard labour not exceeding six months.[73] Before this period magistrates were able to use their own discretion in punishment. Minchin, magistrate in Sydney 1820–21, ordered lashes on the breech (i.e., buttocks) for instance, fifty lashes on the back and fifty on the breech formed a common punishment. The early Judge Advocate's Bench seems to have regularly ordered 100 lashes for offences such as the theft of promissory notes, street robbery and house robbery.

For country magistrates the difficulty was when to stop punishment and they ordered further punishment for contempt of court or refusal to obey orders. When John Middleton, servant to Hannibal Macarthur, the magistrate, was charged with neglect and insolence at Argyle, he was ordered to receive seventy-five lashes and return to his employer; he refused to return and received a further twenty-five lashes.[74] It was but a short step to punish convicts for refusing to divulge information when the magistrates were certain they were guilty of theft. John Brackfield's servants, for instance, told their employer that they would never tell where they had got spirits. Magistrates, local gentlemen, dealt in the realm of character and re-offending; if they were certain of an offence, they would order punishment until proof could be obtained. This realm sometimes correlated with statute law and sometimes did not. Illegal punishments and the transferring of offenders were the results of such activity and the former was the centre of inquiry.

Punishment of female convict offenders did not depend on the lash: magistrates resorted to the Female Factory or local gaols as places of confinement. The indefinite nature of sentences or their length meant that women in their punishment were closely linked to the prison as an institution. The Female Factory became the centre of debates over reform in the colony and a new effective Factory was ordered to be built by Macquarie. As an institution it was both a holding house and a place of punishment. For the courts it was the latter. In 1822, when the Factory was organised into the class system, which divided women into three classes according to their reason for being sent there, this use of the Factory as a place of imprisonment became clearer.

For convicts the system of punishment which operated in the colony was aimed at both the body and the mind: punishment of the body sought to instil terror into male convicts and punishment of the mind through imprisonment in a cell would instil reform in the woman herself. Though the Female Factory may have been resorted to because there was simply no other kind of punishment available, the moral decision to imprison women rather than physically beat them was made. This distinction in modes of punishment, whether deliberate or not, may be linked to the rhetoric of colonial administrators who saw women in terms of their sex and men in terms of their labour.[75] Convict women were the first to experience nineteenth-century prison relations in the colony. Though such influences are apparent in the specially marked clothes introduced for male convicts in the barracks in 1819, the barracks were not used as a place of punishment.

As well as corporal punishment, magistrates before 1824 ordered male convicts in Sydney to terms in the gaol gang. The gang worked about the town of Sydney and was thus subject to considerations of measurement of time, production etc. They resided at night in the gaol. Such a sentence did not mean that the convicts sentenced were no longer labourers. The same principle was used in the later years of the period by country magistrates sentencing convicts to a time in the ironed gangs.

For offences deemed serious or repeated offences convict men and women were transported, by both magistrates and criminal courts, to terms at the prison settlements of Newcastle, later Port Macquarie, and later still Moreton Bay. Penal settlements moved further up the coast because the settlements outgrew their penal function. They resembled the early settlement of Sydney and similarly concentrated on labour value for men. Women were engaged in some field tasks but the distinction between them and men was discussed in 1819 by Alexander Riley; he said that Newcastle was least effectual as a place of punishment for females, 'who from the difficulty of finding proper places of confinement in the Coal River and from the disproportion of the sexes there obtained the means of enriching themselves from the connections they formed.'[76]

Thus the difficulties of finding accommodation and the problems of gaining some means to pay for lodgings occurred in the penal settlements as much as in the towns. The principles of settlement organisation did not differ.

Relocating or retransportation was meant to be utilised carefully by magistrates. It was complained that they used it indiscriminately. In 1819 the magistrate Cartwright was asked about the practices of magistrates of sending convicts to Coal River, or Newcastle:

> They professed to send more to the Coal River but incorrigible offenders and the term for which they were sent was fixed according to the nature of the offence. I do not recollect the particular reason for sending them during the governor's pleasure except it were to prevent their returning till there was hope of their reformation. I believe this was not the practice when I acted as magistrate.[77]

That other magistrates sent convicts to Newcastle or Coal River for the governor's pleasure, i.e. for an indefinite term, was claimed by Macquarie in 1820 and the records bear this out. In April 1820 Campbell, Colonial Secretary, sent a circular to magistrates:

> No convict or prisoner of the Crown is to be transported to Newcastle or elsewhere otherwise than by the sentence of the Criminal Court or by a Bench of Magistrates which must at all times consist of two J.P.'s and the sentence of such bench must limit and define the term of such transportation on the day sentence is pronounced and on no occasion must be left open (as is frequently the case at present) for the governor's pleasure or to refer to any interposition of his excellency thereon.[78]

Before 1820 the concern that 'incorrigible offenders' would return to the place of their offence *overrode* legal considerations about the validity of the sentence. In 1828 another circular indicated that magistrates were still involved in such sentencing practices. The circulars set out two classes of offences. The first class contained 'all crimes and misdemeanours punishable with death, the second class consists of drunkenness, disobedience of orders, neglect of work, absconding or desertion, abusive language to employers or overseers and other turbulent or disorderly conduct'.[79] Minor offences could be punished by whipping or other corporal punishment, removal to some other part of the colony and hard labour. For the first class or greater offences, punishment could extend the time of the offender's transportation or transportation to a penal settlement. The circular noted:

> the second class of offences comprises such only as are enumerated above—And it is to be observed that *absconding* with whatever frequency it may be repeated and whether it be from ordinary service or a penal settlement is always to be considered as an offence of the second class only.[80]

The circular continued:

> From these decisions it is evident that great care ought to be used both to avoid mistaking either the first and second class of offences or the two subdivisions of the first class and also to designate them correctly in proceedings, Returns and other documents so as to show at once without further reference or explanation that such a mistake has not been made.[81]

As in the use of torture, magistrates were considering factors other than the strict application of the law. The practice of keeping in the lower courts cases that should have been passed on is also evident in court records, particularly in those of the Judge Advocate's Bench. In 1816 Owen McNally was charged with stealing a writing desk, the property of Robert Campbell. It was not valued. His punishment, however, was equal to that of the criminal court: 'To be flogged at the cart's tail in the market place Friday next 100 lashes, confined in a solitary cell on bread and water for two calendar months and afterwards to be sent to Newcastle to hard labour for the space of three years.'[82]

McNally was a convict and it was convicts who were kept in the lower courts for serious offences: this might be related to labour value but it could also be related to the wish of magistrates to punish incorrigibles themselves. This practice occurred in England and has been related by historians to legal technicalities. Justices could manipulate the seriousness of an offence by undervaluing stolen goods.[83] In New South Wales magistrates may well have been exercising the same prerogative. They also used torture in questioning, transferred cases to the criminal court and wrote letters to influence a conviction. Their references to the public mind and the public good suggest that they saw themselves as arbiters not only of law but of morality and the quality of life in their local areas.

Until 1824 free persons were either punished by these magistrates or sent to the criminal court for consideration. After 1824 they appeared before the Quarter Sessions in their local areas to be tried by juries of their peers. In 1825 three magistrates, Wentworth, McLeod, and Lawson, provided their opinion on the nature of these juries: they wrote that trial by jury 'generally produced beneficial effects more particularly, as regards Petty jurors it is equally clear to us that some of the privileges of jurors have been used as a medium for private and improper purposes'.[84] The magistrates Wemyss, Oxley, Berry, Rossi and Balcomb wrote that in 'our own unanimous opinion the Juries have conducted themselves with great propriety'.[85] These differences are essentially regional ones: the latter magistrates were from Sydney, the former from Parramatta. In country areas suitable jurors were chosen from 'yeomen'[86] rather than the small shopkeepers and artisans of Sydney. Magistrates were more likely to imagine or perceive links between the defendant and the accused in country regions. The magistrates also sentenced Quarter Sessions cases despite the fact their direct link in deciding guilt was taken from them.

For the early magistrates' benches the distinction between convict and free was not an easy one to make and according to magistrates themselves it was also difficult for them to ascertain. Samuel Marsden came before Bigge in 1820 and said he could not tell free from convict.[87] The New South Wales Legislative Council in 1828 concluded that magistrates had great difficulty 'discriminating between those persons who were amenable to [summary] jurisdiction and those who were in the ordinary jurisdiction of the law'.[88] We can ascertain punishment patterns before 1824 through examination of these cases where the defendant is listed as free and the offence was one related to a free population.

Freed women were sentenced to terms in the Female Factory alongside convict women, or sentenced to gaol for offences related to drunkenness and vagrancy. In policing and punishment free women were not distinguished from convict. The reason for Factory punishment can possibly be related to the events described to Wylde by Mrs Eliza Bent:

I understand there is no place of separate confinement for females sentenced to Sydney gaol . . . two girls of honest repute was sauntering about with their mistresses . . . and stepped over a part of the wall belonging to the domain . . . were seized by a constable and conveyed to Sydney gaol where they were placed without any ceremony. The constables received two bottles of rum for their exertions and the poor girls were compelled to spend a night or two in that gaol exposed to all the insults which the worst of the convicts chose to offer them.[89]

The Factory may well have been seen as a more suitable place of internment. Punishment of free men was commonly a term at Newcastle or imprisonment. Minchin referred to a 'house of correction' in his sentencing which is an obvious reading of a guide for magistrates, because no house of correction existed in the colony. If they were sent to Newcastle they were caught up in convict labour, while imprisonment meant they were, alongside women, associated with notions of incarceration.

Sentencing both at magisterial level and at Quarter Sessions level was strongly related to the personality of the sentencing magistrate. The treadmill figured largely in 1824 but not in 1828 because of the particular whims of the magistrate involved. Minchin favoured lashes on the breech, whereas the country magistrates preferred lashes on the back. The Quarter Sessions were more likely than the magistrates' benches to return a finding of not guilty.

The personality of the particular person sentencing becomes crucial in the Court of Criminal Jurisdiction and the Supreme Court. While there were set punishments for offences, the Judge Advocates and judges each placed their own stamp on the punishment they ordered.

Judge Advocate Wylde, who arrived in the colony in 1816, favoured solitary confinement as a punishment for both men and women. His first sentence involving it entailed six months' solitary confinement for a woman charged of theft, Sarah Grey.[90] He sent a circular to all of the magistrates in the colony requesting their opinion of solitary confinement and claimed himself that 'it was an excellent punishment if properly applied'.[91] Wylde's enthusiasm for this mode of punishment certainly derived from the popularity of it in discussion in England. Through solitary confinement the prisoner would contemplate his or her wrongdoings and repent. That this type of punishment was applied diligently to women in the colony implies that it was they who were first considered in this light, it being necessary for them to reform and repent.

Wylde and Bent both utilised the death sentence extensively: it was the most common punishment for men after transportation to Newcastle. Executions were crowded; convicts were paraded to watch and crowds gathered on the streets. The execution was conducted as in England and much attention was paid to the last words of those about to be hanged. Sometimes the defendants clarified their role in the crime: Geary, for instance, exonerated a man who had been hung for an offence which Geary had committed.[92] Sometimes they swore their innocence or blamed others for the offence. The *Gazette* reported executions in detail, recording the 'melancholy spectacle' with references to hell and damnation.[93] If a confession was made and God implored to judge the defendant well in heaven, the defendant became quite exonerated by the newspaper and a reference was made to dignity.[94] Reading the *Gazette's* pages we become spectators ourselves at the scene and we hope for what the *Gazette* hopes, a full confession, explanation and repentance. Ninety-five persons were executed between 1819 and 1824.[95]

That transportation and death continued to figure importantly in the punishments of the later Supreme Court is evidence of the convergence of New South Wales patterns of punishment with those of England. But the use also of solitary confinement and imprisonment in the Factory reveals that new notions of the prison were operative in New South Wales. They, combined with hard labour in irons, created a particular brand of colonial punishment which echoed the tensions in the sentence of transportation itself. Labour and reform, confinement and economy were also implicit in the sentencing pattern of all the courts. Women found themselves within the emerging nineteenth-century pattern of punishment. Reform was combined with incarceration. Convict men were punished corporally through the exigencies of labour. This, like the sentence of death, relied upon the terror of the example. Punishment in an iron gang, like assignment, was to effect reform through labour; it was also economical, as were sentences to penal settlements.

Punishment could be modified by the government, and prisoners could be pardoned from the death sentence. The governor's office played an important bureaucratic role in the punishment system. For example on 14 October 1826 the Colonial Secretary wrote to the Sheriff concerning the hanging of Griffiths and seven others at Parramatta:

> The prisoners and their escort will move from Sydney Gaol at 5.00 am for execution at Parramatta. The bodies are to remain suspended through the whole day in the evening they are to come down in the usual manner or at the applications of friends or relations.[96]

Three days earlier the Colonial Secretary had written to the Civil Engineer so that gibbets would be erected.

The bureaucratic role which the governor played gave him opportunity to change sentences, to pardon, to ask why sentences were so harsh or so lenient. His overseeing could alter the pattern of magisterial or criminal court sentences. He wrote to ask for the release of prisoners, to ask for the opinion of the clerk of the Quarter Sessions on sentences, to remit fines. That mercy resided with the governor can possibly explain the prevalence of the use of the death sentence by Wylde and the early Supreme Court. Pardons from that sentence do not seem common in the colony. These sentences, though, were reserved for bushrangers, the offence deemed most serious by judges, governor and counsel alike. We should not be surprised that Donohue regarded himself as 'dead meat already'.

Bodies were asked for after hanging, wakes were held and people sang and drank all night. The courtroom and punishment were ritualistic, and this ritual extended into the houses and public houses of the colony.

For all their involvement in tracking, suspecting, informing and giving evidence, the lower orders of the colony could only watch hangings or punishments and sing and dance at wakes. Once a man or woman had been hanged, the rowdiness, the clamour to speak or the silence began once again.

Notes

1 This ritual has been well described by D. Hay, 'Property, Authority and Criminal Law', in *Albion's Fatal Tree*, p. 27.
2 Reported in *Sydney Gazette*, 17 June 1826.
3 R. vs Henry Crane, C.C.J., September 1822, 20.
4 Papers relating to the Conduct of Magistrates in New South Wales, in directing the infliction of Punishments upon Prisoners in that Colony, House of Commons, 17 April 1826, in *British Parliamentary Papers*, reprinted, Irish University Press, vol. 3: *Correspondence and Papers relating to the Government and Affairs of the Australian Colonies, Australia*, p. 269.
5 See A. C. Castles, *An Australian Legal History*, p. 185.
6 R. vs Edward Hoar, C.C.J., December 1823, 55.
7 R. vs James Crow, William King, James Kirton, C.C.J., December 1820, 326.
8 R. vs Patrick Hogan, Peter McCue, John McKay, C.C.J., June 1820, 60.
9 *Sydney Gazette*, 17 January 1827.
10 C. H. Currey, *The Brothers Bent*, pp. 50–1.
11 *ibid.*
12 Grand Jury Presentment, Parramatta Q.S., February 1825.
13 *Sydney Gazette*, 12 January 1830.
14 R. vs Edward Melville, C.C.J., March 1822, 70.
15 R. vs Dominick McIntyre, Daniel Turney, C.C.J., June 1820, 586.
16 R. vs Francis Williams, C.C.J., March 1822, 101.
17 R. vs Hugh Taylor, Edward Smith, C.C.J., April 1822, 4.
18 R. vs William Brown and others, C.C.J., December 1820, 295.
19 Richard Kelly, Windsor Q.S., July 1827, 30.
20 *Sydney Gazette*, 25 September 1819.
21 R. vs John Gilchrist, C.C.J., June 1819, 86.
22 *ibid.*
23 *Sydney Gazette*, 30 September 1824.
24 *ibid.*
25 *ibid.*, 14 April 1825.
26 *ibid.*, 8 July 1826.
27 *ibid.*, 22 November 1826.
28 *ibid.*, 16 May 1827.
29 *ibid.*, 6 August 1827.
30 *ibid.*, 13 February 1828.
31 *ibid.*, 9 May 1828.
32 *ibid.*, 27 February 1830.
33 *ibid.*, 28 May 1828.
34 *ibid.*
35 *ibid.*, 16 January 1828.
36 A. Portelli, 'Oral Testimony, the Law and the Making of History: The April 7 Murder Trial', *History Workshop*, 20, Autumn 1985, pp. 5–35.
37 *Sydney Gazette*, 28 July 1821.
38 *ibid.*, 10 April 1819.
39 See Currey as quoted by Castles, *An Australian Legal History*, p. 48.
40 R. vs Caleb Wilson, C.C.J., 28 March 1814.
41 *ibid.*
42 Reported in *Sydney Gazette*, 25 September 1819.
43 *ibid.*, 29 May 1813.

44 *ibid.*, 25 March 1820.

45 Currey, 'Chapters on the Legal History of New South Wales, 1788–1863', p. 141.

46 *Sydney Gazette*, 21 October 1824.

47 Letter included in miscellaneous papers, S.C.C.J., June 1824.

48 *Sydney Gazette*, 17 June 1824.

49 *ibid.*, 25 August 1824.

50 *ibid.*, 15 November 1826.

51 *ibid.*, 14 May 1827.

52 *ibid.*, 28 February 1830.

53 *ibid.*, 17 June 1826.

54 *ibid.*, 25 February 1830.

55 *ibid.*, 27 April 1830.

56 *ibid.*

57 *ibid.*, 12 January 1830.

58 See 'Domestic Violence' in Chapter 3, above.

59 *Sydney Gazette*, 16 April 1827.

60 *ibid.*, 9 May 1827.

61 *ibid.*, 18 April 1827.

62 *ibid.*, 14 May 1827.

63 *ibid.*, 15 July 1826.

64 See W. R. Cornish et al., *Crime and the Law in Nineteenth-century Britain*, pp. 8–9; S. McConville, *A History of English Prison Administration*, vol. 1: *1750–1877*, London, 1981.

65 Gustave de Beaumont, Alexis de Tocqueville, *On the Penitentiary System in the United States*, Manhattanville, 1833, p. 138.

66 *ibid.*, p. 139.

67 Jeremy Bentham, *Panopticon vs New South Wales*, privately printed, 1802.

68 de Beaumont and de Tocqueville, *On the Penitentiary System in the United States*, p. 139.

69 A. G. L. Shaw, *Convicts and the Colonies*, p. 17.

70 R. McGowen, 'The Image of Justice and Reform of the Criminal Law in Early Nineteenth Century England', *Buffalo Law Review*, vol. 32, no. 1, Winter 1983.

71 Bent to Cooke, 10 May 1810, *H.R.A.*, 1, VII, p. 51.

72 J. H. Plunkett, *The Australian Magistrate: A Guide to the Duties of Justice of the Peace*, Sydney 1835, p. 270.

73 McLaughlin, 'The Magistracy in NSW', M.A. thesis, University of Sydney, 1973, pp. 267–8.

74 John Middleton, Argyle Bench of Magistrates, 3 April 1826.

75 Michael Ignatieff suggests that to see a neat change from the customary traditional methods of punishment to newer scientific notions is an incorrect approach. See Ignatieff, 'State, Civil Society and Totalizing Institutions', in Cohen and Scull, *Social Control and the State*.

76 A. Riley, Evidence, Select Committee of House of Commons on the State of the Gaols, 29 March 1819, in *British Parliamentary Papers*, reprinted, Irish University Press, vol. 1: *Crime and Punishment, Prisons*, p. 18; 'connections' means sexual relations.

77 Evidence of Richard Cartwright to Bigge Inquiry, B.T. 24, p. 5275.

78 Circular, Campbell to Magistrates, 20 April 1820, Bigge Inquiry, B.T. 24, p. 5270.

79 Circular to Magistrates re Summary Trial, 30 September 1828, AO 2/8328.

80 *ibid.*

81 *ibid.*

82 Owen McNally, P.M.B., 5 April 1816.

83 J. M. Beattie, *Crime and the Courts in England*, pp. 284–5.

84 D. McLeod and others to Brisbane, 10 October 1825, Brisbane Letter Book, ML. A1559–1.

85 J. T. Campbell and others to Brisbane, 2 October 1825, *ibid.*

86 Depending on the region, 'yeomen' could be quite poor. The native youth of Windsor, for example, sat on juries.
87 Marsden, evidence to Bigge Inquiry, B.T. 8, p. 3421.
88 Report of Legislative Council, Inquiry into Alleged Illegal Punishments.
89 Eliza Bent to Wylde, 16 April 1818, *H.R.A.*, 1, IV, p. 239.
90 Returns Court of Criminal Jurisdiction 1816–24, Sarah Grey, January 1821.
91 J. Wylde, evidence to Bigge Inquiry, B.T. 7, p. 3074.
92 The man was George Bowerman.
93 *Sydney Gazette*, 9 January 1830.
94 See 'Domestic Violence' in Chapter 3, above, for the *Gazette* on the Mary Minton case.
95 Abstract of Returns, Court of Criminal Jurisdiction, *H.R.A.*, 4, 1, p. 479.
96 Colonial Secretary to Sheriff, 14 October 1826, Col. Sec., Copies of Letters to Judicial Establishment, A.O. 4/3736.

9

CONCLUSION

When a solicitor rose to address the court and argued than an emu could not be considered food under English law, he was arguing legal technicalities in an English mode. His audience consisted not only of the officers of the court but also a ragged collection of the public who may have come only to see a good performance, a custom which was also English in origin. Apart from the shufflings and whispering of the public, the process of trial was carried on with careful regard for proper speech and proper silence. To us, the courtroom is a scene; it has a careful balance.

This is unlike the series of actions that led to this courtroom scene. While the concerns of the accused may centre on conviction, they need not be our concerns. The point at which a criminal case begins to emerge is fraught with power relations. Complainants, informers, witnesses and defendants, together with constables, made colonial law. There is no careful balance here.

Law has a peculiar relationship to everyday life: in law the historian deals with a realm of symbol, speech and silence that arises in situations of conflict or crisis. But law is not universal: it relates to specific social conditions. A convict and indeed a convict's person was most affected by the loss of rights entailed in transportation. However, transportation involved the valuing of labour. It was this valuing which determined how the law would intervene in the person of the convict. It was valuing only partially enshrined in law[1] and indeed it was created in the colonial labour market. Historians have debated whether labour ameliorated or negated the prison that New South Wales was meant to be.[2] If we shift the focus of research to ask how this valuing of labour affected the intervention of law in the person, we find an enormously complex process by which law defined movement, space, ownership by accepting the employer's definition of a convict offence. And it is employers, and therefore the law, which utilise new ideas of what a labourer, male or female, is.

In the town of Sydney during the Macquarie period the convict was defined by the court as waged labourer. The extreme application of notions of measurement by officials such as Druitt illustrates how quickly philosophies, or perhaps misunderstood philosophies, can be put into practice. But this was greatly aided by the bargaining of them as 'owned' and exchangeable labour. The anonymity of employer and servant and the failure of employers to measure female labour occurred in the modernisation of domestic service in England. So this too was new. Farm labourers and country labour in general demonstrated a different set of relations which was closer, similar to plantation labour. Food and clothing, essential to everyday life, were at issue. The law in practice essentially saw male and female convicts as subject to different rules and as inhabiting different worlds. For the male, labour was central: the control over his person was determined by his value as labourer. For the female, the person was governed by notions of sexuality, and suspicion played an important role in management. The law intervened in sexual use of the body and in delineation of property. Thus we have the law involved in the modernising of labour and gender relations.

Such attitudes concerning the valuing of labor were adopted, albeit shakily, by administrators because New South Wales was not a plantation economy. Convicts were not goods to be sold. New ideas concerning penal practice applied to women first but we can also see in the layout of power relations a constant tension between punishment and the market and notions of gender. The tension between labour and punishment has been well recognised in colonial historiography. This book furthers investigation of the sheer complexity of those labour relations and the depth of those views concerning gender.

A colony perhaps provides a raw, open environment for application of new theories.[3] The colony was not dominated only by a proscriptive law, because these attitudes to the person were reflected in use of law by the ordinary population. What was male and female was clearly distinguished in both property and violence cases. Suspicion appeared more often in the construction of female guilt and there was a female realm of theft that seems considerably different to female urban or rural theft in England. For the administration, the person was something new, something particular to the colony. We see adoption here of ideas not yet put into practice in England. Whether this concept of the person was something new for the ordinary population is difficult to ascertain, given the lack of comparable work in England.

The debate over the role of women in colonial New South Wales has essentially concentrated on the dominant role of the colonial administration with its notions of personal morality and rejection of those notions by ordinary men and women.[4] Magistrates certainly asked questions and made decisions from this perspective, but all levels of the population held notions about signs of female guilt which sometimes clashed and sometimes combined. Women also held notions of 'manliness' of proper behaviour for men but these notions were validated only when women as wives and mothers were protected by the law in cases they brought against their male partners. Cases were slowly built up and distinctions between male and female operated at every step.

What is to be male or female influences all social interaction. In this realm we are dealing with the most intimate aspects of life. The convict system created an environ-ment for street policing which concentrated on male and female in different ways and which partly contributed to the pattern of arrests for theft. Another aspect was women's seeming familiarity with use of the courts for highly personal cases. The law selectively intervened in society because of these different considerations of gender.

Such processes of selective intervention were also clear in the construction of the offence of bushranging. The circumstances of the convict colony gave rise to an offence which involved both rejection of the colony and dependence on it. It was inspired by circumstances in Ireland, perhaps, but it was a colonial offence. The reaction to it and the fears expressed were related to the 'character' of the population. The imagined drama of bushranging gave rise to new methods of policing; the offence and its policing began to focus on the receiver. The offence also gave rise to two economies, the economy of informing and obtaining rewards and the economy of receiving, hiding and transferring stolen property. Harbouring possessed an etiquette, a careful exchange of stolen goods and services. Bushranging was a culture produced both by the offence and its policing.

New methods emerged also in the policing of street offences and house searches. The 'character' of the population also informed the development of the offences relating to vagrancy and drunkenness. But this policing was fuelled by the willingness of all levels of the population to appear in the courts to give evidence. Again, this created a culture of hiding, exchanging and informing. The colonial economy gave rise to a set of offences concerning money, exchange, debt and trespass. It was very easy to transgress financial relations in the colony or to be accused of transgressing them. The courts could serve many purposes and these added to the effectiveness of colonial law and authority. As well, assault cases developed out of social relations which seem very fragile: insults to status were tied to the presence of the convict system.

But this public world was, again, profoundly affected by the different roles for male and female. Women used the courts for highly personal disputes, and community atti-tudes distinguished between signs of male and female guilt. Constables arrested men and women for different reasons and communities waited out a pregnancy to appear in the court and give evidence of child murder.

While New South Wales was like England in that all levels of the population had access to law,[5] authority does exist only in the fact of use. This is where Langbein's critique of *Albion's Fatal Tree*[6] is lacking. As we saw in Chapter 1, it not only presents a mechanical perspective of law, but it also fails to see that the point at which a criminal case begins to emerge is fraught with power relations. Regardless of who used the courts, there were decisions made at every point of the legal process as to what was a male, what was a female, and what signified property, violence and guilt. The editors of *Albion's Fatal Tree* recognised the need to explore such areas further, and subsequent work has concentrated on regional studies. But New South Wales was more than a region of England.

The appearance of the court and the attitudes of judges and magistrates give the impression that New South Wales was almost 'altogether English'. An emu, however, is not English, nor was torture a nineteenth-century English legal practice, nor was the structure of power in the courtroom entirely English. While some aspects of English authority, as described by Hay and Brewer and Styles, operated in the colony—the 'potent fiction' of rule of law for instance[7]—there were also particular attitudes attached to the convict system which altered the nature of authority in the colony. The starting point of this book was not the courtroom or the gallows but what Douglas Hay has recently called 'popular attitudes formed at the boundaries of appropriation and control', and what Michael Ignatieff has called the 'recurring battle' between institutions and those subject to them, the experiential aspect of law.[8] Investigations of these areas have only just begun in England,[9] so there is some difficulty with comparison.

The 'potent fiction' of rule of law certainly is evident in popular use of the courts, not only by complainants but also by those many people who informed or who stood and gave evidence. As I have said, the motivations of these people may have been other than to obtain justice, but they still were seen to be obtaining it. Complainants, informers, witnesses and defendants, alongside constables and magistrates, made colonial law. Defendants, however, were also isolated by particular means and it was these means which were particularly colonial. Unfortunately some of the more detailed work of legal historians remains bound up with the Hay debate. Hay himself recognised complexities in popular use of law and it is to be hoped that this study has partly contributed to this recognition. Historians such as Cynthia Herrup and J. M. Beattie provide further analysis and description of the process of law from deposition to indictment to trial. There are many divergences in the colony from this, as has been recognised by A. C. Castles who is continuing this work. As a social history this work does not deal with those comparisons which concern Castles. In terms of analysis of the nature of authority in the colony, my focus on depositions implicitly redefines authority.

Peter King in his analysis of decision-making in English criminal law has written, 'the key decision-maker in eighteenth-century criminal law was the victim himself'. King does not use this to discredit Hay's work nor to agree with Langbein. In his recognition that 'the English labouring poor made extensive use of the courts for their own purposes'[10] he also sees that the courts worked in the interests of a propertied elite. He argues for more complex research into usage of law. King's request for analysis of complexity is similar to Douglas Hay's, and it is partly in response to such questions that my study of depositions originated. It is not a question of who used criminal law or how they used it, but a question of what power relations are involved in what people understand as law.

Notes

1 For the law regarding transportation and its practice, see Chapter 2.

2 This has been debated by Hirst, *Convict Society and Its Enemies*; see also R. Hughes, *The Fatal Shore*, London, 1987, pp. 283–382.

3 See R. S. Hill, *Policing the Colonial Frontier*, Wellington, 1986.

4 Alford, *Production or Reproduction?*; Robinson, *The Hatch and Brood of Time* and *The Women of Botany Bay*; Sturma, 'Eye of the Beholder', *Labour History*, no. 34, May 1978; Aveling, 'She Only Married to be Free', *Push from the Bush*, no. 2, November 1978; Atkinson, 'Four Patterns of Convict Protest', *Labour History*, no. 37, November 1979.

5 See Brewer and Styles, *An Ungovernable People*, pp. 11–20; P. King, 'Decision-Makers and Decision-

Making in the English Criminal Law 1750–1800', *Historical Journal*, vol. 27, no. 1, 1984, pp. 56–8. King argues, 'The law was available to labouring and middling men in the second half of the eighteenth century as a means of protecting their property.' He adds that middling men had influence in the judicial process, particularly as jurors.

6 Hay, et al., *Albion's Fatal Tree*.
7 *ibid.*, Brewer and Styles, *An Ungovernable People*.
8 Hay, 'War, Dearth and Theft in the Eighteenth Century'; Ignatieff.
9 Brewer and Styles, *An Ungovernable People*; Herrup, *The Common Place*.
10 P. King, 'Decision-Makers and Decision-Making'.

Appendix

The numbers of cases for which depositions survive are given below.

Judge Advocate's Bench
1810, 116
1811, 107
1812, 77
1813, 73
1814, 40
1815, 8
1816, 22
1817, 15
1818, 24
1819, 24
1820, 10
Total, 516

Police Magistrates' Bench
1812, 85
1815–16, 303
1820–21, 586

Argyle Bench of Magistrates
1827, 84

Supreme Court of
Criminal Jurisdiction
1824, 60
1825, 113
1826, 100
1827, 133
1828, 136
1829, 355
1830, 356
Total, 1,253

Court of Criminal
Jurisdiction
1810–15, minutes - 12
1816, 27
1817, 104
1818, 127
1819, 84
1820, 121
1821, 155
1822, 182
1823, 113
1824, 45
Total, 958

Liverpool Bench
of Magistrates
1824 and 1826, 314

Goulburn Bench
of Magistrates
1828, 94

Quarter Sessions
Campbelltown, 43
Liverpool, 120
Newcastle, 90
Parramatta, 141
Sydney, 825
Windsor, 356
Total, 1,575

Bibliography

Court Records: Criminal Courts

Archives Office

Bathurst Bench Book, 27 September 1825–1 August 1826, 2/8323.
Baulkham Hills Returns, X660.
Court of Criminal Jurisdiction, Informations, depositions and other papers 19 boxes, T1-15.
——, Minutes, 1810–15, 5/1119.
Judge Advocate's Bench, S2771–S2775.
Petty Sessions, Reports of Prisoners Tried: 1822, 1824 Parramatta X643: 1826, Parramatta X660; Sydney 1824, 1827 (1 month), 1828, X660.
Police Magistrates Bench: Proceedings, 17 July 1815–15 July 1816, 9/2643.
Quarter Sessions, Depositions:
  Windsor, 1824–1830, 4/8470-4/8483.
  Sydney, 1824–1829, 4/8438-4/8450.
  Parramatta, 1825–1830, 4/8424-4/8429.
  Liverpool, 1824-1828, 4/8395-4/8401.
  Campbelltown, 1828–1830, 4/8383-4/8384.
  Newcastle, 1826–1829, 4/8418-4/8423.
Return of Prisoners Tried, October 1816–February 1824, X275.
Supreme Court of Criminal Jurisdiction, Depositions and other papers, 21 boxes, T128-149.
——, Informations, 21 boxes, T19-40.
——, Returns of Prisoners Tried, X727–8.

Mitchell Library

Argyle Bench Book, 1828.
Goulburn Bench Book, 1827–29.
Liverpool Bench Book, 1824, 1826.

Dixson Library

Sydney Bench of Magistrates, 1815–16, D.L. Spencer 154.
Sydney Bench of Magistrates, 1820–21, D.L. Spencer 54.

Government Records

Archives Office

Apprehension of bushrangers, confidential letters, 4/7089.
Circular re law governing summary trial, 30 September 1828, 2/8328.
Colonial Secretary, Copies of proclamations, 5/2756.
————, Letters from private and official persons, 4/1618.
————, Letters received, 1788–1826, 4/1719–4/1820.
————, Letters to judicial establishment, 4/3736–4/3715.
————, Letters to private and official persons, 4/1618.
————, List of convicts assigned, not mechanics, 1822, 4/5700.
Copies of letters sent within the colony, 4/3521.
District Constables' notebooks, 4/1220.
Governor, Letters received, 4/1672.
Judge Advocate, Letters received, 5/1112.
List of Government and General Orders, 4/7089.
Police Rules and Regulations, 4/7098.
Supreme Court, Civil Jurisdiction, Process Papers, 1815 and 1817–24, 9/2251-8.

Mitchell Library

Attorney-General, Correspondence, A165.
Bonwick Transcripts, Records of questioning at Bigge Inquiry, 1819–20.
Brisbane Letter Book, A1559, FM4.
Census 1806, A4428.
Census 1828, Alphabetical Returns of Female Prisoners in the Colony, H010/28.
Colonial Secretary, Circular to Magistrates concerning Functions, 1820, A797.
Governors, Missing despatches and enclosures, A1267.
Judge Advocate, Draft letters of Agreements, Indentures, Assignments, A3620.
————, Register of Assignments and other Legal Documents, S/1113.
Macquarie Memoranda, A772.
Macquarie Papers, A1508.
Returns, Superintendent of Carpenters, 1811–17, A2086.
Solicitor-General's Letter Book D(TAS 3–13).
Windsor Commissariat, Ration Book, A803.

Newspapers

Sydney Gazette
Australian
Blossom, 1828
Monitor

Private Papers, Mitchell Library

Betts, John, Diary 1829–33, B782.
Campbell, J. T., Notebooks, B418.
Farm Workbook, Stonequarry, A2884.
Field, Barron, Letter to Marsden, 16 December 1824, Af23/2.
Forbes, F., Private letters, A1819.
Hassall, G., Correspondence, vol. 4, A1667.
Hammersly, G. T., 'A Few Observations on the Situation of Female Convicts', A657.
Harris, J., Papers, A1597.
Howe, John, Papers, MSS 106.
King, P. G., Letter Book, C187.
———, Papers, A1976.
Lawson, William, Papers, A1952.
Macarthur Papers, A2920.
Marsden, S., Essays, MSS 18.
———, Journals, A1997.
———, Papers, C244.
Piper, J., Papers, A256.
Wentworth, Darcy, Medical notebooks, B196.
———, Papers, A752–8.
———, Police reports and accounts, 1810–27, D1.

Contemporary Printed Sources

Bannister, S., *Statements and Documents relating to proceedings in N.S.W., 1824*, Cape Town, 1827.
Bentham, J., *Panopticon vs N.S.W.*, London 1802.
Burn, R., *The Justice of the Peace and Parish Officer*, 7th edn. 3 volumes, 1762.
Cottu, M., *The Administration of the Criminal Code in England*, London, 1820.
Howe, A., *Party Politics Exposed. Letter to Secretary of State for the Colonies*, Sydney 1834.
Law Magazine, January 1832.
Maconochie, Captain ———, *General Views on the Social System of Convict Management*, Hobart, 1839.
Papers Relating to the Conduct of Magistrates in N.S.W., 1826.
Parliamentary Documents, 1811–32.
Parliamentary Documents, 1826–32.
Plunkett, J., *The Australian Magistrate: A Guide to the Duties of Justice of the Peace*, Sydney 1835.
Votes and Proceedings of the Legislative Council, 1824–1837.

Reprints

Chitty, J., *A Treatise on the law of the prerogatives of the crown and the Rights and Duties of the subject*, London, 1820, reprinted 1969.
British Parliamentary Papers, reprinted, Irish University Press, Shannon, 1968: vol. 1: *Crime and Punishment, Prisons*; vol. 3: *Correspondence and Papers relating to the Government and Affairs of the Australian Colonies*; vol. 6: *Transportation.*
The New South Wales Calendar and Post Office Directory, Sydney 1832, reprinted 1966.

Articles and Books

Abbott, G. J., and Nairn, N. B., *The Economic Growth of Australia, 1788–1821*, Melbourne, 1969.

Alford, K., *Production or Reproduction? An Economic History of Women in Australia, 1788–1850*, Melbourne, 1984.

Allen, J., *Sex and Secrets*, Oxford, 1990.

Anderson, M., 'The emergence of the modern life cycle in Britain', *Social History*, vol. 10, no. 1.

Atkinson, A., 'Women Publicans in 1838', *Push from the Bush*, no. 8, December 1980.

——, 'The Moral Basis of Marriage', *Push from the Bush*, no. 2, November 1978.

——, 'Four Patterns of Convict Protest', *Labour History*, no. 37, November 1979.

Aveling, M., 'She Only Married to be Free; or Cleopatra Vindicated', *Push from the Bush*, no. 2, November 1978.

Bailey, V., *Policing and Punishment in Nineteenth-century Britain*, Brunswick, 1981.

Bashar, N., 'Rape in England between 1550 and 1700', London Feminist History Group, *The Sexual Dynamics of History*, London, 1983.

Beattie, J. M., *Crime and the Courts in England, 1660–1800*, Oxford, 1986.

——, 'The Criminality of Women in Eighteenth-century England', *Journal of Social History*, vol. 8, 1974–5.

Berg, M., Hudson, P., Sonenscher, M., eds, *Manufacture in the Town and Country before the Factory*, Cambridge, 1983.

Bossy, J., *Disputes and Settlements*, Cambridge, 1983.

Brewer, J., and Styles, J., eds, *An Ungovernable People: The English and their Law in the Seventeenth and Eighteenth Centuries*, London, 1980.

Butlin, S. J., *Foundations of the Australian Monetary System, 1788–1851*, Sydney, 1968.

Cameron, I., *Crime and Repression in the Auvergne and Guyenne, 1720–1790*, Cambridge, 1981.

Castles, A., *An Australian Legal History*, Melbourne, 1982.

Clark, M., 'The Origins of the Convicts Transported to Eastern Australia 1787–1852', *Historical Studies*, no. 7, 1956.

Clarke, S., and Donnelly, J. S., *Irish Peasants, Violence and Political Unrest, 1780–1914*, Manchester, 1983.

Cobb, R. C., *The Police and the People, French Popular Protest, 1789–1820*, Oxford, 1970.

Cohen, S., and Scull, A., eds, *Social Control and the State: Historical and Comparative Essays*, Oxford, New York 1983.

Cornish, W. R., Hart, J., et al., *Crime and the Law in Nineteenth-Century Britain*, Irish University Press, 1978.

Currey, C. H., *Francis Forbes*, Sydney, 1968.

——, *The Brothers Bent*, Sydney, 1968.

Daniels, K., *So Much Hard Work: Women and Prostitution in Australian History*, Sydney, 1984.

Davis, N. Z., 'The Reasons of Misrule: Youth Groups and Charivaris in Sixteenth-century France', *Past and Present*, no. 50, 1971.

Demos, J., *Family Life in Plymouth Colony*, New York, 1970.

Earnshaw, B., 'Convict Apprentices 1820–1838', *Push from the Bush*, no. 5, December 1979.

Eley, G. and Hunt, W., eds, *Reviving the English Revolution*, London, 1988.

Ellis, M. H., *Lachlan Macquarie*, Sydney, 1947; reprinted 1970.

Fairchilds, C., 'Masters and Servants in Eighteenth-century Toulouse', *Journal of Social History*, Spring 1979.

Finnane, M., *Policing in Australia: Historical Perspectives*, Sydney, 1987.

Fitzpatrick, B., *British Imperialism and Australia, 1783–1837*, London, 1939.

Fletcher, B., *Ralph Darling: A Governor Maligned*, Oxford, 1984.

——, *Landed Enterprise and Penal Society*, Sydney 1976.

Flaherty, D., 'Crime and Social Control in Provincial Massachusetts', *Historical Journal*, vol. 24, no. 2, 1981.

Foster, S., 'Convict Assignment in New South Wales', *Push from the Bush*, April 1983.

Foucault, M., *Discipline and Punish: The Birth of the Prison*, Harmondsworth, 1975.

——, *The Order of Things: An Archaeology of the Human Sciences*, London, 1970.

Galenson, D., *White Servitude in Colonial America: An Economic Analysis*, Cambridge, 1981.

Garrioch, D., *Neighbourhood and Community in Paris 1740–1790*, Cambridge, 1986.

Genovese, E., *Roll Jordan Roll: The World the Slaves Made*, New York, 1974.

——, *The Political Economy of Slavery*, Toronto, 1967.

——, and Genovese, E. Fox., *Fruits of Merchant Capital*, Oxford, 1983.

Gilbert, A. D., and Inglis, K. S., eds, *Australians: A Historical Library*, Sydney, 1987.

Gilbert, A. N., 'Military and Civilian Justice in Eighteenth-century England: an assessment', *Journal of British Studies*, vol. 17, no. 2, 1978.

Ginzberg, C., *The Cheese and the Worms*, London, 1980.

Greenberg, D., 'Crime, Law Enforcement and Social Control in Early Colonial America', *American Journal of Legal History*, October 1982.

Grimshaw, P., et al., *Families in Colonial Australia*, Sydney, 1985.

Hay, D., 'War, Dearth and Theft in the Eighteenth Century: The Record of English Courts', *Past and Present*, no. 95, May 1982.

——, 'The Criminal Prosecution in England and its Historians', *Modern Law Review*, vol. 47, no. 1, 1984.

——, et al., *Albion's Fatal Tree*, Harmondsworth, 1975.

Hecht, J. J., *The Domestic Servant in Eighteenth-century England*, London 1956, reprinted 1980.

Herrup, C. B., 'Law and Morality in Seventeenth-century England', *Past and Present*, no. 106, February 1985.

——, *The Common Peace: Participation and the Criminal Law in Seventeenth-century England*, Cambridge, 1987.

Hersh Kowitz, L., and Klein, M. M., *Courts and Law in Early New York*, Port Washington, 1978.

Higgs, E., 'Domestic Servants and Households in Victorian England', *Social History*, vol. 8, no. 2, May 1983.

Hill, R., *Policing the Colonial Frontier*, Wellington, 1986.

Hirst, J. B., *Convict Society and Its Enemies*, Sydney, 1983.

Hoffer, P. C., and Hull, N. E. H., *Murdering Mothers: Infanticide in England and New England, 1558–1803*, New York, 1984.

Hufton, O., 'Women and Work in the Family Economy in Eighteenth-century France', *French Historical Studies*, vol. IX, Spring 1975.

——, 'Attitudes towards Authority in Eighteenth-century Languedoc', *Social History*, vol. 3, no. 3, October 1978.

Hughes, R., *The Fatal Shore*, London, 1987.

Jones, D., *Crime, Protest, Community and Police in Nineteenth-century Britain*, London, 1982.

Jones, D. V. J., 'The New Police, Crime and People in England and Wales, 1829–1888', *Transactions of the Royal Historical Society*, 5th Series, vol. 33, 1983.

Kaplan, S. J., and Koepp, C. J., *Work in France*, Cornell, 1986.

Kaplan, S., ed., *Understanding Popular Culture*, Cornell, 1984.

King, H., 'Some Aspects of Police Administration in N.S.W. 1825–1851', *Journal of the Royal Australian Historical Society*, vol. 42, 1956.

King, P., 'Decision-Makers and Decision Making in the English Criminal Law 1750–1800', *Historical Journal*, vol. 27, no. 1, 1984.

Langbein, J., *Torture and the Law of Proof: Europe and England in the Ancien Regime*, Chicago, 1976.

————, 'Shaping the Eighteenth-century Criminal Trial, a View from the Ryder Sources', *University of Chicago Law Review*, vol. 50, no. 1, Winter 1983.

————, 'Albion's Fatal Flaws', *Past and Present*, no. 98, February 1983.

Laslett, P., *Household and Family in Past Times*, London, 1972.

Le Gates, M., 'The Cult of Womanhood in Eighteenth-century Thought', *Eighteenth-Century Studies*, no. 10, 1976.

Lemire, B., 'Consumerism in Pre-industrial England: The Trade in Secondhand Clothes', *Journal of British Studies*, vol. 27, no. 1, January 1988.

Linebaugh, P., '(Marxist) Social History and (Conservative) Legal History: A Reply to Professor Langbein', *New York University Law Review*, vol. 60, no. 2, May 1985.

Linge, G. J. R., *Industrial Awakening*, Canberra, 1979.

McFarlane, A., *The Justice and the Mayor's Ale*, Oxford, 1982.

McGowen, R., 'The Image of Justice and Reform of the Criminal Law in Early Nineteenth-century England', *Buffalo Law Review*, vol. 32, no. 1, Winter 1983.

Marcus, G. E., and Fisher, M. M. J., *Anthropology as Cultural Critique*, Chicago, 1986.

Maza, S., *Servants and Masters in Eighteenth-century France*, Princeton, 1983.

Medick, H., 'Missionaries in the Row Boat: Ethnological Ways of Knowing as a Challenge to Social History', *Comparative Studies in Society and History*, vol. 29, no. 1, January 1987.

Merrit, A., 'Methodological and Theoretical Implications of the Study of Law and Crime', *Labour History*, no. 37, November 1979.

Morris, R., *Government and Labour in Early America*, New York, 1946.

Neal, D., 'Free Society, Penal Colony, Slave Society, Prison', *Historical Studies*, vol. 22, no. 89, October 1987.

————, 'Law and Authority: The Magistracy in New South Wales 1788–1840', *Law in Context*, no. 3, 1985.

Nicholas, S., ed., *Convict Workers: Reinterpreting Australia's Past*, Cambridge, 1988.

Passerini, L., *Fascism in Popular Memory*, Cambridge, 1984.

Portelli, A., 'Oral Testimony, the Law and the Making of History: The April 7 Murder Trial', *History Workshop*, no. 20, Autumn 1985.

Prude, J., *The Coming of Industrial Order*, Cambridge, 1983.

Ranum, R., and Orrest, R., *Rural Society in France*, Baltimore, 1977.

Ritchie, J., *Punishment and Profit*, Melbourne, 1970.

————, *Lachlan Macquarie*, Melbourne, 1986.

Robinson, P., *The Hatch and Brood of Time*, Oxford, 1985.

————, *The Women of Botany Bay*, Oxford, 1989.

Rude, G., *Criminal and Victim*, Oxford, 1985.

Ryan, L., *The Aboriginal Tasmanians*, Brisbane, 1981.

Saunders, K., *Indentured Labour in the British Empire, 1834–1920*, Canberra, 1984.

Schedvin, C. B., 'The Nomadic Tribes of Urban Britain: A Prelude to Botany Bay', *Historical Studies*, no. 18, 1978.

Segalen, M., *Love and Power in the Peasant Family*, Oxford, 1983.

Sewell, W. H. Jr, *Work and Revolution in France*, Cambridge, 1980.

Shaw, A. G. L., *Convicts and the Colonies*, London, 1966.

Smith, A., *The Wealth of Nations*, London, 1776.

Stansell, C., *City of Women: Sex and Class in New York 1789–1860*, New York, 1986.

Stearns, D. N. and C. Z., 'Emotionology: Clarifying the History of Emotions and Emotional Standards', *American Historical Review*, vol. 90, no. 4, October 1985.

Sturma, M., 'Eye of the Beholder: The Stereotype of Women Convicts 1788–1852', *Labour History*, no. 34, May 1978.

Styles, J., 'Sir John Fielding and the Problem of Criminal Investigation in Eighteenth-century England', *Transactions of the Royal Historical Society,* 5th Series, vol. 33, 1983.

Sydney Labour History Group, *What Rough Beast,* Sydney, 1982.

Thompson, E. P., 'Eighteenth-Century English Society: class struggle without class?', *Social History,* no. 3, 1978.

———, 'Time, Work Discipline and Industrial Capitalism', *Past and Present,* no. 38, 1967.

———, *Whigs and Hunters: The Origin of the Black Act,* Harmondsworth, 1975.

Tomer, N., 'A Torrent of Abuse, Crimes of Violence between Working-Class Men and Women in London, 1840–1875', *Journal of Social History,* Spring 1978.

Trumbach, R., 'London Sodomites, Homosexual Behavior and Western Culture in the Eighteenth Century', *Journal of Social History,* vol. 11, 1977–78.

Vaissey, D., 'Court Records and the Social History of Seventeenth-Century England', *History Workshop,* no. 1, Spring 1976.

Ward, R., *Finding Australia,* Melbourne, 1987.

Weekes, J., *Sex, Politics and Society,* London, 1981.

Windschuttle, E., *Women, Class and History,* Melbourne, 1980.

Williams, J., 'Irish Female Convicts and Tasmania', *Labour History,* no. 44, May 1983.

Wilson, S., 'Language and Ritual in Marriage', *Push from the Bush,* no. 2, November 1978.

Windeyer, W. V. J., *Lectures in Legal History,* Sydney, 1957.

Yarwood, A. T., *Samuel Marsden, The Great Survivor,* Melbourne, 1977.

Yi-Fu Tuan, *Topophilia,* Princeton, 1974.

Zehr, H., *Crime and the Development of Modern Society,* New Jersey, 1976.

Theses

History

Belcher, M., 'The Child in N.S.W. Society, 1820–1837', Ph.D., University of New England, 1982.

Crowley, F. K., 'Working-Class Conditions in Australia, 1788–1850', Ph.D., University of Melbourne, 1949.

Heath, L., 'The Female Convict Factories of N.S.W. and Van Diemen's Land. An examination of their role in the control, punishment and reform of prisoners, 1804–1854', M.A., Australian National University, 1978.

King, H., 'Police Organization and Administration in the Middle Districts of N.S.W. 1825–1851', M.A., University of Sydney, 1956.

Liston, C. A., 'New South Wales under Governor Brisbane 1821–1825', Ph.D., University of Sydney, 1980.

McKinnon, J. A., 'Convict Bushrangers in N.S.W., 1824–1834', M.A., La Trobe University, 1979.

Sturma, M., 'Vice in a Vicious Society', Ph.D., University of New England, 1980.

Wills, A., 'Criminal Life and Criminal Justice: Six Provisional Courts of Paris, 1791–1792', Ph.D., University of Washington, 1975.

Law

Currey, C. H., 'Chapters on the Legal History of N.S.W.', LL.D., University of Sydney, 1929.

McLaughlin, J. A., 'The Magistracy in N.S.W., 1788–1850', M.A., University of Sydney, 1973.

Neal, D., 'The Rule of Law in a Penal Colony: Law and Politics in Early N.S.W. 1788–1840', LL.D., University of N.S.W., 1986.

Index

Names of complainants and defendants are not given in this index.

299